# DR. ECKENER'S
# DREAM
# MACHINE

# DR. ECKENER'S
# DREAM
# MACHINE

*The Great Zeppelin and
the Dawn of Air Travel*

## DOUGLAS BOTTING

HENRY HOLT AND COMPANY    NEW YORK

Henry Holt and Company, LLC
*Publishers since 1866*
115 West 18th Street
New York, New York 10011

Henry Holt® is a registered trademark of
Henry Holt and Company, LLC.

Library of Congress Cataloging-in-Publication Data
Botting, Douglas.
Dr. Eckener's dream machine : the great Zeppelin and the dawn of
air travel / Douglas Botting.—1st ed.
p.   cm.
Includes bibliographical references and index.
ISBN 0-8050-6458-3 (hb)
1. Graf Zeppelin (Airship)  2. Flights around the world.
3. Eckener, Hugo, 1868–1954.
I. Title: Doctor Eckener's dream machine.  II. Title.

TL659.G7 B68 2001
629.133'25—dc21                                        2001024770

Henry Holt books are available for special
promotions and premiums. For details contact:
Director, Special Markets.

First Edition 2001

*Designed by Paula Russell Szafranski*

Printed in the United States of America

1  3  5  7  9  10  8  6  4  2

*Dedicated to the memory of Dr. Hugo Eckener
and the passengers and crew of the* Graf Zeppelin,
*an international brotherhood and sisterhood of
sixty men and one woman from ten nations, who
with courage and comradeship set out on the first
circumnavigation of the planet by passenger aircraft:*

*Lakehurst to Lakehurst (United States)
Friedrichshafen to Friedrichshafen (Germany)*

August–September 1929

*"The* Graf Zeppelin *is more than just machinery, canvas and aluminium. It has a soul."*

Lady Grace Hay-Drummond-Hay (1929)

# Contents

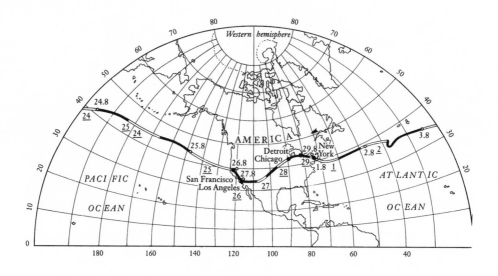

The route is drawn in a line of two tones:
white corresponds to the distance covered by day;
black corresponds to the distance covered by night.
Dates in local time are indicated by the underlined numbers.
The days and hours of Central European time are indicated by
the numbers which are *not* underlined on the open dots.

The International Date Line is drawn on the Pacific Ocean
and passes through the Bering Straits then follows the 180° meridian.
Crossing this line, the local date changes from the 25th to the 24th.

The dotted lines on the lower map show the routes of the first
Zeppelin passenger flight to America and back in October 1928.

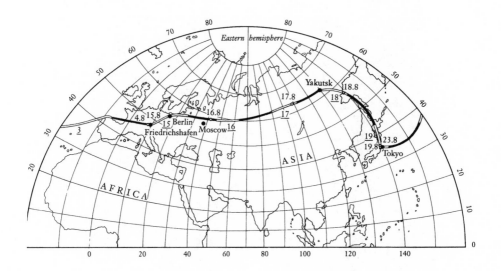

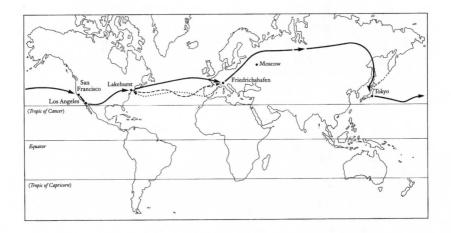

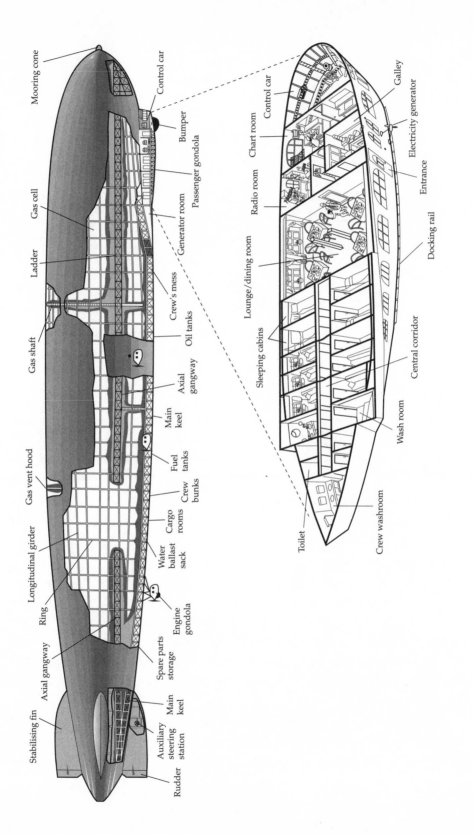

Mooring cone

Control car

Bumper

Passenger gondola

Generator room

Crew's mess

Oil tanks

Axial gangway

Main keel

Fuel tanks

Crew bunks

Cargo rooms

Water ballast sack

Engine gondola

Spare parts storage

Ring

Longitudinal girder

Gas vent hood

Gas shaft

Ladder

Gas cell

Axial gangway

Stabilising fin

Main keel

Auxiliary steering station

Rudder

Control car

Chart room

Radio room

Lounge/dining room

Sleeping cabins

Wash room

Central corridor

Crew washroom

Toilet

Docking rail

Entrance

Electricity generator

Galley

# Preface

Recently I was asked in a BBC radio interview what four great journeys of travel and exploration of the past I would like to have been involved in, given my own previous background as a traveler and explorer. I replied, Alexander the Great's long march to India, Captain Cook's first voyage in the South Seas, the first moon landing—and the pioneer around-the-world flight of the *Graf Zeppelin* airship, across lands and oceans rarely or never seen before from the air.

Though the other three great journeys have been recounted many times, that of the *Graf Zeppelin* has not. The central core of this book, therefore, is the *Graf*'s first-ever passenger circumnavigation of the globe by air, based on the reports and recollections of those who were on board, including the man at the heart of the story, the airship's creator and commander, Dr. Hugo Eckener, one of the great protagonists of aviation history.

The world flight is the jewel in the crown rather than the crown itself—the marvelous nub of the story, though not the complete story. Taken as a whole, this is a wonderfully rich saga that takes in many strands of technological endeavor and human derring-do. Almost stir-ringly romantic, it is a true tale of unusual vision and determined ambition on the part of one man and his dedicated aides to crack the technology and master the expertise of rigid airship flight against all odds (war, disaster, penury, Hitler). The goal was to achieve the world's first transoceanic air service, a trail blazed around the planet by the *Graf Zeppelin,* one of the most spectacular technological and operational marvels of its age and the most successful and best-loved aircraft ever built: Dr. Eckener's dream machine.

# DR. ECKENER'S
# DREAM
# MACHINE

# Prologue:
# On First Sighting
# the Dream Machine

The mass of the mighty airship hull, which seemed matched by its lightness and grace, and whose beauty of form was modulated by delicate shades of colour, never failed to make a strong impression on people's minds. It was not, as generally described, a "silver bird soaring in majestic flight," but rather a fabulous silver fish, floating quietly in the ocean of air, and captivating the eye just like a fantastic, exotic fish seen in an aquarium. And this fairy-like apparition, which seemed to melt into the silvery blue background of the sky, when it appeared far away, lighted by the sun, seemed to be coming from another world and to be returning there like a dream. . . .

*Hugo Eckener*

## Chapter One

# The Dream Machine

One o'clock in the morning, Thursday, August 15, 1929. The Kurgarten Hotel at Friedrichshafen on the German side of the Bodensee, the great inland sea also known as Lake Constance. The lake is calm now; a soft summer night wind whispers about the little wooded lakeside town; the moon is clear and bright, the stars strewn across the sky like sparks.

But it is not a quiet night. Tossing restlessly in his bed in his upstairs room, Max Geisenheyner, a forty-five-year-old German magazine editor and special reporter for the *Frankfurter Zeitung,* is kept awake by the racket of the party downstairs, a band playing, dance music, bursts of song and laughter, footsteps on the gravel path outside. The hotel—the whole town—is restless, keyed up, waiting expectantly for the big spectacular at dawn. All of Friedrichshafen high society is here, and people from miles around.

Down in the brightly lit salon and out on the broad, flower-decked terrace overlooking the lake, the party is in full swing. Leaning against a balustrade, Léo Gerville-Réache, a good-looking, rather wistful young French newspaper correspondent with delicate features and skin the color of mahogany—his mother is Indian—stands lost in thought. In a few hours' time he will be off on a fantastical journey from which he may never return. "I've got a little trip for you, Léo," his editor in chief at the *Le Matin* office in Paris told him a month ago.

Geisenheyner, head on pillow, stares blankly into the dark. It's the middle of the week, but it sounds like a Saturday night. Half the world's press corps, it seems, and no doubt half the VIPs and their friends and well-wishers, are throwing a farewell party. The whole place is full of foreigners. A Japanese couple are taking a late-night stroll in the moonlight, the diminutive wife shuffling along the gravel path in her wooden sandals and blue-and-white-striped kimono. Her head is on his shoulder, his arm is around hers. Perhaps they fear they will never see each other again. A couple of stiff and very correct Englishmen. A resigned, homesick (or perhaps hungover) American. An elegant Frenchman who moves like a dancer and never goes anywhere without a pretty young girl called Rozille in tow. A Russian, a Spaniard, a Swiss, not to mention all the Germans—Berliners and locals alike. Some are reporters, others are travelers. Even the king of Sweden is here, and the American ambassador and the Japanese ambassador too. All are here for the same reason. They've come from all over the world to see the big show.

Geisenheyner dozes, dreams fitfully as the rhythmic beat of the Boston two-step throbs up from below. He is woken abruptly by the night porter banging on the bedroom door. "Time to get up! Cars leave in half an hour sharp!"

It is three in the morning. Time to go. The music stops, the couples untwine. The foyer of the hotel is emptying. People are scurrying toward the line of cars parked in the courtyard, headlamps blazing. Outside, all is commotion. Through the streets thousands of people are making their way to the great hangar at the edge of town—on foot, on bicycles and motorbikes, in cars. It is still dark, but the streets are brilliantly lit by the lights of the procession of cars, and among them the dark flood of pedestrians.

The car bearing Geisenheyner and some of the others is blocked at the airfield entrance by a dense, swarming press of people. A guard at the gate is checking the papers of every would-be voyager. Geisenheyner hands him his pass and the car is waved through.

The long dazzling beam of a searchlight lights up the surrounding fields and the heads of thousands of people pressing close to the airfield perimeter. Directly in front lies the larger hangar, 787 feet long, 138 feet wide, and 115 feet high, lit with a ghostly blue-green phosphorescent light like some avant-garde Berlin stage set. Geisenheyner and the others get out of the car, pick up their hand baggage—their suitcases were weighed and loaded the previous evening—and stumble forward toward the hangar. What they see inside stops them dead in their tracks.

Here, in a vast aeronautical cathedral, held down by sandbags, its gondola lightly balanced on the slender trestles of its fragile cradle, stands a flying machine resembling a gigantic steel shark with huge fins, the size of an ocean liner. Seven hundred seventy-five feet long, it virtually fills the giant hangar. It is so vast that a ten-story building, or a church complete with steeple, could fit inside it—as, for that matter, could an entire express train. This is the grandest and most luxurious aircraft yet to take to the air, one of the great inventions of aviation history and one of the most spectacular technological and operational marvels of its time—the airship LZ-127, *Graf Zeppelin*.

"This is the amazing contraption we're going to entrust ourselves to on our madcap adventure," Léo Gerville-Réache notes, "across Europe, Asia, the Pacific, America, the Atlantic—the world!" The first around-the-world passenger flight in history, a proving flight to end all proving flights, designed to demonstrate the commercial potential of international airship travel once and for all.

"Everyone who goes in," writes Max Geisenheyner, "draws back amazed at the sight of the overwhelming brilliance of the glittering swan's feather of lights draped all over the great hulk of the ship. Thousands of tiny glowing light bulbs are suspended over the engine cars high above us, the propellers are entwined with them, they fill the whole vast space with a kind of frenzy."

The hangar is swarming with people. Several hundred ground handlers are at their posts. Ropes and lines stretch in all directions. Orders go hither and thither, shouted through megaphones. Security guards form a cordon around the gondola to head off would-be stowaways, while passengers and their friends and well-wishers crowd around. Dr. Hugo Eckener himself, the *Graf Zeppelin*'s commander and the greatest airshipman the world has known, in leather flying jacket, winged collar, and commander's peaked cap, can be glimpsed from afar, patrolling the hangar, supervising everything.

The *Graf* (as the ship is popularly known) is weighed off, gassed, watered and victualled up—and ready for boarding. A shudder goes through the crowd, a mixture of anticipation and apprehension, as the departure time draws near. "Is my luggage in my cabin OK?" Gerville-Réache asks the cabin boy by the airship's passenger door. "*Le Matin,* cabin 3, bottom bunk." Twenty kilos per passenger is the baggage limit. Anything in excess will be left behind.

The order comes to embark, and the line of security guards buckles as the crowd lurches toward the gondola. Slung well forward under the hull, the gondola is nearly a hundred feet long and twenty feet wide, with the control room, chart room, radio room, and galley at the forward end and the passenger accommodation occupying the rest. By the open entrance door stands a senior watch officer, Captain Hans von Schiller, and the chief steward, Heinrich Kubis. Von Schiller calls each of the passenger's names—German names, American names, Australian, English, French, Spanish, Russian, and Japanese names— starting with the sole female passenger.

"Lady Grace Hay-Drummond-Hay, *bitte sehr.*"

Lady Hay-Drummond-Hay is a London-born Englishwoman with a Scottish title, a petite, pretty, dark-haired, elegant woman in her mid-thirties, a star journalist for Hearst Newspapers in America. It is the press magnate William Randolph Hearst and his newspaper empire that has put up most of the money for this venture. Wearing a cloche hat and with a fashionable stole around her neck, she clambers up the short wooden gangway—*Himmelstreppe,* they call it, steps to heaven—shows her Hamburg-Amerika Line ticket and enters the ship.

Others quickly follow. Dr. Jerónimo Megías, the king of Spain's personal physician-in-ordinary. Sir Hubert Wilkins, MC (Military Cross), a calm, composed, and neatly bearded Australian, one of the world's greatest polar explorers. Baron Heinz von Perckhammer, a

German news cameraman with an outsize personality. Commander Charles Rosendahl, leading American airshipman and commander of the U.S. Navy airship *Los Angeles,* representing the American Navy Department. Commander Fujiyoshi, head of aviation in the Japanese Imperial Navy and a qualified airship captain in his own right, traveling to Tokyo as the in-flight representative of the Japanese government, his face brimming with enthusiasm for the impending adventure. William Leeds, a high-spirited twenty-six-year-old multimillionaire from New York, married to the Grand Duchess Xenia of Russia and heir to a tin-plate fortune, the richest man on the flight, going around the world on the *Graf* for the hell of it, with a wind-up gramophone in his hand luggage. Professor Karklin, a geographer and Russia's leading meteorologist, the Soviet government's eyes on the ship. Karl von Wiegand, American-German reporter for Hearst, with a revolver and a box of cartridges in his pockets, discreetly presented to him by a friend a minute or two before, with the words "As a last resort."

Altogether there are sixty-one people on the flight—twenty passengers (thirteen of them journalists and photographers) and forty-one crew (watch officers, navigators, helmsmen, radio operators, engineers, mechanics, electricians, cook, and cabin staff).

Max Geisenheyner's name is called but he doesn't hear; he just stands there, dapperly dressed in check suit, matching waistcoat, and chipper bow tie, clutching two cabin bags, a briefcase, binoculars, eight chocolate bars, a red sweater, and two overcoats against the cold of the nights in the upper airs, lost in wonder at the sight of the great ship towering silent and motionless above him. Not until Captain von Schiller cheerily claps him on the shoulder does he clamber up the little wooden gangway and go through the passenger door into the body of the ship.

Passing the hatch to the all-electric galley on the right, Geisenheyner turns left and enters the lounge-cum–dining room that runs the whole width of the ship, with four windows and four tables in each corner, each table with four chairs and a sofa, electric lights in the ceiling, and dark, wine-red patterned wallpaper and matching carpet and curtains—the whole effect like a cozy, well-appointed, old-fashioned Bavarian country hotel. Though the lounge is small, it offers the most palatial passenger accommodation of any aircraft in existence. At this moment, however, confusion reigns. Passengers are jostling at the windows to say their last good-byes to friends outside, hand baggage is strewn around, and Ernst, the fourteen-year-old cabin boy, struggles back and forth ferrying bags to their owners' cabins aft of the lounge.

Captain von Schiller does everything to accommodate the passengers, shows them to their cabins, hands out flight plans, answers the stupidest questions with a twinkle in his eye—an elegant, good-looking man of thirty-eight who is unfailingly helpful and content—"an idealist," Geisenheyner discerns, "only wanting to serve his beloved Zeppelin."

Eventually there is only one person left at the foot of the *Himmelstreppe*—an eagerly expectant stand-by passenger by the name of Nelson Morris, from Chicago.

Schiller shakes his head. "Sorry, you can't come." The ship is full, he tells the devastated American, there's no way it can possibly take another person. The weight of the cargo and personnel on board has been measured to a nicety—not forgetting the 880 pounds of airmail. The ship has been searched for stowaways—they happen—and none has been found. An extra passenger and his baggage is way beyond what the ship has been trimmed for—its safety and that of its passengers would be in jeopardy. The disappointed around-the-worlder turns sadly away.

Zero hour is approaching. "There is babel on board," observes Lady Hay. "Ten different nationalities are taking stock of each other. The Japanese have the biggest contingent. Amongst them are several of the prettiest kimono-clad girls carrying bouquets of flowers to give to their three travelling friends. All wave Japanese flags. They call for me at the window and shout: *Banzai! Banzai!* Our hearts are beating faster and there is a tenseness among us all as the quietly efficient ground crew goes about its work. All are impressed with the deep importance of the occasion."

Then there is trouble. Dr. Eckener has caught sight of Bill Leeds's gramophone on a window ledge in the *Graf*'s passenger lounge and takes strong objection to it. The machine not only represents excess weight, in his view it also sends the wrong message. Though he does not give himself airs, for all his fame and acclaim, Eckener does not suffer fools gladly either, and he can be brusque with anyone he feels is wasting his time or is ignorant or incompetent.

"This music box," he growls at the millionaire, "has nothing to do with what amounts to an expedition."

Whereupon he picks the offending machine up, clambers out of the airship with it, and dumps it in a distant corner of the hangar. Leeds, following behind him, retrieves his gramophone, takes it back into the gondola, and puts on a record of one of his wildest fox-trots. Dr. Eckener is first dumbfounded at this, then furious, then swears he is going to have this recalcitrant passenger's baggage reweighed, at which point Leeds, with a heavy sigh, hands the incensed commander his suitcase and shirts and pajamas and tells him: "Throw those overboard, but leave my gramophone alone!"

Given what he has had to pay for a ticket—seven thousand dollars (over fifty-five thousand dollars in today's money)—he reckons he has the right to have a little fun in the air. So it is settled.


The ship is ready. Its beautiful, torpedo-shaped bow stands poised, brilliantly illuminated in the hangar lights. Last farewells are exchanged, last kisses snatched with loved ones on the ground. Dr. Eckener embraces his wife one last time and without ceremony climbs on board. The *Himmelstreppe* is taken away, and the passenger door shut.

Heads lean out of the saloon's open windows; hands stretch out in a final gesture of good-bye. *Gute Reise!* voices cry. *Auf wiedersehen! Bon voyage! Adios! Banzai! Good-bye!* The restraining sandbags are being removed from the gondola's docking rails. The great ship is buoyed up by the seventeen enormous gas cells full of lighter-than-air hydrogen inside its rigid, fabric-covered hull of duralumin struts and frames and girders, each cell lined with a lightweight gas-tight "gold-beater's skin" made from the intestinal membranes of some fifty thousand cattle. It hovers just above the hangar floor, weighed off fore and aft with meticulous exactness, for it is clear of the hangar roof by only a foot or two. A little water ballast is spouted out through a couple of hoses to correct the trim one last time, and then an order is given: "Remove supports!"

The ground officer blows a sharp blast on his whistle. Another order is barked through a megaphone: *Zeppelin, marsch!*

It is 4:25 A.M. An army of ground handlers two hundred strong begins to haul the leviathan out of its hangar, walking the ship forward with quick, rhythmic steps and a steady, highly coordinated pull on the handling lines. From the passengers' vantage point it looks as though they are carrying the vast bulk of the *Graf* on their backs. The great ship is starting with all the smoothness and precision of a train gliding out of a station.

The crowd of privileged well-wishers, family, and friends runs after it. Most are waving and laughing, a few are in tears. Countess von Brandenfels Zeppelin, daughter of the founding father of this whole enterprise, shouts a last farewell to Lady Hay.

Soon the *Graf* is gliding smoothly out into the open, onto the take-off field, with the forlorn figure of Nelson Morris, suitcase in hand, running alongside the gondola door in a desperate hope that at the last second it will open and he will be hauled on board.

The first flush of dawn is tingeing the sky, and its wan glow casts an eerie light over the scurrying well-wishers. Through one of the saloon's windows Lady Hay throws a bundle of last-minute copy down to a Hearst Press colleague to radio through to the American papers in time for the morning editions—it is still yesterday evening in the States. "How these newspaper men envy us," she observes. "What a great and glorious privilege it all is." She throws a kiss to them all, and then another order is given.

*Taue los!*—Let go lines!

The handling lines are let go; the ship hangs in the air at the height of a man's shoulders, restrained only by the men clinging on to the gondola's rails. Alone of the crew, Captain von Schiller is still down on the ground, darting hither and thither, making final pretakeoff checks. Finally he stands motionless, facing forward, arms outspread—an "all's well" signal to the commander on the bridge—then springs into the rear engine car, the last man on board.

Another shrill blast on the whistle.

*Schiff hoch!* comes the command. Up ship!

The group of handlers holding the control car by its docking rails literally throws the giant ship into the air. In total silence Dr. Eckener's dream machine, almost as long as the *Titanic,* twice as beautiful and three times as fast, soars vertically into the sky like a bubble rising in a pond, buoyed up by over three million cubic feet of invisible, odorless, flammable, and potentially explosive hydrogen.

"Oh, God," groans the distraught Nelson Morris, dropping his suitcase to the ground. "Oh, *Hell!*" Newsmen gather around him, mutter consoling words. "I don't blame the Zeppelin officials," Morris tells them. "I guess I'll go to Paris now, then get a steamer home."

Steadily, effortlessly, the ship rises, hull exactly parallel to the ground, floating up into the still dark sky in uncanny silence. It is like going up in a lift—or, more exactly, a free balloon. "This falling upwards into the sky," one *Graf* passenger was to recall, "is beautiful and intoxicating. It is entirely different from the alarming take-off of an aeroplane. It gives one the complete illusion of having escaped the bondage of the earth's gravity. One floats, suspended from a huge gas-bubble in the sky."

Already the well-wishers and bystanders are sixty feet below. There is a last fluttering of passengers' hands in the saloon windows. The vast crowd around the airfield perimeter stares up in hushed expectation.

"À Dieu vat!" Léo Gerville-Réache, totally transfixed, intones an ancient prayer, "We're going to try and fly round the planet! And I'm one of them! It's a great, an immense moment. The black tree tops are tinged with the first faint rose of a dawn I shall never forget."

At a height of 150 feet, Dr. Eckener in the control room gives the order: "Clutch in propellers!" Then finally: "Full ahead engines!"

The five enormous prop engines slung in their pods outboard of the hull, fueled by a special, virtually weightless gaseous fuel called *Blaugas,* which resembles propane, are roaring now. The *Graf* begins to surge forward. The aerostatic lift provided by the buoyant gas cells is now supplemented by the aerodynamic lift provided by the elevators and the forward thrust of the propellers. Inside the ship the engines' noise is perceptible only as a soft hum, and the slipstream sounds like a waterfall along the hull. There is no vibration, no bumps.

The giant ship is not so much flying as swimming through the air like a giant fish.

Down on the ground the band begins to play. It is 4:34 A.M. Four minutes behind schedule.

"Straight as a ramrod the ship is climbing upwards," Max Geisenheyner writes in his notebook. "Down below there's no one to make any decisions now. Already we are over the other side of the Bodensee. The broad surface of the earth rises up out of a white haze. The sun hangs on the horizon like a rose-red lamp in a blue-green heaven." It is a warmish morning and the air is still, as so often at dawn; hence the early start.

"It's unique!" exclaims the normally taciturn retired Swiss colonel and oil tycoon Christof Iselin, staring through the window as if mesmerized. "Unique, unique, unique!"

"Ya somos prisoneiros a bordo del *Graf Zeppelin*," Dr. Megías scribbles in his notebook. There is no way out. They are committed.

As the five propellers begin to drive the ship toward a cruising speed of seventy miles per hour—top speed is nearly eighty—Eckener orders a course northeast toward Berlin, and the coming day, and the great wastes of Russia and Soviet Asia beyond. To the crowd below the *Graf* looks like something utterly fantastical—"a fabulous silvery fish," Eckener himself was to put it, "a fairy-like apparition, which seemed to melt into the silvery blue background of the sky, coming from another world and returning there like a dream—an emissary from the Island of the Blessed in which so many human beings still believe in the innermost recesses of their souls."

As the *Graf Zeppelin* begins to melt into the dawning day, bearing its passengers and crew away on their great adventure, the crowd breaks into a single rapturous roar and the band continues to play.

Only 21,200 miles to go, vast wastelands and vast oceans to cross. The voyage has begun.


"Next stop Tokyo!" shouts Captain von Schiller, bouncing brightly into the lounge from the bridge forward.

Tokyo is sixty-five hundred miles away. No aircraft has ever flown so far in one hop, and there is nowhere to land between here and there.

The only other way to get to Tokyo is by steamer (six weeks there, six weeks back) or by Trans-Siberian Railway across Bolshevik Russia and a steamer from the Pacific terminus (one month there, one month back).

Captain Lehmann, the executive officer—a civilized, genial man of forty-three, artistic and well-read, with immense experience and character, second only to Eckener in the Zeppelin service—comes in next, all smiles. "The ship's a bit heavy and inclined to sag through the air," he informs the passengers. "But that won't last for long."

Captain Hans Flemming is in command on the bridge, with Dr. Eckener by his side. This is the sharp end of the control car, the head of the ship, whose forward windows provide an unimpeded view dead ahead, below, and on both sides. Here the ganglions of the *Graf Zeppelin*'s brain, so to speak, are hard at work keeping the required course, height, speed, trim, buoyancy, and lift, along with all the other arcane and intricate technicalities of long-distance rigid airship flight.

Here the two servo-assisted control wheels are kept manned in four-hour watches day and night from takeoff to landing. On this watch the elevator coxswain who mans the *Höhensteuer* (elevator wheel), which maintains height and trim fore and aft and is situated at the back of the bridge on the left, is Dr. Eckener's son, twenty-seven-year-old Knut, "shyest of the shy." Above him are the crucial tools of his trade—altimeter, variometer, inclinometer, air and gas thermometers, and gas-cell gauge. The *Seitensteuer* (rudder wheel), which keeps the ship's course with the help of large illuminated magnetic and gyrocompasses, engine telegraphs, gas and ballast controls, and a good-luck mascot in the form of a long-legged rubber toy bird called Hans Huckebein, is positioned right at the front of the bridge in the middle of the wide forward windows. In calm conditions like now the rudder needs only a pound or so of hand pressure on the helmsman's part to hold course—in bad weather it can take as much as forty-five pounds.

In the control car, meanwhile, Captain Eckener is at his command post, staring fixedly ahead, studying the horizon, noting the weather signs, feeling the air currents, watching the world revolve under his feet as the miles pass by. He is rarely off duty. His keen eyes rarely miss a sign. Every change in the shape of the clouds, the look of the wind on water, the color of the horizon, has a meaning for him. His gift for reading the weather and predicting winds and turbulence and frontal activity is almost preternatural. "The Doctor was born," it is said, "knowing what tomorrow's weather will be."

The sky is his true habitat, his workplace and home away from home. It is here the full breadth of his experience and expertise is brought into play at any time of day and night. It is here he is required to make his most complex and momentous decisions. It is here he will stay on duty for virtually an entire flight when circumstances require it, taking a snack now and then, sleeping hardly at all. On the first transatlantic flight the previous year, he slept for only 8 hours of the 112-hour voyage, a feat of endurance remarkable for a man of sixty-one. Constantly he gets out of his wicker armchair on the starboard side of the bridge to go forward to the big window up front and stand there in silent concentration, brow wrinkled, studying whatever lies ahead. Experience, thoroughness, concentration, caution—these are the essential prerequisites of the airship commander. "As every-where in airship flight," he pronounces, "Prudence is the mother of Wisdom."

No one has been so much as scratched on any of his zeppelin flights. An airshipman of genius, master of the theory and practice of aerostatics, the science of lighter-than-air flight, with his gray-bearded face, measured voice, and captain's cap he presents a figure of complete authority and trust. As one of his crew put it: "If the old man says the weather's going to clear, well it's going to clear. The sky wouldn't dare do otherwise."

Dawn is breaking with wonderful pastel shades in the east, and soon the sun is peering over the edge of the white fog coverlet that spreads like a thick veil over the ground. It is shakedown time for the passengers on board the *Graf*. "What if you have to make a forced landing in Siberia?" a reporter asked Eckener at the preflight press call. "What about the mixture of fuel and hydrogen on board?" inquired another. "About as explosive as dynamite, surely?" The passengers have all had to sign an indemnity preventing them from claiming against the Zeppelin Company in case of an accident. Such cares trouble none of them. "Il fait clair, il fait doux, il fait gai," croons Gerville-Réache, his fears evaporating with the light. For some of them this is an experience like no other. Eckener wants to demonstrate how normal life can be on an intercontinental zeppelin airliner, and the passengers immediately settle into a routine.

But routine the experience can hardly be. Staring down at the tidy little towns and villages of southern Germany rolling by below—"From five hundred meters up," notes one passenger, "both beings and things have an unbelievable neatness about them"—Max Geisenheyner is suddenly struck by an incongruity he has never been aware of before, for this is the first time he has ever flown. From his perspective his boots are bigger than the houses down there, bigger even than the church steeples. He has a momentary sense of panic—will the whole orb of the Earth be as unreal as this?

He turns away from the window and its irresistible but vertiginous view, picks up his hand baggage, and carries it through a door at the rear end of the lounge and along a narrow corridor to his berth. There are ten double cabins all told, five on each side of the corridor. Another German journalist, Gustav Kauder, from a Berlin press agency, occupies the lower bunk in his. The only person not to share a cabin is Lady Hay-Drummond-Hay. As a result, one passenger is without a cabin—Dr. Seilkopf, the *Graf*'s German in-flight meteorological adviser, who is accommodated in the officers' quarters inside the hull.

Geisenheyner's cabin, like all the others, is cozy and neat but with walls that are no more than flowered chintz stretched from floor to ceiling. Though the cabins are small, they contain almost every comfort and convenience—a luxurious silk-covered settee that converts at night into two berths; a small, curtained window with a miniature vase of flowers on the ledge; a tiny bedside table; a folding stool; a rack for hats; pouches for shoes; and two wardrobes, each less than four inches deep (to save space), with a length of patterned cloth for a door (to save weight), and an electric light in the ceiling. All in all it resembles a wagon-lit sleeping compartment on a deluxe train. Through a small chink in the ceiling of his cabin, Geisenheyner can peer into a section of the ship's cavernous hull and study the intricate geometric pattern of its infrastructure, in which its huge gas cells are enclosed—the bare bones, the lungs and essence of a rigid airship.

At the aft end of the gondola, on either side of the corridor, are two toilet rooms with flush toilets, and two washrooms, each with a circular stainless-steel washbowl, soap dispenser, and adjustable mirror. There is no bath or shower—water is too precious on such a long flight. Rather than venting the waste water from the toilets, it is stored for use as ballast.

Aft of the passenger section of the gondola, inside the hull itself, lies the crew accommodation, consisting of three messes and space for slinging navy-style hammocks on either side of the lower catwalk that runs the length of the ship. Here too lie the fuel tanks, generator room, water-ballast bags, cargo hold, and spare-parts store. This vast interior contains the heart and guts of the great ship, an eerie, mysterious world to which entry is normally forbidden to all but crew. The entire space is filled with darkness, the smell of bitter almonds, and the batlike flapping sound of the fluttering fifty-foot gas cells, which keep the colossus in the air, suspended in two long rows down the whole length of the interior. "The thrill of it never wore off," one passenger recalled after being allowed privileged entry into this haunting place. "In the surrounding obscurity, the flapping and cracking of the balloon cells became magnified and reverberated with a hollow echo. I was surrounded by a labyrinth of girders, rafters, lattices, trusses and buttresses, a jungle of steel and aluminium." Only a few hundred feet below this secret world lay the cities, mountains, and rivers of planet Earth, sliding past at sixty miles an hour.

They have been airborne for half an hour, and coffee is being served in the lounge. Bill Leeds puts another record on his gramophone, back in pride of place on the window ledge, and Mr. Kitano, the Japanese journalist from the Asahi Press, dances a Charleston solo by himself in a serious, preoccupied kind of way, like a morning workout. "Do we have to?" von Wiegand remonstrates with Leeds. Dance music at five in the morning would destroy anyone's appetite for breakfast. "Not mine," retorts Leeds, who has partied all night at the hotel and—so far from Prohibition America—wants to carry on. But he finally gives in and turns the music off.

Amid such incongruities, the *Graf Zeppelin* throbs along over the fields and hamlets of rural Germany. In a day and a night it can cover seventeen hundred miles, in three days over five thousand miles, or more than a fifth of the world's circumference—and a good deal more than that with a following wind. There are virtually no other aircraft in the sky, no air traffic restrictions, no regulations on altitude. Like a silver fish—for the ship's fabric outer cover is painted with a silvery aluminum paint to reflect the rays of the sun—the *Graf* swims where it will, steadier than an ocean liner.

The official rule of zeppelin flying is never to fly lower than two and a half times the length of the ship above the ground—in the *Graf*'s case, around twenty-three hundred feet. But experience has shown that it is actually *less* dangerous to fly lower, since the wind is generally calmer nearer the ground, and flying lower also conserves gas, which will otherwise blow off through the automatic valves as the ship climbs higher. So often, as now, the *Graf* will sidle over the miracles of the planet at an altitude so low that even small birds can be clearly seen fluttering for cover, and dogs can be heard frantically barking at the giant predator overhead. Passengers sit mesmerized, staring down as if in a dream at the world gliding past barely a thousand feet beneath them, every detail of town and country plain to see. As the *Graf* is not pressurized, the windows can be opened and closed at will. And since a layer of air clings to the fabric skin of the ship when it flies, there are no winds blowing through the windows, so the ship seems to be cradled in an everlasting calm. Among those with a window view is Sir Hubert Wilkins, staring transfixed with his seasoned explorer's eyes, occasionally tapping out a few words on the typewriter beside him.

From his unusual vantage point he watches nature awakening in the pristine Arcadian countryside of southern Germany down below— large owls flapping heavily away, wild boars scampering off among the open timber, three red deer racing for cover, two great bucks running and stopping, running and stopping, large flocks of great white geese, billions of cabbages, ripening cornfields where the shadows spread like lace, two oxen pulling a wagon stampeding in panic and overturning in a gutter amidst wild confusion as the *Graf* drones overhead.

"We begin to look forward with expectancy to a wonderfully enlightening voyage," observes Sir Hubert gravely. "We hope to make an historic voyage and bring back observations which will be valuable in the future when airships bring East and West civilisations within a few days of each other."

All on board are aware that they are participating in one of history's great technological adventures while traveling in Pullman-class comfort—no heating, no smoking, no bath or shower, but cozy cabins to sleep in, a plush little wine-red lounge to sit in, and special Zeppelin porcelain to eat gourmet food from while watching the wide world go by, miraculous in every detail. Lady Grace Hay-Drummond-Hay loves the airship almost as much as she adores its captain. "The *Graf Zeppelin* is more than just machinery, canvas and aluminium," she notes. "It has a soul. I love the airship as if it were something alive, a being animated by life, responsive, grateful, capricious and loveable."

By half past six they are above the ancient city of Ulm on the Danube, carefully overflying its cathedral spire, the tallest in Europe. In the bright, cut-glass rays of the rising sun, the ship carries on over Swabia and Franconia, and toward seven o'clock they are over Nuremberg, traveling at full speed to the northeast, so that the old city, with its castle and roofs and ancient winding streets, seems to whisk past as in a dream.

Over Nuremberg, breakfast is served. Sausage and ham, fruit and jam, coffee and condensed milk. Lady Hay, Sir Hubert Wilkins, Captain Lehmann, and Colonel Iselin from Zurich sit at one table. The news photographer Robert Hartmann and the art photographer Baron von Perckhammer sit at another. The baron, an old China hand from the Tyrol, sports unconventional attire—baggy breeches down to the knees, clog boots, no socks. Spotting this, Captain Lehmann, a former officer of the German Imperial Navy, remarks loudly, "I would like to see all the passengers dress in evening dress for dinner, as on steamships."

During breakfast Dr. Eckener comes in from the bridge. "One egg," he orders. "And coffee." He is looking a little more haggard than usual. Since beginning the countdown to takeoff yesterday evening, he has managed only two and a half hours' sleep. The passengers crowd around him, shake his hand, pass the time of day with the man who stands center stage in this enterprise. Though he has been under intense pressure for many hours, Eckener remains courteous and polite. He looks avuncular, but this can be misleading. It is said of him that he is made of "sugar and steel." He is not always easy to get along with; he has a natural tendency to take charge of everything; he sometimes refers to himself as a troublemaker. But today he is sugar. He was sixty-one only a few days ago, but he is still in his prime, a big man, and strong, with bright blue eyes in a forceful grizzled face that is topped with a crew cut and ends with a little pointed goatee beard.

Hugo Eckener has a personal magnetism that dominates any crowd or gathering. Even American presidents and hard-nosed corporate chiefs succumb. It isn't that he is rich and powerful, for he is neither—though he *is* famous and influential. It isn't his physical presence, either, for he is not especially impressive physically, nor is he exceptionally handsome; he is getting on in years now, he likes his food and puts on weight, and his clothes are ill-fitting and covered in cigar ash. His charisma comes rather from those outward expressions of the masterful and keenly intelligent man within.

To his fellow zeppelin officers and crew, he is always "Dr. Eckener" or "*Herr Doktor,*" never "Hugo" or "*du.*" He commands with an authority that is both autocratic and paternal. To his men he is like a father—severe in mien, demanding of duty, critical of underperformance; but fair, impartial, and accessible, rarely losing his temper or his self-control, and respecting them all to a man. He is revered, for they know that no airship could be in abler or safer hands. "Having the old man in command," they say, "is as good as having life insurance."

Eckener has lived almost half his life in pursuit of the dream of a passenger liner of the skies that will rival those of the seas, carrying travelers through the lower currents of the air from continent to continent in the same aura of luxury, safety, and reliability as the *Ile de France* and *Europa* provide on the oceans below—but in a fraction of the time, in days rather than weeks and months. In order to achieve the goal of the world's first intercontinental air service, he has built the *Graf Zeppelin,* the most successful and best-loved airship ever built.

The *Graf* looks good, handles well, and feels safe. And though Eckener has always regarded it as the guinea pig of airship travel, a trailblazing demonstration and training ship rather than the flagship of the fleet, it is now the regent of the skies. It is to the *Graf* that Eckener entrusts his dream voyage, the world flight, the greatest aerial venture in history, designed to prove to the world that rigid airship travel is safe and reliable, and to initiate the era of transworld passenger air services, with the Atlantic route to America as the prize.

Encountering the renowned airship commander close up for the first time, Léo Gerville-Réache's mind is set at rest: "Until I actually met Dr. Eckener I thought the idea of flying round the world was a fantastical dream," he jots in his notebook, "but now I've met him I'm completely convinced about this incredible gamble."

Before returning to the bridge after his hurried breakfast, Eckener gives Hearst reporter Karl von Wiegand a progress report: "We are now up to two thousand five hundred fifty feet, but as soon as we get over these little hills of middle Germany we'll come down lower. I have shut down one motor and we are now running at seventy-one land miles an hour on four motors. I want as near as I can get to one hundred percent reserve fuel for the time we reach Siberia."

As photographers scamper through the length and breadth of the ship, and journalists tap out their first stories in their cabins, and the young late-nighters—the Americans Leeds, Jack Richardson, Joachim Rickard, and Rosendahl—catch up on their sleep, Dr. Jerónimo Megías decides now is the time to send a radio message to King Alfonso XIII—the first to be transmitted from the *Graf* on this voyage.

"*Su Majestad!*" the doctor reports, "The great adventure begins. We are bearing NE towards Northern Siberia, on a straight line to Tokyo. Commander Eckener and I respectfully salute Your Majesty."

A short while later Captain von Schiller comes aft to brief the passengers. This is not a cruise, he reminds them, it is an expedition. This is the first flight in history to cover more than ten thousand kilometers in one hop. There are going to be no railway stations, no stopping places, no waiting rooms. Water is going to be in short supply, so they must use it sparingly. When they wash in the morning, they should just dip their little finger under the tap and wipe it round their face.

Everyone likes von Schiller. More importantly, they all trust him: tall, clean-cut, and well presented in his navy-blue officer's uniform, courteous and imperturbable. Moreover, he knows his job and his ship down to the smallest twitch and rivet. He is the reassuring interface between the professionals in the control car and the passengers in the saloon, between the deadly serious business of circumnavigating the Earth in an experimental flying machine the size of an ocean liner and the mind-blowing experience of taking an Earth-orbiting sky ride with an uncertain outcome.

"Germany is such a beautiful country!" writes Geisenheyner, entranced by the aerial panorama of his homeland in the late summer sun. "Town after town, village after village, so neatly arranged, the countryside so carefully tended. From here to the horizon, from east and west, the railway lines glint light and dark. If we have to come down here we can take a gentle stroll to the next railway station. If the same fate befalls us in Russia we'll be facing a forced march of some five hundred kilometres. But we don't think about such things. We don't want to come down. We want to go on and on, day and night, night and day."

The possibility of a forced landing in the Siberian wilderness is one that Eckener has had to provide against, though he prefers not to mention it. The fate of the Italian airship *Italia,* which crashed near the North Pole with substantial loss of life while attempting an exploratory trans-Arctic flight only a year before, is still fixed in people's memories. So, at great cost in terms of weight, the *Graf Zeppelin* is carrying an arsenal of rifles and ammunition for protection against wild beasts and for hunting game when supplies run out should worse come to worst.

Shortly after nine o'clock they are over Leipzig, half an hour later Wittemberg, not long after that Potsdam, with the palace at Sans-Souci, the castle, orangery, and peacock island laid out clear and sharp beneath them. And then, at half past ten, Berlin, the capital.

"The foreigners on board have eyes on stalks now," notes the reporter from the *Frankfurter Zeitung* with patriotic pride as they reach the southwest suburbs. The *Graf* flies in via Charlottenburg and over the Tiergarten, the Reichstag, and the Brandenburg Gate. Airplanes come up alongside and swoop and spiral and dive in salute. Dr. Eckener takes the great ship down to two hundred meters, and at a little before eleven o'clock it is flying very low and slow, down the capital's principal avenue, Unter den Linden. The flags are flying from all the buildings in honor of the *Graf*'s arrival, the people are crowding the rooftops, every vantage point is taken, even the tallest monuments are swarming. The radio tower was sold out by eight this morning; the buses in the streets, even the trains, have stopped; the children have been let out of school, they are packed into the parks with hands held up to the sky; and the crowds in the streets are roaring in greeting. The clamor of the people and the hooting of the cars comes up loud and clear.

Over the polytechnic school the *Graf* drops a big bag of postcards for forward mailing. Geisenheyner tries a more direct means of communication: "I take a napkin from the table and wave it out of the window. It flutters in the slipstream like a flag. I'm hoping my mother out on her balcony down there on the fourth floor in Regenburger Strasse will see it and I'm sure if she does she'll realise it's me!"

Beautiful, valiant, and all-conquering, the *Graf Zeppelin* is widely seen as a shining example of German inventive genius and courage; Hugo Eckener, a metaphor for Germany's postwar longing for honor, decency, and prosperity, is already the nation's hero. There are other theories to explain the *Graf*'s universal popularity. To Freudians it is simply a floating phallic symbol, a giant erection in the sky. Followers of the pioneer Austrian psychiatrist Alfred Adler interpret it as overcompensation for the national inferiority complex. For Marxists, however, it is obviously an escapist conjuring trick, aerial cakes and circuses to divert the masses from the real business at hand: the class struggle.

In their hundreds of thousands the people stare upward—proud, entranced, longing, wistful—as the ship makes its way at slow speed and low level northeastward across a metropolis seized with zeppelin fever. Young and old, male and female, rich and poor, high and lowly, Communist and Nationalist—all are united in a single, upturned, beatific grin. From an international conference in the Wintergarten comes a radio greeting: "We greet the *Graf Zeppelin* as an ambassador of good will to the entire world."

It is Hearst's star reporter, Lady Hay, who duly reports the *Graf*'s arrival over the German capital, dropping her "copy" via a little parachute over Berlin airport, along with some rolls of film. The story will be blazed in front-page headlines in America's morning papers:

Cheering Multitudes Fill Berlin Streets as Ship Passes, Lady Hay Radios
EXCLUSIVE BY LADY DRUMMOND-HAY
Famous Correspondent Who Is Taking The Hearst-Zeppelin
Round-World Flight

It takes half an hour to cross Berlin. By twelve they are over Stettin, Poland. Here they make a course change to east-northeast, heading for Danzig. They have been flying for six and a half hours now—for most of that time at a height of one and a half times the ship's own length above the ground. In the navigation room of the control car, with its wide chart table and drawers full of charts, silence reigns. No one talks. A side window is open. Concentration is total. The atmosphere is quiet, controlled, professional.

A meteorological ("met") report comes in from the state-of-the-art radio room—in constant shortwave radio contact around the globe, working round-the-clock receiving met reports and sending endless progress reports to the king of Spain and press dispatches in half a dozen languages—and its implications are studied by senior watch officers Captain Ernst Lehmann and Captain Carl Hans Flemming. Both are veterans of zeppelin flight—Lehmann the commander of the first airship to fly for more than a hundred hours nonstop, Flemming the holder of the unbroken world altitude record for airships: twenty-four thousand feet. Next to them stands the ship's meteorologist, Dr. Seilkopf, specially attached to this flight from the German marine observatory in Hamburg.

At length Captains Lehmann and Flemming move off through a door that leads to the forward part of the control car—the bridge. Here, in this almost cloistered atmosphere of purposeful calm, Dr. Eckener, seated in his favorite chair, has ample opportunity to reflect on where he has come from and where he is going on his life's mission, on his temerity in setting off around the globe in a flying machine bigger than a battleship across lands and seas never before seen from the air—and actually hoping to get away with it.

He has thought about it often, the defining moment, the surprise encounter that led to it all. And now—Mother Russia by the evening, with a bit of luck. "Captain Flemming, Sir, the latest position report, if you'd be so kind."

All through the remaining hours of daylight, Dr. Eckener's dream machine, with its sixty men and one woman on board, rumbles east toward the Soviet frontier and the gates of Asia.

## Chapter Two

# The Dreamer and the Dream

*I suppose we shall soon travel by air-vessels; make air
instead of sea voyages; and at length find our way to
the moon.*

LORD BYRON (1822)

The encounter that had led Hugo Eckener to his post on the bridge of the *Graf,* heading for Siberia, following a line around the planet, had happened nearly a quarter of a century before, on an afternoon in February 1906. He was living in his modest house on the edge of Friedrichshafen with his wife and children, writing his book on aspects of contemporary economics, a quiet, studious, aesthetic, intellectual family man heading for early middle age, trying to earn a living as a freelance journalist, minding his own business.

I was working in the garden, and our maid came to me, quite excited, to say that Count Zeppelin was ringing the doorbell. I told her to invite the Count in and show him into the living room, where I would join him immediately. I pulled off my working-smock, tried to make myself presentable for the prominent visitor, and went into the room. Here I found the old gentleman in meticulously correct morning clothes, with silk hat and yellow gloves, the courteous and distinguished aristocrat which he was at all times.

I was curious to know what had caused him to call on me. He drew a copy of the *Frankfurter Zeitung* from his coat pocket, pointed to an article signed "Dr. E.," and asked if I had written it. I said I had, whereupon he said he wanted to thank me for the friendly tone in which I had written about him personally, but he wished to discuss further with me some inaccurate statements included in my article.

The old count, as "Dr. E." well knew, did not have a wildly favorable reputation locally. The "crazy count," the "mad inventor," was how they spoke of him, "the aerial dreamer down at the lake." Nearly six years before, in the summer of 1900, he had launched the first of his amazing flying machines: LZ-1, Luftschiff Zeppelin (Zeppelin Airship) Number One. The huge contraption had lumbered into the air above Bodensee for a few minutes, proved difficult to control, and descended to the lake again. Judged useless by the official observers, it was dismantled and sold for scrap.

Then, to the surprise of all, in January 1906 the crazy count was back, hell-bent on another perilous ascent with another amazing flying machine, LZ-2, better if not bigger than the one before, and Hugo Eckener was commissioned to write a report about it for the papers. The maiden flight did not go well. A strong wind got up, blowing the zeppelin over the land. Then the engines and steering failed, and the airship crashed and was totally wrecked, fortunately without injury to its inventor and captain, Count Zeppelin, or anyone else on board.

In his newspaper account of the debacle, Eckener described the machine as wanting in many respects, though he tried to be constructive rather than damning. "There were moments," he wrote, "particularly at the beginning of the flight, when the airship flew wonderfully well." But irritatingly, from the count's point of view, Eckener's report had in general been highly unfavorable, pointing out his airship's technical failings and unsatisfactory flight capabilities with unblinking candor. A few weeks after the calamity, therefore, the count decided to pay the doctor a visit and talk the thing through man to man. This meeting was to prove the turning point in the zeppelin story.

There had been nothing wrong with his latest ship, Count Zeppelin assured Dr. Eckener, except that it had no stabilizing fins at the stern, no *Empennage,* as he called it, such as an arrow has to enable it to fly straight. He was going to carry on in spite of everything, he said, and his next ship would have stabilizing fins so it could hold a steady course.

"His statements convinced me," Hugo Eckener was to recall:

> And when he extended a very friendly invitation to me to call on him whenever I wanted information on any question, I accepted gladly, perhaps more from a human interest in the personality of the Count himself than from any real interest in his ideas on airship construction. But when he invited me to dinner a few days later, I went with a faint and not entirely agreeable premonition that the visit might lead to a relationship that could influence my future life and work to a great extent. The result was more far-reaching than I ever suspected.

Count Ferdinand von Zeppelin, cavalry general turned aeronaut, was born on July 8, 1838, near Konstanz on the Bodensee in the southern German state of Württemberg. The world he was born into was the old, comfortable, nearly feudal world of the German aristocracy, a military-cum-aristocratic system whose benefits were to bring him advantage and whose connections were to afford him easy access to the ruling elite of the land. One of the hallmarks of this world was a patriotic devotion to the pursuit of arms and the arts of war. It was therefore a natural step for him to join the Württemberg Military Academy at the age of seventeen, and for almost four decades he was to pursue his military career with great dedication and ability in war and peace—until the catastrophe that was to change his life, and history.

In the summer of 1863 the twenty-five-year-old count took himself off to America as the king of Württemberg's military observer in order to follow the progress of the American Civil War. For a few weeks he was attached to the headquarters of the Army of the Potomac; he was nearly captured in a cavalry skirmish in Virginia; he had an audience with Abraham Lincoln; then, after less than two months with the Union Army, he turned his back on the war and headed north to explore America's frontier wilderness. On an adventurous canoe trek he traveled through the Great Lakes in the company of two Russians and their native guides, subsisting on water rats (cooked at first, raw later) before finally returning to civilization at St. Paul, Minnesota, on August 17. There, by chance, an event occurred that in time was to have some bearing on the zeppelin saga. On the very day he reached St. Paul, a German balloonist who had served in the Union Army inflated a large ex-army observation balloon across the street from Zeppelin's hotel, and two days later he took Zeppelin up in a brief tethered ascent—his first, and for many decades his only, experience of manned flight.

Though half a century later he would claim that this ascent marked the beginning of his interest in the possibility of dirigible flight, in fact it seems to have done no such thing, merely confirming the value of balloons for military observation. What the balloon ascent *had* done, crucially perhaps, was to introduce him to the basic notion of manned flight. So when, a decade later, in March 1874, the German postmaster general, Heinrich von Stephan, founder of the World Postal Union, wrote a remarkably prophetic article on the subject of world postal service and airship travel, Zeppelin (then on convalescent leave after a riding accident) was interested enough to read it.

"Providence has surrounded the entire earth with navigable air," declared the postmaster general. "This vast ocean of air still lies empty and wasted today, and is not yet used for human transportation." The count was fatally hooked. In this he was not alone. Since earliest times man had longed to take to the air and soar toward the sun like a god. But it was not until the end of the eighteenth century that human beings finally succeeded in rising into the skies in the world's first successful aircraft, the balloon. The first to fly were two Frenchmen, Pilâtre de Rozier and the marquis d'Arlandes, who in November 1783 made a short ascent from Versailles in a large and beautiful paper balloon full of hot air from a wool and paper fire. They were followed less than a fortnight later by Professor Jacques Charles and Marie-Noël Robert in a hydrogen balloon launched from the Tuileries in Paris—the first industrial use of this lighter-than-air gas, which had only recently been identified. So began man's long and hazardous climb toward mastery of the air.

Simply to float in the air was not enough, though. Almost at once the early aeronauts experienced the limitations of balloons. It was impossible to steer them. You went where the wind took you. And all too often it took you where you didn't want to go. "The vehicles, Sir," pronounced Dr. Johnson, "can serve no use until we can guide them. I had rather now find a medicine that can cure an asthma."

The balloon needed power to propel it and a rudder to steer it by. If ships of the sea had sails, why shouldn't ships of the air have them too? And oars? And paddles? Why not flap wings like a bird? Why not use real birds to pull the balloon through the sky? As each new invention failed, the aeronauts tried something else. They tried man power to drive paddle wheels. They tried clockwork to drive airscrews. They even tried primitive rocket power. But nothing would budge the balloon from its obstinate windborne course. Bit by bit, as the decades passed, the basic elements of a truly dirigible balloon— streamlined envelope, ballonet, rudder, propellers, trim weight, and load-bearing keel—were worked out. What was still lacking was an engine powerful enough to drive the balloon against the wind yet light enough to be lifted into the air.

Then, in 1852, a French engineer called Henri Giffard tried steam. In a gondola laden with a steam boiler, five hundred pounds of coke, and a three-horsepower engine of his own design, all slung below a 144-foot-long balloon full of flammable hydrogen, Giffard chugged away from the Paris Hippodrome at a steady six miles per hour, landing safely seventeen miles later at the successful conclusion of the first powered flight in history.

Giffard's flight was a milestone—but no more than that. Practical powered flight still eluded man, and this was still the situation twenty-two years later, when Count Zeppelin first became fired by the dream posited by the German postmaster general. The idea of a worldwide airship service profoundly fascinated him from that moment on. The difference between his thinking and anyone else's to date was its scale. What he had in mind was a colossus operating on a global remit.

In notes he scribbled in his diary after reading the article, under the heading "Thoughts about an airship," he set down his ideas concerning the kind of aerial ship he imagined could perhaps negotiate "the navigable air." His specifications were extraordinary in their prescience. "The craft would have to compare in dimensions with those of a large ship," he noted. "The gas volume so calculated that the weight of the craft would be supported except for a slight excess. The ascent will then take place through forward motion of the machine, which will force the craft so to speak against the upward-inclined planes. . . . The gas compartments will be divided into cells which can be filled and emptied individually."

Though Count Zeppelin was neither a trained engineer nor an aeronaut and had no precedent to go on, his sketches and notes reveal a breathtakingly bold and ambitious idea, which in concept, design, scale, essential features, and specifications—an airship over seven hundred thousand cubic feet in capacity, carrying cargo, mail, and twenty passengers, with a rigid structure of vertical rings held in position by longitudinal girders, a row of some eighteen separate gas cells between the rings, and a fabric outer cover—was in effect a primitive, albeit theoretical, prototype of the later passenger zeppelin *Bodensee,* which took to the air forty-five years later. At a stroke, he had hit on the solution to the fundamental problem of airship design—how to make an airship big enough and strong enough to carry a useful payload of passengers and freight. He had done so by inventing, in a brief fit of inspiration, a unique form of flying machine—the rigid airship.

There remained an apparently insoluble problem—the power plant. Steam had been tried in 1852, gas in a tethered ascent in 1872, but both were unsatisfactory, with a crippling power-weight ratio, and dangerous. At this point nothing suitable was in existence. The count was ahead of his time; his plans were to remain stillborn, buried as scattered notes among his papers, for another quarter of a century.

For the next ten years or so, Count Zeppelin pursued his military career in the Prussian-dominated German Imperial Army. Steadily he rose through the hierarchy. He took command of a regiment. He assumed the rank of colonel. He was appointed military attaché to the Württemberg embassy in Berlin. Two years later, in 1885, he was made Württemberg's ambassador to Berlin. It was then that he chose to make his first move to turn his airship dream into reality.

His reasons for doing so were both military and patriotic. It had come to his attention that the French army had developed a remarkable nonrigid airship, called *La France*. In 1884, powered by a novel new electric motor and flown by two officers of the French army balloon corps, Captains Charles Renard and Arthur Krebs, this airship had become the first aircraft in history to return to its starting point against the wind. The performance and usefulness of the new French ship were wildly exaggerated, but Count Zeppelin was greatly alarmed. Germany's traditional enemy—thirsting for revenge after its defeat in the Franco-Prussian War—had stolen a march on the Fatherland and now had the potential to threaten it from the skies with whole fleets of airships, or so he thought.

In 1887 the count resurrected his earlier ideas for a rigid airship and sent a memo to his friend King Wilhelm of Württemberg, urging an immediate start to a military airship development program. The type of airship he had in mind was basically his own. Originally conceived as a long-range civil air transport, or air cruiser, as he called it, he now saw it as primarily a military weapon. "It should have a very large lifting capacity," he told the king, "in order to carry personnel, cargo or explosive shells. All three requirements demand a very large gas volume, hence a very large airship." With transcendent vision he concluded: "Airship travel will certainly be of inestimable importance, not only for warfare but also for general commerce (shortest route across mountains or seas, and for exploring the earth—North Pole and interior of Africa)."

Count Zeppelin never envisaged involving himself in such a program, but his circumstances were soon to change. As the Württemberg ambassador in the Prussian capital, his task of promoting Württemberg's interests without offending Prussian sensibilities was a delicate one—too delicate, it proved, for a man as staunch and forthright as Zeppelin. In 1890, shortly after resigning his ambassadorship and returning to the Württemberg army as a cavalry brigadier, he wrote a secret memo to Kaiser Wilhelm II protesting the fact that the Württemberg army was always under Prussian command. The kaiser took strong objection, and so did the Prussian general staff. Not long after, the count was removed from his command on the trumped-up grounds of failing to properly carry out his orders in the army's autumn maneuvers. He had no option but to resign his commission and abandon his military career with the rank of lieutenant general (ret.)—a shattering blow to a man of his capabilities and sense of honor, and a total surprise to all who knew him.

The count's dismissal from the elite military body he had served faithfully throughout his career was the greatest and most traumatic event of his life. "It is God's will," he noted in his journal. "May He give me the strength to bear it and do the best I can. Amen."

Count Zeppelin was fifty-two when his career was so brutally and dishonorably ended. He was virtually unemployable in any political or diplomatic capacity. Unless he found something else to engage his undoubted energy and talents, he was doomed to rot in enforced retirement on his lonely estate. A much later psychological study of the count at this point of psychic trauma concluded that in order to survive he would have to undergo massive overcompensation:*

> Thus emerged a psychologically modified Count Zeppelin. Beneath his quiet and courtly manner would be a patriot even more fervent for his German *Vaterland,* even firmer in his Swabian loyalties, and resolutely intent to show up Prussian military posturing by developing a weapon of war that would overshadow Berlin's other technological innovations. Zeppelin projected his drive for professional and personal rehabilitation onto a new plane of activism—quite literally into an aerial machine that would move majestically above his beloved Germany, humble his enemies at home, and defeat imperial enemies abroad.

Since he had nothing else to do, and since nobody else would do it for him, he would build his own airship himself, and thus match the French and save the Fatherland. To the secretary of the king of Württemberg he wrote in June 1891:

*Professor Henry Cord Meyer, *Count Zeppelin: A Psychological Study* (Auckland, New Zealand, 1998).

I have the honour to ask you to inform His Majesty that I intend soon to build aerial vehicles, which I am satisfied will be dirigible even in wind currents. My airships are designed to facilitate rapid transport regardless of terrestrial obstacles and will thus be of greatest importance for military and especially naval purposes. Before taking any other steps than to apply for a patent, I consider it my duty to alert the Imperial Government to my invention.

The odds were hugely stacked against him. He had never built such a thing in his life—never built anything, in fact—and neither had anyone else. He had the idea, but that was all. He did not know where the money was going to come from, or the materials, or the expertise to build it or fly it. All he had was his determination, his strength of character, his conviction—and one great breakthrough.

The missing link in the count's original design of all those years ago had been the power plant. The electric motor of the French dirigible *La France* had proved next to useless, for the batteries to drive it weighed more than half a ton each and were used up in no time. But in 1885 the German mechanical engineer and inventor Gottlieb Daimler developed the first successful petrol-fueled high-speed internal combustion engine, with a power-weight ratio so massively reduced that the following year he was able to drive a four-wheeled carriage with it, and later a boat. Here at last was the power plant that was to drive motorized vehicles of the future on land, water, and in the air. In 1888 Dr. Karl Woelfert successfully used a primitive two-horsepower Daimler engine to drive a small dirigible balloon a short distance in a test flight at Cannstatt, in Württemberg. But it was not until the young Brazilian aeronaut Alberto Santos-Dumont successfully demonstrated small petrol-driven hydrogen-filled pressure airships in flights in and around Paris at the turn of the century that safe and practical dirigible flight was truly born.

Suddenly the groundbreaking zeppelin-type rigid airship was no longer a theoretical invention but a potentially practical machine. With no precedent to guide him, the count improvised the technology as he went along. He was helped in this by a young engineer called

Thomas Kober, who shared both his enthusiasm and his ignorance. Kober's first design for a powered rigid airship cargo carrier was a considerable departure from the count's original inspired concept of 1874, owing more to the railway transport system than anything aeronautical—in effect it was an "aerial express train," consisting of a powered towing section pulling two unpowered sections for passengers and freight ships. In the hope of obtaining government funding for the development of this project for military purposes—reconnaissance, communication, reinforcement, bombardment of enemy forts and troops, and the like—the count submitted his plans to the Prussian war ministry. Not surprisingly, they were rejected. Plans for a more conventional single-structure airship were also turned down on the grounds of structural frailty and insufficient power. The only alternative was to fund the construction of his invention himself.

The count bombarded anyone he thought could assist him, from emperor to king to general, from business tycoon to engineer to balloonist. But still the authorities remained skeptical or indifferent. "May all be valid," noted the kaiser in response to one of the count's petitions, "but where's the money coming from?" The war minister was blunter. "Pure Jules Verne!" he scribbled in the margin of one of the count's more ambitious memoranda.

Then in 1896 a chink of light appeared. The prestigious Union of German Engineers invited the count to address a meeting in Karlsruhe. The king of Württemberg came to listen, as well as many of his prominent courtiers and several hundred engineers and businessmen. This time the count changed his tack somewhat. He did not talk about bombs and troop movements and spy flights over enemy territory, but about international commerce, world airmail, polar exploration, scientific reconnaissance over unknown lands. "I have solved the problem," he told his audience, "by the simple sober thinking of a serious man endowed with common sense. . . . My system is the best. If airships are ever possible, they will be mine."

That meeting was to prove a milestone in rigid airship history. Later in the year the Union of Engineers recommended that support be given to the count's project. Zeppelin launched an appeal for funds and founded the Joint Stock Company for the Promotion of Airship Travel, with its headquarters in Stuttgart. Though he succeeded in raising just over half the eight hundred thousand marks he needed to build his first airship, and had to meet the balance out of his own assets, he was now in a position to start work.

In June 1898 construction of the first Zeppelin airship, LZ-1, began in a big floating wooden hangar (it would be easier to come down on water than on land, the count reckoned, and the hangar could be turned into the wind whatever the direction) on the Bodensee by the village of Manzell, near Friedrichshafen, a place known to the count for its gentle winds and stable weather, for he had spent his boyhood in the nearby family castle of Girsberg.

With painstaking care, the first ship of a great new line was put together. The count worked in lonely isolation, far removed from the military establishment and the armaments industry that might have been expected to show an interest, cold-shouldered by his own class and gently mocked by the locals. When a newspaperman sought to interview him about his work, the count brushed him off with the words: "I am not a circus rider performing for the public. I am completing a serious task in the service of the Fatherland." For two years the count and his handful of specialist helpers battled against a daily plethora of new technological conundrums, until finally the extraordinary structure was completed.

The rigid airship conceived by Count Zeppelin was a revolutionary departure from the typical nonrigid airship of the period, which was essentially a small pressure airship consisting of a rubberized fabric gasbag that kept its streamlined shape by virtue of the pressure of the lifting gas inside; it was in effect little more than an elongated balloon that could buckle under structural and aerodynamic stresses. Not even the larger semirigid airship, which had a keel that could carry gondolas, engines, and other loads, could compare with the zeppelin, whose framework maintained its streamlined shape regardless of whether it was inflated with gas or not. This rigid structure permitted the possibility of a very much bigger ship, and therefore a very much greater volume of lifting gas, and therefore (since the lifting capacity of an airship increases with the cube of its dimensions) a very much more useful lift and payload that could be carried across far greater distances.

Four hundred and twenty feet long and just over thirty-eight feet in diameter, LZ-1 was, by the standards of its time, a vast miracle of intricate engineering, a gigantic experimental flying machine. The first zeppelin had a lift of over twenty-seven thousand pounds, but so heavy were the aluminum frame, engines, and ballast that it could lift a payload of only 660 pounds, even though the seventeen huge gas cells suspended inside the hull contained almost four hundred thousand cubic feet of buoyant hydrogen.

Hydrogen was to be the Achilles' heel of the airship concept in general. The most basic element of the universe, and the lightest of all atoms, it had been used to inflate and lift into the sky virtually every balloon and experimental airship since the second balloon flight in history back in 1783. The problem with hydrogen, however, is that it is flammable and, once ignited, will burn with an unquenchably intense flame and explode when mixed with air. Its proximity to the primitive petrol motors of the early airships was therefore always a permanent source of danger—though it was a petrol fire rather than a hydrogen fire that pioneer airshipmen feared most.

Not that Count Zeppelin was particularly burdened with that thought. In any case, there was no alternative, neither then nor for many years to come. Coal gas (or town gas) was unsuitable for anything but a small balloon, while helium, the second lightest gas after hydrogen, and safely inert, had not yet been located and extracted and was not to become industrially available (as a by-product of the American natural gas industry) till the 1920s. So Zeppelin and his successors had no option but to bite the bullet and take the risk—with what consequences they would in due course discover.

Word had got about, and on the evening of July 2, 1900, a festive crowd of some twelve thousand Germans, Austrians, and Swiss had gathered on the shore of the lake or taken to the water in a flotilla of rowing boats, yachts, and motor launches to watch this historic event. When all was ready, by way of a ceremonial overture Count Zeppelin took off his hat, called for silence, and led everyone in a short prayer. Then the zeppelin was drawn out of the hangar on its giant float by a small launch and handling crew, and the five participants in the world's first rigid airship flight went out by boat to board the ship's gondolas. Count Zeppelin and his friend the physicist Baron von

Bassus boarded the forward gondola; the journalist and African explorer Eugen Wolff boarded the rear gondola; mechanic Eisele manned the forward engine and mechanic Gross the rear engine. At three minutes past eight the handling crew on the float let go of the gondolas, and the first zeppelin rose into the air and golden dusk. Then, powered by two marine engines with the combined horsepower of one Volkswagen Beetle, and captained by a former cavalry general whose knowledge of how to fly an airship was entirely theoretical, it moved slowly forward. Count Zeppelin and his companions were setting off into the unknown.

As an object, the technological embodiment of an idea, the LZ-1 was fabulous to behold. It was not very well streamlined; in fact, it was crudely pencil-shaped, and it was not particularly beautiful either. But in terms of scale it was awe-inspiring. Never in human history had anyone had the hubris to attempt to fly anything quite so colossal up to the heavens. Judged as an aerial voyage, however, the colossus's maiden flight was rather less than fabulous. The LZ-1 took off slowly and ponderously, with its nose pointing sharply into the air. The three-hundred-pound movable weight brought it to an even keel, but then the weight jammed in the forward position and one engine stopped. As the nose began to dip, ballast had to be released in large quantities to prevent the ship from going nose-first into the water. In a flight of only eighteen minutes, LZ-1 covered no more than three and a half miles. Even earlier, less ambitious, nonrigid airships had flown a greater distance at a higher speed with superior maneuverability.

The crowd lining the shore and watching from boats on the water was not disappointed, however. It had been an extraordinary spectacle. More critical was a reporter sent from a Frankfurt newspaper. The count's experiments, he wrote the next day, "while extremely interesting, have undoubtedly proved conclusively that a dirigible balloon is of practically no value." The giant ship made only eight miles per hour, he noted, and suffered from a serious design fault in that the rigid hull was not rigid at all but hogged under load, with the middle bent upward and the two ends sagging down. The military commission formed a similarly adverse opinion. LZ-1, they reported, was "suitable for neither military nor non-military purposes."

Dr. Hugo Eckener, thirty-two-year-old economics journalist and occasional contributor to the *Frankfurter Zeitung*, had missed LZ-1's first flight because he had been on a sailing holiday in the Baltic. He had read the press accounts, though, and was aware that "the solution of a significant as well as a difficult problem was being pursued over Lake Constance." However, he did watch the second flight on October 7, 1900, not because he had any special interest in the old count's airship or in technology in general, for that matter, but because the *Zeitung* had commissioned him to cover the story as their local stringer, reckoning it wasn't worth sending their regular reporter down again.

Clad in his long autumn coat and soft hat, Eckener watched the proceedings through his telescope from the shore at Manzell. A little steamer puffed out to the floating hangar and towed the giant contraption out into the open; tiny human silhouettes swarmed over the long raft on which the ship's gondolas rested; and the crew members climbed on board. Eckener could just make out the diminutive figure of Count Zeppelin, with his long white moustache and jaunty white yachting cap. Then the airship's Daimler engines spluttered to life, and the crowd cheered as LZ-1 floated upward and then rumbled off toward the middle of the lake for a flight that was to last eighty minutes—and would have lasted longer if someone hadn't put distilled water into the petrol tanks by mistake.

Eckener reported to his paper afterward:

> Certainly the airship proved itself manoeuvrable. Amid cheers, it rose calmly and majestically into the air. It hovered over the lake, making small turns about its vertical axis. It also turned slightly about its horizontal axis, remaining steady and calm, always at about the same height and above the same place.

He found little else to enthuse about. "There was no question of the airship flying for any appreciable distance or hovering at various altitudes," he noted. "One had the feeling that they were very happy to balance up there so nicely, and indeed the fine equilibrium of the airship was the most successful aspect of the whole affair. But under what circumstances were the modest results, which I have described, achieved? Under the best possible conditions—an almost complete calm!"

Eckener went on to criticize the inadequate steering, the crude sliding weight to change pitch and attitude, and above all the lack of power, for he reckoned the average speed of around fifteen miles per hour was too slow to allow the ship to stand still in even a moderate wind, let alone make progress against it. He even wondered whether what he took to be maneuverability was actually the ship's being moved about by slight shifts in the air currents above the lake. It was an interesting experiment, he concluded, but not exactly promising. He didn't expect to see the thing again.

Three days later the count took his ship for a third trial flight, watched by the king and queen of Württemberg. Though this flight was brief, the ship managed to increase its speed to seventeen miles per hour before the framework began to bend and the flight was aborted. The count now believed his invention had shown enough promise to earn the backing of the government. He was mistaken. With all his funds exhausted, he had no alternative but to dismantle the LZ-1, sell off the aluminum, motors, workshops, and hangar, fire the workers, close down the organization, and pay off the stockholders and creditors. His private means were exhausted, and he was forced to dismiss most of his servants, sell his horse and carriage, and curtail all his living expenses. The count and his wife and daughter, if not exactly beggared, were condemned to live some distance beneath their aristocratic expectations. "I shall not go on building any more," he announced. "The world will never know how good my airship is." One member of his staff he did keep on, however. This was a shy, secretive, prickly but brilliantly talented design engineer, Dr. Ludwig Dürr, who had joined the company the previous year at the age of twenty-one and was promoted to chief engineer when his predecessor refused to fly on LZ-1 because the count was unable to obtain insurance for the ship. To retain Dürr was a shrewd move on the count's part, for the young engineer was to go on to design every other zeppelin in history.

◆　◆　◆

What followed were wilderness years for Count Zeppelin and his engineer. After the debacle of the LZ-1, Zeppelin wrote to a friend who was ill, "I too have become an invalid: my heart is broken." Neither the German navy nor the army had any use for his unproven invention, judging that in its present form it had little capability either as a long-range strategic scout or as an aerial bomber.

But the count persevered. In 1903 he launched a nationwide appeal for funds, firstly through the widely circulated magazine *Die Woche,* then by a carefully targeted mail shot: "I appeal to the German people," he wrote in a letter directed at sixty thousand of the country's leading citizens, "to sacrifice themselves for my undertaking and to support me in my persevering duty. Any sum will be welcome."

But the public now had no time for the "crazy inventor," and all they came up with was a paltry 8,000 marks. A member of the Union of German Engineers told the count to his face, "The monster will never rise again." But again the king of Württemberg came to the rescue. In 1904 he authorized a state lottery that raised 124,000 marks. To make up the balance of the capital sum needed to build a second airship, the count persuaded business associates to make lump-sum donations, and he mortgaged his wife's estates in Latvia for 400,000 marks.

If Count Zeppelin was a persevering man, he was not always a lucky one. Five years were to pass between the last flight of his first airship and the first flight of his next—a period in which the Wright brothers made the first successful airplane flights in America, while in France the Lebaudy semirigid airship became the world's first practical dirigible. Finally, LZ-2 was built and launched from its hangar on the edge of the lake at Manzell. Ludwig Dürr had made some improvements on the previous ship. Though slightly smaller than LZ-1, the new zeppelin was a lot more powerful, with two Daimler engines delivering eighty-five horsepower each, compared with the puny fifteen horsepower of LZ-1. The sliding lead weight that had caused such a problem on LZ-1's maiden flight had been replaced with small elevators and rudders under the hull; the inclusion of triangular section girders in the main hull structure did much to increase the ship's rigidity and resistance to bending forces.

◆ ◆ ◆

Dr. Hugo Eckener had never had the slightest interest in aeronautics. Born on August 10, 1868, the eldest of four children of Johann Eckener, a cigarette manufacturer in the cosmopolitan Baltic seaport of Flensburg, Germany's northernmost city, and his wife Anna, the young Hugo was brought up as a devout Protestant in a liberal bourgeois household. It was an age when manned flight was possible only by gas balloon, of which there were precious few in Flensburg. Hugo's preferred medium was not air but water. Flensburg was set on a picturesque fjord that wound down to the sea between beech forests on either shore. The young Eckener would spend every available moment sailing down the fjord or out along the seacoast, or walking in the woods, and often he would play truant from school to pursue these passions. Sailing was his paramount interest, and it was through sailing that he acquired his extraordinary ability to read the weather in all its guises.

Though he was only an average pupil at high school, with a faint bent for physics and math and a distinct liking for music and poetry, he came into his own when he went to university in Munich, avidly pursuing a wide range of intellectual interests, from the history of art and of civilization to logic and aesthetics and medieval literature. At the age of twenty-two, a broad-shouldered, blond-haired young man, he moved on to the University of Berlin to take a degree course in pure philosophy, his latest passion, but after graduation, with no clear idea what profession he would follow or how he would live his life, he decided to follow a more practical line of studies and enrolled at the Institute for Experimental Psychology, which Professor Wilhelm Wundt, one of the founders of modern behavioral psychology theory, had founded in Leipzig a few years earlier. It was here that Eckener wrote his thesis, "Variabilities in Human Perception," and took his doctorate summa cum laude.

Shortly before Eckener left Leipzig at the age of twenty-four he was offered a post at the University of Toronto to set up and direct a new Department of Psychology. But though his insight into the workings of the human mind was to prove useful in his future life, he was already finding experimental psychology a rather narrow field. He was becoming interested in sociology and economics, which seemed more relevant to the big issues of national life. Unable to make up his mind, he decided to enlist for his national service, serving for a year in the 86th Fusilier Regiment and leaving with the rank of sergeant. After returning to Flensburg he devoted himself to his economic studies, occasionally writing articles for the local Flensburg newspaper, and gathering material for his book, *Arbeitsmangel oder Geldknappheit* (Job Shortage or Financial Squeeze).

In his spare time he made long sailing trips in the Baltic, honing his navigation skills and his feel for the sea and the weather. On one of these he was joined by his best friend, Friedrich Maass, who brought his young sister Johanna with him. Johanna was petite, pretty, blue-eyed and long-haired, and seemed to know almost as much about boats and sailing and navigation as Hugo. They arranged to meet again. Later, on holiday in the Swiss resort of Davos shortly before Christmas 1895, he wrote her a letter which revealed the lyrical romanticism behind his bluff and sometimes austere exterior: "My Johanna, you are my love, my desire, my joy, my happiness, you are the air I breathe, my reason for living. Will you love me, will you be mine forever? Body and soul? Will you?"

In 1897, the year before Count Zeppelin founded his Joint Stock Company for the Promotion of Airship Travel, they married. They spent their honeymoon in Switzerland and Italy, then—since Hugo was not exactly hard up, thanks to his endowment from the family tobacco company—sailed across to Egypt, where they stayed the best part of half a year.

When they returned to Germany they settled in Munich, but not for long. Hugo Eckener was not a big-city person: too much commotion, too much noise. He needed peace and quiet in which to write. He also needed a mild climate to help him recuperate from a lung infection, which he feared might be tuberculosis, from which his father had died. One day the couple saw an advertisement in the paper for a house in Friedrichshafen, a quiet, attractive backwater town on Lake Constance, just across the water from Switzerland, blessed with one of the mildest and healthiest climates in the whole of Germany, and a place, moreover, where one could go sailing to one's heart's content and walk among mountains. Here Hugo could afford to live as a private scholar and occasional contributor of articles on art, music, and literature to a variety of upmarket newspapers.

In the summer of 1899—when Count Zeppelin was wrestling with the technological intricacies of the world's first rigid airship, LZ-1—Hugo Eckener and his wife and their two daughters, Lotte and baby Hanneliese, moved to the small town that would be their home for the greater part of their lives, only a mile or two from the hangar at Manzell, where the count's airship was taking shape.

Not long after Count Zeppelin's first encounter with Dr. Eckener, following the debacle of LZ-2's brief flight, the two men met for dinner at the count's hotel, the Deutsches Haus. Short, stocky, and driven, the count was also at that particular moment an outraged and recriminating man. To his younger friend he spelled out (not entirely fairly) the full extent of the malignant hostility with which his airship concept had always been regarded in government circles, and how callously the technicians, scientists, and industrialists who had once backed him now cold-shouldered him and would have no more to do with his venture.

It was at this meeting that Eckener made a fateful commitment. Only an unremitting educational and publicity campaign, he said, could turn the zeppelin enterprise around. An important factor in such a campaign would be a cult of personality—the engaging and ever newsworthy personality of the count himself. "I told the Count," Eckener related later, "that in view of the great progress with internal-combustion engines, I believed in the practicality of his ideas and that I would try to publicise his cause. He accepted my offer with thanks, though perhaps with some scepticism. Personally I was more optimistic."

Eckener's first act was to serve as a testimonial witness to Count Zeppelin's memorandum, "The Truth about My Airships," which was sent to the Prussian minister of war in Berlin on February 10, 1906. Almost certainly it was also Eckener who persuaded the count to release the memo to the press. The die was cast. In effect, Eckener had talked himself into a job, or talked the count into giving him one, as some people saw it. For reasons that not even he could fathom—perhaps because his life lacked a focus and a cause, perhaps also because the count's ambitions for his giant airships deeply intrigued him—Eckener perceived that life might never be the same again.

"I realised that I would have little time for my previous intellectual pursuits," he later wrote, "and I would have to devote most of my life to the Zeppelin project. And the changing fortunes of the Zeppelin during the next three years brought me to the point where I was to demonstrate the worth and capabilities of the rigid airship not only with the pen but also eventually with the steering-wheel in my hand. Thus the philosopher and economist was turned into an airship man."

None of this happened immediately. In 1907 Eckener and his family moved back to his home town of Flensburg. He was still trying to finish his book, still writing cultural pieces for the papers, and for the next few years he was involved with the zeppelin project only on a part-time basis—"more of an astonished spectator of these events," as he put it, "than an active participant. These were not merely my own experiences, but those of the entire German people. They were so exciting and tumultuous that they could be described without exaggeration as a portion of the great history of the German people."

At first Count Zeppelin had been devastated by the loss of LZ-2. "I shall build no more airships," he declared. But already a ground swell of sympathy was growing for this plucky old aristocrat, bravely taking on the future only to be scythed down repeatedly by fate. Within a short time after the demise of his second ship, he had been presented with the money for a third—250,000 marks from a lottery conducted in the state of Prussia, and another 100,000 marks as a gift from the kaiser himself. By May 1906 the new ship, LZ-3, was under construction at Manzell. It was identical in almost every respect to its ill-fated predecessor; it even included the very engines that had caused the LZ-2's demise. The one seemingly small but significant modification was the inclusion of two pairs of large horizontal stabilizer fins at the stern, intended to control the violent pitching that had been experienced on LZ-2's only flight.

The impact of Dürr's stewardship of the new zeppelin's design and construction was obvious from the moment the ship left the ground. LZ-3 represented a quantum leap in zeppelin capability. In a maiden flight of two hours, seventeen minutes, the ship achieved a speed of over twenty-four miles per hour while carrying a record load of sixty-two hundred pounds (most of it water ballast) and eleven people in its open gondolas. The government immediately donated half a million marks to help the count develop the zeppelin into a potential war machine and promised that if he could achieve a flight of twenty-four hours' duration, it would buy one of his ships outright.

Not only had the zeppelin's performance improved, but so had the public and military perception of it, although the latter remained doubtful about the giant zeppelin as a front-line weapon and inclined to favor its smaller, cheaper, more mobile scouting rivals, the nonrigid Parseval and the Prussian Airship Battalion's semirigid types. But nothing could deflate the count's soaring ambitions. "I can assert today," he wrote to the imperial chancellor at the end of the year, "that I can demonstrate the possibility of constructing airships with which five hundred men with full combat equipment can be carried for the greatest distances." ("Oh, no!" an incredulous official had scribbled in the margin. "Don't even think about it!")

In the summer of 1907 Zeppelin and Dürr worked away at modifications that could enable LZ-3 to meet the government's challenge. By now the principles of airship flight were well understood. Unlike an airplane, a heavier-than-air craft that can fly only as a result of aerodynamic lift (the effect of the airflow over the wings, caused by the plane being propelled forward by its engines), the airship is able to fly mainly as a result of the aerostatic lift provided by a lighter-than-air gas, like hydrogen—though it can also generate aerodynamic lift, and even land and take off aerodynamically like a plane if need be, by flying at appropriate speed in a nose-up attitude.

It was to assist this characteristic that Zeppelin and Dürr made their most significant modification to the new ship's design—the addition of horizontal tilting vanes (elevators or flaps) that could convert the forward motion of the ship into aerodynamic lift, particularly for takeoffs with greater loads. In normal flight, when the ship was more or less in equilibrium, altitude could also be controlled by these flaps (operated by an elevator wheel in the control car) in the same way that direction was controlled by the rudder.

Though aerodynamic lift was a major capability of an airship, it remained essentially an aerostat: unlike an airplane, it could stay in the sky if its engines stopped. Thus, flying an airship depended to a large extent on constantly adjusting its buoyancy. A ship could be "light" or "heavy" or "in equilibrium" at any given time. This depended on a number of variables, including the temperature of the gas inside the hull and of the air outside, the weight of the load, the amount of fuel consumed or gas vented, altitude, atmospheric pressure, and other factors like the weight of snow or rain that may have accumulated on the outer cover. Flying an airship was an arcane art that took time to learn. If the ship was heavy, the pilot might have to release ballast to lighten the load aerostatically, or obtain aerodynamic lift by flying in a nose-up attitude, or employ a combination of these. If the ship was too light, he might have to release gas, take on sea or rain water, fly in a nose-down attitude, or all of these.

As the summer passed, Count Zeppelin took the new ship on longer and longer flights—of three, four, even seven hours over the Bodensee and the south German countryside. It was an intensive course in zeppelin handling, with the count and his crew learning as they went along. So confident did he become of the safety and reliability of the airship that he even agreed to allow dignitaries like the crown prince of Germany and Countess Hella, as well as his own young daughter and his friend and colleague Dr. Eckener, to go on pleasure flights lasting up to eight hours.

But it was clear that a twenty-four-hour flight was beyond the capacity of LZ-3, and that a bigger ship would be needed to carry the fuel and ballast necessary for such endurance. The government agreed to grant four hundred thousand marks to build a new zeppelin, LZ-4—similar in most respects to LZ-3 but bigger and better and able to lift a load more than half again as large. If the new ship could stay aloft for the stipulated twenty-four hours over a distance of 435 miles, the government agreed to buy both it and its predecessor for 2.5 million marks.

The first endurance trial flight, on July 1, 1908, was sensationally encouraging. With twelve people on board and fourteen hours' worth of fuel, the count set off in command of the first international flight by zeppelin—a cross-country flight to Switzerland across the lake, returning to Manzell by way of Lucerne and Zurich. The flight lasted twelve hours, a world air-endurance record, and the international press seized on the event. It was, Eckener reckoned, the event that made Count Zeppelin a household name, establishing the reputation on which future events would build. The old count's seventieth birthday on July 8 turned into a popular celebration. Streets were named in his honor. Greetings poured in. The king of Württemberg awarded him the Gold Medal of Arts and Sciences. It was the turning point.

Shortly after dawn on August 4, 1908, the LZ-4 took off from the glassy waters of Lake Constance at the start of its twenty-four-hour proving flight to Mainz. The count was confident he could achieve his goal. So, it seemed, was the German nation. As the ship flew in splendid state up the valley of the Rhine, the populace poured out to honor its passing. No other aircraft in the world could aspire to fly around the clock, for hundreds of miles, and return whence it had started. The longest airplane flight in Europe to date had lasted no more than fifteen minutes (though within a few weeks of the zeppelin's long-distance flight, Orville Wright was to make a solo flight of an hour and a half in America). The zeppelin's flight became a triumphal procession: the ship was greeted with salutations of cannon fire from castle battlements, the hurrahs of the crowds in the town squares, and hats waved wildly from cathedral towers. Over Konstanz they flew, over Schaffhausen, Basel, and Strasbourg (then a German city).

In the early afternoon, problems arose. The engines had to be stopped in order to be refueled (a serious design defect). Each time this happened, the ship rose in altitude and blew off hydrogen through its automatic valves; it then became heavy and had to be flown at an upward angle to maintain lift, which, in turn, reduced the air speed to a very slow nine miles per hour. Just after four o'clock, an engine radiator's fan gear broke, and the count had no alternative but to land the ship by the banks of the Rhine at Oppenheim, a few miles south of Mainz, to carry out repairs. By the time these were finished, LZ-4 was too heavy to take off. Only by putting five of the crew and as much gear as could be spared ashore was it able to struggle up off the river, with the help of a tow from a passing steamer.

It was now 10:20 P.M., and darkness had fallen. The ship made it to Mainz in half an hour, then turned for home into a southwesterly head wind. A fan blade broke and had to be replaced. At around half past one in the morning, a crank bearing melted, stopping the forward engine. Then, a little south of Stuttgart, the after engine had to be stopped for refueling. With the headwind freshening and no forward way, LZ-4 was blown backward in the dark. As a matter of urgency, Count Zeppelin decided to bring the ship down so that the forward engine could be repaired by experts from the Daimler works nearby. At 7:51 A.M. LZ-4 touched down in a field near Echterdingen, a village southwest of Stuttgart, scattering cows and sheep as it went.

A vast crowd gathered. Soldiers had to be called out to cordon off the ship and serve as ground crew while engineers from the Daimler works tended the faulty engine. LZ-4 lay quietly at rest in the field, its bow line anchored to a farm wagon. Count Zeppelin had a doze in the gondola, then repaired to the local inn for lunch.

Around three o'clock there was a weather change. A sharp squall sprang up, tore the ship from its mooring, and bore it away side-on, with a soldier and two crew members still on board. One of the crew madly tried to valve gas to bring the ship down, but it snagged some trees, which tore the bow fabric open and ripped a forward gas cell. Gas cells at this time were made of rubberized cotton, and unknown to Count Zeppelin or any of his engineers at this time, such a fabric could emit sparks of static electricity if it rubbed against itself. There was a sudden enormous whoosh of flame as the hydrogen ignited, and then a colossal explosion. At the inn, the count heard the earth-shattering bang and rushed out with all the other guests. In horror he saw in the distance the entire ship consumed in a soaring column of fire. Within seconds it was a burnt-out wreck, though by some miracle the three men on board were saved.

As the count approached the scene, the crowd parted silently to let him pass, the men doffing their hats like mourners at a funeral. The count's head was bowed, and he looked old and broken. Staring for a moment at the smoldering wreckage, he turned and without uttering a word left the scene. Now seventy years old, he was sure no zeppelin would ever take to the air again.

David Lloyd George, a British cabinet member and future prime minister who happened to be visiting Stuttgart, arrived at the scene soon after the fire. Later he recalled:

> Disappointment was a totally inadequate word for the agony of grief and dismay which swept over the massed Germans who witnessed the catastrophe. There was no loss of life to account for it. Hopes and ambitions far wider than those concerned with a scientific and mechanical success appeared to have shared the wreck of the dirigible. Then the crowd swung into the chanting of "Deutschland über Alles" with a fanatic fervour of patriotism. What spearpoint of Imperial advance did this airship portend?

The extraordinary phenomenon Lloyd George observed was the beginning of what was to become known as the "Miracle of Echterdingen," deriving from the German people's perception of the role and symbolic import of Count Ferdinand von Zeppelin in their lives. With a nudge here and there from his publicity assistant, Dr. Hugo Eckener, the count's image as a national folk hero was being reshaped, fact and myth merging into the form of the heroic inventor, an emblem of German pride, honor, and endeavor. Shops sold zeppelin sweets, cigarettes, harmonicas, yachting caps. There were zeppelin streets, squares, parks, roses, and chrysanthemums. Newspapers followed his every move, recorded his every utterance. Holidaymakers in the thousands arrived in excursion steamers and circled his floating construction hangar, cheering their heads off. And his wondrous flying machine, the most awesome creation ever to challenge the skies, was seen as a symbol of German aspiration and achievement.

It was now a matter of national pride that the great man should be helped to develop his great invention, and the whole country rallied to the old count's aid. On the day after the accident, contributions toward the cost of a replacement ship began to pour in to his headquarters—from the kaiser, from the rich, from savings under beds, from Germans living in faraway lands, from the bowling club in Baden who sent 150 marks and the mining association of Essen who sent 100,000. Those who had no money sent sausages, hams, wine, a pair of hand-knitted woolen socks. A little girl wrote from Mainz:

> Mummy carried me from my bed out on the balcony. The sky was dark with many stars, and I saw the Zeppelin and heard its humming noise. It was so pretty. But on the next day we heard the terrible news that the beautiful airship had burned up. Then I cried an awful lot and told Mummy to send the Count everything in my piggy bank, so he could build a new airship.

Count Zeppelin had not lingered at Echterdingen but set off for home, worn out and very low. If Zeppelin was despondent, Eckener was unaccountably ecstatic. "When the Count returned dejectedly to Friedrichshafen the next day," he recalled, "and was met at the station by a silent, bareheaded crowd, I greeted him with the words, 'My congratulations, Your Excellency!' He looked at me with amazement when I told him that already during the night several hundred thousand marks had come in as a fund for a new ship. Yes, it was a miracle!"

"Well, then," replied the count, perking up mightily, "we'll go on ahead!"

By the end of the day money equal to the cost of the wrecked LZ-4 had come in, and the total of contributions from all sources would amount to 6.25 million marks. "The desire of the German people to send forth airships built on my system to span the world," the count wrote in a widely disseminated thank-you letter to the nation, "will give me the courage and the strength to continue my project."

The rehabilitation of the career and honor of the count was in hand. The words "airship" and "zeppelin" had become synonymous. On November 10, 1908, the kaiser himself came to Friedrichshafen, proclaimed Count Ferdinand von Zeppelin the greatest German of the twentieth century, and awarded him the exalted Prussian Order of the Black Eagle. The army, concluding that now might be a judicious moment to buy their first zeppelin, purchased the renovated LZ-3 and renamed it Z-1, the first of a not-very-long line of army rigid airships.

Forever after the count always spoke of the Echterdingen disaster as his *glücklichster Unglücksfahrt*—his "luckiest bad luck trip."


At first it seemed there was no looking back for Count Zeppelin and his brainchild. On September 3, 1908, with enough capital to put the whole venture on a sound basis for the first time, he founded his own airship construction company, Luftschiffbau Zeppelin, appointed a hardheaded business manager by the name of Alfred Colsman as managing director, and took possession of a large open area of ground just north of Friedrichshafen as the base of the enterprise. Here in due course a large double hangar was erected for the construction and storage of future airships, while subsidiary companies were brought into the burgeoning Zeppelin conglomerate to provide specialist products and services.

The old, seigneurial, pioneering stage of the Zeppelin venture was at an end. As if to underline the change, Alfred Colsman's first act as business manager was to recruit Hugo Eckener as the company's full-time director of public relations in 1909. This was not only a significant moment in the zeppelin's history, but also a decisive turning point in Eckener's life. By now he had become beguiled by the zeppelin dream, the call of the sky, the challenge of a problem he knew he could help solve. His book on economics had just been published in Leipzig. Most of the rest of his life would be dedicated to the zeppelin.

One of the first aims of the new company was to build a big new airship to replace the one lost at Echterdingen. Against the advice of the skeptics, the army, having bought the renovated LZ-3, also agreed to purchase the next zeppelin to come off the production line at Friedrichshafen, the LZ-5. In the spring of 1909 the new ship succeeded in making the longest powered flight to date—a triumphal thirty-seven-hour, thirty-nine-minute tour over 712 miles via Ulm, Augsburg, Nuremberg, Bayreuth, Leipzig, Schweinfurt, Würzburg, Heilbronn, and Stuttgart. The flight ended only when an exhausted Ludwig Dürr, asleep on his feet at the elevator wheel, rammed the ship's nose into a large pear tree during an intermediate landing near Göppingen. With the nose sawn off and patched up, the ship returned safely to base the next day, but it still failed to meet army speed and height requirements, and as a result the army declined to purchase the next ship, LZ-6, identical in all but detail to LZ-4 and LZ-5, preferring to rely on their own smaller but proven Parseval nonrigids.

Deprived of any more focused purpose, the new zeppelin became a kind of symbolic ambassadorial demonstration ship, a patriotic crowd-puller. Its technology was barely up to its aspirations, and it broke down and force-landed continually for all sorts of mechanical and meteorological reasons; but as a showstopper (at the International Aviation Exposition at Frankfurt, for example, doing VIP cruises up and down the Rhine) or soaring totem of imperial pomp, it did its stuff, thanks to the mind-over-metal determination of Count Zeppelin.

On August 27, 1909, the kaiser sent the count a telegram: "I request Your Excellency to advise by return mail when you will come to Berlin with the airship; since I will begin a Scandinavian vacation on 29 August, the flight cannot be later." The count had no option but to comply, and though one engine broke down, one propeller stopped, and another dropped off en route, the crippled ship struggled to the capital and proceeded on a stately tour over the rooftops to the cheers of the enthralled populace before landing in front of the kaiser, the royal household, and all the top brass of the state. Afterward the count and his crew were guests at a party with the kaiser at the Imperial Palace in Potsdam.

None of this was very profitable business, however. The army was still dissatisfied with the performance and reliability of the trial-and-error zeppelin airships, and again the count entered a period of bitter frustration. To the kaiser he fired off a recklessly unconsidered letter of invective and complaint, bewailing the fact that his airships had been so disregarded: "I have been ridiculed, pitied and variously held suspect—just as in earlier times! If I should die before I am given an opportunity to show what I can accomplish, it will be a great loss for Germany. Should war break out, I hope that I will be permitted to lead the best of my available airships into battle myself."


The count began to run out of funds again and sought the advice of Alfred Colsman. Until the army came to share the Zeppelin Company's view of the military potential of its rigid airship as a weapon of war, some other purpose would have to be found for it. Colsman, thinking laterally, came up with an idea. If we can't have a zeppelin air force, he suggested, why not have a zeppelin airline? Why not capitalize on the popular enthusiasm for the zeppelin by starting an airship service to carry fare-paying passengers? The airline could place orders for its ships from the construction company. The count agreed, but with extreme reluctance. As Colsman later explained: "In the use of his ships to earn money, he saw his ideas being profaned. . . . The enterprise remained for him, the feudal aristocrat and former military man, a tradesman's undertaking. . . ."

The German Airship Transportation Company (Deutsche Luftschiffahrts Aktien Gesellschaft, or DELAG) was founded on November 16, 1909, with the modest capital of $750,000. The long-term aim of the company was to link the major cities of Germany, and perhaps later the rest of Europe, with a zeppelin passenger service. In effect it was meant to be the world's first airline, though in reality it never managed to run a scheduled service or link German cities in any meaningful or reliable way. The Hamburg-Amerika Line steamship company acted as sponsor and booking agent, and a number of cities keen to have a passenger air link—Baden-Baden, Cologne, Dresden, Düsseldorf, Frankfurt, Gotha, Hamburg, Leipzig, Munich, and Potsdam—were prepared to provide landing fields and hangars.

In the summer of 1910, DELAG commenced operations with a new Zeppelin passenger airship, LZ-7, the first ship to be given a name: *Deutschland*. Four hundred eighty-six feet in length and 683,000 cubic feet in capacity, the ship was larger than its predecessors, and of necessity a great deal more comfortable. In addition to a crew of eight or nine, the *Deutschland* would carry up to twenty-four passengers in all the luxury that money—and the ship's lift—could bear. The passenger compartment was constructed as an integral part of the ship, with walls and ceiling of mahogany plywood, carpeted floors, and rich mother-of-pearl inlays on the pillars and ceiling beams. Seated in wickerwork chairs by large sliding windows, passengers could enjoy a panoramic view of the world few had ever seen.

The inaugural flight of the *Deutschland* took place on June 28, 1910. This was the first commercial flight of the first commercial aircraft, at a time when airplanes were still small and fragile—though only a few weeks before, a plane had made the first double crossing of the English Channel without landing, and only a few weeks later another was to make the first flight over the Alps. Oddly, Count Zeppelin had always believed that the future in the air would eventually belong to the airplane, but he also thought it would be many years before planes surpassed the big airships as a practical form of transportation. Not that the *Deutschland* was all that practical. Like virtually all its successors in that experimental prewar period, it suffered from inadequate engine power, which meant that its speed was insufficient to cope with even a moderate head wind.

With twenty-three journalists and an ample supply of caviar and champagne on board, the *Deutschland* took off from Düsseldorf and proceeded downwind toward the picturesque Wupper Valley, under the command not of Count Zeppelin—who was on an expedition to Spitzbergen with the kaiser's brother to reconnoiter the chances of a Zeppelin flight to the North Pole—but of an inexperienced captain from the Prussian Airship Battalion. The captain's first mistake was to take off before receiving a meteorological report. His second was to proceed before the wind, so that when the wind grew stronger and the ship turned for home, it could make no headway. Then one engine broke down, and the ship was driven stern-first into a towering thunderstorm, which tossed it up like a balloon to thirty-five hundred feet, causing it to lose large quantities of gas and plummet helplessly into the Teutoberger Forest. Fortunately, it did not catch fire and no one was injured, except for a crew member who broke a leg when he jumped from the after gondola. But the *Deutschland* was a total wreck.

One immediate consequence of DELAG's disastrous start was Colsman's appointment of Hugo Eckener as the company's flight director, with the tasks of demonstrating the usefulness and safety of zeppelin airships, flying them himself, training others to fly them, organizing flight operations, and supervising construction. For this daunting raft of responsibilities he was to be paid the then-not-inconsiderable salary of one thousand marks per month. "I personally had to assume the difficult task of proving the capabilities of the Zeppelin airships," he wrote later. "This caused me many sleepless nights, and tortured hours, before success was achieved."

For a start, the ships were too slow to be flown safely in anything but a gentle breeze, and no one had yet worked out how to handle their vast bulk on the ground. Eckener himself was completely unqualified for the job. He had flown in airships as a passenger and once or twice had held the wheel, and though as a small-boat sailor he had become an uncanny reader of weather conditions—a crucial attribute for an airship commander—he was now being asked to train pilots before he had been trained himself. But he was a quick learner, and Count Zeppelin, now a veteran pilot, was a masterful teacher. In short order Eckener earned his International Aeronautical Federation Airship Pilot's License (Germany) No. 10, and he was very soon to demonstrate a mastery of airship handling that was never surpassed— but not before he had brought the whole enterprise, and his own life and the lives of others, to the brink of catastrophe.

LZ-7's less than brilliant beginning was followed a few weeks later by LZ-6's more than dazzling end, when the ship was spectacularly destroyed in its hangar by a fire started by workmen cleaning the gondolas with petrol. A replacement ship, LZ-8, *Deutschland II*, enjoyed an even briefer flying career than its DELAG predecessors. On May 16, 1911, under the command of Eckener on his first flight as a zeppelin captain, the new ship was walked out of its hangar at Düsseldorf in blustery conditions by a three-hundred-strong ground crew for the start of its latest aerial excursion. Suddenly it was caught by a gusty crosswind, wrested away from its handlers, and smashed down broken-backed, with its forward section coming to rest on top of the hangar and its tail impaled thirty feet up a high windscreen fence that was there to prevent just such mishaps. Again no one was injured, and the shocked passengers and crew were able to scramble down fire ladders to safety.

For Eckener the experience was a salutary lesson. So far virtually every zeppelin in the world's first airline had come to grief. Though the public and the press—even those members of the press who had nearly breathed their last in the first *Deutschland* accident—still remained staunchly behind the zeppelin experiment, the commander of the ill-fated *Deutschland II* saw things differently.

If he had had his way, Eckener would not have dreamed of taking the *Deutschland II* out of the hangar, let alone off the ground, in the conditions prevailing on that day. He had been pressured into doing so by the passengers, who were there for the thrill, and by the spectators, who were there for the spectacle. After the debacle, he vowed that such a thing would never be allowed to happen again. "I paid for my weak-kneed decision," he would comment later, "by damaging the ship so badly she had to be almost completely rebuilt, and thereafter was cured of such impulsive acts."

Henceforth the paramount priority of the zeppelin commander at all times would be the safety of the passengers and crew, and therefore of the ship. No external pressure of any kind—public, commercial, or political—would be allowed to compromise that golden rule. It was not easy. "A refusal to fly," Eckener noted, "would make us look ridiculous and damage the enterprise; while an irresponsible decision to take off could endanger the ship. How many times in such circumstances have I cursed the fate that made me an airship captain."

Eckener decided the time had come to give DELAG's amateurish operations a great shake and set them down on a more rigorously professional basis. The first step was to intensify crew training. A second was for the company to organize its own weather-forecasting service, with meteorological stations at each zeppelin base, for Eckener perceived that meteorology and navigation were the keys to successful operational flying. Another innovation was to improve ground handling safety by installing docking rails and trolleys to which the zeppelin could be attached while being walked in or out of its hangar in gusty conditions, thus preventing a recurrence of the *Deutschland II* accident. Finally, something would have to be done about engine performance and reliability, which had so far been poor. At Eckener's insistence DELAG turned from Daimler to Maybach, a company specializing in airship engine manufacture, for the new 145-horsepower plants to be fitted to the latest ship of the line, LZ-10.

What Eckener had initiated was a revolution in the theory and practice of rigid airship operations. "More and more we learned to overcome our difficulties," he summed up, "by making proper arrangements and developing a sure skill. The DELAG fulfilled its main purpose, which was to train a nucleus of qualified commanders and steersmen, and above all to develop a familiarity with the elements in which the craft had to fly in the ocean of the air, with all its dangerous tricks. The DELAG became the university of airship flight."

Thanks in part to the new outlook instilled by Eckener, LZ-10, the *Schwaben*—named for the duchy of Swabia, where Count Zeppelin was born—was to break the cycle of launch and destruction that had gone before. A little smaller but a lot more maneuverable than the *Deutschland* rigids, the new zeppelin proved to be the airline's lucky ship, at least for a time. Fitted with three of the new Maybach engines, the *Schwaben* could get up to a top speed of forty-five miles per hour on a good day, and after entering service in July 1911 it was to fly the length and breadth of Germany under Dr. Eckener's expert command.

The *Schwaben* and its able commander saved the passenger zeppelins—with the help of the weather. Eckener recalled:

> That marvellous summer of 1911, with its three months of practically unbroken fine weather, was a perfect godsend. No longer were the flights daily exposed to the threat of weather disasters. For weeks and months our pilots flew in calm safety and began to understand and master the strange new element. Nature, "who hates man's handiwork," can at times be kind and gentle. But woe to him who disregards her warnings and grows incautious! It was caution which the *Schwaben* pilots learnt to exercise more and more as public confidence slowly returned. They could not risk losing it again.

Though airplanes were snapping at the great airships' heels— achieving heights up to a thousand feet, speeds up to a hundred miles per hour, distances in excess of 1,250 miles (St. Louis–Chicago–New York, in stages)—and though other countries, notably France and Britain, were developing airships of their own (the British were completing a modest rigid airship called the *Mayflower*)—no airplane or foreign airship could remotely compare with the *Schwaben,* the first successful commercial zeppelin.

Though DELAG was never able to fulfill its mission of operating a scheduled intercity airline—providing instead short-haul air tours of the German countryside, with occasional diversions to a neighboring city if the wind was in the right direction—a flight on the *Schwaben* was still a fabulous event, especially in an age unused to viewing the Earth from the sky. In the luxuriously appointed passenger gondola, complete with a "Ladies' Corner" and a washroom with basin and toilet, the smartly dressed passengers would sit at small tables near the open windows, looking down at Germany rolling by while feasting on caviar, lobster, capon, and cold Westphalian ham, washed down with Rhine wine and champagne, 1842 cognac, and "Sherry pale very old," all served by a steward in uniform and peaked cap. For the privilege they paid a hefty two hundred marks for a one- or two-hour flight, and up to six hundred marks for a longer sortie—the equivalent of three months' pay for an average German worker. None doubted it was worth the money, and few felt the slightest fear. "Anxiety and scruples fall to pieces," claimed the English-language version of the DELAG brochure, "and flit away like floating bits of fog."

Even after the *Schwaben* was accidentally destroyed in a fire on the ground in 1912, the fare-paying public continued to pour on board the remaining ships. By 1913 three more ships had been added to DELAG's commercial Zeppelin fleet: the *Viktoria Luise,* named after the kaiser's daughter and operating out of Frankfurt; the Hamburg-based *Hansa,* which made DELAG's first overseas flight to Copenhagen in September 1912; and the *Sachsen,* based in Leipzig. Thanks to Dr. Eckener's operational doctrine of safety first, DELAG ships made hundreds of flights between the spring and autumn of 1913 without mishap.

Count Zeppelin the genius inventor, Dr. Dürr the master builder, Dr. Eckener the ace flier, Herr Colsman the business mastermind—under this extraordinary quartet the future of DELAG and the Zeppelin Company seemed secure. To the German people the zeppelin was a symbol of their world leadership in science and technology, its seventy-six-year-old inventor the greatest popular hero since Bismarck.

But neither the army nor the navy was as enthusiastic about the zeppelin as a military weapon as Count Zeppelin hoped they would be. "The *thing* itself is not very safe," commented navy chief admiral Tirpitz after the Echterdingen disaster. "Whether the *concept* is safe is very much in dispute." Though the zeppelin's potential as a strategic scout or bomber was considerable, its actual performance was less convincing, and under Count Zeppelin's excessively cautious leadership, improvement was slow.

It was largely the pressure of public opinion that forced the hands of the army and navy chiefs. Following the success of the DELAG operations, both arms were prompted to send their crews for training on DELAG airships and to place orders for military zeppelins, the army taking eight in the run-up to World War I, the navy two. None of these ships was fit for war service. Too small, underpowered, vulnerable, insufficiently equipped—really they were experimental ships, flying test beds for the true aerial warships to come. Both the navy ships soon met with disaster. The L-1* was forced down in the North Sea by bad weather and sank, with the loss of fourteen lives, in September 1913— the first fatalities in zeppelin history. A month later the L-2 was destroyed shortly after takeoff on a test flight at Johannisthal, Berlin, when its hydrogen was ignited by a sparking petrol engine and the ship fell in flames, killing all twenty-eight people on board.

After the disaster at Johannisthal, the naval airship division had no military airships and no chief, for he had been killed in the accident. Very soon it had no Count Zeppelin either, for in a stand-up shouting match with the naval minister at the funeral of the L-2's victims, he blamed the navy for the catastrophe and was promptly sidelined by an irate Tirpitz. Though Zeppelin remained the company's figurehead at Friedrichshafen, he was no longer in control and had little say in future events. From now on it would be Alfred Colsman and Hugo Eckener who would direct the company. Bitter, dispirited, and indifferent, the old aristocrat largely turned his back on his invention, busying himself instead with plans for a giant five-engine *Staaken* bomber plane, commenting toward the end that "whatever was done with the airships was all the same to me."

Ultimately the invention had outrun the inventor. Count Zeppelin's unswerving devotion to the primal idea, his refusal to undertake

---

*All German civil Zeppelins were numbered in order of production, the number being prefixed with the letters "LZ" (for *Luftschiff Zeppelin*, meaning Zeppelin Airship). Most German army Zeppelins also bore the prefix "LZ," but navy Zeppelins simply had the letter "L" (for Luftschiff).

basic research into structures and aerodynamics, his almost pigheaded refusal to accept expert advice or entertain the possibility that some of his developmental solutions might be flawed—merely, as one historian put it, "making empirical modifications as experience dictated"—had begun to stifle the development of the unique machine he had labored so long to bring forth. Now, forty years after the count had first grappled with the concept, it would be left to others to push it through to fruition in the forcing house of war.

"In the final analysis," Hugo Eckener was to tell an audience of workers, officials, and international aviation experts at the Zeppelin works many years later:

> Count Zeppelin was not an inventor. He was not just some dabbler caught up in a technological problem, with a single-minded devotion to his conception as some sort of salvation for mankind. His airship was not an end in itself. It was rather a means to an end. He hoped to serve his Fatherland with it, to create greater security and military strength for Germany. Count Zeppelin was basically a politician at heart, in the broadest sense a politician of genuinely statesmanlike dimensions. Under the threatening pressures of his times his concern and thoughts were always for Germany's national welfare.

In the spring of 1914 construction began on a brand-new ship of greatly advanced design: LZ-26. With a properly streamlined hull, a new light alloy called Duralumin* for the framework, simple cruciform fins and control surfaces at the stern, improved propellers and enclosed gondolas, this was the first truly modern zeppelin. But LZ-26 was never to take a single fare-paying passenger. Before it had even made its first test flight, the Zeppelin enterprise and the entire world were overtaken by history.

On August 3, 1914, Germany declared war on France, and at midnight on August 4 Britain declared war on Germany. Nothing would

---

*The name given to a family of aluminum alloys containing small and varying amounts of copper, as well as iron, magnesium, manganese, and silicon.

ever be the same again. On August 7 the *Sachsen* made the last DELAG passenger flight. Almost as soon as it landed it was taken over by the German army, as were the other two ships of the line, and later the new LZ-26. Though their crews were to continue to fly the ships, they now wore the uniforms of the army reserve.

In four years of passenger service, the DELAG ships had made over two thousand flights and flown over one hundred thousand miles, carrying 34,028 passengers—10,197 of them fare-paying—in complete safety. But now the old count's original dream for his beloved zeppelins was to be fulfilled. Now they would carry bombs instead of passengers in their bellies.

Into the vacuum left by the count's departure stepped the new chief of the naval airship division, *Fregattenkapitän* Peter Strasser, who would prove one of the outstanding German leaders of the war in spite of his relatively lowly rank—an officer of drive, imagination, and ability, dedicated to the cause of the airship in war and possessed of an intelligence and charisma that enabled him to influence the innermost circles of high command.

Strasser had been appointed to his new command two weeks after the loss of the L-1 and was learning airship handling from the commander of the *Sachsen,* Captain Ernst Lehmann, himself a former Eckener trainee, at the time the L-2 was destroyed. His first acts following the loss of the navy's entire zeppelin fleet were to requisition *Sachsen* as a training ship and to retain Eckener and Lehmann to direct the training program for the crews who would fight the zeppelin campaign.

In May 1914 the navy took delivery of a new replacement zeppelin, L-3, a copy of the L-1, totally inadequate for the demands of the looming crisis but a ship nonetheless. And so the zeppelin went to war—the army airships scattered around the rim of the Reich like fragile and lonely outposts of empire, with no effective center of command; the solitary navy ship L-3 still training its crews, cheered on by kaiser, public, and press, who truly believed that here was a war-winning weapon in a conflict that would last only a few months.

## Chapter Three

# The Dream Becomes a Nightmare

*War in the air is here—and here to stay.*
COUNT FERDINAND
VON ZEPPELIN (1915)

W hen Germany went to war, only one man in the zeppelin camp was skeptical—Dr. Hugo Eckener himself. Privately Eckener was against the war, which, he believed, Germany could not win. "Peace nourishes," he once said, "war devours." But whatever his personal standpoint, it took second place to his sense of public duty, for he was also a patriot and would do whatever he could to defend his country. On the outbreak of war he wrote to his brother-in-law Friedrich Maass explaining that he felt it his duty to enroll in the naval airship service in this time of national crisis. The navy was short of pilots, he wrote, so he would be taking command of L-5 when it was completed next month. His heart was heavy when he thought of his family, but he had to contribute his knowledge and experience to the cause. It was not necessarily a death sentence, he reassured his brother-in-law. Though he was opposed to the use of airships over land—artillery fire would be too lethal—he was strongly in favor of their deployment at sea, where it was easier to evade the enemy.

"However, a military airship is no life-prolonging device," he acknowledged, "and we have to be prepared for everything. Naturally, I have only one request to make to you: Look after Johanna and the children, should the need arise! Your promise to do so would take a great burden from my heart. Your advice and support would be needed, and maybe also material assistance." The navy would pay dependants' benefits in the event of his death in action. "In other respects," he concluded, "my financial situation is bad, as you well know."

Eckener duly reported as a volunteer airship captain, hoping to be given command of a war zeppelin, but instead the admiralty ordered him to duty as an instructor of airship commanders, based at the naval airship division's headquarters at Nordholz, on the North Sea coast near Bremerhaven, with the honorary rank of lieutenant commander. At forty-five, they argued, he was too old for active service, and, more importantly, he was far too valuable training the commanders and senior crew of the expanding airship service to be risked in combat.

So Dr. Eckener stayed in the rear, a crucial component of the zeppelin war but an unusual one in that he remained a civilian among warriors. This did not escape the notice of the king of Saxony when he visited the training ship *Sachsen*. When the king asked him why a naval zeppelin's commander was addressed as "Doctor," Eckener told him that he was a doctor of philosophy. "Well, then," the king replied, "you don't know much about *airships,* do you?"

In fact, no one in the world, then or later, knew more about airships than Eckener. As director of airship training for the Imperial German Navy, he played no part in the actual military direction of the zeppelin war or the formulation of its grand strategy, but in reality he was never far from the heart of it. He did not just train a large percentage of the commanders, officers, and crew of the naval zeppelins, imbuing them with the highest standards of operational skills, he was also, as airship advisor to the leader of the naval airship division, Captain Peter Strasser, close to the driving force of the zeppelin war.

Now thirty-eight years of age, Strasser was a determined, sometimes ruthless martinet with an almost fanatical belief in the zeppelin's historic destiny as a war-winning weapon. Eckener was fascinated by Strasser, a fierce, taut, utterly professional officer but also a sensitive, deeply repressed man—"a confirmed bachelor," it was sometimes said with a nudge and a wink—for whom Eckener gradually formed both a respect and a liking. "He is a queer, strangely taciturn fellow," Eckener wrote to his wife. "Driven by unbridled ambition and the demon of his will, he doesn't share a great deal of interest with 'mere mortals.' But I have a lot of sympathy with this rare fellow."

For as long as they served together, Strasser and Eckener were the outstanding personalities at Nordholz. Not for nothing was Eckener known to the personnel there as "the Pope," because his pronouncements on zeppelin flying were judged infallible, and Strasser as "the Kaiser," because his word was their command. The working relationship of these two zeppelin devotees was crucial. Without Eckener's experience, Strasser could get nowhere. Without Strasser's dynamic leadership, there would be nowhere to go. "It was Eckener's operating knowledge and Strasser's military spirit," Lehmann commented, "that cemented the organisation into one of efficiency."

With the advent of the war, the domain of the zeppelin would extend far beyond its native sphere of operations. England was to become a routine call, and many war zeppelins were to perish over that foggy, darkened, hostile land. Later they would range far and wide, from one end of Europe to another, and eventually beyond, into skies that had never before seen airborne human beings. In the process, the design and capabilities of the zeppelin airship would be transformed.

For the aging Count Zeppelin, the war brought a moment of fulfillment for his airship. He had always seen his invention as a war machine. Here at last was the chance to reveal its worth to a Fatherland at war. The situation at the start was not auspicious, however, as Germany was in no position to conduct an air war on any front. Though the army had six military zeppelins and requisitioned the peacetime passenger ships *Viktoria Luise* and *Hansa* to join the *Sachsen* (mainly for training only), the navy had only one ship and was seven-eighths below its authorized establishment, with only three crews, none of them trained for attack operations.

Nor did the Zeppelin Company at this stage possess the means to build new or replacement ships in the time and numbers required, and ancillary equipment for combat missions was lacking. There were as yet no aerial bombs and no bomb sights, so bombing was carried out by the simple expedient of throwing artillery shells over the side of the gondola, causing trivial damage. Nor had the German high command worked out any clear strategy for zeppelins in a combat role. Four of the army's six zeppelins were shot down by enemy ground fire while on scouting missions in the first few weeks of the war, confirming the army's grave doubts as to the airship's effectiveness as strategic scout, due to its vulnerability (even to rifle fire) and inadequate speed, altitude, and payload.

Initially the role of the navy airships was seen as conducting daylight reconnaissance flights over the North Sea to detect the movements of enemy ships and submarines. But though the range and endurance of the zeppelin, far in excess of any airplane of that time, made it ideally suited for the role of long-distance scout, few naval officers had yet thought that potential through. Under the pressure of war the situation changed rapidly, and the high command turned to an infinitely more aggressive and spectacular role for the zeppelin—the strategic bombing of enemy cities, in effect waging war against the enemy home fronts and war economies as a way of exerting pressure on their political leaders and forcing them to sue for peace. "Such attacks," reported the deputy head of the German naval staff as early as August 20, 1914, "may be expected to cause panic in the population which may possibly render it doubtful that the war can be continued."

Four days after that declaration, on the night of August 24–25, army zeppelin ZIX bombed Antwerp in Belgium, the first city in history to be bombed from the air, killing or wounding twenty-six people. This was the harbinger of one of the most extraordinary campaigns in the history of war. Though the cities of every enemy nation were valid targets—bombing raids were planned (though not always carried out) on targets as far apart as Bristol in the west to Moscow and even (in time) Baghdad in the east—it was against the English, and particularly against London, the political and commercial heart of the British Empire, that the great weight of the zeppelins' war effort would be thrown. So the world's first strategic bombing campaign was born. But so long as the kaiser expressed diffidence about bombing Britain on account of his blood ties with the British royal family, it remained only a plan.

At this point the zeppelin remained an exotic and dilettante adjunct to the German war machine, so the first German bomb to fall on British soil was dropped by a lone navy warplane, which three days before Christmas Eve 1914 attacked Dover Castle, leaving a crater in a garden and smashing a few windows. A month before, three British Avro bombers had attacked the Zeppelin works at Friedrichshafen, though they inflicted no damage on the zeppelin then being built.

It was Strasser who changed the situation. His ethos was precisely that of the song German children were singing in their schools:

*Fly, Zeppelin,*
*Help us in the war,*
*Fly to England,*
*England will be destroyed by fire,*
*Fly Zeppelin.*

Strasser was convinced his fleet of zeppelin bombers could bring the war to a speedy end by paralyzing the enemy's industry and transportation, diverting troops and materiel from the fighting front to the defense of the home front, demoralizing Britain's people, and forcing the Allied governments to sue for peace.

Under Strasser's dynamic and aggressive leadership, the naval airship division was swiftly geared up for all-out war. Within four months of the outbreak of hostilities, there were twenty-five airship crews either in service or in training under Eckener at the naval airship school at Nordholz, and some 3,740 officers and men stationed at nine airship bases, most of them along Germany's north coast, where the land was flat and the North Sea approaches the English mainland direct and unhindered. Nordholz, "the most God-forsaken— one might almost say the most man-forsaken hole on earth," as one zeppelin officer put it, was Strasser's headquarters for one of the boldest, most fantastical, most misjudged campaigns in the history of war.

To meet the challenge of the war in the air, control of the Zeppelin Company was taken over by the government, and its design and production program was hugely expanded to fulfill a construction quota of twenty-six new military airships, bigger and better than any that had been built so far, for delivery in the coming year. The Zeppelin Company, with a greatly expanded engineering force and a second construction works at Potsdam, Berlin, embarked on an ambitious research-and-development program that was to accelerate during the course of the war to a point where the Zeppelin became an unchallenged world leader among airships. Applying the very latest scientific methods, the most advanced engineering skills, and the highest-quality construction materials, the new generations of zeppelins were greatly enlarged and refined. The new ships were better streamlined, with simpler, more effective fins and control surfaces, enclosed control cars, and more powerful engines, and they were armed with specially designed aerial bombs. At the airship bases, revolving hangars were built to accommodate the zeppelins easily, whatever the direction of the wind.

While the Zeppelin Company built the airships, Hugo Eckener trained the personnel who would fly them—a thousand officers and men on a total of fifty ships, flying out on training flights off Germany's North Sea coast day after day, when the weather allowed. Sometimes he took his trainee crews on operational exercises in support of the fleet, as little as a hundred miles off the English coast, tracking British submarines, and reporting back to base, out all day and sometimes all night. In the process he developed an expertise in rigid airship handling unsurpassed by anyone on the planet. The secret was simple but not obvious, he found. You did not fly an airship like an airplane—you sailed it like a sailing boat. "Not for nothing," he told his trainee captains, "is a Zeppelin called an air*ship*."

The army also built up its zeppelin service, establishing bases along the Western Front and down the length of the Eastern Front, from the Baltic to the Balkans. But lacking a leader as dynamic as Strasser, the army's service never achieved the size or potency of the navy's. By the beginning of 1915, the navy had the means to carry the battle to the British. Then, on January 10, a telegram was sent from the kaiser to the commander of the German fleet: "Air attacks on England approved by the Supreme War Lord." The first Battle of Britain was about to begin.

◆ ◆ ◆

Nine days later three zeppelin raiders set out across the North Sea. One ship, commanded by Lieutenant Baron Treusch Horst von Buttlar Brandenfels, with Strasser himself on board, turned back with engine trouble. The other two came in over the Norfolk coast. Hans Fritz in L-3 was the first zeppelin commander to bomb a target in Britain, unloading his bombs over the port of Great Yarmouth and killing the first two Britons to die in an air raid. Late that evening zeppelin L-4 bombed King's Lynn, killing two of its inhabitants, whose death certificates ascribed their demise to "the effects of the acts of the King's enemies."

For the Germans it wasn't much, but it was a start. The British people reacted with curiosity and contempt rather than panic, but the press waxed hysterical. THE COMING OF THE AERIAL BABY-KILLERS raged one headline. The German press saw the significance of the first raid differently. "The most modern air weapon," ran one, "a triumph of German inventiveness and the sole possession of the German forces, has shown itself capable of carrying the war to the soil of old England." German airships would raid other cities in other enemy countries—Belgium, France, Greece, Poland, Romania, Russia, with attempted raids on Italy and even Egypt—but it was Britain that would bear the brunt of the first all-out effort to bring a country to its knees from the air.


It was at Nordholz that Hugo Eckener spent most of the war. Though he missed his wife and children and sometimes grew weary of the monotony of the place, he took pleasure in doing his duty by doing what he loved best—flying airships and inculcating others in the art.

In the main Nordholz was a dreary spot, especially when foul weather prevented flying for days, or even weeks, on end. It was not so much a town as a railway station in the middle of a bare flatland of woods and meadows. At the airship base nearby, the officers, including Eckener, lived in the casino (officers' mess), though zeppelin crews slept in quarters in the hangars, for they had to be ready for anything at any time. Often a commander and crew could be on standby and confined to base for an entire week, and every day the airships had to be checked to make sure the mice were not eating the gold-beater's skin of the gas cells, and that the ships were not getting heavy and crushing their frames against the ground. There was little to do off duty, except go to the railway restaurant for a beer or shoot rabbits and quail. There was no library, and sweethearts and wives were seldom seen.

The most Eckener ever saw of the operational arena of the zeppelin in combat was on occasional forays out over the North Sea on a training ship. In March 1915 he was on board naval zeppelin L-9 for a long reconnaissance flight in support of the High Seas Fleet's defiant breakout from the British blockade. Eckener was elated to be in the action. "What a great day for naval airship flying!" he wrote to his wife. "By 3 P.M. we were already off the Dogger Bank, only a hundred sea miles from the English coast." The view from three thousand feet up, he went on, was "imposing," and the sunset over the sea that evening the most glorious he had seen in the last ten years.

It was soon clear that the early type of zeppelin raider, such as Eckener's L-9, was inadequate for the job. In cold weather it could barely manage to reach the coast of England carrying a minimal bomb load of half a ton. In warm weather, with less lift, its performance was even worse. By April 1915, however, the first of a new breed of million-cubic-foot zeppelins, L-31, came into service, with a sufficient range to cross all the way to the west coast of England carrying two tons of bombs. Five hundred thirty-six feet long and well streamlined, with four powerful Maybach engines driving seventeen-foot propellers of laminated West African mahogany and American walnut to a maximum speed of sixty miles per hour and a cruising speed approaching forty miles per hour, the new ships represented a major advance in zeppelin design.

Virtually all zeppelin raids on Britain would follow the same broad pattern. They almost invariably took place at night and during the dark of the moon, when the ships were less visible to ground defenses and fighter planes. The zeppelins would take off from their bases in the late morning or early afternoon and make their landfall over the coast of England at dusk. They would aim to come in over their targets—assuming they could find them—in the darkest hours of the night and be well on their way back to Germany by dawn.

In May 1915 the kaiser finally sanctioned the bombing of military and strategic targets in London, and on the last day of that month a zeppelin appeared over the capital for the first time. This was the brand-new L-31, commanded by Captain Erich Linnarz. From the control car he was astonished to see the lights of the city glowing like an aurora on the horizon. "London all lit up and we enjoyed total surprise," he reported later. "Not a searchlight or anti-aircraft gun was aimed at us before the first bomb was dropped." L-31 was over the city for just ten minutes. During that time it dropped 154 bombs, killing seven people, injuring thirty-five, starting forty-one fires, causing considerable damage, and reinforcing the confidence of Germany's leadership in the zeppelin's potential for crippling the British war effort.

On September 8 Lieutenant Commander Heinrich Mathy led the first truly devastating air raid on the very heart of London. Mathy was not only the most outstanding of the zeppelin commanders in the war, but also, at least in his report of this raid, the most eloquent. As the sun set in the west, his zeppelin was still at a considerable distance out over the North Sea, he recorded. Below them it was rapidly getting dark, but up where they were it was still light. Off to one side another zeppelin was visible against the clear sky, gliding majestically through the air. A low, mistlike fog hung over the spot in the distance where England was. Then the stars came out, and the air grew colder. They took another pull at their thermos flasks and had something to eat. As they neared the coast, Mathy set the elevator planes to climb still higher so that the noise of the engines would not disclose their presence too soon. Before long it was time for the machine-gunners to set off to their gun nests up on the top of the hull, in case of attack from fighter planes, and everyone else went off to their action stations. It was a cold, clear night with no moon, and it would be difficult for anyone looking up from the ground to judge distances or to get an accurate range on a rapidly moving object.

The mist disappeared. Off in the distance they could see the River Thames, which pointed the way to London. It was an unconcealable, indestructible guidepost, and a sure road to the great city. The English could darken London as much as they liked; they could never eradicate or cover up the Thames. Not that the Thames was the only way to come in on a raid on the British capital. London was under blackout, but on this summer night it was sufficiently well lit at ten o'clock for Mathy to be able to see its reflected glow on the sky nearly forty miles away.

Soon the city was outlined, still and silent below in the distance. Dark spots stood out from blue lights in well-lit portions. The residential areas were not particularly blacked out, but it was the dark spots Mathy was after, and he bore down on them, for they marked the city. There was no sign of life, except in the distance—the lights of what were probably trains. Mathy gave the order for the bomb releases to be activated and the big incendiary and high-explosive bombs to be checked and primed. He picked out St. Paul's Cathedral and laid a course for the Bank of England, on which he aimed to drop the biggest bomb in air-war history to date (a 660-pounder) and at a stroke destroy the financial center of the British Empire. All seemed very quiet; no noises came up from below to penetrate the sound of the sputtering motors and whirring propellers. Then, in the twinkling of an eye, all that changed.

Mathy reported:

> A sudden flash and a narrow band of brilliant light reached out from below and began to feel around the sky, then a second, third, fourth, fifth, and soon a score of criss-crossing ribbons ascended—tentacles seeking to drag us to destruction. Then from below came an ominous sound that deadened the noise of motors and propellers, little red flashes and short bursts of fire. From north and south, from right and left, rolled up from below the sound of guns. When the first searchlights pick you up and you see the first flash of guns, your nerves get a little shock, but then you steady down and put your mind on what you are there for.

Mathy had spent a week in London six years previously and was familiar with the layout of the inner city. His first splatter of incendiaries and high explosives hit a residential district near the British Museum, others cut a swath across the capital as he steered for the landmark of St. Paul's Cathedral, which he hoped would lead him to his main target, the Bank of England.

American journalist W. E. Shepherd watched Mathy's progress from Fleet Street and described the scene:

> The traffic is at a standstill. A million quiet cries make a subdued roar. People stand gazing into the sky from the darkened streets. Among the autumn stars floats a long, gaunt Zeppelin. It is dull yellow—the colour of the harvest moon. The long fingers of searchlights, reaching up from the roof of the city, are touching all sides of the death messenger with their white tips. Great booming sounds shake the city. They are Zeppelin bombs—falling—killing—burning. Lesser noises, of shooting, are nearer at hand, the noise of aerial guns sending shrapnel into the sky.
>
> Whispers, low voices, run through all the streets.
>
> Suddenly you realise that the biggest city in the world has become the night battlefield on which seven million harmless men, women and children live.

The British had a battery of guns under the cover of St. Paul's Cathedral, and Mathy could see their flashes as they belched shrapnel at him. As L-31 came directly over the target, Mathy shouted an order down the speaking tube to the Lieutenant bomb-aimer: "Fire slowly!"

The thunder of the British guns mingled with the explosions of the German bombs. Mathy could see flames everywhere. Then he was over Holborn Viaduct, letting fly at Holborn Station, trying to hit London Bridge and coming under fire from the guns in the Tower of London. L-31 was enjoying a charmed life. The London defenses were putting up a vigorous firefight, but nothing struck home and no fighter plane came roaring in. Over Liverpool Street Station Mathy shouted the order: "Rapid fire!"

"The bombs rained down," he was to report later. "There was a succession of detonations and bursts of fire and I could see that we had hit well and apparently caused great damage. Having dropped all the bombs, I turned for a dash home. We had not been hit. Several times I leaned out and looked up and back at the dark outlines of my Zeppelin, but she had no holes in her grey sides. The main attack was made from 10:50 to 11 P.M. It lasted just ten minutes." Though Mathy missed the bank, he started huge fires among the textile warehouses beyond St. Paul's, causing damage estimated at over half a million pounds.

No one in Britain was unmoved by the coming of the zeppelins. The sight was so extraordinary—beautiful and unearthly, fascinating and menacing. D. H. Lawrence saw Mathy's zeppelin overhead that night. He wrote to his friend Lady Ottoline Morrell the next morning:

> We saw the Zeppelin above us, just ahead, amid a gleaming of clouds: high up, like a bright golden finger, quite small, among a fragile incandescence of clouds. And underneath it were splashes of fire as the shells fired from earth burst. Then there were flashes near the ground—and the shaking noise. It was like Milton—"then there was war in heaven." But it was not angels. It was that small golden Zeppelin, like a long oval world, high up. It seemed as if the cosmic order were gone, as if there had come a new order, a new heaven above us. I cannot get over it, that the moon is not queen of the sky by night. . . . So it is the end—our world is gone, and we are like dust in the air.

George Bernard Shaw first set eyes on this nocturnal apparition from the garden of his home in Hertfordshire, north of London. To his friends the social reformers Beatrice and Sidney Webb, he wrote:

> The Zeppelin manoeuvred over the Welwyn valley for about half an hour before it came round and passed Londonwards with the nicest precision over our house. It made a magnificent noise the whole time; and not a searchlight

touched it. What is hardly credible, but true, is that the sound of the Zepp's engines was so fine, and its voyage through the stars so enchanting, that I positively caught myself hoping next night that there would be another raid.

At first the Londoners had crowded the rooftops to watch. Now they poured into the underground stations to escape.

On October 13, Heinrich Mathy again set out to raid London at the head of a flotilla of four other zeppelins. The only ship to get through to its target directly was the L-15, commanded by Lieutenant Commander Joachim Breithaupt on his first raid over England. At around 10 P.M. he arrived above the Houses of Parliament. A late-night debate was in progress in the House of Commons, but as the guns opened up all around, the word "Zeppelins! Zeppelins!" spread among the assembled Members of Parliament. Abandoning the affairs of state, they tumbled out of the chamber to watch. "There she is!" cried one MP, pointing into the starry sky. Then two searchlights caught the zeppelin in their gleam. "In their radiance," a reporter recalled, "she looked a thing of silvery beauty sailing serenely through the night, indifferent to the big guns roaring at her from Green Park."

Over Charing Cross Station, Breithaupt let go his first salvo. His primary targets were the Bank of England and the British naval headquarters at the Admiralty, but his bombs fell short and instead he hit the crowded West End theater district just to the north of the Strand. Though one bomb killed seventeen people in Wellington Street—the largest number killed by a single bomb in any air raid to date—the crowded hotels, restaurants, and theaters were mercifully spared.

Early in January 1916 Vice-Admiral Scheer took over as Commander-in-Chief of the German High Seas Fleet. Scheer was committed to increased aggression against Britain, and almost at once began to form a close working partnership with Peter Strasser, to whose Naval Airship Division he gave his total support. The zeppelin war was resumed with a vengeance, and even though it was the depths of winter Strasser committed his airships to a bombing campaign that ranged from London and the south to Edinburgh in the north.

At the end of January nine zeppelins set off to attack the industrial cities of the Midlands and the north, flying in total darkness through wintry weather over snowy, windswept landscapes, and suffering navigational errors and mechanical failures that greatly handicapped their efforts to blitz Sheffield, Manchester, and Nottingham, though they succeeded in hitting other places, Burton-on-Trent most severely of all. For nearly a week in early April zeppelins took off almost every day to strike at industrial and commercial targets throughout Britain in a campaign without parallel in the air war, seriously damaging Sunderland and destroying a whisky warehouse near Edinburgh in a spectacular fire. Though a few ships were lost—notably Joachim Breithaupt's L-15, which was forced down in the sea off Kent, where the crew were rescued by a British destroyer—the German airshipmen were to look back on this period as the high point of their war careers. Their efforts were not matched by results, however.

The zeppelin was a powerful psychological weapon but it was not nearly so devastating as the Germans believed. Often the zeppelins were miles off course, and most of their bombs missed their targets. On one occasion zeppelin L-20, groping blindly around Scotland in dense fog looking for Edinburgh, bombed a castle in the Highlands in the mistaken belief that it was a coal mine, then came down beside the German steamer *Holland* to ask for directions and found it was in the latitude of the Orkneys, and finally crash-landed in a fjord in Norway, where most of the crew were interned. So many bombs landed in fields that the British government seriously thought the Germans were trying to destroy crops and livestock as part of the war effort.

No one had worked out just how great a weight of high explosives and incendiary bombs would be required to bring down a nation with the industrial and military might of Britain, or whether a handful of zeppelins at a time could fulfill such a mission. Moreover, British interceptor aircraft were faster than the zeppelins, which were inflated with flammable and explosive gas, and were thus doubly vulnerable.

It was not the actual damage inflicted on Britain by the zeppelins, which was relatively slight, but the threat they posed that helped the German war effort. Halfway through the war they had managed to tie up in anti-aircraft defenses in Britain over seventeen thousand officers and men, all of whom would otherwise have been more effectively employed in France and other theaters of war.

Meanwhile, at Nordholz, the tireless Dr. Eckener continued to train the zeppelin bomber crews of the not-very-distant future. Flying a zeppelin was such a complex business that in peacetime it could take up to two years to train a crew, and even longer to pass a commander as properly qualified. Under the pressure of the war, however, this was reduced to a crash course of ten to twelve weeks. Eckener's own flight manual imparted to his trainees the secrets of his mastery of airship flight—"careful, conservative and prudent airship handling," as one expert put it, "together with a profound knowledge of the physical laws and weather conditions governing the operations of the monster gasbags."*

For his trainee aircrews, Eckener was a compelling, meticulous, and exacting instructor. No detail was too minor to impart, nothing too trivial to overlook. He taught his pupils not only how to fly a zeppelin by the book, but also how to improvise and continue to fly it when the book let you down. "Your compass has dropped overboard!" he would roar. "You haven't got a sextant. So what are you going to do now, eh?" On one occasion a resourceful trainee responded to this question by coyly pulling a tiny instrument case out of his back pocket, containing a miniature compass and sextant. "Did I see right?" demanded the dumbfounded Eckener. "I must get one of those for my own emergency kit!"

"Beim landen zeigt sich der wahre Künstler," Eckener always said. "You can tell a true artist by his landing." His own mastery, especially on water, was always amazing. "No one could land a Zepp on water like the good doctor could," recalled one student pilot. But teaching others how to do it was another matter. "Pull up, man!" Eckener bawled at one trainee commander as he tilted the ship's bow straight at the deep. "We don't want to turn into a U-boat quite yet!"

Whenever a trainee executed a difficult maneuver correctly, Eckener would take a thick cigar—gold dust in wartime Germany—out of his bag and announce: "We're all going to smoke this in the

---

*Dr. Douglas Robinson, Introduction to Hugo Eckener, *Brief Instructions and Practical Hints for Piloting Zeppelin Airships* (Dallas, 1964).

casino when we get back, so I hope you'll remember me kindly in the future."

It was an intensive and exhaustive program. Trainee flight engineers were seconded to the Zeppelin works and the Maybach motor works at Friedrichshafen for three weeks' further specialist training. The tests at the end of the course were supervised by Eckener himself. Only the best got through—and they were very, very good.

During the spring of 1916 there was a pause in the bombing campaign on England. The zeppelins were now increasingly reserved for naval reconnaissance operations during the run-up to the confrontation of the British and German fleets at the Battle of Jutland at the end of May. Shortly afterward a new generation of super-zeppelins entered service, marking the biggest advance in airship construction and design in the war. The first of these radically improved ships, the L-30 (LZ-62), undersides blackened to show up less in the searchlights, arrived in the early summer of 1916. Six hundred fifty feet long and nearly eighty feet in diameter, the new ship was a custom-built strategic air bomber almost as big as the biggest battleship afloat, a huge and beautiful vessel kept aloft by 2 million cubic feet of hydrogen in nineteen enormous gas cells.

On operational flights the new ships carried a crew of twenty, clad in leather flying suits lined with fur against the cold, stationed in the four enclosed gondolas suspended under the hull. The front part of the forward gondola was the control car, measuring a meager six and a half by nine feet. Here the commander, flight officers, and steersmen flew the zeppelin, controlled the raid, and, with luck, navigated a course with the help of a limited range of basic instruments—a small liquid compass, an altimeter, a thermometer, and an airspeed meter, and occasionally radio bearings, which were generally misleading and which could give away a ship's position to the enemy. To combat the growing strength of the British air defenses, the new zeppelins were fitted with up to ten machine guns—two in the control car, two in the after engine car, one in each of the side gondolas, one in the rear gun pit abaft the rudders, and three on the top gun platform, toward the bow. In two bomb rooms, forward and aft of amidships, the super-zeppelins could carry nearly five tons of bombs, including four fat and devastating 660-pounders, forty smaller explosive bombs, and sixty incendiaries. The six big Maybach motors were capable of driving forty tons of airframe and twenty-five to thirty tons of fuel, lubricating oil, water ballast, machine guns, ammunition, bombs, and personnel through the air at a maximum speed of sixty-two miles per hour and a maximum ceiling of 17,400 feet (limited to 13,000 feet on raids). As twentieth-century strategic bombers go, the L-30 and its sister ships were relatively primitive, but by the standards of their time they were a technological phenomenon. Theoretically they had sufficient range to fly to New York and back.

Strasser pinned his hopes on these new ships. "The performance of the big airships has reinforced my conviction that England can be overcome by airships," he reported, "inasmuch as the country will be deprived of the means of existence through increasingly extensive destruction of cities, factory complexes, railroads, docks, harbor works with warships and merchant ships lying therein. The airships offer a certain means of ending the war."

On September 2 Strasser launched the biggest raid of the war. Sixteen giant ships rose into the air from Germany's North Sea bases that night. Never again were so many airships to fly in the sky together at one time, for waiting for them in England were two new British weapons: the high-altitude airplane and the incendiary bullet.

First to fall victim to the British fighter planes' incendiary bullets was the SL-11, a rigid airship similar in many ways to the zeppelin; it had a generally superior streamlining but an inferior plywood framework, manufactured by a rival firm in Leipzig, the Schütte-Lanz Company.

To the horror of the German airship crews over London that night, but to the jubilation of the massed English citizenry that sang and danced for joy in the streets of London—and as far away as Cambridge and Windsor—the SL-11 fell through the sky like a fiery meteor, burning with an intense incandescent white flame, and finally came to Earth in a field near Cuffley, north of London, with the loss of all on board.

News of this cataclysm profoundly dismayed the crews of the naval airship division. Death by fire in the air was the ultimate vision of nightmare. The crewmen did not wear parachutes, which added too much weight to the ship's load, but some men preferred to jump anyway rather than be burned alive. Only three men ever survived being shot down in a flaming zeppelin.

One was Alfred Mühler, steersman of the army zeppelin LZ-37, which was bombed from above by a British naval pilot while flying home across Belgium after a raid on England on June 7, 1915. Almost blown in two by the explosion, the airship came down in flames over the town of Ghent. Knocked unconscious in the crash, Mühler came around to find himself on a bed with a nonplussed nun staring down at him. In a million-to-one chance he had been flung through the roof of a convent when the ship's control car struck it, and he fell unerringly straight into the nun's bed, which cushioned his fall and saved his life.

Only two other German crew members were known to have ridden a burning zeppelin down and survived. Both were from L-48, which crashed in flames in a field at Holly Tree Farm near Theberton in Suffolk. Surviving both the fire and the fall, dazed mechanic Heinrich Ellerkamm found himself in the wet grass of an English meadow in the cool of the early morning. Horses galloped past. A wild duck flapped through the glimmering sky, quacking madly. Low overhead a British fighter plane was circling. The pilot spotted the young German he had just tried to kill and gave him a cheerful wave. Villagers were running across the field, and from the control car came the sound of groans. Ellerkamm went to investigate and found Watch Officer Otto Mieth lying in the wreck. He was suffering from burns, and both his legs were broken, but he would live. With the help of the villagers, Ellerkamm pulled the young officer out and lay him on the grass. Then one of the villagers took Ellerkamm to his house. He was in shock and in pain, and in the hands of the enemy, but life had never seemed so sweet.

As British air defenses stiffened, so the terrible vision of zeppelins falling like blazing comets through the night sky over England was repeated time and again. Even the finest commanders succumbed— even Heinrich Mathy, the greatest of them all, whose flaming descent in L-31 was described by one British eyewitness as "probably the most appalling spectacle associated with the war which London is likely to provide." L-31 smashed into a field near Potters Bar. Eighteen of the crew had stayed with the ship in its descent and been burned beyond recognition. One had jumped from a great height, and his body was found in a field some distance from the wreckage. "So great was the force with which he struck the ground," reported a London journalist who reached the scene, "that I saw the imprint of his body clearly defined in the stubbly grass. There was a round hole for his head, then deep impressions of the trunk, with outstretched arms, and finally the widely separated legs. Life was in him when he was picked up, but the spark soon went out." It was Heinrich Mathy.

At the funeral, as a mark of respect, Mathy's black-palled coffin was carried by officers of the British army. "With his going," one zeppelin man later wrote, "the life and soul of our airship service went out too." When two other airships went down in flames over England shortly after, it was clear that the balance of the air war had changed.

Hugo Eckener made no secret of his conviction that in war the zeppelin was ideally suited to long-distance scouting operations in support of the fleet out at sea, where it was difficult for the enemy to locate it and bring it down, but that it was totally unsuited for raiding operations overland, where it was at grave risk from ground and air defenses. In his heart of hearts he was opposed to the waste of life, of friends and comrades, that the bombing campaign against England entailed, even though he believed Germany's cause was just.

On May 27, 1917, he wrote to his wife in great excitement following a long flight that once more proved his point about the zeppelin's usefulness in operations at sea:

> Yesterday we were on a long flight from four in the morning to eight in the evening in weather so clear that we could look out over half the North Sea to the Dogger Bank. It was very interesting. We hunted an English U-boat till it dived, then went off with a German torpedo boat flotilla.

> We scouted around in a circle twenty miles out from the torpedo boats and reported five Dutch cargo ships, so the torpedo boats gave chase. "These damned German airships make tough Sea Police!" they must have thought. "The moment you set off across the North Sea, they set a fleet on you."

The German army, which broadly shared Eckener's doubts about the zeppelin's capabilities as a weapon of war over enemy-held land, chose to disband its airship fleet in favor of long-range airplanes, now coming into production, and for a while the navy seemed inclined to follow. To replace a zeppelin was a slow and very costly business, to train a senior flight officer an even slower process; and if the current rate of losses continued, the naval airship division would run out of both the machines and the men to fly them. Count Zeppelin himself had steadily lost interest in his zeppelins, believing the era of the airplane had finally arrived, as he had always forecast it would. Even Peter Strasser, now promoted to leader of airships, conceded that the damage they inflicted on the British war effort was negligible but argued against their disbandment on the grounds that their psychological impact on the civil population in England justified their continuing operations—a thesis that was as wrong in this war as it would be in the next.

If it was to continue, the zeppelin bomber would have to adapt. The only way to deal with high-altitude fighters firing incendiary ammunition into flammable gas was to operate at heights the fighters could not reach. The Zeppelin Company designers, under Dr. Dürr, were compelled to accelerate the advance of airship technology. The British fighters could generally fly to a ceiling of between eleven and thirteen thousand feet. The new generation of airships, the so-called height-climbers, would aim to operate at twenty thousand feet or more. To reach such heights the ships would have to be made drastically lighter. So one engine, machine guns, and crew quarters were taken out; fuel capacity was reduced, bomb load reduced by half; and the control car was made smaller and the hull structure lighter.

Count von Zeppelin did not live to see his primal concept evolve into the elegant height-climber. He died in the early spring of 1917, a few months before the new ships were introduced into service. At a stroke the height-climbers rendered the British air-defense system obsolete. Neither fighter planes nor anti-aircraft fire from the ground could reach them. As they underwent further development, these zeppelins improved their performance to a point where they could carry three tons of bombs to a height considerably in excess of twenty thousand feet. To further obfuscate the enemy, observation cars could be let down on cables, swaying invisibly beneath the clouds while the airship remained in hiding above them.

The problems posed by these new high altitudes were multifarious. Engines and even compasses froze, oil lines snapped and windows cracked, men fell unconscious from lack of oxygen or vomited uncontrollably after inhaling compressed oxygen from primitive breathing apparatuses contaminated with oil and glycerine. Static electricity flew out of their fingers, haloed the lookouts' heads, and flickered around their fur collars and the machine-gun sights. It was so cold some of the men wore newspapers under their fur-lined flying suits, but they still got frostbite. Sick and exhausted in the strange winds of the upper air, they drifted far from their targets and dropped their bombs harmlessly into the sea or empty fields.

The difficulties of navigation alone made nonsense of Strasser's ambitions for his new superbombers. Dead reckoning at sea and pilotage over land were more difficult than ever. Landmarks and targets were either totally invisible because they were below cloud level, or barely visible because they were so far away. Drift was difficult enough to measure at the best of times, but in the little-known winds of higher altitudes it became virtually impossible. Radio communication was still in its infancy, and bearings from German stations were not only misleading but gave the zeppelins' positions away to the enemy.

By the late summer of 1917 the zeppelin was being phased out in favor of the airplane, both for air raids over England and for strategic scouting over sea. Soon formations of long-range Gotha and Giant bombers were raiding London and other key targets regularly, effectively, and with relative impunity. Scarce raw materials such as aluminum and rubber were diverted from airship to aircraft production, and zeppelin manufacture was reduced to a rate of one every two months. To protect the ships of the naval airship division from terminal depletion, the order was given that future raids over England were to be carried out only on very dark and cloudy nights, and then only exercising extreme caution.

To send even the most high-tech zeppelin on a raid on a cloudy night during the dark of the moon was a triumph of will over reality, as was spelled out in the "silent raid" of October 19, 1917, so called because the ships flew so high they could not be heard from the ground—the most ambitious but also one of the most calamitous raids of the war. Strasser's plan was to strike at the industrial centers of the English Midlands, but the huge flotilla of giant airships had barely reached the coast of England when it was struck by a violent northerly gale that scattered the ships before the wind, sweeping them helplessly south over a pitch-black England far below at speeds of forty-five to fifty miles per hour. To identify a target in such conditions was an impossibility. The best the commanders could do was make educated guesses and release their bombs blind into the void, hoping they would hit something useful. Only L-45, fortuitously driven across London by the wind, managed to bomb an identifiable target. The rest were so wildly off target that they did not just bomb the wrong objective, they bombed the wrong country: one commander who thought he had wrecked the industrial heart of Birmingham was later found to have bombed Arras, in France.

Getting safely back to Germany in these conditions was even more perilous. From their control cars four miles up in the night sky, the crews could see the flash and flicker of gunfire along the Western Front and realized to their dismay that this was where the wind was driving them. One by one they were swept into the maw of the battlefield. L-44 was shot down by French guns, with the loss of all hands. L-49 was forced down by French fighter aircraft and the crew taken prisoner by a bunch of sprightly old French boar hunters armed with hunting guns. L-50 crash-landed in the same place but was then swept away with four men still on board and vanished without trace over the Mediterranean. L-45, out of fuel and lost, its crew exhausted, made an emergency landing in the Provençal Alps; all on board survived after an extraordinary flight, which had taken them, as one crew member put it, "from Denmark to the Riviera by way of London and Paris in twenty hours." L-55 and Lieutenant Commander Hans Flemming managed to overfly the Western Front by climbing to a height of twenty-four thousand feet—a world record for airships, unbeaten to this day—but was wrecked when, flying at an angle of forty-five degrees and running out of fuel, it made a forced landing in Thuringia. The remaining six zeppelins made it safely back to their bases, but the loss of five of the most advanced height-climbers on a single and for the most part futile raid plunged the service into deep gloom.

Strasser began to turn in on himself. Eckener noticed this and did what he could. "Peter is rather pleased with me staying on another day," he wrote to his wife on December 12, 1917, "as he is very lonely in his pad, having cut himself off completely from the people at the Mess. For the majority of the officers he is far too tough and hard. All he can think of is his responsibility, and he is not easy to get on with. But he is an excellent man and stands head and shoulders above the average. Such distinctive personalities usually have a lot of enemies."

Only one event brightened the gloom for German airshipmen: the forty-two-hundred-mile solo flight of zeppelin L-59 to Khartoum and back in an attempt to bring supplies to German forces cut off by the British in East Africa, the longest nonstop journey so far made by air. Though the flight had little impact on the course of the war, it was to have a momentous consequence for the zeppelin's postwar future. The captain of L-59, one of the most advanced of the war zeppelins, was Lieutenant Commander Ludwig Bockholt, who earlier in the year had become the first airman to capture a ship on the high seas by landing alongside a Norwegian schooner carrying war materials to Britain and sending a boarding party across in the zeppelin's lifeboat.

On November 21, 1917, L-59 set off from Jamboli, Bulgaria, the most southerly of the German airship bases on the Eastern Front, for a flight of a distance never attempted before, under conditions never before experienced by an airship. Thousands of miles to the south, German East African forces under General Paul von Lettow-Vorbeck were fighting a rearguard action against the British in the Makonde Highlands (now part of Tanzania). Cut off from reinforcement and supply, waging an almost guerrilla war in the wilds of the African bush, the German forces were running out of ammunition, medical supplies, and other materiel. With sea and land routes cut off, the only way to them was by air, and the only aircraft then in existence that was capable of delivering cargo such enormous distances without landing and refueling was the latest mark of zeppelin.

Laden with fifteen tons of medical supplies, thirty machine guns, 230 machine-gun belts, and several hundred thousand rounds of rifle ammunition, L-59 flew south via Turkey and Crete to Egypt, and then into the desert. No airship had ever flown over such a hostile landscape, a scorching wilderness offering little prospect of a safe landing in an emergency, the sand so bright in the sun it gave the crew of twenty-two intense headaches and hallucinations. So violent were the hot air currents that the ship sailed along like a liner in a heavy Atlantic swell. The crew were seasick, and the elevator man needed all his strength to hold the wheel steady.

Across the trackless wasteland, Bockholt steered his course, mostly by celestial navigation, for landmarks were few and meaningless. At sunset on November 22 he arrived at the Nile near the second cataract above Wadi Halfa and carried on through the starry night toward Khartoum. Ahead lay sub-Saharan Africa, the wastes of Kordofan, the swamps of the White Nile, the rain forest of the equatorial highlands, the grasslands of Tanganyika.

Early on the morning of November 23, L-59 was 125 miles west of Khartoum. At this point a radio message was received from the German admiralty in Berlin that effectively aborted the mission and saved the ship. Lettow-Vorbeck's forces had been overrun by the British, the signal read. L-59 must turn back immediately. In fact, German naval intelligence was misinformed: Lettow-Vorbeck's forces were holding out, but Bockholt had no alternative but to obey his orders.

On the morning of November 25, the L-59 returned safely to its base in Jamboli, and its crew staggered stiffly down to terra firma, cold and tired, some feverish. In the first intercontinental flight in aeronautical history, they had flown a total of forty-two hundred miles in ninety-five hours; they had enough fuel left for another sixty-four hours' flying. It did not escape the attention of many in the zeppelin business, Dr. Eckener above all, who as technical adviser had supervised the L-59's preflight preparations at Jamboli, that if the airship had flown in a different direction it could have crossed the Atlantic and bombed Chicago.

There was no happy end to the Africa ship's story. Surprised to see L-59 returning safely home, high command had to work out what to do with it. Long-range bombing seemed the obvious answer, and plans were proposed to attack British installations in Brindisi, Naples, Malta, Tripoli, Cairo, Port Said, Suez, Aswan, and Baghdad. On March 10, 1918, Bockholt bombed Naples; on March 20 he attempted to attack Port Said and the British naval base in Crete. On April 7 he took L-59 across the Balkans to the Strait of Otranto on his way to bomb the British naval base in Malta. He never got there. That evening a German U-boat commander observed "a gigantic flame, which lit the entire horizon bright as day for a short time and then slowly fell to the water." Little trace was found of the L-59, and it was concluded that the ship's hydrogen had been ignited by that most feared of inboard mishaps, a petrol fire.

Three months before the destruction of the L-59, on January 5, 1918, the big naval zeppelin base at Ahlhorn had been reduced to rubble in a series of explosions, the exact cause of which was never determined. Four of the hangars and five airships were destroyed; ten men were killed, 134 injured. It was a black day in zeppelin history, but worse was to come. With Ahlhorn inoperative, morale running down, and confidence in the zeppelin as an aerial bomber in steep decline, zeppelin raids against England were scaled down.

For Hugo Eckener, life was at its bleakest. "Having sneaked out of the Casino, I sit quietly in my room, getting plastered on a bottle of Burgundy," he wrote to his wife in early February. "I feel a bit melancholy about this never-ending monotony and the dismal pressure of the eternally immutable confusion of war which will just not budge or come to a solution." He wasn't the only one. "Peter Strasser escaped from the bad weather and went to Hamburg," Eckener went on. "I have no idea what he is doing there."

With the war to all intents already lost, it seemed Strasser still dreamed of dealing England a critical blow by smashing London. On August 5, 1918, for the last time, five huge dirigibles headed west for England. In L-70 was Strasser himself. L-70 was a triumph of zeppelin technology: the fastest, biggest, and finest airship yet to be built. It was nearly seven hundred feet long, had a gas capacity of 2,195,800 cubic feet, could carry up to 3.5 tons of bombs, climb to twenty-three thousand feet, and fly at up to eighty-one miles per hour with its seven Maybach high-altitude motors. But though it was the acme of zeppelin design, it was already a weapon of the past, sent into battle as the consequence of fanatical belief and wishful thinking.

At 9 P.M., approaching the coast of England while it was still light, Strasser radioed his last command to the four older-type ships in his formation: "To all airships. Attack according to plan." That signal was to betray him to the English defenses. Within the hour thirteen fighter aircraft had taken off from Yarmouth air station to intercept the zeppelins. Though Strasser might be regarded as the supreme zeppelin strategist, his operational experience on raids was limited, as was that of L-70's captain, the inexperienced Lieutenant Johann von Lossnitzer. Approaching the enemy coast at seventeen thousand feet, Strasser was confident he was out of reach of enemy fighters. He was wrong. Three of the British fighter planes climbed to within shooting range of L-70. While one high-speed de Havilland D.H. 4 two-seater attacked from below, another closed in from the opposite direction. One of the pilots was Major Egbert Cadbury, who later described his attack on Strasser's ship: "I approached it from the stern, about three hundred feet below it, and fired four drums of explosive ammunition into its stern, which immediately started to light. As I was doing this, one of the other pilots was flying over the top of the Zeppelin and to his horror he saw a man in the machine-gun pit run to the side and jump overboard."

Bursting into flames, Strasser's ship sank by the stern and began its long and terrible fall to the sea below. All on board perished. Strasser's body, which showed no signs of burning or injury, was recovered and buried at sea. It was thought he might have died of a heart attack during the long dive. The other zeppelins in the raid aborted their mission and made it safely back to Germany.

Hugo Eckener was shattered. The next day he wrote in despair to his wife:

> You may have read it by now: Last night my good comrade Strasser was lost over England in the L-70. This is a

hard blow for the Naval Airship Division. It is also a painful blow for me, who was this excellent man's friend. Any rough and uncomfortable aspects of the man are now as nothing, compared with the feeling that he was an exemplary warrior and ultimately a good man, a diamond in the rough. . . .

There is no telling yet what is going to happen now. The Naval Airship Division will carry on, but Strasser will remain irreplaceable.

Eckener was weary at heart. Germany was losing the war. The zeppelins had been blown out of the sky. He ended his letter on a resigned note: "I doubt whether I shall be staying here much longer now. I am no longer required here, and it was only Strasser's friendship that would not allow me to leave. I shall file another application to be released from my contract."

On August 9 he wrote again to his wife: "The old Count would be shocked to see how many lives of good men his weapon is costing. Of course, it is the same with aeroplanes. The 'latest weapon' is a lethal instrument." And five days later: "My comrades are going, one by one, and these days I cannot get out of my head the verse we once learned at school: 'Now I shall be very much alone, the Lords lie in death. . . .'"

On October 13 two zeppelins were sent out on a long-range reconnaissance mission over the North Sea. Commanding one of the ships, the L-65, was Lieutenant Werner Vermehren. Many years later he was to tell the present author: "They are a thing of the past now. But they were a thing of the past then. They had given their all. And it was not enough." No zeppelin would fly in the war again.

The war, it was clear, was lost, and the terms for the peace laid down by the Allied Powers, it was equally clear, would reduce Germany to impotence and beggary. Though Hugo Eckener was at heart a man of peace, he was not inclined to end the war on any terms if to do so spelled the ruination of all. On October 27, 1918, just over a fortnight before Armistice Day, he wrote to his brother suggesting that they should fight on rather than accept an ignominious and crushing peace.

But the following day, October 28, the mutiny that had erupted among the disaffected men of the German High Seas Fleet spread to the naval airship division. The zeppelin crews remained loyal to the kaiser, but the mutinous ground crews took over the bases, arrested their officers, and sent them home. By November 9 all the remaining zeppelins had been deflated and hung in their hangars. Two days later the war came to an end.

The German airships had significantly increased the war-weariness of the British populace, diverted troops and materiel from the fighting front, and fulfilled the will of the German people to strike at the enemy heartland in retaliation for the blockade of the Fatherland. But the cost had been atrocious. Nearly a hundred zeppelins had served with the German army and navy in the war—most of the zeppelins ever built. The naval zeppelins bore the brunt of the combat, and by the end of the war fifty-three of the navy's seventy-three ships had been destroyed, while 40 percent of their crews were dead. This represented the greatest percentage loss of any command of any nation in World War I. Only the German U-boat navy and Royal Air Force bomber command in World War II were to suffer comparable percentage casualties. Most of Germany's experienced airshipmen had perished, and though army airships had suffered slighter losses, it was plain that as a weapon the zeppelin had failed.

For such an enormous cost in ships and lives, courage and know-how, the return had been puny. Far from knocking Britain out of the war, the campaign had inflicted the smallest pinprick on the British war effort: 196 tons of bombs dropped in a total of fifty-one raids, 557 British dead, 1,358 injured, total damage amounting to rather more than £1.5 million, over a third of it caused by Heinrich Mathy in just two raids on London, especially that of September 8, 1915.

The year 1915 had been the high-water mark of the zeppelin campaign. In 1916 the British effectively organized their defenses, forcing the zeppelins to operate at such high altitudes that their efficiency as strategic bombers was greatly reduced. By then the airplane was already surpassing the airship in every aspect of performance except long-range scouting over great distances, a role for which the zeppelin was supremely suited but for which it was very seldom used. In the end, the zeppelin, hailed as a war-winning weapon, proved a vulnerable and spectacular failure.

As an aircraft, however, the zeppelin had proved itself beyond any doubt and had set performance records far ahead of those of any other type of aircraft, including the endurance record of 101 hours set by Ernst Lehmann's LZ-120 over the Baltic in July 1917, the height record of twenty-four thousand feet by Hans Flemming's L-55 over the Western Front in October 1917, and the nonstop distance record of forty-two hundred miles set by Ludwig Bockholt's L-57 on its marathon flight from Jamboli to Khartoum and back in November 1917. Developed and refined in the crucible of total war, the airship had developed to a point where in terms of design, build quality, and operational expertise the Zeppelin Company now found itself in a position to run the world's first intercontinental passenger airline—if the world would let it.

In February 1915, just as the zeppelin war against England was about to accelerate, American journalist Karl von Wiegand interviewed the old Count Zeppelin about his views on the future of airships in war and peace. The count was in no doubt that Germany would win the war in the air:

> I still have one great ambition. I would wish that a Zeppelin be the first vehicle to link Europe and America by air. I would like to live long enough to pilot one of my cruisers over the ocean to America, where many years ago I made my first balloon ascent. This war has interrupted my plans in this direction. Some day travel by air will be the quickest and safest way possible. In this respect Zeppelins have a great future. Relatively few people know the feeling of comfort and security that a Zeppelin gives. They will play a great role in the future of travel and conduct of the mails.

Chapter Four

# Dreaming of America

*Dr. Eckener is a modern Columbus.*

PRESIDENT HERBERT HOOVER (1924)

The war was lost. In the peace, the victorious Allies were determined to dismantle Germany's capacity to wage war, zeppelins included. Though Hugo Eckener had survived, along with zeppelin designer Ludwig Dürr and the company's business manager, Albert Colsman, the zeppelin airship itself had almost ceased to be. Those that remained after the hostilities were either destroyed in their hangars by aircrews and ground crews determined that they should not fall into the hands of their erstwhile enemies, or were eventually surrendered to the Inter-Allied Control Commission as war reparations, for there was keen interest in future airship development in countries outside Germany.

Germany in defeat was not only defenseless but penniless too, ruined by more than four years of total war and before long by the crippling terms of the Treaty of Versailles. Politically, too, Germany was in a parlous state. The kaiser, whom the Allies blamed for the war, had been deposed and sent into exile, and in place of a monarchy there was now the well-intentioned but weak and vulnerable democracy of the Weimar Republic.

Germany had few friends in Europe, and its former enemies remained largely hostile, especially France and Britain, both of which seemed determined to destroy the German airship industry: the former for reasons of revenge, the latter to secure a monopoly in global airship transport for itself. Only the United States could be seen as a potential partner nation in the future. That country was not a signatory of the Versailles Treaty and would not share in the redistribution of surviving zeppelins among the Allies. The U.S. Army and Navy saw a future for zeppelin-type airships as long-distance scouts and were even prepared to cooperate with the Zeppelin Company to have one built—if this were permitted.

At Hugo Eckener's home in Friedrichshafen, the first Christmas of the peace was a time for both thanksgiving and uncertainty. Though the future looked bleak, there was still much to be grateful for. The family was together and intact—Eckener's wife Johanna, now forty-seven, their daughters, Lotte and Hanneliese, nineteen, a chemistry student who would tragically drown in a boating accident in the Bodensee a few months later, and their son, Knut, who had been just under the age for military conscription.

From the point of view of the Zeppelin Company, too, there was much to be grateful for. The airship works, the hangars, and the company's model estate for its workers at the edge of town had survived, and plant, plans, and core personnel—the industrial base and intellectual property of the enterprise—were ready to be put to use again should the opportunity ever arise. Such was the unique pool of experience acquired by the officers and crews of the wartime navy and army airships during the most extensive rigid airship operations in history—some 4,720 operational flights all told, covering a total of around 1.25 million air miles.

In Eckener's view, one clear message came through those early postwar months. Though the zeppelin had been defeated as a weapon of war, or at any rate as a strategic bomber over hostile territory, it had been proven beyond doubt as a potential form of air transport in peacetime. Eckener had emerged not only as the greatest rigid airship pilot of all, but also as the great proselytizing visionary of transworld

airship flight. In the New Year of 1919, therefore, he and his colleagues at Friedrichshafen began to make plans.

Almost immediately after the Armistice two separate proposals
had been hatched to fly zeppelins to the United States as a way of
seeking reconciliation and bringing Germany's plight to the attention
of the American nation. The first plan involved one of the finest zeppelins, L-71, under the outstanding wartime commander Martin Dietrich. The second was the brainchild of one of the most senior and
successful zeppelin commanders, Captain Ernst Lehmann, whose aim
was (as he put it) "to re-establish Germany in the eyes of the world"
by flying the L-72 to the United States and back without landing—a
phenomenal ambition, for it would entail not only the first crossing of
the Atlantic by air, but by far the world's longest flight to date. Perhaps fortunately, the government in Berlin withheld its permission,
and both these desperate projects were abandoned. It was left to the
Zeppelin Company to hatch more considered plans of its own.

With Hugo Eckener as its operational director and Count Zeppelin's nephew Baron von Gemmingen as its chairman, the company's
plan was to revive the old prewar DELAG intercity service, initially
to run short-haul passenger flights between Friedrichshafen and
Berlin, connecting the south of Germany to the capital using a small
airship that could do the journey in six hours, compared with twenty-
four hours by train.

Within two months the final plans for the new DELAG ship, numbered LZ-120 and christened *Bodensee,* were finalized and approved,
and in six months more the construction of the first postwar zeppelin
was complete. Though it was a modest ship in terms of size, with an
overall length of just under four hundred feet and a gas capacity three
and a half times less than that of the biggest of the wartime zeppelins,
the *Bodensee* was not only the world's first fully streamlined rigid airship but also the fastest airship yet built, with a top speed of over
eighty-two miles per hour. With a crew of sixteen and upholstered
seating for up to twenty-six passengers, a VIP cabin, washrooms, and
a buffet with electric cooker and refrigerator, the gondola of the new
ship resembled the interior of a deluxe passenger express train, with
the control car at the front.

On August 20, 1919, the *Bodensee* made its maiden flight, followed four days later by its first scheduled flight to Berlin, under the command of Hugo Eckener. Altogether there were a hundred flights to the capital and back before the end of the year, with intermediate landings at Munich, conveying a total of over twenty-five hundred passengers. The fastest flight over the 370-mile route took a little less than four hours, a sixth of the time taken by train. For the better part of its short career, the *Bodensee* was a well-patronized passenger aircraft in a world where there were as yet few rivals; it even made a flight to Stockholm, with a view to extending the route to Sweden. In December the *Bodensee* was laid up for a refit and modification, by which time a slightly larger sister ship called the *Nordstern,* intended for the Friedrichshafen-Berlin-Stockholm run, had been built to the same plans.

At this promising point came disaster: the U.S. secretary of war terminated the company's second big project, a proposed super-zeppelin, LZ-125, intended for the U.S. Army Air Service, on the grounds that technically the United States, having declined to ratify the Treaty of Versailles, was still at war with Germany.

Then a second catastrophe struck. Under the punitive terms of the Versailles Treaty, the Zeppelin Company was ordered by the Inter-Allied Commission of Control to cease operations and surrender its two airships in partial compensation for the zeppelins that had been destroyed by their crews after the war instead of being handed over to the Allies as war reparations. *Nordstern* was delivered to France in June 1921 and *Bodensee* to Italy in July. Forbidden by the treaty to build any military airships or any commercial ones with a gas capacity of more than a million cubic feet—too small for the Atlantic service—the Zeppelin Company found itself in a state of crisis. The Allies were dismantling airship hangars throughout Germany, and it seemed that any day the construction shed at Friedrichshafen would be razed too, the Zeppelin personnel dispersed, and the dream extinguished forever. Already the workforce had been cut from its wartime peak of 13,600 down to only 550.

Reeling from these setbacks, for want of any alternative the company turned in desperation to manufacturing aluminum pots and pans. The makers of airships at the cutting edge of technology were condemned to churn out everyday kitchen utensils, while their former enemies and present rivals forged ahead, utilizing the plundered products of their own genius and invention, and competing technologies began to catch up.

In the arena of early postwar aeronautical endeavor, the Atlantic was by far the greatest prize, and the competing efforts to make the first crossing by air almost overlapped. Significantly, from Eckener's point of view, the first aircraft to conquer the challenging expanse of ocean and link the New World and the Old by air was not an airship but an airplane. Between May 16 and 21, 1919, an American Curtiss NC-4 flying boat, flown by U.S. Lieutenant Commander Albert C. Read and his crew, succeeded in crossing the Atlantic west to east by stages from Newfoundland to Lisbon, with two stops in the Azores. A little over a fortnight later came the first nonstop crossing, by a converted twin-engine Vickers Vimy bomber flown by two British pilots, Captain John Alcock and Lieutenant Arthur Whitten-Brown, who crossed from St. John's, Newfoundland, to a patch of soft bog in Galway, Ireland, in a time of sixteen hours, twenty-seven minutes, at an average speed of 118 miles per hour.

Both these flights were essentially demonstrations of pure endurance by airplanes carrying crew only and no excess baggage. Though they marked the future potential of planes, they offered little immediate prospect of commercial transoceanic air traffic. The third transatlantic flight, barely a fortnight after Alcock and Brown's, however, did just that. The British rigid airship R-34, a modified copy of the zeppelin L-33 and the first and smallest airship ever to attempt the Atlantic crossing, took off from East Fortune, Scotland, on July 2 under the command of Major George H. Scott to make the first east—west crossing (the hard way, against the prevailing winds), arriving at Hazelhurst Field, Long Island, New York, virtually out of fuel after a flight of 108 hours, the longest by any aircraft to date.

As it happened, the first man to arrive in America from Europe by air was Major J. E. M. Pritchard, who parachuted out of the ship to supervise the landing arrangements. As he floated to earth he was pursued by a posse of American newsmen in automobiles. "Major

Pritchard, Sir," they cried as he landed with a painful bump, "what is your first impression of America?" Rubbing his sore back, the major replied with a single word: "Hard!"

On July 10 the R-34 returned to Pulham, England, after a west-east crossing of only seventy-five hours with following winds, thus completing the first double crossing of the Atlantic by air—and the first transatlantic flight to follow a commercially viable route out and back, carrying a commercially viable number of people (thirty all told).

Perhaps under the stress of circumstances, the Zeppelin Company began to crack up at the top. First the chairman, Baron von Gemmingen, fell seriously ill and resigned. Then his natural successor, Albert Colsman, who knew the company inside out, was ruthlessly ousted by Eckener. Colsman was a German businessman of the old school—stiff, correct, autocratic, inflexible—and it was clear to Eckener that he was not the man to carry the enterprise through in the very different climate of the postwar world, particularly where American big business was concerned. Eckener not only knew that America was the zeppelin's only hope of salvation; he also saw the company's destiny as wedded to the future of the commercial zeppelin airliner, while Colsman saw his remit as saving the company from extinction by any means, including ending the production of airships and turning to more profitable consumer products. In 1922, at fifty-four years of age, Eckener took over as business director of the Zeppelin Company, becoming chairman two years later. From this point forward, his and the zeppelin's story were one. Only a superhuman effort on the part of Eckener and his employees, inspired by his leadership and example, virtually without pay and sometimes without equipment, kept the dream alive.

From a room on the second floor of the Luftschiffbau-Zeppelin administration building in Friedrichshafen—a book-lined, cigar-fumed room more like a university professor's study than a business director's office—Eckener began to plot the difficult way ahead. Working tirelessly, he kept tight control, personally accounting for every mark and pfennig spent, demanding the utmost from all his staff, even taking English lessons, knowing that it would be the key language of the future (before long he could recite Shakespeare and Mark Twain by heart). Whenever there was an airship to fly, it was Eckener who would methodically plan the details of the flight: route, timings, costings, and above all the crucial publicity campaign that he saw as vital to drumming up public support at home and abroad.

"Business-wise the Zeppelin airship was a highly speculative venture," a Berlin banker noted. "Particularly since it was having to prove its economic practicality in the very worst years. It was a tribute to Eckener's sound business judgement and his handling of Luftschiffbau-Zeppelin's finances that he was not only able to keep the company running but was actually able to expand its operations at the very time that larger, older, and more established firms were having to close their doors."

To save the enterprise, Eckener began to look abroad. He discussed the possibilities of zeppelin development in America with the U.S. Army and Navy, the Goodyear Tire and Rubber Company of Akron, Ohio (resulting in the Goodyear-Zeppelin Corporation, formed to exploit the Zeppelin patents), with Henry Ford, and with banks. He put out feelers to Czechoslovakia and Japan, sought to join forces with a French consortium, negotiated endlessly with the Spanish about a possible zeppelin airline to South America, and even tried to involve the British, who were more interested in obtaining zeppelin designs and know-how than in saving the German airship industry.

The United States offered some hope. Impressed with the operational performance of German zeppelins during the war, the U.S. Navy was keen to build or acquire large rigid airships of its own to act as long-distance scouts and the eyes of the fleet. Two such airships were ordered in 1919—Zeppelin Rigid 1, or ZR-1 (rechristened *Shenandoah*—"Daughter of the Stars"), built by the Americans themselves as a pirated copy of the wartime Zeppelin L-49; and ZR-2, built by the British as the R-38, based on designs of their own. Both were to prove disastrous failures. The R-38 crashed, with great loss of life, after breaking up during violent low-level maneuvers over the River Humber in August 1921, and four years later ZR-1 was destroyed in a line squall over Ohio, killing many on board.

Undeterred by the loss of ZR-2, the Americans placed an order with the Zeppelin Company for a new German-built ship of some

2.6 million cubic feet, the smallest that could safely fly the Atlantic (though the British R-34 had been smaller). The contract was signed in June 1922, but not before Eckener agreed to pledge the assets of the company as security in case the ship was lost on her delivery flight to the United States, as no insurance company was willing to underwrite it. In securing this contract, Eckener saved the Zeppelin Company and the zeppelin concept in Germany from extinction, at least for the moment. It was not, however, a business deal in any conventional sense. The new zeppelin was essentially a reparations ship, compensation to the value of 3 million marks paid in the form of an airship whose cost had been met by the German government.

The new ship—designated LZ-126 by the Zeppelin Company, ZR-3 by the U.S. Navy—was of a fully streamlined design, representing an advanced version of the wartime high-altitude zeppelins in some regards, but with features of the small commercial airships *Bodensee* and *Nordstern* thrown in. LZ-126 was intended as a training ship for the U.S. Navy and built under navy supervision. But in order to conform with postwar international law, which required that the new zeppelin be used for civil purposes, it was designed to carry twenty passengers and was the first airship ever to provide sleeping accommodation for passengers on long flights. Both passenger quarters and control room were accommodated in a seventy-five-foot-long gondola built directly onto the forward part of the keel, which in addition contained a radio room, electric kitchen, washrooms, and toilets. Unlike previous zeppelins, the outer cover was coated with "dope"* mixed with powdered aluminum, which gave it a silvery look and enhanced its already beautiful lines.

LZ-126 was not only the largest zeppelin yet built, but with its five specially developed Maybach V-12 engines, capable of getting its speed up to just under eighty miles per hour, it was also one of the fastest. Since there were no further orders in the offing, and everyone concerned with the project believed it would be the last of the line, its work force built it with loving care and meticulous attention to detail,

---

*The dope was a solution of cellulose nitrate or acetate in acetone, which was applied to the outer cover in order to tauten and waterproof it.

so that it should be as perfect as could be, a magnificent example of a vanishing breed, the admiration of the aeronautical world.

The appearance of this symbol of German inventive genius on test flights in September 1924 provoked wild enthusiasm, for this was the first zeppelin to be seen over the Fatherland for five years and might very likely be the last. But some patriotic fanatics viewed the transference of such a masterpiece of German technology as nothing short of treachery. Threats were made against Eckener's life if he went ahead with the America flight, and a would-be assassin with a gimpy leg and a sawn-off rifle was apprehended while skulking around the Zeppelin shed at Friedrichshafen. Even the president of the Reichsbank, Hjalmar Schacht, joined in the recrimination: "This is the last airship of German manufacture," he raged, "because it is *German*. Hate, revenge, envy and stupidity still live!"

Eckener could have done without the politics, for the flight itself was a daunting enough prospect. Though the ship handled well, Eckener in private viewed the transatlantic flight—the first ever undertaken by a zeppelin airship—with some trepidation, for neither he nor anyone else in Germany had any experience of the weather of the middle Atlantic, and the ship's gas volume and fuel endurance margins were too small to allow for navigational or operational errors.

"It was clear that not only the lives of the participants but the fate of the Zeppelin idea would depend on our success," Eckener was to write afterward. "A failure would, in these circumstances, have meant the end of the company in Friedrichshafen and with it the only place where the rigid airship tradition and the belief in its future were still alive."

The departure from Friedrichshafen, scheduled for October 11, 1924, proved troublesome. When Captain Flemming weighed the ship, he found it puzzlingly tail-heavy. A search revealed two stowaways in the stern portion—a reporter from the International News Service and a photographer from International Newsreel who had sneaked on board in work clothes hoping for a scoop. A second attempt to get the ship airborne was aborted when unusually warm atmospheric conditions made it impossible to get lift-off without dumping fuel. Eckener had no alternative but to postpone the flight until six the following morning.

There was some derision amongst the watching crowd, who thought Eckener had lost his nerve, and even his own officers believed he was being overcautious. To his daughter Lotte, who had come to wave farewell, he explained: "I am completely indifferent to what the public think. It is the biggest mistake you can make to allow your decision to be forced on you by public opinion. Supposing we had come to a sticky end. Do you think the public would have cared because we took a risk to please them?"

A little after daybreak next morning, October 12, the anniversary of the day Columbus discovered America and twenty-four years and a day since Eckener had set eyes on his first zeppelin, the latest and possibly last zeppelin of all took off on its maiden Atlantic voyage. On board was a crew of twenty-seven, including Eckener's most able watch officers (no fewer than five of them with masters' tickets as rigid airship pilots), together with four observers from the U.S. Navy and Army. The voyage was to test to the full Hugo Eckener's gifts as a navigator of airships and a reader of weather. With the North Atlantic dominated by low-pressure areas and very strong head winds, he had chosen to cross by the southern route via Cape Finisterre in Spain and the Azores—a course four hundred miles longer in distance but a lot shorter in time. Flying over the mouth of the Gironde in France, LZ-126 reached the Atlantic coast. "We crossed with feelings of tense expectation, perhaps with inner jubilation," Eckener wrote. "Before us lay the boundless plain on which we were to discover for the first time whether airships could be safely navigated across it. Our dreams and our hopes were on the verge of fulfilment."

Leaving Europe at Cape Finisterre, LZ-126 reached the Azores around noon the following day. By now the weather had changed, with a strong southwest wind reducing the ship's speed to little more than twenty-five miles per hour. This was a potentially alarming situation, for at the present speed it would take a further seventy hours to reach New York, and there was enough fuel for only fifty. Eckener realized he needed to take stock of the whole Atlantic weather pattern in the hope that he could find some other way through. Meteorological reports from two U.S. Navy cruisers that had put to sea to provide assistance if required suggested that to the far northwest, in the vicinity of Newfoundland, lay a low-pressure center that might be put to use.

Eckener was about to take his first lesson in transoceanic pressure flying, a technique for harnessing the circulation of the air. He changed course toward Newfoundland, knowing that in the northern hemisphere he could make use of the counterclockwise air circulating around the north side of the low to minimize head winds and, he hoped, take advantage of any tail winds that might be blowing. A similar but opposite technique could be utilized around high-pressure areas, where the air circulated in a clockwise direction. As he expected, on the afternoon of the fourteenth, the third day of the flight, the ship picked up a following wind from the east that bore it toward the coast of America at a steady seventy-eight miles per hour. In the early hours of the fifteenth they were over Boston, and by breakfast time they were off Sandy Hook in the run-in to New York.

"The bay and the low shore were shrouded in a light morning mist," Eckener wrote, "but the fantastic shapes of skyscrapers towered above it and gleamed in the rising sun. The imposing picture which this overpowering giant metropolis of daring and enterprising spirit offers to the arriving stranger, appeared to us with a double beauty, a fairy tale city to which we had abruptly come out of the dark, empty sea."

As the din of the city's fire sirens and the hooters of every seagoing vessel in the harbor filled the control room with their clamor, Eckener was moved to scribble a message addressed to the entire city and its people. He attached it to a small parachute and tossed it out of a control car window.

> *New York, we salute you!*
> *The ZR-3 dips its bow and sends sincere greetings to the people of America.*
> *We hope that our transatlantic flight will be the forerunner of a fruitful epoch of cordial co-operation between our two nations in developing Count Zeppelin's immortal achievements in the conquest of the air by lighter-than-air craft.*

*Thus we will work hand in hand at the task of bridging time
and distance, thereby binding all nations of the Earth more
closely together.*

*ECKENER*

After a triumphal loop over the Statue of Liberty, Eckener took
the ship up above the city in a broad spiral to a height of over ten
thousand feet—an extraordinary sight for the mass of New Yorkers
below—releasing gas and trimming the ship for landing before setting
course for the naval airport at Lakehurst.

By 9 A.M. on October 15, 1924, after a flight around one-fifth of the
Earth's circumference in a total of three days, nine hours, and two
minutes, they were safely down at the Lakehurst naval air station in
New Jersey, to a welcome such as they had never experienced in their
lives. Eckener received a signed receipt for his airship, which was later
christened *Los Angeles* ("because it came to us like an angel of peace")
by First Lady Grace Coolidge. As a highly successful training and
experimental navy airship, the *Los Angeles* was to prove the best rigid
America ever had, flying a total of nearly five thousand hours in an
unblemished career of eight years.

The first transatlantic zeppelin flight stirred mass enthusiasm in the
United States, especially among the sizeable German-American com-
munity. For Eckener and his crew the flight was an unqualified triumph. "The flight across the ocean brought us valuable experience,"
he reported later. "We had found that certain weather conditions
could be used to our advantage to make our journey faster and safer.
Furthermore, we had seen that atmospheric turbulence in the line
squalls had not been in the least dangerous to our ship. This was an
important discovery."

The flight was also of immense importance in helping to further a
postwar rapprochement between Germany and the United States. At
the moment of touchdown there had been a welcoming message from
President Coolidge, and Eckener and his officers were summoned to
Washington for a special reception with the president at the White
House. "The Zeppelin did more good for Germany," read one news-
paper, "than a dozen ambassadors." Another hailed its commander as
"Germany's greatest and only diplomat." Yet another voted Eckener

man of the year, the visionary protagonist of a forward-looking idea: "the conquest and command of the skies."

The first half of November was taken up with receptions, banquets, lectures, and press conferences all over America. Once Eckener sat down to lunch with eleven hundred of the most important businessmen in America. Another time a theater audience burst into a rendering of "Deutschland über Alles" in his honor. He was awarded countless citations. That of the Detroit Aviation Association was typical, acclaiming him and his zeppelin for "the remarkable achievement of uniting for the first time the continents of the old world and the new world with a span of only sixty-six hours between coastal ports."

During the first half of November, Eckener, accompanied by his senior Zeppelin officers, Lehmann and von Schiller, traveled the breadth of America to make contacts and try to establish the groundwork for a proposed international airship service. Already the previous year the Goodyear-Zeppelin Corporation had been founded to further the development of rigid airship flight and to ensure, by sharing Zeppelin patents and engineering expertise, the continuance of the zeppelin concept in America if (as seemed possible) it came to an end in Germany. The principal airship-orientated corporation in America, the Goodyear Tire and Rubber Company of Akron, Ohio, whose president, Paul W. Litchfield, was almost as committed an airshipman as Hugo Eckener himself, owned two-thirds of the shares; Luftschiffbau-Zeppelin owned the remaining third. All patents owned by the Zeppelin Company were transferred to Goodyear, while Goodyear made their own airship patents available to the Germans in Friedrichshafen. Captain Lehmann, as the Zeppelin representative of the new company, was about to move into his office at Goodyear headquarters in Akron, and the Zeppelin Company's leading design engineer and stress analyst, Dr. Karl Arnstein, was on the point of setting sail for America with twelve other airship engineers from Friedrichshafen to help build America's own rigid airships of the future along zeppelin lines.

In November 1924 Eckener returned by sea to Germany, "full of joy and satisfaction," he said. The cities and towns were decorated with flags, church bells rang, and newsmen reported that "Germany has re-established itself in the eyes of the world." Dr. Eckener had become the new father figure of the nation, the man who most filled his fellow citizens with pride, and one of the best-known and most admired Germans in the world. But he came back to nothing.

The great hangar, scene of so much excitement and high hopes only a few weeks before, was now empty and echoing, "like a deserted ball-room on the morning after." Nothing could hide the fact that, as things stood, the ZR-3's flight to America was the last flight of the last Zeppelin airship, and the Zeppelin Company was nothing more than a name, with no ships and no plans. Short of a miracle, the zeppelin was now an invention that, as far as Germany was concerned, was soon to be consigned to history. But a ground swell of support for the zeppelin cause was growing both at home and abroad, and Eckener was encouraged when the eminent Swedish explorer Sven Hedin formally approached the German government in Berlin with the idea of using a zeppelin to retrace the steps of Marco Polo across Central Asia to Peking. The zeppelin enterprise should not be brought to an end, Hedin argued; otherwise the world of science would lose a unique research tool, particularly in the fields of photography and cartography. Eckener himself was full of enthusiasm about using a zeppelin for the long-distance exploration of little-known lands. The question was, what zeppelin?

It was obvious to Eckener that the company must either formulate a target and a plan, or perish. In his own mind the target was clear: the giant rigid airship had only one possible role, one niche that no other form of aircraft could fill. Only the big rigid was capable of transporting an economically viable load of passengers, air mail, and cargo between continents in comfort and at a speed vastly greater than that of the ocean liner, the only other form of intercontinental travel. The demand for such a form of travel was potentially enormous, particularly for the route between Europe and America (though a Far East service via India was a possible option). For a transatlantic airline comprising three passenger zeppelins, landing facilities, and hangars, Eckener reckoned the capital outlay would be around 35 million marks. On the basis of the likely returns from passenger, freight, and mail receipts on an average of a hundred Atlantic crossings per year, plus receipts from other sources, such as advertising and airport tourism, he reckoned that bankers could expect an attractive 35 percent return on their original investment—if they chose to make one.

Immediately upon his return to Germany, Eckener began to draw up a plan. He needed to build a demonstration ship to show the world the potential and practicality of international commercial passenger flight by zeppelin. But how was he to raise the money to build one? It cost millions of dollars to build a zeppelin—almost as much as a battleship—while airplanes cost only thousands. Germany was in a state of economic crisis, and in any case its aviation advisers were almost to a man fighter pilot veterans from the war who were convinced the civil and military future in the air lay with the airplane.

That left the public. Although Eckener well remembered how the nation had rallied to Count Zeppelin's appeal after the disaster at Echterdingen, he had doubts about trying it again. "A whole people will not enthuse twice over one and the same cause," he remarked. But there was no other option. So in August 1925, to coincide with the twenty-fifth anniversary of the first zeppelin airship, a nationwide appeal—the "Zeppelin-Eckener Fund of the German People"—was launched. Eckener and his leading officers—Hans Flemming, Hans von Schiller, Anton Witteman, and Max Pruss, all of whom had taken part in the flight of LZ-126—traveled the land to lecture the populace about the transatlantic flight and to drum up donations for the new ship of the future. In the course of a year Eckener himself gave over a hundred illustrated lectures, from one end of the country to the other, to packed town halls, clubs, schools, civic centers, universities, and business banquets, with other trips to the lands of the German minorities beyond the Fatherland's frontiers: Austria, Switzerland, Poland, Hungary, Romania, and the Baltic states. "It was perhaps the most exhausting work I have ever done in my life," he was to comment when it was over.

In the middle of all this came a lucky break. In October 1925 Germany's former enemies signed the Treaties of Locarno, allowing Germany to join the concert of Europe as an equal partner. Limitations on the size of future airships were rescinded. It was now possible to build a much larger passenger zeppelin than originally envisaged—not of optimum size (cost and hangar size prevented that), but large enough for Eckener's immediate ambition to operate a transatlantic zeppelin for fare-paying passengers, mail, and freight—"an airship in which one would not merely fly," he said, "but also be able to *voyage,* a Zeppelin that was also a training ship with a pioneering mission, not only for airships but also for all kinds of flight above the oceans."

Though the 2.5 million marks raised by the Zeppelin-Eckener Fund was less than half the money required to build a transatlantic airship, it was enough to start construction. Later Eckener was able to extract a further million marks out of his grudging government, and Colsman was obliged to find the balance out of Zeppelin Company funds. The new ship, LZ-127, was designed by Ludwig Dürr, who had designed every Zeppelin built in the last twenty years, except for the very first. From the outset LZ-127 was intended to be the best and biggest zeppelin yet to take to the skies, representing the cutting edge of zeppelin workmanship and technology of its day. The only practical limitation to its proposed volume and configuration was the size of the hangar in which it was built, which was rather too low, resulting in the ship's slender and elegant-looking but rather inefficiently streamlined shape—like a pencil rather than a cigar.

Although the new ship owed something to the design of the LZ-126, it incorporated a number of improvements. The control room was placed farther forward, giving the commander and his watch officers and helmsmen a much better view in all directions. The helmsmen now had servo-operated controls, which made handling easier and less tiring. The old magnetic compass, on which it had been difficult to read a change of course of even several degrees, was replaced by a gyrocompass, which clearly showed a course change of only one-tenth of a degree. The powerful 2,650-horsepower Maybach engines gave a cruising speed of 71.5 miles per hour. They could be run on petrol or Blaugas, a mixture of acethane, acetylene, butylene, methane, propylene, and hydrogen, which was almost weightless, meaning that as it was used up during the course of a flight the ship's weight remained virtually unchanged, and it was therefore not necessary to valve off crucially valuable hydrogen in order to maintain level buoyant flight. The Blaugas was contained in twelve fabric bags inside the hull, which altogether held nearly a million cubic feet of it—enough for a hundred hours at cruising speed. The ship also carried enough conventional petrol for 67 hours' cruising, and on long flights would carry enough fuel of both kinds for 118 hours' cruising, an average of eighty-four hundred miles.

On July 8, 1928, the anniversary of Count Zeppelin's birth, the new ship was christened *Graf Zeppelin* by his daughter, Countess von Brandenstein-Zeppelin. He had named the new ship after the old count, Eckener explained, "in order to connect the final decision concerning the value and significance of the builder and his airship concept with their confirmation in this ship fated by destiny. The result would be either victory and fame, or final downfall and the end of a defective concept."

And so was born LZ-127, *Graf Zeppelin*, familiarly known as the *Graf*—Dr. Eckener's dream machine.

In initial trial flights the new ship proved itself satisfactory in every respect, with a greater useful lift than anticipated, good maneuverability, and a top speed of over eighty miles per hour. The usual thirty-six-hour endurance flight, set for September 18, took the *Graf Zeppelin* down the Rhine, over the cheering cities of Cologne and Düsseldorf, to the Hook of Holland and the North Sea, and thence to Harwich on the east coast of England—the first zeppelin to be seen in those parts since the war. Then Eckener turned the ship back to Friedrichshafen on a long loop via Hamburg, Kiel, Berlin, and other large cities, in each of which the great ship was greeted with universal jubilation and hailed as a technical masterpiece and an envoy of the German people for peace and international reconciliation. The *Graf* had proved itself in every respect.

"What the ship was to demonstrate was of epochal significance," Eckener wrote. "She was to prove that passengers could now be carried across the Atlantic Ocean by air in speed and safety, and with all the comfort and pleasure which the modern traveler demands. Up till then this had been a wishful dream, which other types of aircraft had not fulfilled so far. But we were sure that we could do it, and we hoped that our flight would strengthen the moral and political success that had resulted from the ZR-3's ocean crossing. I never dreamed that we would be placed in mortal peril en route."

The *Graf Zeppelin*'s departure was scheduled for October 10, but the omens were bad. The Atlantic weather map was a nightmare, one severe depression following another, with winds up to storm force ten. Cargo ships were sending distress signals, the great ocean liners were twenty-four hours late butting their way to New York. A flight via the steamer routes across the middle Atlantic would be folly, Eckener reckoned. The southern route via Gibraltar, Madeira, and Bermuda was too long: "The speed of an airship is its most important advantage, so how could one emphasise speed by taking the longest route?" As for the northern route via the north of Scotland, Iceland, and Newfoundland, with all its fogs and low clouds and rocky coasts, that was too risky with the navigational aids then available. "Thus I vacillated, discouraged and uncertain," Eckener wrote, "between the Scylla of a long southern route I did not care for, and the Charybdis of a northern route decidedly dangerous in the circumstances."

In the end he decided that the only option was to postpone the departure altogether. The crowd of many thousands wandered away, disappointed and disgruntled. "Just look at what they mean by the regularity and punctuality of airship travel," Eckener overheard one of them say. But later that morning a terrific storm swept over Friedrichshafen, and blew all day. Now everyone complimented him on his expertise as a meteorologist and the wisdom of his decision to postpone the flight.

"When I went to bed that night," Eckener would recall, "the wind was howling past my bedroom and the rain beat against the panes. I have hardly ever passed such a restless night. I spent it listening to the constant whistling of the wind in the shingles and the splash of rain against the window. I got up every hour to look out and went back to bed cursing that the Lord in his wrath had made me an airship pilot."

By the time he reached the airship shed at six the next morning, the weather was almost calm and dry. Preparations were already being made for takeoff. Baggage and mail were being stowed on board the ship, the engines were running thunderously in a final preflight test, the gasbags were having a last fill of hydrogen. In conference with his senior watch officers, Flemming and von Schiller, it was soon clear that the Atlantic weather fronts allowed only one route to the west: the southern route via Gibraltar, after all.

In addition to the forty crew members, sixty-six thousand items of airmail, and a pet canary, there were twenty passengers—among them Count Zeppelin's son-in-law Count Brandenstein-Zeppelin, the Prussian minister of the interior, four representatives of the German air ministry, two foreign airship experts, six representatives of German and international newspapers, two artists to depict whatever the photographers could not, and an insurance expert to assess the risks of commercial airship flights.

For a while it looked as though one of the passengers might not make it. When the airship was ready to be brought out of the shed, it was discovered that Lady Grace Hay-Drummond-Hay of the Hearst Press had not yet finished her toilette at her hotel. Then there was a commotion. Figures could be seen scampering in breathless panic through the workshops and into the hangar—her ladyship herself, her chauffeur, and the hotel porter, laden down with overnight cases and small packages.

"Hurry! Hurry!" Dr. Eckener roared at her through the control-car window, barely able to suppress his mirth. The boarding steps had already been removed, so Lady Hay had to be bodily manhandled up through the gondola door. No sooner was she on board than she rushed to a window in a state of great agitation. "For goodness *sake!*" she yelled. "My *coat!*"

"A cold chill seized me," she wrote. "In the hurry and rush I had left in my room at the hotel the new coat which Mr. Gordon Selfridge, the millionaire American storekeeper in London, had especially designed for me. Could anything be more tragic? I felt it could not. Thrusting a money note into the hotel porter's hand, I fairly prayed him to rescue it for me."

The *Graf*'s command was gallant enough to send a fast car to the hotel to fetch the coat, returning with it in a short while, to the rapturous cheers of everyone on the airship and in the hangar. At last the great ship could be set in motion by the rope spiders and trolleys, and carefully hauled out onto the takeoff field.

At 7:45 on the morning of Thursday, October 11, 1928, the *Graf Zeppelin* rose into the sky above Friedrichshafen at the start of the first-ever commercial passenger flight from the Old World to the New. Flying over Konstanz, the birthplace of Count Zeppelin, the ship headed down the Rhine through Switzerland to Basel, then shaped course over France, following the Rhône valley through Languedoc and Provence and over Avignon to the river's estuary. At 4:20 P.M. the *Graf* crossed the French coast and headed across the Mediterranean toward Barcelona on the northeast coast of Spain.

Between six and eight that first evening Lady Hay sat in the navigation room watching the sunset. Though this was her first ride on a zeppelin, it would not be her last, and before long she would come to be known as "Lady Zeppelin." Born of a professional family in London in the early 1890s, her life had never taken the conventional path of the average middle-class Victorian English girl. Ambitious, charming, and attractive, she had traveled widely and had succeeded as a reporter in the hurly-burly of Fleet Street's all-male preserve. At the age of twenty-eight she had married a Tangier-born Scottish aristocrat, Sir Robert Hay-Drummond-Hay, a huntin'-and-shootin' Arabist and diplomat who was nearly fifty years her senior. Following his not-unexpected demise, she had traveled in China, then returned to Fleet Street, soon moving on to become the English correspondent of the Hearst Press.

Now she was sitting on the bridge of the *Graf Zeppelin* with Hugo Eckener, watching the coast of northern Spain grow sharper and blacker against the setting sun. "The golden ball of the sun sank lower and lower toward the horizon," she wrote. "The shores of Spain took on gleaming clusters of sparkling lights as one by one the tiny fishing villages illuminated themselves against the darkness."

But it wasn't just the magic of space and distance that so entranced her: it was also the unique experience of traveling in this way—above all, perhaps, the magnetic personality of the man now sitting beside her on the bridge of the *Graf,* feeding bread and apple from his supper to his pet canary. Hugo Eckener was, she reckoned, the first true genius she had ever got to know. "Dr. Eckener is an artist," she perceived. "That is why some people do not understand him. . . . Few know him as I have been privileged to see him—the whimsical wit, the sweet-natured student and thoroughly loveable, unspoiled giant of the century."

The lights of Barcelona were reflected along the silvery hull of the giant ship, and the crowds could be seen running about excitedly in the streets below. Then the *Graf* was over the dark Spanish interior. At 5:40 the next morning everyone on board was woken by Captain Flemming calling out "Gibraltar!" They turned out sleepy-eyed in their night attire—"a regular pajama party," noted Lady Hay—for a farewell look at the brightly shining lighthouse of Ceuta on the African side of the straits and the famous rock on the other as they bore down toward Cape Trafalgar, the jumping-off point for the Atlantic crossing. "What surprises would we find this time," Eckener asked himself, "in the broad expanse of the spiteful and incalculable North Atlantic?"

Dawn, breaking in shades of lemon, pink, mauve, and blue, promised another fair-weather day to come, the trackless immensity of the silver-flecked ocean stretching to infinity before them—and not another aircraft in the whole of that boundless space, only the shadow of the *Graf* on the sea.

The key to smooth and comfortable airship flying was the handling of the elevator and rudder wheels. Only men who had an almost instinctive feel for the movement of the ship were chosen for the jobs of elevator and rudder helmsmen—men who could "read" the ship's responses in wind and storm, updraft and turbulence, anticipate and correctly judge the delay and subsequent behavior of the ship in reaction to any movement of the elevator or rudder wheels. Every helmsman on the *Graf Zeppelin* possessed these qualities in different ways and in varying degrees; some passengers could tell by the change in the movements of the ship that there had been a change of watch. Generally the ship was kept so steady that even in stormy weather, when the passengers could see the waves breaking on the sea below, the wine did not even slop in their glasses.

The rudder helmsman's job had been made easier by the introduction of an automatic pilot that enabled him to hold a course within half a degree in steady weather, or within two degrees in gusty weather. For the elevator helmsman there was no such aid, however, and he continued to control the pitch and attitude of the ship manually. His job was to limit the rise and fall of the bow to five degrees by all possible means, for this was the angle at which a bottle of wine would keel over on the dinner table. Normally the elevator man kept a four-hour watch, but in very windy or stormy conditions the strain of the job was so great that the watch was limited to two hours.

An improvement that both eased the strain on passengers' nerves and improved the efficiency of the ship was the change in the method of taking altitude "shots." The ship's altitude was measured by a conventional aneroid altimeter that registered the barometric pressure. But because of changes in atmospheric pressure during the course of a flight the altimeter's readings could be wildly inaccurate, by as much as five hundred feet, so at intervals the altitude had to be checked in other ways. One method, much more accurate but not popular with the passengers, involved echo-ranging altitude measurements made with a nonbarometric apparatus called the Echolot. The duty navigation officer in the control car would fire a gun loaded with a blank cartridge straight down at the sea, and then measure the length of time the echo took to come back. The altitude was automatically indicated on an electric meter, accurate to within a yard over a height range of three thousand feet. The trouble was that gunshots in the environment of a gas-filled zeppelin could prove alarming to passengers, especially at dead of night. Later a compressed-air device was installed instead, which produced an ultrasonic and therefore silent, but no less accurate, "shot." A more popular method from the passengers' point of view entailed dropping an empty bottle (usually a mineral-water bottle, since wine bottles came in too many shapes and sizes) out of the control car window and timing its fall to the sea with a stopwatch, which enabled the altitude to be calculated to an accuracy of thirty or forty feet.

The position of the ship at sea was calculated in the conventional way: by taking a fix on the sun or stars and using the drift sight to take drift readings to measure the angle between the axis of the ship and its track over the water; at night a powerful searchlight mounted under the hull abaft the control car was used for this purpose. The highest drift angle ever recorded on the *Graf* was a massive forty-nine degrees. The accuracy of the navigators in plotting the ship's position by dead reckoning was formidable. On a later ocean crossing, for example, they picked their way across eighteen hundred miles of ocean and arrived over their first landfall dead on course and only a minute or two off their projected arrival time.

As the *Graf Zeppelin* began its ocean crossing, it picked up a tail wind, and by two in the afternoon it was over Madeira—mountainous little islands, bright green vineyard terraces, whitewashed houses, winding trails, peacock-blue sea—pinpointed with unerring accuracy by Dr. Eckener's sophisticated system of dead reckoning. This was their last glimpse of land before they reached the eastern seaboard of the United States. The real test now truly began.

From the outset the overriding concern had been weight and safety, two elements of zeppelin design and operations that were inseparably linked. Every pound of weight counted. The airship itself weighed many tons, but even eight ounces could make all the difference between ascending and descending, so exquisitely was the weight balanced. So on this trial flight some rudimentary items were in short supply. There were no mirrors in the cabins, for example—or, for that matter, electric call bells, for fear that a spark might ignite the hydrogen and blow up the ship—and both food and water were rationed, to the extent that bottled water ran out on the first day, and the wine was running out by the second.

"This is a picnic life," noted Lady Hay. "It is a huge experiment. The tiny electric kitchen is inadequate to supply luxuries for passengers as well as cook innumerable cans of steaming food for the forty members of the crew—at least 180 meals a day in a tiny kitchen only a few feet square." Not that the passengers suffered too much. Meals were simple and informal but adequate—eggs and coffee for breakfast, soup, meat, and stewed fruit for lunch, bread and sausage for dinner. At 4:30 the steward would smuggle some English tea to the only English national on board, sneaking into Lady Hay's cabin with a teapot secreted under his white overall and a buttered roll in his pocket. Other passengers plundered a luxury basket of dainties including caviar, foie gras, and bottled pears, washed down with vintage cognac distilled in the year of Napoleon's march on Moscow, the gift of a connoisseur from Berlin.

The only passengers with any reason for complaint were the newsmen, who could not radio their stories home because the radio was mostly taken up with weather reports. "The wireless service is another thing which can stand improvement," wrote Lady Hay in her own unsent dispatch. "But the passengers are all happy and pleased with the voyage, voting airship travel the best method for long trans-ocean journeys. The Zeppelin swings in space like a cradle, swaying gently to the lullaby of the winds on the silver canvas. The only one who is not actually enthusiastic is the American Gilfillan, who feels the privation of not being able to smoke. He says he smokes more than 100 cigarettes a day."

Frederick Gilfillan, a wealthy American financier who lived in Switzerland, was known as the "mystery man" to the other passengers—an irascible, neurotic loner. No one quite knew who he was or why he was there. All they knew was that he complained loudly and endlessly of just about everything to do with the *Graf Zeppelin*. The coffee was terrible, the air bad, the ship slow, the bed hard, and the service awful.

That evening, some 250 miles south of the Azores, nearing the middle of the Atlantic, the ship received a weather report from the Azores weather station warning that a storm front was approaching from the northwest. On the bridge for much of that second night the watch could see vivid lightning flashing along the northern horizon. "Towards midnight," Eckener recorded, "the entire northern heavens were aflame with almost incessant lightning. It was a grandiose spectacle, but at the same time disturbing." An influx of cold air was extending far to the south from the northern cyclonic storm, and in due course it would reach the ship, bringing with it severe turbulence and violent squalls. "I must admit," Eckener wrote, "that I experienced a feeling of great tension over what the next hours would bring."

The *Graf* was a largely unproved craft. Its maiden flight had taken place less than a month before, and on none of its six short proving trips had it encountered bad weather. Eckener felt sure the ship's structure could survive very bad weather intact, and in any case it was believed that squalls over the sea were not as violent as those over land. "But that was only a theory," he added, "and had to be proven by practical experience, which we still lacked."

For a few hours they flew on in calm weather, but the wind was steadily increasing, and the atmosphere became so sultry that Captain Lehmann in his cabin above the control car was unable to sleep. "It was very disagreeable," Eckener recorded, "for something *had* to happen." It was no great surprise when, at about six o'clock on Friday morning, the second day of the flight, he saw "a blue-black wall of cloud of very threatening aspect advancing towards us at great speed from the northwest." Stretching from horizon to horizon halfway between Spain and the coast of Virginia, this menacing atmospheric barrier represented a violent cold front, bringing with it wind, rain, and turbulence of a level that was potentially catastrophic for an aircraft the shape and size of the *Graf Zeppelin.*

Around daybreak it started raining heavily, and at breakfast time it began to grow dark. Glancing out of the window, Lieutenant Commander Charles E. Rosendahl, the U.S. Navy observer and the commander of the *Los Angeles,* recognized the squall characteristics of the bilious sky. "Such atmospheric conditions are always attended by vertical currents," he wrote. "Being intensely interested in the handling of the ship in such a situation, I went up into the control space to observe."

By now Eckener realized that a severe test of the ship was imminent and sent for his most experienced elevator man, Albert Sammt (future watch officer—and survivor—of the *Hindenburg*), to take over the elevator controls from the less experienced man on duty. But it was too late. For reasons that are not entirely clear, Eckener did not reduce power, and before Sammt could take over the wheel, the ship ran straight into the squall front at full speed. At a combined speed of almost 150 miles per hour, the great storm and the great ship smashed into each other.

It was 8:25 A.M. Breakfast was being served in the saloon, and Lady Hay-Drummond-Hay was sitting in a chair with her back to the bow when she was aware that a terrific wind had sprung up. Suddenly the ship's nose dipped steeply down, as if it were diving into the sea, sending chairs and tables skidding the length of the saloon, and cups and saucers and tea- and coffeepots hurtling along the floor, and pinning Lady Hay in her seat against the forward wall of the saloon. Then, in a frantic effort to pull the ship out of its dive, the elevators were pulled too suddenly upward.

Commander Rosendahl on the bridge could see what was happening. As the ship's nose started to rise, the elevator man, a green hand under instruction, became confused. Instead of putting the elevators into the "down" position to lift the tail, he put them in the "up" position, thus accelerating the downward movement of the stern and the upward movement of the bow. Lehmann and Rosendahl spotted the man's error and yelled at him. Another officer sprang to the wheel and took over control, but by now the ship had acquired an extreme nose-up angle—perhaps twenty-five to thirty degrees by Rosendahl's calculation, "pointing towards the moon" in the passengers' view—before the upward thrust of the bow was checked. The loss of the British rigid airship R-38 seven years previously was attributed to just such an error.

On the bridge, the watch officers, Eckener included, were sent sliding down the deck, and in the navigation room the books and charts fell off the navigator's table with a thud. Eckener grabbed a girder to keep his balance, aware of a "horrible racket" from the saloon and the kitchen, where pots, pans, and kettles fell with a clatter to the deck and against the door. "Amidst the noise, which was increased by the crash of thunder," recalled Eckener, "it was impossible to tell if the hull structure was breaking up. Mutely we looked enquiringly at each other, wondering what was coming next."

"Unutterable confusion," reported Lady Hay. "Chairs, tables crashed in a heap. Crockery slid to the floor, smashing the lovely blue and white Zeppelin chinaware. Coffee, tea, butter, sausages, marmalade formed a glutinous mess and overspread the unlucky ones sitting with their backs to the stern. I, in my chair, slid the length of the saloon, crashing into the unfortunate artist, Professor Dettmann, who in turn fell over Robert Hartmann's movie camera, which fell full weight on Frederick Gilfillan."

Lady Hay, her breakfast in her lap and all over her face, was seized with determination to save her precious coffee, for which she had waited two and a half hours, but as the ship pitched and bounced heavily through two or three lighter squalls, it went all over Colonel Herrera, the Spanish airship representative on board, while Robert Reiner of Weehawken found himself sitting, "aggrieved and surprised," in the lap of artist Theo Matejko. "Breathless moments passed," recalled Lady Hay, "leaving not a few blanched faces, and the thought—we were facing death."

"I've lost my coffee!" she cried. Then, overwhelmed by the ridiculousness of the sight before her, she laughed out loud. "It was not lack of a realisation of the danger on her part," recalled her Hearst colleague Karl von Wiegand. "She knew. But that laugh broke the tension of a momentary deathlike silence as the ship righted itself." It was, reckoned von Wiegand, a singular example of a woman's nerve and bravery, "surpassed by not one man's nerve." In the narrow corridor a petrified Mr. Gilfillan accosted the remarkably calm Englishwoman with the grim question: "Have you ever faced death before?" She laughed again. "In sharp contrast to her usual quiet poise and reserve," noted von Wiegand, "the darker the situation seemed to grow, the more animated and lively she became."

Going forward to the bridge, Lady Hay found the atmosphere was now one of responsible concern rather than alarm. Dr. Eckener was pacing up and down looking serious (as he often did), Captain Flemming was calmly drinking hot coffee from a flask, Captain Lehmann's characteristic cheery smile remained intact, Rosendahl, who had been on the bridge since the first weather warning, looked grave. But at least the *Graf* had not broken up in the turbulence like the American rigid *Shenandoah*. The control-room floor was flooding with rainwater, so that the duty watch had to take off their shoes and socks, but that mattered little. The engines were humming along, at half speed now, and for the moment the rudders and elevators were answering as they should. "I was very well satisfied," Eckener wrote later. "Out here, over the warm ocean, we had managed to overcome a squall which probably ranked as the most severe the North Atlantic could produce."

But the ship had not emerged unscathed. "Suddenly the hatch leading into the car from the keel above slammed open," recalled Rosendahl, "and a panting, white-faced member of the crew tumbled down the ladder and in jerky sentences told of damage to the ship aft." The violence of the storm had torn away the lower part of the port horizontal stabilizer's doped cotton cover. The torn fabric on the fin was streaming loose, and there was a real risk that the rudder or elevators would be jammed, or that if the upper cover of the fin gave way, the ship would be rendered uncontrollable, a balloon adrift at the mercy of the wind.

This was an emergency of the greatest gravity. Eckener's decision was immediate. He ordered the engines to slow speed so as to reduce the aerodynamic load on the damaged fin, then called for volunteers to go aft to try to carry out repairs. Four men stepped forward, among them Eckener's son, Knut, and the senior elevator helmsman, Albert Sammt. After walking aft along the *Graf*'s interior catwalk, the men clambered up onto the windswept top of the ship, then worked their way to the seventy-five-foot-long fin of the port stabilizer, cautiously crawling through the intricate maze of its Duralumin interior to reach the tapering outer edge, from which streamed the flapping shreds of its torn fabric cover. This was perilous work. The metal structure was wet and treacherous underfoot. There were no lashing lines to secure the men, so they tied themselves to each other like mountaineers. The fin lurched up and down. Wind and rain beat about them. Even at low speed the slipstream swept over the fin at forty-five to fifty-five miles per hour, threatening to tear them from their handholds and hurl them headlong into the sea. Fifteen hundred feet below they could see the surging waves of a storm-swept ocean. "You can imagine their position," remarked Rosendahl, "if you picture a steelrigger clinging to the skeleton of a skyscraper while it rushed and bounced through space."

Meanwhile Eckener's position was no less acute. The ship was in a storm, with a vital part damaged. Speed had to be reduced to protect the men carrying out the repairs, but without sufficient headway it was impossible to control the ship, and there was no way of predicting how much longer the storm would continue and with what violence. There had to be a compromise, a fallback position. A distress call was not the best way to promote the safety and virtues of transoceanic zeppelin travel, particularly on a maiden Atlantic flight, but the interests of the passengers were paramount. Eckener decided he had no alternative but to radio an urgent message to the U.S. Navy Department requesting them to send a fast ship to the *Graf*'s position, and called on the American Rosendahl to draft the signal:

> Position Lat 32N, Long 42W, course for Cape Hatteras x Proceeding half-speed about 35 knots airspeed on account of damage to cover of port

> *horizontal x Effecting repairs as conditions*
> *permit x Request surface vessel proceed along*
> *our course and stand by x Request weather con-*
> *ditions to westward x In rain squalls at*
> *present . . .*

With the ship running at such slow speed it proved impossible to send the signal at first because of the low power generated by the outboard wind generator. Half an hour later the emergency battery generator was brought into use, and an Italian steamer in the vicinity picked up the signal and passed it on. Before long the crews of a number of U.S. Navy destroyers along the Atlantic coast were being recalled and full steam was worked up in readiness to deploy.

Rumor of this signal caused no little stir among the passengers. Was this an SOS? Were they in serious danger? Were they going to ditch? Were they asking for a tow the rest of the way? The passengers had got over their first fright, but anxiety now returned. The unhappy Mr. Gilfillan, in the second day of total nicotine deprivation, spent most of his time flat out on his bunk, lamenting his decision to embark on this adventure in the first place. "We should have been provided with parachutes," he complained later, "so that we could bail out when we'd had enough." No survival aids were normally provided on passenger zeppelins because of the extra weight they imposed.

Later Lady Hay wrote to her mother:

> Eckener should never have sent for the ships—it was not necessary and proves that he has lost his nerve. The two men who kept their nerve were Knut Eckener and Captain Lehmann. Personally I would not hesitate to make the trip again in the *Graf Zeppelin*. I have every confidence in her, I have every confidence in the motors, and the crew. I was never afraid. I had no sensation of fear, although I fully realised the gravity of the situation and nothing was hidden from me.

Eckener called the passengers for a briefing in the saloon. Some of them, he noted, were quite depressed and frightened, while others were full of confidence. "Foremost among the latter was brave little Lady Hay. She greeted me with a gay smile and remarked, looking at the broken china on the floor, 'The good old Count has been in a surprising and expansive mood! Well, if we have to, we can get along without cups and saucers.'" Told about her cheerful pluck at the first near-catastrophic moment of crisis, he commented, "Such coolness, particularly in a woman, could well have prevented the development of a spreading panic."

Eckener's manner was brisk, confident, serious. He told the assembled passengers about the damaged fin, the repair party trying to put it right, the emergency radio signal. It would take a U.S. Navy ship three days to reach their position, he explained, but the *Graf* was in no present danger, and even if it proved impossible to repair the fin, ballast could be released to lighten the ship and keep it in the air long enough to reach the rendezvous position. "If the worse comes to the worst," he assured the passengers, "a destroyer will certainly pick us up."

"It's after 2 and there's no sign of lunch," Lady Hay noted in her minute-by-minute diary:

> I know there are practically no plates left, but is there no food? Anyhow, the Zeppelin has been presented with hundreds of complimentary packets of sweet biscuits, honey cakes and chocolates, specimens of which my table is well loaded with. I'm getting thoroughly spoiled by stewards and passengers. That's the one advantage of being the only woman, and I am feminine enough to revel in small attentions. Things are getting back to normal. This morning's experience is the most marvellous advertisement of the stability and safety of the Zeppelin and Eckener's fine commandership.

Up on top of the ship, the repair work on the fin had begun under almost impossible conditions. Three-quarters of the lower covering had gone, and the volunteers did their best to cut away the loose fabric and lash down what was left. Inside the ship other crewmen had rigged up a screen of blankets to prevent the wind coming through the gaping hole in the fin and tearing the gas cells. As the minutes passed it was clear that the ship and the lives of everyone on board depended on the desperate struggle to save the port stabilizer.

Meanwhile the *Graf* began to sink. To reduce the speed of the slipstream around the damaged fin, Eckener had ordered the engines to be throttled back still further. This had substantially reduced the aerodynamic lift provided by the ship's forward speed. At the same time, the *Graf* had accumulated six to eight tons of rainwater on its outer surface, which substantially reduced its aerostatic lift, and without sufficient speed to compensate for this burden, it was no longer able to maintain height. Minute by minute, Eckener and Watch Officer Flemming watched the ocean rising up to meet the ship. Eckener did not reveal his thoughts, but Flemming could guess them only too easily. Increase speed, and his son might be swept off the outer surface along with the others. Fail to increase speed, and in time the ship would be lost with all the people on it. Flemming stood with one eye on the altimeter and one on his commander. Eventually he was forced to speak: "*Herr Doktor,* we're losing too much altitude. We've got to do something."

Eckener stared ahead.

"*Herr Doktor,*" Flemming spoke again, "we are down to nearly three hundred feet. I must have two engines or we lose the ship."

Eckener looked at Flemming in an absent way. "Send a man aft," he ordered, "and tell the repair team to stop work and get off the stabilizer until we get the airship up again."

The *Graf Zeppelin* was now a good deal less than half its own length above the sea. "*Herr Doktor,*" said Flemming, "by the time he has gone the length of the ship it will be too late."

Eckener said nothing. He clenched and unclenched his fists, stared fixedly down at the sea below, shoulders hunched. His only son was dear to him, but there was a golden rule: passengers' lives and the ship have priority over individual members of the crew. His hands fell to his side. "You are right, Captain Flemming," he said.

"Eckener's face suddenly aged," reported Karl von Wiegand, who was on the bridge at this moment. "He looked out of the window from his favourite place in the corner of the bridge. He swallowed hard. Huskily came the command . . . 'Start the motors.'" The ship began to pick up speed and gain height. "There is no telephone communication from the bridge to where the fin is," reported von Wiegand. "What Eckener lived through only he and his God know."

After an agonizing wait, news came to the bridge that the emergency work party, Knut Eckener included, had safely withdrawn from the surface of the fin and would return to it when speed was again reduced. "It was a very disagreeable game to play," Eckener would recall, "increasing and decreasing the ship's speed, enabling the men to work during the period of reduced speed."

But it worked. After an hour and a half, the emergency repairs were complete, and the ship was able to go ahead at around three-quarters speed without overtaxing the stabilizing fin. During the next three or four hours, the job was finished sufficiently for the fin to be fully operational, provided they encountered no further squalls. "The men who had volunteered deserved the highest praise," Eckener wrote. "I must admit that I felt some parental pride that my son had been one of those who volunteered, and not the last one either."

The weather was improving all the time, and they made such good progress that by noon Eckener felt justified in sending a second signal to the U.S. Navy Department to say that help was no longer required. But he was not completely at ease. New weather reports indicated a series of deep depressions strung out across the North Atlantic. It was all too possible for a squall front to extend down to the *Graf*'s more southerly route. Eckener wondered how an already damaged ship would come out of it. He felt aggrieved. "On our first flight with the new 'passenger ship,' which was to provide a convincing demonstration of the practical usefulness of the airship in commerce over the ocean, why did this same ocean have to play its autumn tricks with such malice? I was very upset about this, even though I kept up a calm appearance for the sake of the passengers."

His dilemma was acute. The proving flight was in danger of becoming a *dis*proving flight. Already the *Graf* was one day overdue, and this could extend to two. Already the world knew it had been damaged in a storm, and very possibly it was thought lives had been put at risk as well. "If I take the long way round every time I meet up with a storm," complained Eckener, "people will say that the *Graf Zeppelin* is a fair-weather ship."

During the following night and much of the next day, Saturday, October 13, the *Graf Zeppelin* continued to make good progress. Though facilities were rapidly running out—no fresh water (only boiled ballast water), food running low, no wine, no electricity for cooking—spirits were buoyed by the possibility of arriving in New York in time for dinner that evening. But near Bermuda the west wind got up, and yet again Eckener could see the way to America barred by a darkening, menacing change in the weather, with fog and low scudding clouds, and every prospect of violent squalls once more. Word spread among the passengers that there was little likelihood of their arriving in America that evening, or even the next day. "Mr. Frederick Gilfillan, more despondent than ever," observed Lady Hay, "was telling his cabin mate that he wished to goodness he had had the presence of mind to bring a revolver with him 'as nothing is worse than lingering torture.' He murmured hoarsely, 'It may take six or seven hours to die by drowning.' "

To raise morale, the indomitably cheerful Captain Lehmann began a long walk through the length and breadth of the ship, from crew quarters in the hull to the passenger saloon inside the gondola, serenading all and sundry with his accordion music. But Lady Hay noted, "The ship's officers look tired, specially von Schiller, he is pale and terribly weary round the eyes. Dr. Eckener too must get some sleep, he has sacrificed himself in every way, his rest, his strength, and in yet another manner which can only be told later—a drama as poignant as an epic of ancient heroism."

On the bridge Eckener was faced with a quandary. "What to do?" he wondered. "Turn aside farther south to Florida? I could not make up my mind to do it, for that would involve a detour of ten or twelve hours more and put the capabilities of the Zeppelin in an unconvincing light. Then should we plunge into the storm-front with a crippled ship?" He called for the flight engineer and asked if he thought the damaged fin could weather another squall. The engineer was doubtful. "The decision I now made was the most difficult and critical of the whole flight," Eckener wrote. "I decided to go through the storm." Turning to Karl von Wiegand, he said, "We must tunnel through this wall of wind." Von Wiegand thought Eckener looked so tired—he had hardly left his post on the bridge night or day, and he took all his meals there—that he went to his cabin and brought him a glass of vintage brandy, for which Eckener was grateful.

Toward midnight the ship entered its second squall front. As the temperature plummeted from seventy-three to forty-six degrees, a sure sign of violently contrasting air masses, the *Graf* bucked and bounced in the wildly raging turbulence, and rain and hail lashed the outer cover and windows of the gondola. Crowded at the saloon windows, the passengers stared into the blackness of the storm, not a light to be seen anywhere, reliving their ordeal of thirty-six hours before.

On the darkened bridge there was a busy, concentrated silence. In the navigation room Commander Rosendahl and a meteorologist from the German transportation ministry pored over the weather charts, plotting the latest data from U.S. meteorological stations. The ship was at half speed now, and at times, butting the headwinds, ground speed was down to near zero as Eckener cautiously felt his way forward, trying to spare the damaged fin. This time both rudder and elevator men handled the ship faultlessly, keeping the ship on course and, as far as possible, in straight and level flight.

An hour later the turbulence began to lessen, and they entered calmer and drier air. Except for a small rip in the upper cover, the fin had held. At last Eckener felt he could relinquish the bridge and snatch a short nap after being on duty on the bridge for twenty-seven hours without a break. The American coast was only five hundred miles away.

Eckener was greatly concerned that news of his SOS to the U.S. Navy might have undermined confidence in the zeppelin's safety and reliability. His fears were unfounded. The news of his dire predicament, fighting valiantly against disastrous storms in the wastes of the mid-Atlantic, gripped the imagination of the American nation and wrung its people's hearts.

The *Graf Zeppelin*'s flight had been front-page news in America from the moment of its takeoff. Virtually every paper had devoted most of its front page to daily news of the *Graf*'s progress across the

Atlantic, usually accompanied by a map showing the airship's course and the distance it had covered to date. When Rosendahl's call for help was picked up, the coverage turned from news to drama. ZEP FIGHTS FOR LIFE, ran a typical banner headline in letters inches high. ECKENER BATTLES THE ELEMENTS, *GRAF* FEARED DESTROYED.

The ship's radio silence, caused by the failure of the radio generator when the *Graf*'s speed was reduced following the damage to the stabilizer fin, served only to raise emotion in America still higher. Countless messages were radioed to the ship on its call sign D-E-N-N-E, but no replies came back. The fear grew that the *Graf Zeppelin* had gone down. Then Rosendahl's second call came through, followed yet again by radio silence. The American nation, indeed the world, was gripped again with an agony of hope and fear. The *Graf,* it seemed, was still out there, battling storm and sea. ZEPPELIN FORCED OFF COURSE, blazed the *New York Herald Tribune*. WANDERS NEAR BERMUDA, IGNORES NAVY CALLS.

In New York on Friday night a Catholic priest and a Presbyterian minister joined in an interdenominational service on radio station WOR, during which a minute of silent prayer was followed by the latest reports on the *Graf*. In Hampton Roads, Virginia, three U.S. Navy cruisers were on stand-by to give help if required, along with eighteen destroyers at Charleston, South Carolina. At Lakehurst the officers and men of the naval air station waited and waited for the overdue airship, along with families and friends of passengers and crew, and many of the world's press. When finally a signal was picked up from the *Graf,* a brief position report indicating the ship was making headway toward the Virginia coast, there was hysteria and relief. Scores of messages of welcome and good luck jammed the ship's hard-pressed radio room.

All Saturday zeppelin watchers took up their positions on rooftops and other vantage points along America's East Coast. In Atlantic City the mayor asked the seaside hotels to keep their lights on that night to act as beacons for the incoming airship. At Lakehurst a flood of people from New York, Philadelphia, Baltimore, and as far away as Ohio was homing in on the airship field by car, motorbike, bus, and a special train. By midmorning on Sunday, October 14, a festive crowd 50,000 strong was packed into the air station, and as the day wore on the crowd swelled to almost 250,000, according to some estimates, so that the approach roads became impassable with stalled lines of traffic eight miles long. All day the crowd waited—elated, noisy, and expectant.

The media were there in force, too, and no less expectant. NBC planned a live coast-to-coast commentary describing the arrival of the *Graf*. CBS hoped to have Lieutenant Commander Rosendahl give a personal account of the great flight the moment he stepped off the ship. Station WOR had hired an airplane with a radio to provide a running commentary of the *Graf*'s arrival over New York.

But the *Graf* never came. By 10:20 that night, it was still 150 miles west of Bermuda, course northwest to Hatteras. All through the night people sat out on beaches, boardwalks, and rooftops searching the sky for the lights of the approaching dirigible. Even toward dawn the *Graf* was still three hundred miles southeast of Lakehurst and several hours away from the coast of the New World.

At breakfast on Monday the passengers were told that since they were only a hundred miles off the coast of America there was no longer any need to ration food and water. The ship's steward served up the best breakfast since the first day of the flight. The passengers crowded the windows, hoping to be the first to set eyes on the New World. They saw their first seagulls, then patches of seaweed. At 9:15 A.M., the Hog Island coastguard station, in Virginia, reported the *Graf* overhead and changing course slightly to north-northwest. At 9:40 the passengers and duty watch spotted a long yellow spit of sand in the gray-green sea. "Land ho!" came the cry. At 10:00 on the morning of Monday, October 15, accompanied by a U.S. Navy plane, which looped the loop in greeting, the *Graf Zeppelin* crossed the American coast six miles north of Cape Charles at the mouth of the Chesapeake Bay.

Instead of flying directly to Lakehurst, Eckener ordered a course change toward Washington and radioed a message of greeting to President Coolidge. The *Graf Zeppelin* might be wildly overdue, it might be bearing a gaping hole in its fin like a wound, it might be running out of food and water, but Hugo Eckener had decided that the inhabitants of the great cities of America along the route to journey's end should be treated to a ringside view of the legendary airship's passing.

At 10:50 the *Graf* was over Cambridge, Maryland. Half an hour later it was throbbing low over Washington, D.C., with an escort of army, navy, and civilian airplanes above, below, and on all sides. It dipped its bow in salute as the president broke off an official reception to go out onto the White House lawn to watch. Chief Justice William Howard Taft leaned across to Justice Oliver Wendell Holmes in the Senate house and whispered, "The *Graf*'s here!"

Standing by Eckener on the *Graf*'s bridge, Karl von Wiegand reported, "As we turned over the White House in Washington, Eckener laughed so spontaneously, so heartily, that it did me good to see him so happy. 'America is good to me and I am grateful,' he remarked."

Just after midday the *Graf* was over Baltimore. In every city and town the people erupted in a bedlam of greetings, church bells ringing, sirens howling, cars hooting, trains whistling, crowds shouting their welcome. Eckener was so touched that he turned to von Wiegand and said, "I'd decided not to visit New York, very much to my regret, because of the condition of the ship and the lateness of hour, but after this reception I must try and show my appreciation." He gave Captain Flemming, in command at the time, a new course change: "From Philadelphia steer for New York and not for Lakehurst. I think we can make it before dark."

Leaving the bridge, Eckener went aft into the passenger saloon, walked up to Lady Grace Hay, and stretched out his hand to her. "Let me congratulate the first woman to cross the Atlantic by air from Europe to America," he said, "and so brave a little lady at that. I am happy to have been able to justify your confidence in our ship and ourselves."

Hearing this, Robert Reiner proposed a toast. "Three cheers for our Lady Drummond-Hay, the bravest passenger amongst us!" The saloon rang with a score of heartfelt male cheers.

When the *Graf* arrived over New York, the city center stopped dead. Offices, shops, and homes emptied in minutes as people swarmed out into the streets and onto the roofs. One man was killed and several injured in the stampede. Subways, buses, streetcars, and automobiles disgorged their occupants, who watched the silver ship pass overhead. The din coming up to the *Graf* almost drowned out the noise of the ship's engines. "All the sirens of all the boats, all the factories screamed at us," Lady Hay reported. "Eckener was terribly emotional, and so was everyone, even Rosendahl the American commander said that it moved him." For an hour Dr. Eckener had the *Graf* tack about the city, then bore away to Lakehurst, sixty miles to the south.

It was dusk when the great ship came in. A crowd of twenty to thirty thousand people still crowded the airship field, many of whom had been there for sixty hours. Also waiting was a U.S. Navy landing party four hundred strong, and 250 newspaper reporters, cameramen, and radio crews who for two days and nights had been sleeping in the giant airship shed and surrounding workshops, with nothing to eat since the previous morning. Reception officials and VIPs were also there, including the German ambassador and the chief of the U.S. Navy's bureau of aeronautics, Rear Admiral Moffett, upon whom the *Graf* inadvertently, but amid much merriment, dropped five hundred pounds of water ballast while it was being trimmed during landing. As the ship sank lower and lower toward the field, the station's landing lights were switched on, and the ground-handling officer signaled with his torch to the *Graf's* bridge, where Rosendahl interpreted the instructions to Eckener and his officers.

Eckener recalled:

> The loud shouts of welcome, cheers and yells as we sank earthwards were like the roaring of a hurricane, and the crowds of people which pressed round the ship, despite heavy police cordons, as soon as she lay on the ground, surrounded her like a wildly tossing sea. In a moment we were hemmed in and neither we nor the ship could move. Luckily it was dead calm, and the ship lay comparatively quiet, otherwise the presence of the closely packed crowd, which included many women and children, could have led to a serious accident. The enthusiasm was such that the normally well-disciplined American public was completely out of hand. In spite of the great and solemn significance of the

moment in which the pioneer airship touched her bumpers to American soil after her eventful voyage, I had to smile as I looked down on the excited crowd.

At six o'clock on Monday evening, October 15, 1928, after a flight which had lasted 111 hours and 44 minutes and covered 6,168 miles, the *Graf Zeppelin* was down at last. "It was the most wonderful experience in my life," Lady Hay wrote to her mother in London a few days later. "It will be something to think about and to dream about for all the rest of my days. I enjoyed every minute of it, I cannot tell you how much I enjoyed it." In her report for the Hearst Press she wrote, "The journey has contributed richly to my emotional life. These few days have been worth years to me. I would travel with the Zeppelin under Dr. Eckener and his crew anywhere in all confidence. If the airship should come to harm, I would weep, because part of my heart would die with it."

The arrival of the *Graf Zeppelin* on American soil was a historic moment and, for Dr. Hugo Eckener, a profoundly satisfying one. It was also utterly chaotic, as Lady Hay observed: "There was a terrible muddle. They took me off first and some officials rushed me to the Customs House because they were afraid the crowd would mob me. Some people did rush at me, and the police hit about them. Finally after a real scramble I got to the Customs House, and there was more fuss, because there were a lot of newspaper people there and they had to be cleared out."

The rest of the passengers and the luggage were a long time coming. A fresh crosswind made it difficult to walk the airship into the hangar. The passengers had to wait two hours in the Customs House for their luggage, and it got terribly hot, what with all the officials and their wives and daughters coming in and asking questions. "I did nothing but sign autographs for an hour," wrote Lady Hay. "We could not leave the Customs House for fear of being mobbed. The crowds were all around the windows. And I could not get any food. I had not eaten since five in the morning when I ate the sausages I had saved from Sunday supper, being too tired to eat them then. Then some thirty Press photographers wanted to take photographs. They had been waiting two days and two nights. A lot of people lost their patience."

When Hugo Eckener finally came off the bridge to the gondola entrance, two large policemen picked him up and carried him on their shoulders through the milling crowd amid a bedlam of cheers. They put him down inside the huge hangar housing the USS *Los Angeles,* formerly the reparations zeppelin LZ-126, which Eckener had flown across the Atlantic four years previously. "There she is," he called out when he saw her, "there's my sweetheart." Then he was led into the improvised press room, where an army of reporters was putting together a story that would eventually occupy a total of three hundred thousand words in the American papers.

Fielding a barrage of questions in his stumbling English, the exhausted hero of the hour, who had managed only eight hours' sleep on the 111-hour flight, puffed gratefully on a big cigar as he talked the newsmen through the crises of the *Graf Zeppelin's* flight. Finally, around nine o'clock in the evening, over four hours after the ship had landed, the last question was answered and the last photo taken, and the sixty-year-old zeppelin commander was driven off to the Lakehurst commander's house for a simple supper and a long, deep sleep.

If the American public had welcomed Eckener as a conquering hero, the nation's leaders lauded him as an honored guest. On the morning of Tuesday, October 16, the German airshipman and his son, along with a detail from the crew and some of the passengers, boarded a special train from Lakehurst to Hoboken Pier on the west side of the Hudson River. There, after a welcome from the city's official host, they embarked on a riverboat for a triumphal cruise downstream to Battery Place, at the far end of Lower Manhattan, where they disembarked into twenty-seven open limousines for a ticker-tape parade up Broadway to City Hall. Eight thousand police had been drafted to line the route, the largest number deployed for the job in the city's history.

The long line of limousines, preceded by an honor battalion of the U.S. Army and a detachment of marines, and accompanied on either side by police outriders on horseback, proceeded slowly through the canyon of lower Broadway's tall office blocks, the air a snowstorm of ticker tape, confetti, streamers, and scrap paper. Eckener stood in the back of his car, waving his commander's cap in the air. Only one other airman had ever been accorded a reception like Hugo Eckener's in New York: Charles Lindbergh the previous year, following his solo airplane flight to Europe in the *Spirit of St. Louis.*

At City Hall the cars stopped and everyone got out to be welcomed by Mayor Jimmy Walker. At the grand luncheon reception inside, the message was German-American solidarity—a posthostilities togetherness largely forged by the emotional fervor generated by the *Graf Zeppelin*'s dramatic flight. On the ship's arrival President Coolidge and Germany's President Hindenburg had exchanged cordial telegrams, and in no time every important American military and political personage was at the German embassy in Washington.

With the German flag hanging side by side with the Stars and Stripes inside City Hall, Dr. Eckener and his crew and passengers joined in a passionate rendition of "Deutschland über Alles." Then the mayor pinned a medal on Eckener's chest—"Germany's flying ambassador," he called him—and declared, "I'm not talking of *improved relations*—I'm talking of *friendship!*" The crowd of invited VIPs clapped and cheered vociferously. For Eckener it was like a dream. Near catastrophe over the Atlantic had turned into heady triumph.

Meanwhile Lady Grace Hay-Drummond-Hay was a focal point of American adulation in her own right:

> I got up at 9. I was thankful to get a bath, and hot food. Then I had to see reporters. They took so much time I did not get lunch till 3.30. Photographers came, the telephone went without stopping all the time, packets of letters poured in. . . . People came up to the room, dashed in, wanting to lend me clothes, thinking I had none, it was the most awful time I ever had. I did not have a minute to breathe in. I had to get my hair washed for the functions at night, and even then there was no privacy—girl reporters came right in and sat with me, the people from the hotel poured in, other people. There was no stopping it. They were as mad as they could be. Nothing stopped them.
>
> I dressed for dinner as fast as I could, but was a bit late. It was a huge dinner at the Ritz Towers, all men, no ladies

except myself. When I came in everyone stood up and yelled themselves hoarse. I sat on the dais with Eckener and the Zeppelin officers. Then without warning they asked me for a speech. I was so surprised that I had no time to be nervous, so I got up and made one. Everyone congratulated me and said that it was a good one, and I know that at least it was sense.

After dinner the procession of cars carried on uptown, taking the celebrity zeppelin guests to the Ziegfeld Theater to see the hit musical *Show Boat*. "The drive to the theatre was a fine sight," Lady Hay reported to her mother:

> We had cars and escorts of motor-cycle police, and cordons of police to keep the crowds back. They pushed and yelled and screamed, the police charged into them, and we dashed in with sirens shrieking like banshees. All traffic gave place, and we were just like fire-engines. Mobs were at the theatre door. When we came in the performance stopped. The actors remained on the stage, while the orchestra played *"Deutschland über Alles"* and "The Star-Spangled Banner." Then there were cheers, disorder, upheaval, and it took a long time to get everyone settled down. The actors stood still on the stage watching! The performance went on, and between the last two acts they had us on stage, with the actors, and microphones, where Eckener, Rosendahl, Admiral Moffett, the Mayor of New York and myself made speeches to the audience which were broadcast and filmed and photographed. No speeches were prepared, of course, and I do not know how I did it. I suppose it was because I was excited.
>
> When the theatre was over about 12:30 we got in these cars again and went to the Capitol cinema. It was more difficult than ever to get through, and the mob seemed stronger than the police. At the cinema they gave me a tremendous sheaf of roses, so big that I could not carry it.

We went in the boxes, and again there was all the music, and standing up, more speeches, more cheers, and yells. We saw the films of our journey. It was very thrilling to see them on the screen. But how tired we were! Two or three of us later repaired to Rigge's for oysters and I got to bed about 2 something. I was so tired I do not know how I fell into bed.

For Eckener and his executive officers, the day was still not over. Almost immediately after the film showing they boarded a train for Washington in time for breakfast with President Coolidge, a later meeting with Herbert Hoover, who had just been elected to succeed Coolidge as president, and a ceremonial wreath-laying at the Tomb of the Unknown Soldier—a singular distinction for a German in those years. And so it went on: receptions, banquets, galas, lectures, requests for appearances from all over the country, "demanding," as Eckener put it, "considerable powers of endurance."

Zeppelin fever had gripped the whole of America. Even the hard-headed financiers, decision makers, and captains of industry who were the real target of this adventure were affected by it. Public support and political goodwill, important though they were, were not enough to underpin a future commercial zeppelin service between Europe and America. Considerable capital investment would be needed to build the ships, put the infrastructure in place, and run a service that had to be safe, reliable, comfortable, and, of course, profitable. With Germany under economic duress, only America could provide the funding for what were beginning to be called the "big-business zeppelins."

Between Eckener's extensive public engagements, which served as publicity for the main purpose of his presence in the United States, he was deep in discussions with many of America's leading bankers, as well as the president of the Goodyear-Zeppelin Corporation. What Eckener was proposing was a joint operation using four supermodern airships of considerably greater size and capabilities than the *Graf Zeppelin*. What the financiers were proposing as a preliminary stage was the founding of an international zeppelin transport corporation, which would research the entire issue of commercial airship transportation. In the meantime, as a result of a separate initiative, the

United States Navy Board had again become interested in another possible use for the rigid airship, whose range and endurance made it a potentially perfect scouting weapon for a nation lying between two oceans.

Lady Hay, too, had been doing her bit for the zeppelin cause. It was heady stuff. The *Graf Zeppelin*'s dramatic flight to America, she was told, had been hailed as "the biggest story since the Armistice." Her own account of it was described by the Hearst editors as "the finest story ever written by a woman," even (so she told her mother later) "the finest story ever written by *anyone*." As the heroine in that drama, she was the coast-to-coast darling of the moment. As the first woman to arrive in America from Europe by air, she had become an overnight entry in the record books—and she was an English milady, and pretty to boot.

In America, perhaps more than in any other country in the world, there was a price to pay for stardom, as Lady Hay soon learned. For a start, it seemed that the public and the press owned her—above all William Randolph Hearst and his mighty press empire, which billed her to its readers as a "remarkable British noblewoman and famous journalist, world-renowned for her beauty, wit and piquant view-point." It was Hearst who separated Lady Hay from Eckener and the rest of the zeppelin contingent at the Warwick Hotel and installed her in a sumptuous penthouse suite in the Waldorf Astoria, New York's premier hotel, no expenses spared.

Her lifestyle there was commensurate with her stardom:

> I have as many as eight reporters at a time in my room, and four or five photographers. Flowers pour in, chocolates, masses of cables from total strangers. I have a maid arranging flowers, and two secretaries working their heads off now. I have to be almost barricaded up here, for it has been terrible, all kinds of people trying to get in. I have a car to ride in, screaming motor-cycle police clear the way and all the traffic stops aside. Can you imagine stopping the New York traffic, and can you imagine the thrill of all this excitement in New York!

Of all the people who landed at Lakehurst on the *Graf,* only Dr. Eckener had been quite as worked off his feet as Lady Hay. It was taking its toll on him, as Lady Hay confided to her mother in a letter home: "He is getting more and more crotchety every day. He is not young and feels it. He is old for his age. He is only about 60, which should be the prime of life, but looks around 70 something." She was almost as exhausted as he was, she went on: "I am sick of it. I want peace and quiet again."

At Lakehurst Eckener had to make a decision. The *Graf Zeppelin* had to face the Atlantic once again and return to its home base in Germany before the truly foul weather came. Though the *Graf* was not just a fair-weather ship, it was not a true all-weather ship or around-the-year aircraft either. It had taken twelve days to repair the damaged fin, by which time it was nearly November, and the weather at Lakehurst had become so unpredictable that even bringing the ship out through the doors of the shed was an increasingly uncertain operation; out over the Atlantic the weather would very likely be a great deal worse. Eckener decided to cancel a proposed demonstration flight over the cities of the Midwest and set a takeoff date for the return journey of Sunday, October 28.

The *Graf* had a full load, including twenty-seven thousand cubic meters of American gasoline, fifteen tons of gasoline-benzol, three tons of oil, six tons of water ballast, forty-eight bags of mail, 330 packages, a bale of cotton, food and drink supplied by a deluxe New York catering firm, a new cook from a German liner, a chow dog, and twenty-five passengers, some of them new, including an American zeppelin enthusiast by the name of Mrs. Clara Adams, replacing Lady Hay, who was remaining in America.

It was not an auspicious departure. Crosswinds forced Eckener to put back the takeoff hour twice, to the irritation of passengers and press alike. It was not until two the next morning, six hours after the scheduled departure, that the *Graf* was heading once again for New York—"a limitless sea of light which stretched in all directions," Lehmann recalled, "so that we asked ourselves in amazement if electric light costs nothing in this blessed land." After taking a turn over the Statue of Liberty, the sirens once more howling below despite the lateness of the hour, they were again heading out over the Atlantic, this time on the shorter, northern route, since by Eckener's reckoning it could hardly be worse than the southern one by which he had come.

Not long after first light, while making an inspection of the ship, Captain Hans von Schiller discovered a stowaway, a blond-haired, eighteen-year-old American from St. Louis, Missouri, who had sneaked on board at Lakehurst carrying nothing but a toothbrush and hidden himself among the mail sacks. Wearing only a pair of velveteen trousers and a red pullover, the boy was so pitifully cold and hungry he could barely speak. Dr. Eckener was not amused, especially as he suspected an American newspaper had put him up to this escapade. But since he could not throw the boy overboard, he sent him to the steward to wash plates and sweep out the cabins for the duration of the flight. "More was radioed about the stowaway," reported Captain Lehmann, "than the real sensation which awaited us off Newfoundland."

The Atlantic is a fickle ocean, and, as Eckener was beginning to learn, late autumn was too advanced in the year for a comfortable crossing by airship. Approaching Newfoundland, the *Graf* found itself heading once again for a frontal squall system. At first Eckener flew low over the sea, picking up speed to a hundred miles per hour in the following wind, but off Newfoundland the *Graf* was forced down to seven hundred feet to get under the thick fog cover, then up to three thousand feet to get above the dense cloud layer. Though the *Graf* was steering an easterly course, a southerly gale gusting up to 115 miles per hour seized the ship, sweeping it three hundred miles northward, at one time proceeding stern first at a ground speed of twenty miles per hour. "We had stumbled into an amazing adventure," Eckener was to write of this experience. "But our *Graf Zeppelin* was equal to such situations."

Towards evening worse was to come, as Captain Lehmann later reported:

> I do not believe that a single one of our men slept during the turbulent night that followed the calm day. It was the

worst night an airship ever lived through, not excepting the years of the war. Whoever lived through that night now knows what an expertly constructed airship, in skilful hands, can endure. Experienced airshipmen and helmsmen were at the controls, and Eckener is a commander the like of which the world has never seen. During this night, when the hurricane almost tore the light but well-made ship apart, I became convinced that the Zeppelin of today need fear no storm in any part of the world.

Eckener was now experienced enough to go through the storm with the engines throttled down. The air currents continued to hammer the ship hour after hour so that it wildly rolled and heaved like a ship at sea and was hardly able to move from its position, marking time with its bow kept into the wind, the waves in the black sea below as high as houses, and icebergs like islands floating by. But this time no damage was sustained; not even a single bracing wire snapped.

Off the coast of Europe the ship was confronted with another low-pressure trough. As Eckener observed, they were as unlucky with the weather going east as they had been coming west. But there were compensations. While the male passengers were busy dancing with the only female on board, Eckener concentrated on steering a more southerly course along the squall front toward the Bay of Biscay, where he hoped to find better conditions. Here he encountered a skyscape so sublime—curtains of rain, sunbeams like celestial searchlights, complete circular rainbows surrounding the ship—that he was determined to have it immortalized. "From the navigational point of view this front appeared extremely threatening," he reported, "but from the artistic point of view it was all the more attractive. I therefore sent for the painter, Dettmann, to come to the control car, and he proceeded to make a number of sketches of the truly grand cloud formations, the airy mountains, imposing turrets and 'Matterhorn' peaks which loomed up in extraordinary shapes and colours in the rising sun. It was like an indescribably beautiful endless panorama, which unfolded before our astonished gaze to port during the next two or three hours."

Toward noon, after a southerly detour to the mouth of the Loire, Eckener decided it was time to break through to the east and head for land. Around 6 P.M. the *Graf Zeppelin* crossed the French coast to complete its return Atlantic crossing, and from the passenger saloon came the sound of cheers and shouts of joy. Ten hours later the *Graf* was coming into Friedrichshafen through a blanket of white fog, unable to see either land or water, until suddenly the curtain parted and, "as by a stroke of magic," recalled Eckener, "the brightly lit airship shed greeted us. . . . It was as if a Higher Power were helping the *Graf Zeppelin* at her home port after the varied and difficult ocean crossing." In front of a crowd of thirty thousand people singing the German national anthem, the church bells ringing and the band playing, the *Graf* nudged down to Mother Earth. "By 7 A.M.," the commander reported, "the ship lay safe and sound in the shed in which she had been created." It was Thursday, November 1. The homeward flight had lasted seventy-one hours, fifty-one minutes.

The *Graf*'s Atlantic flights, for all their setbacks and difficulties, had turned out a great success—"beyond all expectations," in Eckener's view. "We had been able to show that the Zeppelin airship, even in the most unfavourable weather conditions and with a failure of one of her important structural features, could safely cross the ocean." True, there had been shortcomings that would have to be improved: Rosendahl had found the navigation "rusty," the capabilities of the radio room and its operators needed upgrading, as did the catering for both passengers and crew. "The ship had to be faster!" Eckener reported. "This was the first goal to be attained. And we ourselves had to get to know the ocean still better. But this could be done, and we had already learned a great deal on the two journeys."

Above all, the Fatherland was proud of him. The novelist and poet Hermann Hesse, who had once flown with Eckener on the *Schwaben* many years before, spoke for all the German people: "So now, after all these years and fateful events, this man is still at work. He did not become a general in times of war, nor a banker in times of inflation; he still remains a shipbuilder and captain, true to his cause. He has carried on, flying to America at last, and neither war, nor inflation nor personal fate could deter him from doing his duty and asserting his firm will."

◆　◆　◆

The *Graf Zeppelin* was not the only extraordinary marvel of modern science and technology in existence at the end of the 1920s, though it was one of the biggest. In the course of the previous twelve months, for example, penicillin had been discovered, the iron lung invented, the Big Bang theory had had its first airing, and an American astronomer called Edwin Hubble had announced a crucial discovery about stellar systems in deep space; the splitting of the atom was just around the corner, and there were cars that could reach over two hundred miles per hour. In America the talkies had arrived in the cinema, and color television had been transmitted on an experimental basis.

Meanwhile, airplanes had improved by leaps and bounds in recent years. By 1929, performance records included a speed of over 357 miles per hour (British Supermarine S-6), a height of nearly forty-two thousand feet (German Junkers W.34 with a British Bristol Jupiter engine), and a straight-line distance of over forty-nine hundred miles (French Breguet 19). Following the world's first successful liquid-fuel rocket launch two years previously, rocket planes, too, had taken to the skies, and turboprop propulsion was in development.

In conventional airplanes, pioneer airmen had made historic proving flights (many of them prospecting future routes for airlines) from Britain to India, Australia, and South Africa, to the North Pole, and, in November 1929, to the South Pole. Charles Lindbergh, the first man to fly the Atlantic solo in 1927, was the great American hero, while Amelia Earhart, the first woman to fly the same route solo, in the following year, was not far behind. Increasing understanding of the science of aerodynamics, improving technology, better operational procedures, and, in September 1929, the first successful demonstration of instrument flying—enabling a plane "to take off, fly a specific course, and land without reference to the earth"—had hugely improved the safety, reliability, and efficiency of commercial and military airplane flight.

For the *Graf Zeppelin,* still the world's only operational commercial passenger airship, competition was intensifying not only in the air but also at sea. In the summer of 1928, two new luxury ocean liners, the *Bremen* and the *Europa,* the biggest ever built in Germany, had begun service on the Atlantic run, breaking new records for speed and service, crossing in as little as four and a half days—roughly as fast as the *Graf Zeppelin*'s flight to America and a good deal less fraught—on a schedule of one crossing a week, which the *Graf* could not possibly match.

The airplane was cutting into the Zeppelin Company's market niche, especially in its native land. On the *Graf*'s own home patch by the Bodensee, the Dornier company was developing a giant, twelve-engine monoplane flying boat, the Do-X, designed to carry eighty passengers (though it could accommodate many more if required), while Junkers and Fokker were producing large monoplane transports that were becoming the mainstay of the Europewide air network. Commercial airplane services were now operating across the whole of Europe, connecting the major cities of every country with regular passenger flights, many over very short distances but some reaching out to the far periphery: from London to Moscow, for example, and even Basra and Teheran.

Worldwide, the picture was much the same. The larger, three-engined airliners could carry up to twenty passengers, a crew of two or three (around forty fewer than the *Graf*), and a quantity of freight at a speed of up to 110 miles per hour over stages of about five hundred miles for as many stages as there were staging posts. By 1929 British Imperial Airways were running a regular weekly service from London to Karachi via eighteen intermediate stages, using three-engined Argosy and Hercules landplanes and three-engined Calcutta flying boats capable of carrying up to eighteen passengers and a steward, though in the early days they were mainly carrying airmail. In 1919 the world total of miles flown on scheduled airlines (excluding China and Soviet Russia) was approximately 1 million; by 1929 it was 57 million. Similarly, while world passenger figures in 1919 totalled 5,000, by 1929 they had risen to 434,000.

Faced with this revolution in commercial aviation, the Zeppelin Company's small intercity service of the immediate postwar period would by now very likely have been forced out of business. And even with the world-famous *Graf*, the company had to think hard about where its future lay. Though the *Graf*'s flight to America and back had received great public acclaim, it led to no public or commercial contracts, and the future once again looked bleak. Eckener had received a hero's ticker-tape parade down Broadway just like Lindbergh, but unlike Lindbergh, whose solo flight had at a stroke helped create the financial and technological climate that the dramatic development of modern aviation required, Eckener appeared to have created nothing but large crowds in the city streets.


To drum up interest Eckener devised a spectacular public-relations flight for the spring of 1929, inviting a number of important government officials and influential politicians, including the president of the Reichstag and the minister of commerce, on board the *Graf* for what he called "a sentimental journey to Egypt," the so-called Orient Flight, a fabulous aerial voyage during which they could savor at first hand the unique experience of zeppelin travel. There were twenty-seven passengers on board, including a number of news reporters, among them the familiar faces of Lady Hay and Karl von Wiegand. Also on board were sixty-three quarts of wine and 160 bottles of spirits, as well as 330 pounds of airmail letters for the international stamp collectors' market, an important means of funding the flight. The income from the carriage of mail was already proving to be a major contribution to the funding of the *Graf Zeppelin*'s long-distance operations, and the interest shown by stamp collectors in the *Graf*'s highly publicized flights added greatly to the profitability of its airmail service, amounting eventually to some $5 million.

That winter was the coldest in Europe for many decades, and though the *Graf* took off on the first day of spring, the passengers did not take off their winter coats till the ship reached Crete. The flight was an air tourist's dream, as Eckener had intended it to be, one delectable spot and romantically resonant place-name after another, an aeronautical grand tour all the more spectacular for being viewed from the comfort of a well-appointed dining room floating in the sky. By breakfast time they were crossing the French Riviera and watching the dolphins leaping out of the sea. By lunchtime they were bearing down on Elba; by teatime they were circling low over Rome before heading south for Capri and the smoking volcano of Vesuvius, and Sorrento covered in snow.

All day the politicians and government officials stared down entranced. But they were cold. To cross over to the eastern side of Italy, the *Graf* had to be taken up to thirty-six hundred feet, and the temperature on board fell to lower than that inside a domestic refrigerator. By the time they reached the Ionian Sea, it was growing dark, and dinner was served: turtle soup, ham with asparagus, roast beef with vegetables and salad, celery with Roquefort cheese, nut cake from Friedrichshafen, and fine wines. Then, lulled by the gentle lapping of the slipstream and the murmur of motors, the passengers slept, as the ship held its steady course toward the Near East and the Holy Land.

Next morning found the *Graf Zeppelin* over the eastern Mediterranean: Crete for breakfast, Cyprus for lunch, Jerusalem at twilight. A full moon rose red as blood and cast a magical glow over the city. Dr. Eckener ordered the ship's engines to be cut, and the *Graf* hovered in reverent silence over the Holy Sepulchre and the Dome of the Rock. "From below," Ernst Lehmann reckoned, "we must have looked like a fiery chariot. Palestine, the farthest point of our flight, lay at our feet."

The Dead Sea appeared below them as a dark, sheer-sided gorge. Eckener would later recall:

> I now had the idea of offering the guests a sensation of a quite extraordinary kind. The surface of the Dead Sea lies almost 1,300 feet below sea level. We were irresistibly tempted by the opportunity to fly our Zeppelin at an altitude well below sea level. The barely risen full moon shone still with little power, so that the great lake lay reflected in semi-darkness, as mysterious as the nether world. We slowly sank down, carefully feeling our way lower and lower, until we hovered a few hundred feet over the surface of the water. We looked up to the heights towering around us as if from a cellar. It was a strange sensation to be in a ship which ordinarily soars high above sea level, now flying some thousand feet below it. We opened a couple of bottles of Rhine wine and celebrated the occasion, which each of us found unique.

Not even a wartime U-boat had reached so far below sea level.

By moonlight they flew out along the coast of Egypt, then turned north to Greece, reaching Athens at dawn. With reports of bad weather over the Black Sea, Eckener decided to alter his course home and aim for the Adriatic instead, passing the island of Ithaca and, later, Corfu. There remained only the daunting task of crossing the Alps at night in extreme blizzard conditions, not by flying over them but by wriggling through them, hoping that the experience would not undo all the public-relations good that the flight had achieved up to this point.

"The passengers had once more wrapped themselves in their heavy coats," Eckener recalled. "The snow froze on the panes of the windows of the control car and formed an ice layer a quarter of an inch thick, through which we could not see. Navigation on a dark night was hazardous in such circumstances. It was difficult to hold the ship on her course over the Danube valley, between the great heights on both sides." But Eckener kept his nerve, the *Graf Zeppelin* kept its height, and finally the land flattened out below and they were through. By 10:16 they were all safe on the ground at Friedrichshafen, after a flight of exactly eight thousand kilometers lasting eighty-one hours and twenty-eight minutes—the longest yet made by the *Graf* and very possibly one of the most glorious in the history of aviation (in Eckener's view, "perhaps the most splendid that one could make in Europe").

"We were sure," Eckener reported, "we heard it from our passengers in words of enthusiastic thanks, that this flight had created a great impression on every one of them. We were sure that henceforth they would be true friends of the Zeppelin airship. And so it proved." The government ministers and officials had seen for themselves the international goodwill the *Graf Zeppelin* could generate for Germany. Attitudes in Berlin began to change, and it would now be government subsidies as well as income from stamp collectors around the world that would enable the dream machine to go on to achieve its goal.

Then came a near catastrophe that threatened to terminate the zeppelin once and for all. On May 16, 1929, the *Graf* took off from Friedrichshafen for its second transatlantic flight. At midday, heading for Spain, one engine broke down. Off Barcelona in the evening, a second engine broke down. Since there was no hope of flying over the Atlantic in that condition, Eckener turned back toward base, struggling slowly up the Rhône on three engines against the mistral (a violent, cold, dry northerly wind of that region). Then, early the following afternoon, two more engines gave out, for the same reason as the others: severe vibration of the crankshafts caused by modifications that the ship's chief engineer had made to the propeller couplings without consulting the manufacturers.

The *Graf* was now at the mercy of the elements. There was no prospect of making it back to Friedrichshafen and, in Eckener's view, little chance of saving the ship, which drifted before the wind low over the open French countryside. The priority now was to save the lives of the passengers and crew. The great ship's desperate struggle for survival did not go unnoticed by the French, even though on previous flights over France the populace had deliberately ignored the *Graf Zeppelin* overhead, pointedly turning their backs on *les sales Boches*. At this critical point the French air ministry intervened, radioing the *Graf* with an offer to house the crippled ship in the big airship base at Cuers, north of Toulon. Running before the wind, the *Graf* made it safely to the French base and was quickly berthed in the hangar that had once housed the wartime zeppelin L-72 and the postwar passenger ship *Nordstern*. There it remained for two months until new engines were fitted and the ship was able to return to its German home. Little adverse publicity resulted from this potentially disastrous setback.

Eckener now turned his attention to the grandest and most audacious of ventures, a feat that could be undertaken by no other form of aircraft then in existence, one that would make the *Graf Zeppelin* a household name in every land—the first-ever passenger flight around the world.

For most of human history, the only way of circumnavigating the globe had been by sea, or by land *and* sea. A ship of Ferdinand Magellan's expedition of 1519 to 1522 was the first to sail around the world, taking 1,125 days to do so, its crew suffering dreadfully from sickness, starvation, savages, and loss of life, including Magellan's own, on the way. Steadily the time required to complete an around-the-world voyage got shorter, but it required a revolution in transportation—human flight—for circumnavigation to be anything less than a long-term commitment.

Surprisingly, it was not the big long-distance airship that was the first to enter the ring but the small, short-haul airplane. In 1924 four U.S. Army Douglas World Cruiser single-engine biplanes set off to make the first flight around the world. They flew in a clockwise direction on a route plotted to avoid the worst of the world's weather and to be over land as much as possible. Two planes dropped out, but the remaining two completed the twenty-six-thousand-mile course via seventy-two intermediate landings in a total of 175 days (15 days, 6 hours flying time). Four years later, in July 1928, three now almost forgotten heroes of aviation by the names of Henry Mears, a New York theatrical producer, Charles "Bert" Collyer, a U.S. airmail pilot, and Tailwind, a pet Sealyham terrier, circumnavigated the world in a folding-winged Fairchild monoplane, flying round-trip to New York via Europe, Asia, Japan, and British Columbia in the world-record time of twenty-three days, fifteen hours, twenty-one minutes—though strictly speaking this adventure set a world circumnavigation record rather than a purely aeronautical record, for the crew and their dog and plane crossed both oceans by ship.

It was not a world record that Eckener had in mind when he proposed circling the globe in the *Graf Zeppelin,* however, but a proving flight to demonstrate the zeppelin's potential for a worldwide passenger air service. "We knew we had a good and capable airship," he later informed an audience of six thousand members of the National Geographic Society in Washington:

> so we conceived the seemingly fantastic idea of a world cruise, to see other seas and other continents, and to widen our knowledge, above all, to learn what the capabilities of an airship are: how to make utmost use of them, so that regular air traffic may be possible in various zones and climates. A trip round the world, heading over several oceans and continents of entirely different meteorological

conditions, seemed likely to increase our knowledge of the airship's reaction under various circumstances; so at the very beginning, it was actually a flight into uncertainty, to gain wider experience of air navigation.

The proposed flight was also a chance to refute the critics who claimed that airships were only fine-weather craft, too large and clumsy and much too slow for serious commercial traffic. "Such a flight," Eckener declared, "would provide a brilliant testimonial of the endurance and operational radius of the ship, and would promote propaganda for the cause around the world."

There were two problems: funding and routing. The problem of money was solved at a stroke, not by the German government but by a surprise offer from William Randolph Hearst, who was prepared to put up two-thirds of the cost of the venture, some $4,250,000 in today's money, in return for exclusive world rights to the story. When Eckener decided he was unable to exclude the German media from coverage of the flight—they would have pilloried him, he said, and given the undertaking a hostile reception—Hearst reduced his offer by a third to cover U.S. and UK rights only, and to this Eckener agreed. That accounted for rather less than half the total cost of the venture. The rest was to come from German news and newsreel companies, passengers' tickets (at nine thousand dollars per person for a full world-flight fare), and stamp collectors, who were to take an extraordinary interest in special zeppelin stamps and world-flight first-day covers, and pay extraordinary sums for them.

As for the route, the Earth's wind systems in the northern hemisphere favored an eastbound circumnavigation. The main question was which eastbound course to take to reach the Pacific. There were three options. The first was a southern maritime route through the Mediterranean and across the Indian Ocean and China Sea, but this was eighty-seven hundred miles long, approaching the *Graf*'s maximum range and endurance. The second, the so-called direct route, crossing Central Asia to Lake Baikal in Siberia and thence down the Amur Valley to Manchuria and Japan, was only sixty-two hundred miles long but ran the gauntlet of high mountains and perhaps typhoon winds sweeping inland from the China Sea and shrouding the whole of northeast China and Manchuria in rain clouds. A third option involved a zigzag course that led across central Russia and the entire length of northern Siberia, to the barely charted Stanovoy Mountains and the Sea of Okhotsk. Though this was a little longer than the more direct route—seven thousand miles all told—it was a good deal safer, and this was the route Eckener finally chose.

There was one other consideration: the starting and finishing points. Logic and the German nation demanded that the *Graf Zeppelin* begin the world flight from its home base in Friedrichshafen. William Randolph Hearst demanded otherwise. If America, in the form of the Hearst newspaper empire, was putting up most of the money for the flight, that was where it should begin and end—specifically, Hearst insisted, with a circle round the Statue of Liberty in New York Harbor. Eckener went along with this. "How could this ideal be better served," he explained later, "than if America should embrace the German Zeppelin ideal so publicly?"

So, in fact, there were to be two world flights—an American one that went from Lakehurst to Lakehurst, and a German one from Friedrichshafen to Friedrichshafen. The flight out to the American start point began on August 1, 1929, with eighteen passengers on board, and ended at Lakehurst ninety-five hours later. The takeoff from the American start point before a crowd of ten thousand fervent well-wishers began on the evening of August 7, with four new passengers on board (replacing some who had left the ship), a baby alligator, and a nine-month-old Boston terrier pup called Happy. The night departure was an extraordinary sight, as the Hearst newspapers splashed all over the front pages next day:

GRAF OFF ON WORLD TOUR
AIR GIANT HEADS TO SEA FOR EPOCHAL SKY VOYAGE

In the deep darkness of midnight, the *Graf Zeppelin* soared away from Lakehurst late last night on the Hearst-Zeppelin round-world flight.

Gleaming like a huge phosphorescent fish in the moonless darkness, the giant airship hovered for a moment over the flying field; then, as her propellers gripped the air, she sailed away, disappearing toward New York and the Statue of Liberty.

For a moment the huge crowd was silent and the stilly night was broken only by the whirr of the Zeppelin's motors. The sight of the huge ship flying the air, her undersides brilliantly reflecting the rays of a score of searchlights directed on her, left the onlookers too breathless to cheer.

Then a band burst through the silence with a martial air and the spell was broken.

On August 10, after a fast eastward crossing of only fifty-five hours (Statue of Liberty to Land's End, England, in five hours short of two days, New York to Paris in less than forty-eight hours), the *Graf* was back in Friedrichshafen. There was to be a five-day layover to check the ship and engines before the great leap into the unknown, and then the German version of the world flight—the real version, many thought—would begin.

"Go round the world as fast as you can," ran Dr. Eckener's brief from the Hearst Press, "and tell us what you saw."

But it was not quite as simple as that.

## Chapter Five

# The Dream Voyage

*In an airship one does not fly, one voyages.*

DR. HUGO ECKENER

At daybreak on August 15, 1929, the *Graf Zeppelin* took off from Friedrichshafen before an enraptured crowd, and by midday, after the excitement of the *Graf*'s momentous circuit of Berlin, the saloon was turning from an aerial drawing room into a kind of flying recreation room for maturer students. Its four tables served three purposes—to eat on, write on (five typewriters per table), and play on. Each hour had its application. Now it was leisure time. Maps had been hung on the walls. Miniature flags of many nations were scattered around the dining tables. The coffee had rallied the passengers and they were perky and industrious, fiddling with cameras, studying star tables and maps, scribbling in diaries and on postcards to be thrown overboard at the next mail drop. Heinrich Kubis, the chief steward, was going from table to table selling special commemorative zeppelin stamps for the postcards.

Dr. Eckener, after satisfying himself that the crew had settled down to its in-flight routine and the ship was in full working order and correctly on course after taking a half right turn to bear east-northeast toward Danzig, committed the *Graf* to the care of his senior watch officers and sauntered aft to attend to his passengers. He spotted Geisenheyner, winked at him, and grinned. Lady Hay trotted out of her cabin. When she saw Eckener coming she took a red rose and presented it to him. "Our ship's father seems a bit taken aback by this," Geisenheyner noted. "Oh well, when occasion demands, he seems to say. But nothing discourteous against our brave lady fellow traveller. No, he likes her." Lady Hay's first world-flight dispatch for the Hearst newspapers in New York, Chicago, and Los Angeles took up half the front page and the whole of the second. No wonder Dr. Eckener liked her.

The photographers and film people were running around the ship "like headless hares," as one passenger put it. The tripods followed Eckener everywhere. The journalists were made to sit at their typewriters and tap, the cook in his white chef's hat was made to slice ham and dish out eggs and fruit in his little all-electric kitchen, and the passengers were corralled in front of a large map of the world on the saloon wall and told to look curious.

The passengers were getting to know each other. Dr. Jerónimo Megías, the Spanish unofficial emergency doctor on board, a small, well-dressed, cultured, and amiable man, was deep in conversation with Dr. Seilkopf, the German meteorological expert, on the subject of the likely lucky numbers for the next big Spanish lottery. Max Geisenheyner was having a word with Hearst reporter Karl von Wiegand about the risks inherent in the voyage. Geisenheyner had Siberia in mind, but von Wiegand was thinking of Japan, where rioting crowds and a typhoon were forecast. Whatever the risks, the two men agreed, this enterprise had to succeed; the zeppelin idea must not go under.

The language problem made communication difficult among the sixty-one people confined in the gondola's narrow living quarters, slung beneath the ship's vast, gas-filled hull. This was a German ship, and few of the foreigners on board spoke German. Geisenheyner undertook to teach the French reporter Léo Gerville-Réache a few handy German phrases to help him get by on board. "*Keine Ahnung.* No idea," the Frenchman enunciated brightly after his brief crash course. "Wo gibt es hier ein schönes mädchen?" he inquired. "Any pretty girls around here?" His big brown eyes lit up in his exotic, beaming face, for all the world, as Dr. Megías put it, "like a Hindu prince from the banks of the Ganges, a son of the Brahma."

The meteorologist Professor Karklin, the Soviet representative, was a more intransigent problem. He spoke only Russian, which no one else on board understood, but he had learned by rote a set-piece German sentence that he repeated endlessly, irrespective of the context: "Moskau Industrie, viele Leute, Sibirien nicht gut." "Moscow industry, many people, Siberia no good." It helped that Captain Hans von Schiller—"a star in our heaven," Geisenheyner called him—spoke fluent French and English as well as German.

As the ship approached Danzig, the first meal of the Friedrichs-hafen-Tokyo leg was served. The four lunch tables were set with crisp white cloths and specially designed "Graf Zeppelin" pearl-white and blue-and-gold Bavarian porcelain, glassware, and cutlery. The seating was drawn by lots. At the table presided over by the ship's commander the lots went to Bill Leeds, the explorer Sir Hubert Wilkins, Megías, and Lady Hay; they would keep their places for the rest of this leg of the flight. Head Steward Heinrich Kubis and his assistant Ernst Fischbach served up a sumptuous three-course meal prepared by the cook, Otto Manz.

The collective ritual drew the passengers together in communal good cheer. The wine flowed and the first toast was called—*Prosit!*—the glasses clinked and the passengers began to talk, to sign each other's celebratory menu cards. Robert Hartmann photographed Lady Hay sitting at Dr. Eckener's side. "Close friendships are made on board," ran the caption when the photo was published in a Berlin magazine. In spite of the wide assortment of nationalities, this was one of the most congenial gatherings Commander Rosendahl had ever seen. "Truly they were good shipmates," he reported. "Any peace convention or good will gathering would find in our passenger list a good example."

Even Lady Hay, the only woman among sixty men, felt at ease. "Ours is a little republic of democracy," she noted, "where professors, kings' physicians, millionaires, highest naval and army officers, crew, steward and cook all live and fraternise in the most amiable harmony." The German reporter Max Geisenheyner and the Japanese naval officer Commander Fujiyoshi had no language in common, but it didn't seem to matter. "Nice chap," noted Geisenheyner, "dark colouring, black eyes, blue uniform, navy dagger at his side, sparkling personality, thoroughly enjoying himself, laughs at each toast, clinks my glass, bows his head, then down in one."

There was no sign of apprehension on board, either individual or collective. "Flight in an airship is always a surprising revelation to the inexperienced," Rosendahl declared. "The utter absence of noise and vibration; the general freedom from even mild motion or lurching; the missing smoke, cinders and dust of trains; the freedoms and comforts; the splendid food and service; all are indelibly impressive."

During luncheon the *Graf* left Germany proper and cut across a snick of Polish territory toward East Prussia and the Baltic coast. When the politically disputed Free City of Danzig appeared on the port beam, the lunch guests put down their glasses and peered through the windows. Geisenheyner was struck by the improbability of it all. "So here we sit," he mused, "four hundred meters above the earth, on the way to Danzig, thin air twenty centimetres under our feet—and we're drinking Mokka!"

Danzig's welcome was tremendous. In this former German city the *Graf Zeppelin* was seen as a symbol of national rebirth. Airplanes came up to greet the airship. The din of ships' sirens, factory hooters, locomotive whistles, and church bells was terrific, and the doleful tolling of the cathedral bells welled up to them like a plaintive lament as the port saluted the zeppelin overhead. From the streets below came a roar of greeting from tens of thousands of the city's German inhabitants, and then the air filled with the people's hosanna, sung like a magnificat: "Deutschland, Deutschland über alles . . ."

On the bridge, Hugo Eckener, eyes fixed on the eastern horizon, floated over this uproar without paying the slightest attention to it. Then they were over Danzig Bay, crossing into East Prussia and over-flying Königsberg, the capital town, marked by its medieval brick fortresses, where another bag of postcards was dropped overboard as the *Graf* made a decisive turn to the east.

They were running out of German landspace now. After Tilsit came Memmell. Evening was coming on. The land was flat as a table.

Soon they were entering foreign territory. An aircraft with the double white cross of Lithuania on its fuselage appeared alongside, curved and caracoled in salute, then dipped away. The landscape had changed utterly: wretched thatch huts; uncultivated land; not a soul to be seen; a long, straight, badly made road stretching from nowhere to nowhere; a vast swamp as far as the eye could see. Lithuania, it was all too evident even from the air, was poor, run-down, ruined by years of war fought on its sour soil by the armies of those two extinct monarchies, that of the kaiser and that of the tsar.

They were crossing Latvia now, closing on the Soviet frontier, heading for Moscow, where batteries of searchlights were waiting in readiness to greet the *Graf Zeppelin*'s nighttime circuit over the capital. Among the passengers there was a growing sense of disorientation, of entering a great void. "By supper time," observed Max Geisenheyner, "we've forgotten everything. Where we are, that we're going round the world, that we're heading for Russia. We sit, drink, talk, are cocooned in the drone of propellers, whose murmur pours over the whole ship like a waterfall. Already Baron von Perckhammer is on his ninety-eighth postcard, and he has another two hundred and twenty to go. . . ."

At 7:48 in the evening they crossed the Russian border ten miles south of Dünaberg. Comrade Karklin was becoming increasingly nervous and animated. He spent a long time on the bridge with Eckener and Flemming, contemplating the vastness of Soviet territory. With great difficulty he made Eckener understand that the *Graf* had to fly via Moscow. Eckener told him it all depended on the weather reports. Karklin was not satisfied. He went into the saloon, buttonholed and harangued each passenger in turn, pointing at the map: "Siberia no good . . ."

The world darkened. A fabulous sunset gave way to a moonlit night, cool and clear. Dr. Eckener turned in early after nearly twenty-four hours on duty. In their cabins the world voyagers slept as best they could. Some time after midnight Dr. Megías's cabin door slid open, the light was switched on, and the duty radio officer came in, grinning broadly, and handed the doctor an envelope. There was a radio-telegram inside. It was from the king of Spain.

Jeronimo Megias - Graf Zeppelin - Santander,
15.15,30 -

So sincerely grateful for greetings from Eckener
and you, which I return. Wishing you a successful
journey which I am following with interest -
Alfonso R.

"I got very emotional when I read this," Megías was to write. "I really found myself losing touch with reality. Was it really possible that a perfectly ordinary human being lying in a comfortable bed and flying over a Russia he has never seen before at a height of 500 meters and a speed of 150 kph can be woken up in the middle of the night with a message from—of all people—the King of his country?" Bowled over by all this modern technology, he tossed and turned until dawn, Colonel Iselin's refrain endlessly ringing in his ears: "It's unique, unique, unique . . ."

By the early hours Eckener was back on the bridge, wrapped in his black leather flying jacket. A meteorological report came in on the radio. A new depression was forming near the Caspian Sea to the south, and Moscow and other points east reported head winds.

The direct route led via Moscow to Yekaterinburg (Sverdlovsk), where Eckener was planning to cross the Urals. The new weather report changed all that. "Moscow's out of the question," Eckener informed Karklin. "We're changing our course away from Moscow and heading northeast instead—if necessary as far as the Arctic." The Russian was furious. The ship must stay on course to Moscow, he insisted. The *Graf Zeppelin* must appear over the Soviet capital. Those were his instructions, that was the arrangement, this was what Dr. Eckener must do. Hundreds of thousands of people would be lining the city's rooftops in eager expectation of the world-famous airship's arrival. They must not be disappointed.

But to Dr. Eckener the *Graf*'s present mission was clear: to fly around the world in the shortest possible time. The journey was long and the fuel supply limited. No other considerations could be allowed to compromise this mission, not even Comrade Stalin, and certainly not his delegate, Comrade Karklin. "Our safety and our reserves," Dr. Eckener explained later, "could best be assured by the right use of wind conditions and by taking advantage of tail winds if they could be found. It was a fundamental principle with me to take navigational considerations into account first of all, even if political or other disadvantages might ensue. I therefore decided to steer to the north and leave Moscow on our right." Shortly after ordering a change of course he made a formal statement to the pressmen on board, which was radioed to the German ambassador in Moscow: "It is with deep regret that I cannot meet the wishes of the Soviet government. It is such a long flight I cannot assume the responsibility of deliberately and knowingly heading into contrary winds, which would mean retarding us by many hours. Therefore I am deviating back to the upper edge of the high pressure area, now about 120 kilometers away."

Comrade Karklin was downcast. He knew that it was not a good career move to fail to carry through an instruction issued to him personally by the Soviet government. The agitated Russian ran his finger over the maps and weather charts, saying things no one could fathom. He was beginning to make the crew nervous—"and nervousness," noted Geisenheyner, "is the privilege of the passengers, not the crew."

Later the Kremlin would deliver a sharply worded note to the German foreign office, while *Pravda* sternly declared, "The commander of the *Graf Zeppelin* appears to have a political agenda. So he chooses to fly over the old Russia rather than the new USSR. The whole flight has an aristocratic, anti-Bolshevik character. We hereby issue a warning that the road from Germany to Tokyo runs through Moscow."


At one o'clock in the morning the *Graf* crossed the legendary Volga. To the regret of everyone on board, there was not a single boatman in sight. Geisenheyner had been up for several hours. "I can't lie in bed while the sun comes up over Russia," he wrote. "I've got to see my first patch of Russian earth, my first Russian. This is Tolstoy country, the land of the *moujik*, the poor of the earth."

At three in the morning there was a glimmer of light on the horizon. By four, virtually dead ahead, the light began to spread in the east. Then a glowing point of light crept up over the gray-green horizon and within twenty minutes had spread like a broad fire along the dividing line between heaven and Earth.

"We've covered a hundred kilometers and I haven't seen a soul, or even a dwelling," Geisenheyner wrote in his notes. "Then suddenly I spot a couple of peasants in a field. They must have been sleeping there, because they take one look at the airship then run in a panic across the meadows to a little log cabin and disappear inside."

With the help of a freshening tail wind, the ship was making sixty-eight miles per hour on only four throttled-down motors, and by five they were bearing down on Vologda, their first Russian city. The golden cupolas of its forty-eight churches—"not churches now," insisted Comrade Karklin, a diehard Bolshevik, "schools"—gleamed in the streaming rays of the sun. The whole city seemed asleep, but as the roar of the propellers shattered the slumbers of the inhabitants, they rushed out into the streets in their night attire, took one look at the awesome apparition bearing down on them out of the west, then in bewildered panic stampeded back into their homes and slammed the doors. The *Graf,* still droning loudly, passed on toward the east.

The Union of Soviet Socialist Republics sprawled across two continents and covered one-sixth of the entire land surface of the planet. Few, if any, aircraft had ever flown across the entire breadth of this little-known landmass before. All day the *Graf Zeppelin* throbbed eastward across these endless open spaces. "The immense and awesome Russian forest," the French reporter observed, "stretches all the way to the Manchurian mountains and the Sea of Okhotsk. From our present height—around 1,200 meters—we can see as far as 200 kilometres away, and always it's the same mysterious, impenetrable, hostile forest."

Villages were small and scattered. Roads were few and cultivation slight. Communism had as yet had little impact here. Rosendahl was particularly impressed by the number of well-kept churches in this part of the country and the poverty of everything else. The conifer forest grew thicker as they approached the Ural Mountains, and huge forest fires, sixty miles in length and breadth, formed a dense, far-reaching smoke cloud, so that at times the helmsman could see only a hundred feet in any direction. The acrid smell of woodsmoke and vaporizing pine gum permeated the *Graf* for hours, an uncomfortable sensation on an airship filled with hydrogen.

A long flat line of cumulus clouds now stretched directly ahead across their course: the Ural mountains that divided Europe from Asia. In the late afternoon and at a height of thirty-three hundred feet, the *Graf* crossed this historic natural barrier at its lowest point near the city of Perm and descended into Asia.

Here the forest gave way to the vast and primordial marshland of the tundra, stretching forever, monotonous, treeless, and trackless. Hour after hour the *Graf* flew over an endless procession of lakes, rivers, and swamps, great patches of moss and lichen and turbid water that stretched to every horizon, impassable in summer. Such charts as existed for this region were incomplete or wrong. There were no aids to navigation, no beacons, no railroad tracks, not even roads. Over such featureless terrain, the navigators could hold their course only by dead reckoning, using major river systems to take an occasional fix of their position. It was a land, as Dr. Megías put it, "entirely unedited by the gaze of man." Barely a handful of people could have seen even a tiny part of this virgin expanse. "Totally, as a whole, directly from above, we are surely the first to have seen it," Megías wrote. "I experience simultaneously a disquiet both spiritual and mental."

"The landscape became steadily more lonely, even frightening and terrifying," Eckener recorded. "Like an extraordinary decorative carpet it blazed up at us in all its colours—green, yellow, blue, red and orange—horribly beautiful when we thought we might have to land on this carpet and be trapped helpless and lost amid the swamps and countless little streams." It was, he reckoned, truly uninhabitable for man or beast.

For all their many differences—ten nationalities, a wide range of ages (from teens to sixties) and of class—the sixty-one human beings on the world flight formed a group with many qualities the postwar years badly needed, not least a global vision and a concept of international accord that was ahead of its time.

For Léo Gerville-Réache, the urbane Parisian reporter from *Le Matin*, what went on in the *Graf*'s saloon as it circled the world was innately more fascinating than the world it was circling. "Flat country do anything for you?" he jotted in his notebook at one point. "Me neither."

In this respect he was the exact reverse of the explorer Sir Hubert Wilkins, who ceaselessly scanned the world below, ignoring the world within. Wilkins was forty and had spent half his lifetime in one polar region or the other. A pioneer of the use of aircraft for polar exploration, the previous year he had copiloted a plane on a twenty-one-hundred-mile nonstop flight from Alaska to Spitzbergen, a feat for which he was knighted, followed by a six-hundred-mile flight across the Antarctic. It was presumed he had joined the world flight to assess the airship's potential for polar exploration, but Gerville-Réache divined that he had two more overriding preoccupations—first, to get to Cleveland, Ohio, as quickly as possible to marry a pretty young Australian actress, and then, almost immediately after the wedding, to head off for the North Pole in command of a subpolar submarine, the *Nautilus*. Now, sitting by the window, Sir Hubert proclaimed: "If we didn't know it was impossible we might almost think the Zeppelin had flown to the moon or Mars. This view is positively unearthly."

Max Geisenheyner from the *Frankfurter Zeitung* reacted in the same way, writing in his diary: "Muddy mirrors of water between treacherous algae-slimed ponds like fat round mammoths' footprints. Grey-blue walls of cloud in all directions. A brick-red balk of cloud to the west. The sun a flat pale disc. Everything dark and mucky. Turbid, lifeless pools of water. Algae like poisonous verdigris." As he scribbled down his notes someone put a record on the gramophone: "I glimpse a pair of creased grey trousers dancing the Cakewalk. On the gramophone squeaks a flat and sentimental negro voice—and beneath us the bogs blow bubbles after bubbles back at us. Was it not a grotesque conceit on the part of the human spirit to venture over this wasteland at all? If we had to make a forced landing tonight, I don't think any of us would get back alive. The swamp would swallow us up for ever without so much as a glug."

Geisenheyner had felt the first gnawing twitch of fear. So too, perhaps, had his fellow passengers—one of them informed Dr. Eckener that he had lost all appetite for supper. Eckener himself confessed to Captain von Schiller: "Never in my life have I had such a strong feeling of utter loneliness and abandonment as here over the Siberian tundra." At a pinch a zeppelin could make an emergency landing on dry land, Schiller reckoned, or even on the sea, but to go down in these swamps, a thousand kilometers from the nearest settlement, would mean certain disaster.

"How can Dr. Eckener steer his cruiser over this country where identical horizon follows identical horizon?" pondered Léo Gerville-Réache. "This traverse of Siberia is perhaps the most scabrous part of this whole venture." There was no respite. No help from the radio room. The Russian wireless stations were deaf and dumb. "For many long hours now we have had no connection with the civilised world," complained Gerville-Réache. The steppes had no end, their melancholy no limit. In the passenger lounge, the typewriters fell silent. Even Baron von Perckhammer was quiet, and Lady Hay's eyes were unusually troubled.

Siberia was not entirely deserted. From time to time the *Graf* came to a tiny peasant settlement marooned miles from anywhere. Even from a height of two thousand feet the signs were clear for every passenger to read—the inhabitants of these villages were the wretched of the Earth, impoverished, hungry, and deprived. The Russian Revolution had not reached these far-flung outliers of the old Russian Empire, or, if it had, its impact had been zero. Illiterate, ignorant, and superstitious, the peasants all reacted to the arrival of the zeppelin in the same way: in utter terror at what they probably saw as an instrument of the wrath of God or an engine of the Devil.

"Many of the peasants, who have never even seen a train," noted Karl von Wiegand,

mistake the Zeppelin, with its thrumming motors and sylphlike speed and lines, for a celestial monster, ominous and awesome. We saw villagers run wildly into forests and houses and gather around churches, gazing to the sky in awe and terror. They cringed as the *Graf*'s giant shadow overtook their open hiding places. Many of the streets of the small villages were utterly deserted; everybody, apparently, had sought cover. Few people in the world have the comprehensive mental picture of Russia we are getting. It is indescribably empty, dreary and melancholy.

Tea-partying with friends in her cabin (caviar, pâté de foie gras, and jellies—gifts from well-wishers at takeoff), Lady Hay was smitten with guilt when she compared her lot on board the *Graf* with that of the struggling peasantry on the ground. "We—who know of life and have lived—sail along above, enjoying the choicest delicacies of the world," she wrote, "while the poor, hard-working, uneducated peasants below us have to struggle and strive and tear their hands almost to the bone to get their food."

So the day passed. It was getting colder now, and the passengers were wrapping themselves in all the woolly and furry clothes they possessed. Lady Hay emerged from her cabin in a black hat and a leather overcoat over a long felt dress, her feet buried in fur-lined arctics. "She's lost her feminine lines," lamented Dr. Megías, "but then, no one's got time to bother about what colour to wear on lips and cheeks at this juncture." The Japanese had taken to their beds, wrapped in blankets. Even the hardened polar explorer Sir Hubert Wilkins had been forced, amid much banter from the rest, to put on something warmer than his city-slicker camel-hair coat.

Supper was simple fare—sausage and cabbage, cheese, beer, wine, or water. The sun set over the wilderness in splendid radiance. A gray halo announced moonrise. Shortly the moon appeared, red and enormous. In these latitudes the night would last only three or four hours. Gerville-Réache put his watch forward one hour. "Since leaving Friedrichshafen," he wrote, "I have wiped out five hours of my life." Heading due east they had been losing time continually. Twice a day they had been changing the clocks. "By the time we have gone all the way round we'll have lost twenty-four hours," Dr. Megías noted, "and then we will begin to get them back and end up with two days the same."

After supper Bill Leeds put another dance record on the gramophone. The ship's cook, fat and jolly Otto Manz, came into the saloon and began to execute some comic pirouettes. Young millionaire Leeds, burly photographer Baron von Perckhammer in his Tyrolean getup, and veteran reporter Heinz von Eschwege-Lichberg wrapped in a blanket joined in, skipping about and laughing hysterically. "It's curious, this scene," reflected the quiet and dignified Dr. Megías. "Interesting—the psychology of these buffoons from different countries and different social strata, united in pure diversion."

The noise reached the control room, and Captain Lehmann came in from the bridge and courteously announced that the racket was proving a distraction to the proper running of the ship. This was an expedition, he reminded them, not a flying nightclub. Might he, he asked, offer his services to provide a more restful distraction? He came back with his accordion—he was a talented musician who also played the cello and harmonica—and smiling his famous smile began to play: old nostalgic songs, sweet songs, popular works from the German classics, waltzes from *Rosenkavalier*. . . . By the time he finished at one o'clock in the morning, there was a more reflective mood on board.

Dr. Megías tiptoed back to his cabin, where Comrade Karklin, his minuscule two kilos of baggage neatly stowed, was sleeping. The Spanish doctor kissed the little portrait miniature of his mother on the bedside table, a relic he had kept with him since he was an adolescent, "when She went to Heaven," then wearily climbed into his bunk and shut his eyes.

All was calm. The saloon was empty. A couple of empty wine bottles stood on a table. The silent gramophone in the window gleamed in the moonlight. From the passengers' sleeping quarters came snoring and the tap-tap of a solitary typewriter—Lady Hay, alone in her freezing cabin, hammering out her copy to be radiotelegraphed to the States in time for tomorrow's dailies. It would appear in next morning's New York and Chicago papers under a banner headline splashed across the front page:

ZEPPELIN NEARING MANCHURIA

It was actually doing nothing of the sort. Manchuria was a major war zone (Russia versus China, China versus Japan), and was also afflicted with typhoons from the sea. The *Graf* was keeping well away, following an approximation of the Arctic Circle just north of the sixtieth parallel on a course that would take it eventually to the Lena River far to the north.

International interest in the zeppelin's progress remained intense, and in America, Europe, and Japan the public eagerly kept track of the flight. America's leading flat-earther declared that the flight would furnish incontrovertible proof that the world was flat, for otherwise the zeppelin would fall off the bottom of the planet when it got to Tokyo.

In Tokyo, expectations of the *Graf Zeppelin*'s arrival were reaching fever pitch. Emperor Hirohito himself, along with half a million of his subjects, was expected at the landing ground to greet the ship on its arrival, and plans were being made to charter the *Graf* for a special flight over the capital carrying cabinet members and city officials.

They were somewhere near the junction of the Ob and Irtysh Rivers now, Lady Hay typed, three hundred miles northwest of Omsk in the heart of western Siberia. Though they had descended from 3,700 feet to 2,500 feet, it was still penetratingly cold as they ventured farther and farther into the frozen fastnesses.

Lady Hay was no longer alone in her cabin: she had found a new companion who was now sleeping soundlessly on her bed. Though the *Graf* was carefully searched immediately prior to departure, a stowaway of sorts successfully eluded discovery until earlier that day. Hungry, shivering, and distressed, a small black kitten was found in the depths of the ship's vast and complex interior by a rigger on a tour of inspection, and with Dr. Eckener's blessing it was brought to the only woman on board for a little necessary care and affection.

The weather had been good for the whole flight so far, Lady Hay reported; according to Dr. Eckener, after flying more than twenty-seven hundred miles the ship had used only six thousand cubic meters of fuel gas out of the twenty-four thousand it started with and had burned only three tons of gasoline out of its supply of ten tons.

"We are all realising the extraordinary privilege which has been given us to see Russia from one end to the other as no mortal eyes have ever done before," Lady Hay tap-tapped on her typewriter. The view through her window extended for a hundred miles or more, and there was not a railway, a road, or even a trail to be seen. "It seems like a dream; indeed it is a dream—a dream of man's ambition to conquer the elements, to conquer space, to conquer nature's barriers, which since the world began have effectively segregated the races and the peoples of the nations."

The only other passenger still up in the early hours was the young American Bill Leeds, staring down at the darkened Earth for hours, looking for a light, a sign of life. Leeds was not entirely what he seemed. A sportsman and flier as well as a very rich young man, he gave the impression of being a fun-loving playboy, and other passengers, to whom he was known as "Sunshine," teased him about his gramophone and getting up so late every morning. But he was a serious man and highly regarded on the *Graf Zeppelin*. Lady Hay apart, he was the most pro-zeppelin of all the passengers, and almost the only one who preferred to stay on board rather than check in at deluxe hotels during intermediate landings on the world flight. On the bridge he was happy to take the wheel for a stretch. Suspended between heaven and Earth, he liked nothing more than to watch the world down there at night and the stars up there in the sky.

Meanwhile, "in calm and stately flight," as Hugo Eckener put it, the great ship sailed on across this vast region. In the navigation room the lights had been dimmed. A yellowish green moon hung above the horizon, its light reflected back from the mirrors of water scattered across the darkened Siberian landmass. The stars were clear tonight, and frosty and bright. It was difficult to steer an accurate course in the dark over this trackless desert, and now and then the navigation officer, Max Pruss, took a fix on a star with his sextant to check the ship's position.

Dr. Eckener was seated in the dimmed control room, staring out at the bright starlit sky. The *Graf* was passing over the western Siberian territory of Omsk en route to the central Siberian territory of Krasnoyarsk, and through the control-car window Eckener could see the gleam of some unknown river winding down below, a nomad's solitary fire flickering in the wastelands. Somewhere ahead, where the illimitable, godforsaken tundra petered out far to the east, lay a wall of lofty mountains that barred the ship's route to the Pacific. Often cloud-covered, height uncertain, the route through or around them unknown, they greatly preoccupied Eckener's sleepless mind.

All night the *Graf* held a steady course northeast. At dawn on the fourth day of the flight, the mighty Yenisey could be seen dead ahead, and at nine o'clock, after flying over continuous swamplands for twelve hours, the *Graf* reached this great river—"like a safe street,"

Eckener recalled, "that for all its loneliness and remoteness would lead us again to towns and people." Since it was impossible to tell from the maps what point of the river they had arrived at, Eckener was anxious to locate the tiny river port of Imbatsk, which had a weather and wireless station and could serve as a fix and departure point for another compass course. Turning north, he flew down the river at low altitude, not a settlement in sight, not a boat on the broad, powerful stream, until after an hour they turned a corner and found themselves over a wretched little village of some twenty-five huts: Imbatsk.

"Though Imbatsk had twenty-five huts when we arrived, it had only twenty-three after we left," Eckener recalled:

> Apparently our arrival was a complete surprise. Who would have thought we were steering straight for this little hole merely to fix our position? Doors and windows opened and people stuck their heads out to look for the cause of the thunder from the heavens, but most of them quickly drew back, apparently frightened by the sight of the giant heavenly chariot. A heavy two-wheeled cart was slowly plodding down the narrow street between the low huts, and the driver was lazily leaning back on the sacks and dozing. Suddenly he jerked upright, saw the monster close overhead, and jumped off, vanishing into the nearest hut. The horse pulling the cart apparently took fright as well and raced off terrified, dragging the cart behind it. At the next corner it turned so abruptly down a side street that the cart turned over, knocking down a shabby hut and destroying the next one also. We could not follow what happened next, but we jokingly told each other: "Now we're going to have to pay for wilful damage to a peaceful village!"

From Imbatsk they headed due east toward the Tunguska River, following its course for several hours as it twisted through the uninhabited forests en route to Yakutsk. Late in the afternoon their way was barred by a squall line, a wall of black, menacing clouds that darkened the country for miles on either side and reached down to within five hundred feet of the ground. Eckener decided to break through the cloud wall at as great a height as possible and climbed to thirty-three hundred feet, where the turbulence was likely to be minimal. It was the first real storm of the flight so far. Rain beat about the ship, and upward thrusts of violent air threw it up several hundred feet at a time. With all engines at full-ahead, the *Graf* shot through the storm clouds. On the other side of the front the air was pleasantly warm, and the ship flew steadily on to the east, approaching the watershed between the Yenisey and Lena Rivers in a calm, almost windless atmosphere, and as the sun went down the empty plain was flooded with golden light.

The night that followed was no less miraculous, the northern sky straddled with the weirdly beautiful colors of an aurora, a meteor streaking down across the vastness of the Siberian heavens. From the radio room there came a surreal babble of celestial squawk as communication was established with the American legation in Peking. Eckener recalled:

> During the brief night hours a full moon rose, or at least attempted to rise, for it remained low above the horizon to the south, where it rolled slowly along on its brief course like a huge yellow ball. In the north the brightly glowing sky showed that the sun was only a few degrees below the horizon. An American passenger [Bill Leeds] was so fascinated by these theatrical lighting effects that towards 11 P.M., when everyone else had gone to bed for a brief rest, he called for two bottles of wine and spent the night watching the moon and the twilit heavens. I kept him company for a while, for the wine we were carrying on board was not bad at all, and the celestial spectacle was quite extraordinary.

After the short night they came to the remote river port of Yakutsk on a bend of the Lena, a regional capital and the first substantial settlement they had set eyes on in a thousand miles—a town of log cabins and dusty streets, scattered churches and a few grander public buildings, seven hundred miles from the nearest railhead. With due ceremony and solemnity they dropped a large wreath on a parachute into the cemetery next to the cathedral at the edge of town, to commemorate the German prisoners of war who had perished in Siberia during and after the last war. Two more mailbags were also dropped over the side, though the chances that the post would reach its destination were slim. By now all communication with the outside world had ceased: the radio room could no longer pick up any transmissions, not even from Peking, and it seemed no one could hear any signals from the ship—a situation that led to widespread anxiety and rumors that the *Graf* had been lost with all hands.

They turned southeast now, heading for the Stanovoy Mountains and the east coast of Siberia, where the landmass of Asia ends, still nearly five hundred miles distant. This was the most uncertain leg of the flight to date. The world below was as empty as before, a seemingly limitless wilderness of forests and swamps, not fifty habitations to be seen, not a hundred cultivated acres. But as they neared the mountains, the landscape grew more picturesque, and after two hours they crossed the Aldan, a substantial tributary of the Lena, flowing parallel to the base of the mountains.

The Stanovoy extended for some five to six hundred miles along the eastern shore of the Sea of Okhotsk and barred the *Graf*'s route to the Pacific. They had never been charted, and their height was not known precisely, though such maps and handbooks as existed described them as being no more than five thousand feet—substantially higher than the *Graf*'s average altitude level of sixteen hundred feet on this part of the flight, but not insurmountable, even in cloud or fog.

As plains gave way to rolling hills, the ship began to climb, following a valley that the maps showed should take them to a pass through the mountain barrier. They climbed to thirty-three hundred feet, then four thousand, winding their way up through the valley's twists and turns till the full expanse of the Stanovoy's peaks and ridges were revealed, rising ever higher before them as far as they could see. "We were tense with anxiety," Eckener was to recall, "as we watched the valley steadily narrowing and the peaks on either side rising higher and higher."

By midday it seemed they were near the crest, but they were already up to fifty-five hundred feet, and still the top of the pass was above them. A gusty northwest wind had sprung up, rocking and swaying the ship, adding to the anxieties of the passengers and the officers on the bridge, for now they had to worry not only about their height above the rocky ground but also their distance from the rock walls on either side of them, which steadily narrowed to within 250 feet on either side. This was flying without precedent in airship history. Though the *Graf* could probably have reached an absolute altitude of eighty-five hundred feet, it would have blown off a large quantity of its lifting gas in the process and thus become heavy, a potentially dangerous situation if it was loaded down with rain.

On the bridge Eckener and his officers looked tensely ahead as the crest of the pass drew closer. Any error now, any unforeseen trick of wind or weather, and a catastrophe could take place from which the chances of survival were almost certainly zero, even if anyone escaped the crash. Transfixed, passengers and crew alike watched as the ground slid by barely 250 feet beneath them. Once again Lady Hay-Drummond-Hay was the heroine of the hour, just as she had been when the *Graf* took a dive on its first Atlantic flight. "The example and moral support she showed to the other passengers," von Wiegand declared, "proved her to be the true daughter of England—the world's womanhood could have no finer representative on this pioneering flight."

And then a great shout went up in the saloon as well as on the bridge. Stretching away almost directly beneath lay the vivid blue of the Pacific. They were through.

"Now *that,*" Eckener cried out, raising his arms in triumph and glee, "is what you call airship flying!"

"*Thalassa, thalassa!*" cried those who knew their classical history. "The sea, the sea!"

They embraced, they clapped each other's backs, they gripped each other by the hand, they beamed from ear to ear. They had done it. They were safe. Though the helmsmen did not relinquish their grip on the control wheels, their faces registered a joy that was absolute—"the ecstasy of achievement," as Lady Hay put it, still scribbling ferociously, "the almost fanatical joy of successful pioneers."

From Siberian cold to summer seas and warm airs was a transition of only a few minutes. They had entered a new world. "The journey through hostile Siberia was over," Eckener wrote. "The beautiful blue ocean beckoned us and we expected soon to be once more over friendly coastlines and cities."

The *Graf* had flown 5,105 statute miles from Friedrichshafen to the Sea of Okhotsk in just over three days, Eckener told Karl von Wiegand, averaging 68.1 miles an hour on four motors. They had completed the first nonstop flight across Soviet Russia and still had fifty hours of fuel left over, enough to get them across the Pacific to Los Angeles nonstop and achieve another first. But what would the Japanese say, Eckener wondered. Zeppelin fever had gripped Tokyo, and already the crowds were gathering. "They would be even more resentful than the people of Moscow over avoiding their city. On this occasion my political instincts triumphed over my Zeppelin passion and I gave orders to steer south towards Nikolayevsk and Japan."

Flying a zeppelin was an art requiring, among other things, a thorough knowledge of the physics of meteorology, and skilled practitioners were few. No one was more versed in this art than Hugo Eckener. For him every weather report was like a move in a game of substratospheric chess. His aim was to work out what his opponent had in mind, then outwit him, avoiding a threat or taking advantage of it, or even on occasion meeting it head on, always bearing in mind that any miscalculation could end in catastrophe.

The flight across the Sea of Japan was one such opportunity for the ship's commander to demonstrate his mastery of weather and airship flying. It was, he recorded, "a navigationally very interesting part of the journey." While over Siberia he had received a report that a severe typhoon centered over China was moving toward them over the Sea of Japan. Eckener judged that by the time the *Graf* reached this area, the typhoon would have passed through and he might have an opportunity to hook onto its tail and be swept along at a greatly increased speed. He therefore ordered the stern engine, which had been idle for most of the flight, to be started up and, with the help of the extra thrust, began to bear down on the rear of the southerly storm.

Eckener's calculation proved correct. As the ship tucked into the back of the typhoon, its speed went up to around a hundred miles per hour. They were now racing down the narrow Gulf of Tartary, separating Sakhalin Island from the continent of Asia, flying in thick weather, shrouded in cloud without sight of the sea, doing their best to avoid colliding with the high mountains to both right and left. It was, Eckener noted, "a rather unpleasant situation." To seasoned airshipmen it was also rather exciting. "Row after row of fantastically shaped clouds loomed up ahead like threatening gods," Commander Rosendahl recalled of this passage. "They were disintegrating rapidly and had spent their violence in the storm just passed." Even so, it was the roughest ride of the entire trip. "The tail threshed about a lot," von Wiegand reported, "giving us the worst shaking we have had—so Schiller had to take her up to fifty-two hundred feet. I ask you if that isn't daring? But we knew Dr. Eckener knew his business in this most modern science of man's continuous flight in the air."

As dawn broke around five o'clock, the watch officers were at last able to see the water below them here and there, and this enabled them to assess their drift. An hour later they found themselves on the west side of the Japanese island of Hokkaido. With clear weather ahead they had a straight run south along the main island of Honshu, and at five in the afternoon, after a speedy thirteen-hundred-mile flight along the east coast and over the flowered fields of Japan, they came in low for a triumphal arrival over Tokyo and its neighboring port of Yokohama. They had traveled seven thousand miles in a little less than 102 hours, the longest nonstop distance flight ever made. "The task of overcoming the longest and most difficult portion of the flight around the world had been successfully completed," Eckener wrote. "From distant Berlin in the west, an airship had come in less than four days, a distance requiring almost a month by fast steamer and more than fourteen days on the Trans-Siberian Railway. The distant Orient cheek by jowl with Central Europe . . . !"

The world was suddenly a much, much smaller place. The future was already here—and all Japan perceived the fact. The scenes in the Tokyo streets were unparalleled. At the first sight of the approaching zeppelin all the city sirens went off, and hundreds of thousands of people poured out to see the long-awaited colossus; one estimate put the total of people staring skyward from the roofs and pavements at 4 million, and the crush quickly caused the public transport system to collapse. As soon as the *Graf* came swimming in over the capital, the minister of the navy communicated its arrival to the emperor in his summer palace on the seashore, and the emperor conveyed his greetings to Dr. Eckener, the passengers, officers, and crew. As the giant ship circled overhead, radio station JOAK broadcast live commentary of the *Graf*'s arrival throughout the Japanese Empire, and the newspapers issued extras continuously. One of them, *Nichi-Nichi,* printed messages of welcome from around the empire, calling the flight "the greatest accomplishment mankind has achieved."

"Roar after roar of '*Banzai!*' floated up to us," reported Karl von Wiegand. "It was a magnificent welcome to Japan; a spontaneous, popular and official recognition of the *Graf*'s great feat. Dr. Eckener was deeply touched and began to growl to himself, as he usually does when his emotions are stirred, lest he betray his feelings." For the *Graf* the Japanese had coined the title "King of the Air," and for its commander, Hugo Eckener, the typhoon chaser, the epithet "Storm King." The airship was seen as a machine of wonder and magic, its arrival an event of huge historic portent and symbolism. With the coming of the *Graf Zeppelin* it seemed to the multitude below as if a new era had dawned and Japan's age-old isolation had come to an end. To the people on board the *Graf* the clamor and wild excitement in the streets below was almost beyond belief. "Only a poet," Eckener said, "could manage to portray the intense feeling that seized the crowd."

After an hour and a half flying over Tokyo, the *Graf* headed off to the Japanese naval airship base at Kasumigaura, where a vast crowd of a quarter of a million awaited its arrival. Many had come from far away and were wearing traditional costume, the women in kimonos with their babies on their backs. "The Japanese are an emotional race, though characteristically inscrutable of deportment," reported an American journalist who was in the crowd, "and when the *Graf* first passed over Kasumigaura on its way to Tokyo, glistening like a dew drop, it was as if they had seen a prodigy. They were too awed to talk. The tense hush was noticeable everywhere." All that now changed. As the *Graf Zeppelin* nudged down toward the landing field in the last light of evening, the passengers waving handkerchiefs, napkins, and even a tablecloth from the windows, the answering roar of the multitude drowned all other sounds, and when the crowd rushed forward they sent up a cloud of wheat chaff from the adjoining stubble field, which for a moment totally enveloped the great ship.

Looking out on this scene, the vast throng below, the rising moon above, the rosy glow of sunset over the sacred mountain of Fuji-yama in the distance, Watch Officer Max Pruss turned to Lady Hay, seated in her usual place in a corner of the navigation room, and whispered, "It's like a dream." And she thought, "That is what it all seemed like—a dream. A flood of pent-up emotion rushed over me. Some passengers asked how I felt. I was happy and thankful to God, Dr. Eckener and the crew who had brought me safely through the unknown spaces."

The landing lines were dropped, water ballast let go, and the engines shut down. A Japanese band played the national anthem, followed by the German colony bands' rendering of "The Watch on the Rhine," and the great, ghostly airship, silvered by the first beams of the moon, slowly settled to the ground. "So ended," noted the American reporter, "the most thrilling day in Japan since Armistice Day."

Expertly handled by its German-trained Japanese naval ground crew, the zeppelin was squeezed stern-first into its ex-German war-reparations hangar with barely a foot to spare. Finally passengers and crew could disembark, and Lady Hay's little black kitten, too. Immigration and customs formalities were waived, baggage nodded through. The Japanese passengers were besieged by relatives and friends, while the young Americans Bill Leeds and Joachim Rickard begged the first fifty people they met for cigarettes. Sir Hubert Wilkins sniffed the Japanese air. Germany had smelled of new-mown hay and flowers, he recalled, but in Japan he noted "a strong, intriguing odour of the East, not disagreeable, but different."

Eckener looked tired and admitted as much. The moment his feet touched the ground he began to talk about taking off for Los Angeles; it took his mind off the impending ordeal of official receptions and all those speeches. In a large marquee nearby the ceremonies began; they were to continue without cease for the entire duration of the *Graf*'s stay. After clasping hands with the official welcoming party, which included the foremost officers of the Japanese army, navy, and air forces, Eckener addressed the multitude:

We owe it to all the splendid co-operation we had from the weather stations along the route. Germany, Poland, the Soviet Union and Japan all aided us wonderfully in being able to avoid bad weather and hook our craft to the tails of typhoons and go in search of favourable winds.

The *Graf* behaved like the master of the air it is. I never expected such a quick journey. It is the most wonderful, most marvellous journey I have ever had. Nothing could compare with that speedy flight over the utterly desolate regions of Siberia. And nothing could have been more impressive than our battle with the typhoon in our speeding course down the Tartar Strait and over Vulcan Bay.

And our reception here, where no commercial airship has ever touched, is simply stupendous. I thank you so much. Now I must look after my crew for a minute.

News of the *Graf Zeppelin*'s landing in Japan provoked reactions worldwide. In many American cities the progress of the flight had been tracked on billboard-sized maps in cinema foyers and town squares, and when the little zeppelin counter finally came to rest at a place called Kasumigaura the crowds burst into spontaneous applause. JAPAN ACCLAIMS ZEPPELIN ran the front-page headlines in the American papers; TOKYO WILD. The entire first four pages of the Hearst papers were devoted to the *Graf*'s flight to Japan. Even the British, usually dismissive of airships and most things German, hailed it as "an epoch-making event not only in aviation but in international communications." In every restaurant and beer hall of the *Graf*'s small lakeside hometown of Friedrichshafen, toasts were drunk to the zeppelin and all on board her, and in the modest Eckener family home, an atmosphere of quiet contentment prevailed, as the *Chicago Herald-Examiner* reported:

Frau Eckener Happy
Keeps on Knitting

Frau Eckener was quietly happy in her little home today. She is a motherly type of woman and was knitting a sweater when news arrived that the *Graf Zeppelin* had landed. She said: "Isn't it wonderful? We go to sleep when the ship sails away and awaken when it returns. Now I must get on with my knitting."

It was rather different in Japan. The *Chicago Examiner* proclaimed: EXOTIC ASIATIC HORDES AWED BY WORLD AIR TOURISTS! And GRAF ZEPPELIN ENDS EPIC AIR VOYAGE TO JAPAN — PAYS RESPECT TO CAPITAL OF EMPIRE, splashed the *Osaka Mainichi*'s front page.

After speeches and toasts at Kasumigaura, the *Graf*'s passengers and crew were driven off to a teahouse near the capital for the official reception. This was the beginning of what Eckener called the "difficult social and political obligations." It was the part of the flight he had least looked forward to, and his discomfiture was to begin almost at once.

At the teahouse he was confronted by geisha girls. They smiled, bowed, and bent down to unlace his shoes. Horrified, Eckener remembered that one of his socks had snagged on a nail and had a large hole in it. For almost the first time since leaving Friedrichshafen, the unflappable commander was close to losing his nerve. "Nein, nein!" he exclaimed in a panic. "Nein, nein!" In desperation he looked around for help. "Lehmann!" he called out to his senior watch officers. "Flemming!"

The Zeppelin men, the most honored guests of the nation, conferred in low, urgent tones and arrived at a syndicate solution. The commander could not take off his shoes, they explained to their politely puzzled hosts. None of them could. It was against the religion of their country. Their hosts bowed in accord, then whispered amongst themselves before coming up with a compromise: woolen sacks were produced to wrap round the officers' shoes, and so attired they joined the party.

The days in Tokyo were packed. Rarely, if ever, had the Japanese extended greetings on this scale to any foreigners. "The *Graf Zeppelin* has conquered Japan," commented Lady Hay. "Tokyo is Zeppelin mad. There is not a thing they won't do for us. They threaten to kill the crew with kindness. Commander Eckener, usually shy about receptions, has been quite won over." On Tuesday night a state banquet was held for Eckener, his officers, and the passengers at the Imperial Hotel, Japan's grandest, where the passengers were staying, hosted by the foreign minister, the minister of communications, the minister of war, and the admiral of the navy. Lady Hay, whom the Japanese had dubbed "the Queen of the Zeppelin," was the only woman present— "queenly beautiful," as the press described her. Later that evening, in a speech to an audience of two thousand in the Asahi Auditorium, she spoke of the honor of being the only woman on the *Graf*'s world flight, "a recognition and a tribute to the women of the twentieth century who are trying so hard to take their place worthily among the workers and history-makers of their generation."

Next there was tea at the Imperial Palace with the emperor. The Japanese press was printing more column inches about the visit of the *Graf* than any other event in Japanese history, and the wireless and cable routes were busier than they had ever been. On board the *Graf*, lavish gifts from functionaries and well-wishers piled up—ornamental daggers and vases, silk embroideries, a sword and silver cups from the emperor—till there were more than the ship could take and they had to be crated up and sent ahead to Germany by steamer.

It was heady stuff, but wearing. Eckener was uncomfortable, overdressed, and overwhelmed. It was more than a hundred degrees in the shade in Tokyo, and humid. Eckener had only his heavy uniform and normal Western clothes. He badly wanted a lightweight white linen suit, but no tailor had one his size in stock, and there was no time to have one made. Meanwhile, the rich and exotic food and drink upset his stomach, he began to go down with ptomaine poisoning, and in his sweaty clothes he developed a boil on his bottom. He longed to be back in his airship, seated in his favorite chair on the bridge, contemplating the heavens and the Earth, playing chess with God, luck, and the weather. At last came the finale, a grand dinner at the German embassy with the entire German colony in Japan. And then it was over.


Takeoff was set for 4 A.M. on August 22. ZEPPELIN OFF FOR U.S. TODAY proclaimed the Hearst Press headlines. Though the *Graf Zeppelin* had hogged the headlines, a plethora of other flying stories from the last twenty-four hours shared the front page with it. Four Swiss fliers had

Count Zeppelin with his wife, Isabella, and daughter, Hella, in Saarburg in 1890. With his army career in ruins, he was already thinking about "a very large airship for warfare, general commerce, and exploring the Earth." *(Archiv der Luftschiffbau Zeppelin GmbH)*

Under the critical eyes of three junior citizens, the first Zeppelin LZ1 takes off on its first flight above the Bay of Manzell, October 17, 1900. *(Archiv der Luftschiffbau Zeppelin GmbH)*

Crowds gather around LZ3 during an intermediate landing at Konstanz in 1909. *(Archiv der Luftschiffbau Zeppelin GmbH)*

New technology catches up with old: LZ4 and its shadow overtake an express train during a flight to Switzerland. *(Archiv der Luftschiffbau Zeppelin GmbH)*

After bumping into a pear tree in a field near Göppingen in May 1909, LZ5 makes an emergency take-off with a patched up nose to complete an endurance flight. *(Archiv der Luftschiffbau Zeppelin GmbH)*

Watched by a flotilla of onlookers, LZ6 is hauled out of its floating hangar on Lake Constance for a flight in 1909. *(Archiv der Luftschiffbau Zeppelin GmbH)*

BELOW LEFT: Dr. Hugo Eckener, Zeppelin commander and pioneer of intercontinental flight *(Ullstein Bilderdienst)*

BELOW RIGHT: Dr. Ludwig Dürr worked on the construction of all 118 Zeppelins ever built, as chief designer on all but the first. He was a reclusive man and personally preferred to travel no farther than his bicycle could take him. *(Süddeutscher Verlag Bilderdienst)*

An unpromising start to a singular career: Hugo Eckener's first voyage as commander of a DELAG passenger zeppelin in Düsseldorf, May 16, 1911, was marred by a disastrous collision with the hangar roof on take-off. The passengers and crew of LZ8 *Deutschland II* had to be rescued by fire ladders. *(Süddeutscher Verlag Bilderdienst)*

LEFT: A brochure for the 1912 season of DELAG's zeppelin passenger air service. *(Ullstein Bilderdienst)*

ABOVE: The so-called Trinity: Dr. Hugo Eckener, Count Zeppelin, and Captain Peter Strasser at the Nordholz naval airship base during World War One *(Archiv der Luftschiffbau Zeppelin GmbH)*

LEFT: Captain Peter Strasser, the dedicated chief of Germany's Naval Airship Division and the leader of the zeppelin bombing campaign against Britain in the Great War *(Archiv der Luftschiffbau Zeppelin GmbH)*

ABOVE: Lieutenant Commander Heinrich Mathy, one of the finest airship commanders of the war, and his young bride, Hertha, in a honeymoon photo taken at Freidrichshafen in July 1915. A little over a year later Mathy was killed on a raid over London. *(Courtesy Frau Hertha Mathy)*

Zeppelin raider L33 was set on fire by its crew after crash-landing in a field at Little Wigborough, Essex, on September 23, 1916. *(Courtesy of the author)*

In the murk of an early morning mist, the reparations airship LZ126 takes off from Friedrichshafen at the start of the first zeppelin crossing of the Atlantic to America, October 1924. *(Courtesy of the author)*

Dr. Eckener and officers of the LZ126 are welcomed by President Calvin Coolidge at a reception at the White House on October 15, 1924. Coolidge stands sixth from left, Eckener fourth, and Lehmann third. To the right of Coolidge is Secretary of State Curtis Wilbur, with von Schiller third from the right. *(Süddeutscher Verlag Bilderdienst)*

Dr. Eckener (center), Captain Ernst Lehmann (left), and Captain Hans von Schiller (second from right) meet with automobile tycoon Henry Ford (right) to discuss Zeppelin business following the 1924 America flight. *(Archiv der Luftschiffbau Zeppelin GmbH)*

The *Graf Zeppelin* soars over the High Alps on one of its many tour flights over Switzerland. *(Courtesy of the author)*

Dr. Eckener on the bridge of the Dream Machine *(Courtesy of the author)*

The forward part of the *Graf*'s control car during the World Flight, showing elevator man Knut Eckener (left) at the wheel with controls at head height, rudder man (center) at the wheel up front, and Captain Hans Flemming (right) as watch officer in command *(Courtesy of the author)*

Lunch in the *Graf*'s elegant saloon: chef Otto Manz (far left), chief steward Heinrich Kubis (standing near window), and cabin boy Ernst Fischbach (foreground) *(AKG London)*

LEFT: A passenger cabin for two on the *Graf Zeppelin (Courtesy of the author)*

ABOVE: Lady Hay and Dr. Eckener on the *Graf*'s bridge during the first passenger flight to America, 1928. The only female on board, Lady Hay was to become the first woman to arrive in America from Europe by air. *(Courtesy of the author)*

Hugo Eckener and his companions ride down New York's Broadway in a tumultuous ticker-tape parade celebrating their 1928 Atlantic crossing. *(Ullstein Bilderdienst)*

The *Graf*'s shadow glides over the forested swamps of the Siberian wilds on the toughest stage of the 1929 around-the-world flight. *(Archiv der Luftschiffbau Zeppelin GmbH)*

In Japan, crowds mobbed the hangar doors for a glimpse of the fabulous "King of the Air" following its sensational arrival over Tokyo on the 1929 World Flight. *(Hulton Getty)*

Around-the-world passengers and Japanese geisha girls pose for a last photo after lunch at Kasumigaura airship base. Moments later the passengers will embark on the *Graf* for the first nonstop Pacific crossing by air. The King of Spain's physician, Dr. Jeronimo Megias, stands in the center, German journalist Max von Geisenheyner is far left, with Hearst reporters Karl von Wiegand just behind him and Lady Hay just in front. *(Courtesy of the author)*

The moment after the *Graf Zeppelin*'s landing at Lakehurst at the completion of the American version of the World Flight. With nearly twenty-two-thousand miles of the planet behind him, a jubilant Dr. Eckener leans out of the control car window to shake the hands of well-wishers. *(Süddeutscher Verlag Bilderdienst)*

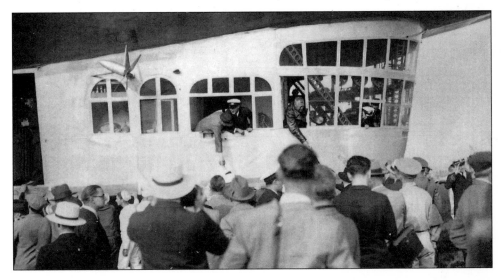

Hugo Eckener salutes the cheering crowds as he rides through New York with the chief of the New York Police. *(Süddeutscher Verlag Bilderdienst)*

The populace of Friedrichshafen welcomes the *Graf Zeppelin* home at the end of the final leg of its historical World Flight. By the end of the journey, it had flown six thousand miles farther than the circumference of the Earth. *(Archiv der Luftschiffbau Zeppelin GmbH)*

The duty mechanics in the port engine gondolas enjoy a privileged view of one of the pyramids of Gizeh during the *Graf*'s Egypt flight in the spring of 1931. *(Courtesy of the author)*

The *Graf* descends to its rendezvous with the Russian icebreaker *Malygin* on the ice-strewn sea off Franz Josef Land during the Arctic reconnaissance flight of 1931. *(Bildarchiv Preussischer Kulturbesitz)*

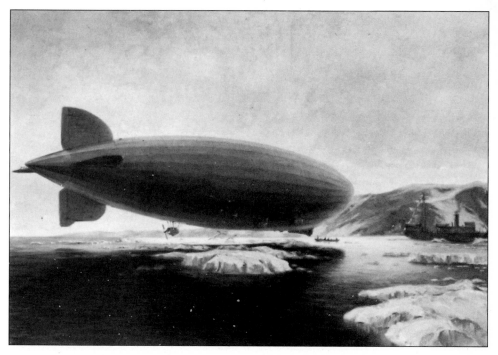

Repairs often had to be made during flight. Over the southern Atlantic in 1933, the soon-to-be-famous German photographer Alfred Eisenstaedt captured a crewman being lowered down the *Graf*'s side to tend to some damaged fabric. *(Rex Features. Life Magazine/Time Warner)*

LZ129 *Hindenburg* under construction at Friedrichshafen. This is a view from the rear of this complex structure, with part of the tail cone standing vertically on the left and part of the tailplane spar sticking out on the right. *(Courtesy of the author)*

In a stiff breeze, the vast bulk of the *Hindenburg* is hauled to earth by a straining naval ground crew and anyone else around during the ship's descent to the Naval Air Station at Lakehurst, New Jersey. *(Ullstein Bilderdienst)*

The noisiest place on the ship, one of the *Hindenburg*'s four engine gondolas, where three mechanics kept two-hour watches by day, three-hour watches by night *(Ullstein Bilderdienst)*

Passengers look down at the incomparable view of the planet through the tilted windows of one of the *Hindenburg*'s spacious promenade decks. *(Süddeutscher Verlag Bilderdienst)*

The *Hindenburg*, the world's
biggest aircraft, flies past the
Empire State Building, the
world's tallest building, on
its way to final destruction,
May 6, 1937. *(Corbis
Bettmann)*

The beginning of the end: LZ129 *Hindenburg* explodes in a hydrogen fire-
ball over Lakehurst field, New Jersey, May 6, 1937. *(Bildarchiv Preussischer
Kulturbesitz)*

perished in a failed transatlantic-flight attempt. An American passenger plane had flown nonstop from California to New York to demonstrate the feasibility of a transcontinental passenger service. A Royal Air Force pilot had reached a speed of 350 miles per hour in a fighter plane. A young American woman pilot had been killed in the Pacific Coast–to-Cleveland women's air race. Even as the *Graf Zeppelin* had been terrifying God-fearing peasants in the Siberian wilderness, it seemed that aviation scientists had been "investigating the flying apparatus that once enabled angels to fly back and forth from earth to heaven in seconds."

During its time on the ground, the airship had been undergoing a thorough overhaul, with a hundred Japanese mechanics working around the clock to repair, refuel, regas, and revictual it for its next great leap across the ocean. Some seventy-five-thousand pieces of mail were already on board. The last items to be loaded consisted of fresh vegetables and dry ice, nine carrier pigeons to carry press dispatches to Tokyo for onward filing to London and New York, and a parachute with which to throw any stowaway overboard—one had already been caught in the hangar earlier in the day, a seventeen-year-old boy dressed in a kimono. As the day progressed, the crowd grew, many arriving on special trains from Tokyo, till around half a million people surrounded the airship field.

A little after two o'clock on the morning of August 22, the passengers embarked for the long haul to America. Professor Karklin was not among them for the next leg of the flight, and three new Japanese passengers replaced the ones who had flown in from Germany: Lieutenant Commander Ryunosuke Kusaka of the Imperial Japanese Navy, Major Schinichi Shibata of the army, and Dofu Shirai, a reporter from the Nippon Demp News Agency, who admitted he was "scared to death."

Red-eyed from exhaustion at the end of the hottest day of the year, Dr. Eckener was on the bridge supervising the countdown to takeoff. Conditions were perfect, the field was brilliantly illuminated by batteries of searchlights and beacons, the ceremonies of departure were on cue, the band played the national anthems of Germany and Japan; toasts were drunk, heels clicked, farewells exchanged, the ground officer's whistle blew, and the ship began to be hauled out of the hangar.

Then came a serious mishap. One of the ground handling trolleys snagged on its rail, forcing the rear engine car sharply down against the hangar floor and snapping one of its struts. The Japanese officer in charge of that section of the ground crew was mortified, believing he would be cashiered on the spot and obliged to commit suicide, along with all his men. But Eckener and von Schiller hastened to his defense. Happens all the time, they lied, could have happened to anyone, soon get it mended, be off by tomorrow at the latest. The passengers were no less laconic. "Now isn't that the dickens!" drawled Bill Leeds.

Although the damage was repaired by midnight, half a gale was blowing across the shed, and it was impossible to bring the ship out. Eckener sat on a chair outside the hangar, determined that the moment the wind dropped he would give the order for takeoff regardless of officialdom and protocol. As always, the ship and the mission were his overriding priorities.

At lunchtime the passengers, who had been camping out in the zeppelin, were taken off to a restaurant in a nearby town. They had barely sat down to table when a phone call came through. Commander Eckener was going to take off at three sharp. All passengers must return to the airship station forthwith. The launch was already in progress by the time they got back. The German ground officers, commanded by Captain von Schiller, were watching the Japanese ground crew's every move. All were determined that this time nothing should go wrong. Just after three o'clock Dr. Eckener joined the Japanese navy officers in the corner of the hangar, where they toasted his success with Japanese wine. Then he walked to the rear of the ship and inspected the repaired engine car for the final time. He stayed on the ground as long as was necessary, and then, as whistles were blown and orders shouted in shrill Japanese, and the *Graf Zeppelin* began to slide slowly out of the hangar, he opened the door and jumped in.

Once the *Graf* was clear of the hangar, the motors were started, the lines cast off, and the order was shouted: "*Lift her! Lift her!*" With one accord the ground handling crew hurled the giant ship into the sky, then stood openmouthed with astonishment as they saw the effect of their action, for the *Graf* was soaring rapidly skyward above their heads. It was 3:13 P.M. on August 23. As the ship floated upward, the passengers broke into cheers audible below, and the crowd on the ground erupted too. "It is impossible to imagine that people as undemonstrative as the Japanese should show so much emotion," noted Sir Hubert Wilkins, observing the scene below from his favorite window seat. "Admirals in uniform danced and shouted like schoolboys. High officials tossed their hats into the air. The ground crew clapped and clapped. Thousands of people roared '*Banzai!*'" Then the rumble of the engines drowned all other sounds as the airship turned toward the east and the ocean and the black storm clouds along the sea horizon. The first nonstop crossing of the Pacific by air had begun.

Tapping away in her cabin amid a litter of geisha-house fans, Japanese dolls, and other souvenirs, Lady Hay wrote an elegiac note of farewell:

> *Aboard the Graf Zeppelin, Aug. 23. - (By Carrier Pigeon)*
> *Japan, like a lovely mirage, beckons tantalizingly from the*
> *fading distance. The garden-like country with its doll-like*
> *houses was a wonderful panorama. We have just come out of a*
> *beautiful dream, a flowery Utopia, where every one is kind,*
> *smiling, helpful and courteous. . . . It is a happy world—this*
> *world of the Zeppelin.*

She entrusted her report to the first carrier pigeon to be released from the *Graf Zeppelin*. Four others were released later, though only two were known to have reached their destination.

To all on board, the Japanese minister of the navy, Admiral Hyo Takarabe, sent a message of goodwill: "We owe it to science, civilisation, humanity and international friendship to forward this noble aerial enterprise, in which we have recognised a significance entitling it to the foremost place in the history of civilisation. . . . We now offer fervent prayers that the ship will navigate the virgin Pacific in safety to the other shore. I bid them bon voyage."

For this historic flight Dr. Eckener was relying heavily on weather data radioed to the airship from a network of weather stations. Such information was critical to intercontinental airship flying, never more so than over an ocean where he had never flown before. The Japanese had completed a weather survey of the western Pacific and reported that the conditions the *Graf* was heading into were good. Seven steamers of the American Dollar Line, strung across the Pacific, had been lined up to provide meteorological reports on the way across, and the San Francisco Weather Bureau would transmit reports twice daily during the *Graf*'s approach to the California coast.

Even before takeoff Eckener was aware that there was a storm front awaiting him out there—the same typhoon that had passed over Tokyo the previous day was now heading out to sea at a speed slower than the *Graf*'s. Eckener knew it would be generating a strong southwesterly wind, which would, if he could somehow take advantage of it, greatly enhance the ship's speed. Living up to his reputation as the "Storm King," he had barely got up to cruising height before he set off in chase of the typhoon. "Within less than three hours," he wrote, "we got into an increasingly stiff north wind—a sign that we were approaching the rear of the typhoon. Towards the east we saw a dark cloud-bank towering, with heavy thunderstorm formations extending far to the south, directly across our course. The sun was setting and illuminated the tremendous cloud-peaks with red-and-gold light. It was an unforgettable picture."

Captain Flemming had the bridge at this point, but Eckener, Lehmann, and von Schiller were there too, with weather expert Dr. Seilkopf at the weather chart, Navigation Officer Pruss at the navigation desk, and Chief Navigation Officer Wittemann on the crucially important elevator wheel. "We had to find a way through the squall-front extending to the south," Eckener wrote later, "so we turned somewhat to the south and soon found a gap between two thunderstorms and slid through."

"Slid" was not exactly the word the passengers would have used to describe that terrifying operation. To the normally unflappable polar aviator Sir Hubert Wilkins, the scene looked "fearsome," with dark, angry clouds low down to a troubled sea, and lightning flickering. "Eckener had no information on the violence of the storm," Wilkins noted. "But he reckoned he had the experience to handle it, so he went straight in."

The *Graf* was caught in an uprushing current of air of tremendous force. In a few seconds it was carried up three hundred feet, then the bow dipped steeply and it plunged downward like a rock. All around, lightning flashed, the first the ship had ever flown through. In Wilkins's cabin a shower of navigation books, almanacs, diaries, protractors, and cameras fell on his head. Two passengers slept through it all, but most of the others rushed into the saloon. Poised and cool as ever, Lady Hay came from her cabin, "her eyes sparkling," her colleague von Wiegand noted, "and with colour in her cheeks that is rarely seen except when danger is present." The Americans Rosendahl, Richardson, and Leeds were leaning out of the windows, watching the play of the elements, and the three Japanese sat as unemotional as statues. Then the ship rose to an even keel, and Wilkins felt a curious motion, "as if walking on a great big rubber cushion."

This was the worst storm the *Graf* had encountered since the beginning of the flight, and in force, though not in duration, it exceeded even the storm that had damaged it on its first Atlantic crossing. "It was sharp, intense and dramatic," reported von Wiegand. It lasted barely half an hour. At the outer edge of the storm the ship rose sharply, but Wittemann at the helm was waiting for this, and with extraordinary expertise he compensated for it with the elevators. Then Dr. Eckener came into the saloon from the bridge. He looked in good spirits, and in his voice von Wiegand detected "a queer little note of triumph" as he told the passengers: "We have broken through. The worst is over."

At dinner that evening Eckener was in the highest good humor, seated at table with von Wiegand, Seilkopf, Iselin, Gerville-Réache, and, as always, Lady Hay. To her and von Wiegand he presented a basket of choice liqueurs and rewarded himself with a glass of sherry from Walter Spiel, the famous restaurateur of Munich. Eckener talked and laughed—what the storm conditions were all about, why men were better chefs than women—"all this," observed Lady Hay, "with a humorous wrinkling of his handsome, weather-beaten face."

In the middle of it all, the full moon rose above the horizon, blood-red and streaked with black clouds. "Have you seen the American moon?" Colonel Iselin cried out. "It's bigger than any moon I've ever seen in Europe—and different!" Eckener was drinking red wine, Lady Hay noticed. That was a good sign: it meant he was relaxed and going to bed for the night. If he had been drinking white wine it would have meant there was an emergency expected and that he was going to stay on the bridge.

But there was one unhappy note. The little black cat that had been the airship's mascot on the flight to Tokyo was missing. It had disappeared during the first day at Kasumigaura, and an intensive search had failed to find it. It now seemed likely that it had walked off the ship after landing and chosen to take up residence in Japan.

For the next four or five hours, following winds pushed the *Graf Zeppelin* briskly along at almost a hundred miles per hour across the North Pacific. Commander Rosendahl, a keen connoisseur of clouds—"one of nature's most beautiful displays"—sat entranced by the richness of the collection. There were what he called "rotting cheesecloth clouds," "smokescreen," "snowdrift," and "whipped-cream" clouds, clouds the shape of skyscrapers and castles, hills and valleys and huge ice fields, then sudden brief gaps where the blue Pacific flashed up like a conjuring trick. Sometimes the ship's shadow went racing along over the cloud mass "like a huge shark swimming alongside," sliding over the tops like a surfboard or canoe, and sometimes gorgeous rainbows formed and melted into thin air, "almost close enough to touch for the pot of gold."

Gradually the ship passed beyond the influence of the typhoon, and Eckener was forced to hunt the sky for favorable wind currents. He headed east-northeast toward the Aleutian Islands, rising from the thirty-fifth parallel of north latitude to the forty-sixth, where the *Graf* entered a zone of westerly winds that pushed it along for the remaining two-thirds of the flight.

Los Angeles was sixty-two hundred miles away, and there was enough fuel on board for a hundred hours' flying on all engines, which was ample. Flight endurance, therefore, was not a problem, though navigation was. The great circle route from Japan to America lay to the south of the Aleutians, the foggiest area of the North Pacific, with fog about 40 percent of the time. Thick, clammy fog or dense cloud engulfed the ship for much of the remainder of the crossing, and when there was no fog there was driving rain and the darkness of night. The *Graf* flew through this atmospheric opaqueness for two days, and for two-thirds of its breadth the Pacific Ocean was invisible to those who were flying over it. For up to twelve hours at a stretch, as Eckener tacked this way and that like a sailing ship's captain, "feeling" for the west-northwest wind he believed was up there somewhere, visibility was less than the length of the ship.

Reckoning the *Graf*'s position and keeping an accurate course through this soup made huge demands on the expertise of the navigators, Pruss and Wittemann. Sometimes the ship was taken up to nearly four thousand feet so that sun observations could be made for course and distance, sometimes down to four hundred to drop flares on the water to calculate drift, or to drop a "fog log," whose explosive echo indicated how far the ship was from the surface of the sea. Without the instruments on the bridge it might have been a losing battle. In pride of place was the efficient but weighty gyrocompass with a vernier attachment, fixed in front of the rudder control man, which indicated immediately the slightest change of course to within a fraction of a degree.

It was the opinion of Sir Hubert Wilkins, who as a polar pilot had a keen interest in air navigation problems such as this, that without this compass and a pilot capable of flying entirely on instruments, an airplane would have found it impossible to keep a course and even stay in the air in these conditions. Though there could be no certainty as to the accuracy of the *Graf*'s navigation until they could take a fix on a known landmark, there was a general feeling in the navigation room that at any given time they were very near where they thought they were on the map.

In thirty hours passengers and crew had only two or three sightings of the sea. Once they saw three white whales, another time several huge sunfish and some monstrous-looking creatures they could not identify. Sometimes, when the gondola was skipping through the tops of the rainclouds, they were entranced by the rainbows and haloes and parabolas that were thrown up around them. During the night they crossed the international date line, the 180th meridian of east longitude, so that when they woke up the next morning it was still the same day it had been when they went to bed. This led to yet another record being broken on this record-breaking world flight: it was the first time that anyone had flown in an airship all day and all night for two Saturdays in succession in a forty-eight-hour period.

As the miles went by and they drew nearer to America, racing along the forty-fifth parallel with a favorable wind behind them, the ship's bow pointing almost directly at Portland, Oregon, the excitement on board grew by the hour, and even among the non-American passengers there was a feeling they were nearly "home." Late on the night of Saturday, August 24, Karl von Wiegand sent his most bullish dispatch to date. They were thundering along on all five engines, he reported, and only twenty-four hundred miles northwest of San Francisco, so they should be in sight of the American coast by eight o'clock the following night. "Marvellous airship," he enthused. "Marvellous journey. Marvellous speed. Absolutely astounding everyone on the *Graf Zeppelin*, including that wise old air hawk, Commander Eckener." For this veteran reporter, a seasoned campaigner in war and peace, nothing in his life had equaled these last few hours on the *Graf*, pounding on to America at nearly a hundred miles per hour, pushed on by a following wind:

> I stood on the bridge at midnight. The *Graf* was quivering as if driven by a great force, racing over the Pacific, dodging the storms, pushing the clouds away. It was very dark, except for the dim light cast over the compass and the various indicators. The helmsmen were silently twirling the wheels. Standing, peering out of the windows to study the heavens and watch for danger signals, or if all was clear, huddled in a chair in the darkest corner—that was Dr. Eckener. Clouds raced by the moon, stars came and disappeared. There was a thrill of exhilaration and a wonderful feeling of freedom. They were hours that can never be erased from memory.

Fog gave way to saturating rain, and soon the bridge was awash. Eckener still had a high fever from his ptomaine poisoning, but he stuck to the bridge as long as he could. Seeing how frail he looked, Karl von Wiegand made him some tea from his own private supply from China costing an astronomical twenty dollars a pound, and next morning Eckener came down to breakfast "looking quite fresh again" and had his first meal in three days.

Toward midafternoon on Sunday, August 25, the *Graf* passed over an American cargo ship, which radioed its position as thirteen miles north of Point Sur, Monterey County, a hundred miles south of San Francisco. The *Graf*'s position, as calculated by the ship's navigation officers after two difficult days and nights of almost continuous dead reckoning, was barely eight miles out; when Rosendahl learned this he burst into spontaneous applause. First to actually sight land, at 3:42 P.M., was Bill Leeds, who suddenly abandoned his caviar and champagne, leapt over to a window to sniff the air, smelled land, and then saw it. Excitement mounted, and soon the bridge and navigation room was crowded with passengers, all straining to get their first glimpse of California from the air. Dr. Megías toasted Eckener, his crew, and his ship. Not even Eckener could conceal his emotion, though he did his best to keep a face like granite.

By late afternoon the bridge officers could see San Francisco dead ahead, and at 6:06 P.M. the *Graf* made its American landfall above the offshore islets of the Farrallones. Just over twenty minutes later, with the Stars and Stripes blazoned across the rudder window, Lady Hay at the wheel and Dr. Eckener murmuring in her ear, "Beautiful, beautiful . . . Nature has been kind to San Francisco," they came flying in over the Golden Gate. The flight had taken sixty-eight hours, twenty-nine minutes, over a distance of 5,380 miles from coast to coast, at an average speed of over seventy-eight miles per hour, the fastest aerial crossing of the most significant span of the Pacific to date, and the longest overwater flight ever made.

Karl von Wiegand's exclusive dispatch to the Hearst newspapers spelled it out:

> On board Graf Zeppelin, *Hearst-Zeppelin World Flight.-*
> Over San Francisco, Aug. 25, -
> The Pacific has been conquered. There will be no other "first flight" over that great ocean.
> This will go down as the greatest of all air adventures up to the present time. It will stir the imagination and inspire coming generations.

Eckener could be a reticent, even dour and withdrawn, man, but for a moment over San Francisco, he lapsed into a rare and heartfelt eloquence:

> As we steered inland at 1,600 feet and viewed the fabulous scene, we were deeply affected and even moved to tears. The setting sun flooded sea and land and the surrounding mountains with warm, golden light and painted an extraordinary picture. And the reception which this beautiful city had prepared for us was no less magnificent. Squadrons of planes flew out to meet us and escorted us past the entrance. The vessels lying in the harbour and at the docks had dressed ship, their whistles sounded a greeting, accompanied by the tooting of thousands of motor car horns in the streets. We needed both eyes and ears to appreciate the enthusiasm of our welcome. Many times had we experienced such receptions, but this one, after our long and monotonous flight above clouds and fog, has remained unforgettable in my mind for its warmth and beauty.

By the standards of the age, the statistics of the flight were stunning: Statue of Liberty to Lizard Point, England—America to Europe—in forty-two hours, forty-two minutes. New York to Paris in less than forty-eight hours. Berlin to Tokyo—Europe to the Far East—in less than four days. Tokyo to San Francisco—Asia to America—in sixty-eight hours, fifty-one minutes. New York to San Francisco via the broad Atlantic, the length of Europe, the breadth of Asia, and the vast expanse of the Pacific in less than seventeen days, with a four-day stop in Friedrichshafen and three days in Japan.

It began to seem possible that the *Graf Zeppelin* might break the around-the-world air record of twenty-three days, fifteen hours, twenty-one minutes, eight seconds, set the previous year by Henry Mears, Charles Collyer, and Tailwind the terrier. By comparison with the *Graf*'s four days' flying time from Germany to Japan, Mears and Collyer's monoplane had taken six days from France to Japan. To beat the record, the *Graf Zeppelin* had to pass over the Statue of Liberty by

4 P.M. on August 31, which meant overflying the Pacific Ocean and the American continent in eight days.

What were the reasons for the *Graf*'s success so far? According to Captain Lehmann, they were careful preparation, a good crew, a good ship, meteorological navigation, and good luck. To this Sir Hubert Wilkins added a sixth element: "Eckener's ability to read weather and judge storms and take advantage of conditions that were totally obscure to most passengers on board." Having weather reports along the route and an expert on board to interpret them was a crucial factor in the *Graf*'s achievement.

Eckener lingered only a quarter of an hour over San Francisco before taking the ship south down the coast toward Los Angeles, 450 miles away. Just before eleven o'clock that night, the *Graf* flew over Hearst Castle at San Simeon, the fabulous estate of the man who had made the world flight possible, the legendary press tycoon William Randolph Hearst. To everybody's surprise, the castle was enveloped in darkness. Nobody, it seemed, was awake, nobody apparently cared that the great ship was passing overhead. And then suddenly hundreds of dazzling lights were switched on, flooding the press magnate's palace and the surrounding grounds. It was, Eckener noted, "a special and memorable surprise," and he immediately radioed the ship's patron with his thanks.

In the early hours of the morning of Monday, August 26, after a leisurely cruise down the California coast, the *Graf Zeppelin* arrived in the vicinity of Los Angeles. It was still dark, but the great city was brilliantly lit with millions of lights patterned in geometrical precision, entrancing all those who were still up to see it, for electric illumination on this scale was still rare, and to be in a position to fly over it at night even rarer. Indeed, for many on board the *Graf*, the most memorable moments of the entire flight were arriving over San Francisco at sunset ("the art of nature," as Lady Hay put it) and over Los Angeles by night ("the art of man").

It was Eckener's most basic rule never to land at a strange field in the dark, so he stood off till dawn while the passengers slept. At five o'clock, as the new day broke, a smoke bomb went off at the landing place at Mines Field, Los Angeles Municipal Airport, informing the ship that the ground crew was in place and all was in order for landing. Escorted by fifty naval planes, the *Graf* headed in out of the pink dawn for the completion of the Pacific leg of the world flight.

On the ground the excitement was intense. Searchlight beams roamed the sky in an attempt to pick out the approaching airship. Half a million people had flocked to Mines Field; their cars poured in in a continuous stream and were parked in every direction for miles around. Twelve hundred police, fire department, U.S. Navy, and Marine Corps personnel stood guard around the floodlit field. Smoking and flashlight photography were strictly forbidden. NBC had organized the most ambitious live outside broadcast in history to cover the *Graf*'s arrival, with a hookup that reached listeners all over the United States and much of the rest of the world, Germany included. In an accompanying aircraft, Herbert Hoover Jr., son of the U.S. president, was giving a running commentary on the *Graf*'s approach, while down at the landing ground NBC commentator Jennings Pierce was peering anxiously through the dawn mists for his first sight of the ship.

The laws of physics governing the behavior of lighter-than-air airships are very different, and rather more complex and contrary, from those governing heavier-than-air planes. The buoyant lift of an airship is greatly affected by the temperature of the hydrogen in its gas cells in relation to the temperature of the surrounding air, and an airship commander ignores this at his peril. At sixteen hundred feet above Mines Field, the *Graf* entered an "inversion," a component of Los Angeles's famous smog, in which the temperature above the interface stood at seventy-seven degrees, while below it registered only sixty-six, due to the cooling effect of the night and the cold air that had flowed down from the mountains. For an airship of the *Graf Zeppelin*'s size, a cooling of the air by only one degree increased the lift of the ship by around 660 pounds. The effect of this differential, therefore, was to make the ship some four thousand pounds lighter as it descended into the colder and denser ground layer, producing a phenomenon an airplane pilot would find mind-boggling.

Simply put, the ship flatly refused to go down. Only by valving a full thirty-five thousand cubic feet of hydrogen, a maneuver that would cause problems when they came to take off later, could the *Graf Zeppelin* be persuaded to come anywhere near the ground. The moment it did so was vividly described by NBC commentator Jennings Pierce: "The Zeppelin is now almost at the mooring mast. We can just barely see it because of the mist over the field. The Zeppelin is nearing the mast and two men atop of it are reaching out to grasp something. The mist is getting a little thicker, but we can just see the *Graf* touching the mooring mast. Yes . . . [excitedly] I think it has! There is a press car roaring across the field!" The giant airship had come sliding from the sky, as one reporter put it, "like a whale with tail lights, her engines drumming the roll call of man's victory over time, space and distance."

It was an achievement that in some quarters was held to augur a new era in worldwide transportation. In Washington the chief of the U.S. Bureau of Aeronautics, Rear Admiral William A. Moffett, predicted that a nonstop around-the-world dirigible service on regular schedules was aviation's next step. In Tokyo the Japanese government announced they would welcome the inauguration of a German-Russian-Japanese airship service. In Berlin the director of the Lufthansa airline company saw the time as near when airships and airplanes could profitably work side by side in commercial aviation. Few doubted that a new era of global air transport had begun.

Eckener and the passengers alighted to the by-now familiar barrage of photographs, interviews, jostles, and cheers. Via NBC radio they broadcast their impressions to the four corners of the world. Dr. Eckener was hailed as the Magellan of the air. Commander Rosendahl declared that dirigible travel might eventually supplant ocean travel: "It's far more pleasant and interesting." Lieutenant Commander Kusaka of the Japanese Navy was impressed by the international harmony on board: "If nations could get on like that, there would be real hope for permanent peace." Lady Grace Hay-Drummond-Hay attracted almost as much interest as the *Graf*'s commander. "I want a manicure, a bath and some sleep," she told a woman reporter. The reporter had expected an Amazon dressed in man's clothing. Instead she met a slim, feminine, good-looking woman in a yellow blouse and modish black hat who looked as if she were on her way to a bridge party rather than disembarking from a historic venture. She had averaged three hours' sleep per night on the Pacific flight, and none at all the previous night. "It was all so wonderful, I didn't want to miss it," she said.

The stopover on America's West Coast was to be a short one. The run for the record for the circumnavigation of the earth was on, and Eckener wanted to be back in the air as soon as the ship was ready for departure. "We sail tonight," he announced, "and for the *Graf Zeppelin* and for Germany a new world record." The planned stay of two to three days was cut to less than one. All invitations were turned down, and the usual round of official functions was reduced to one— William Randolph Hearst's grand banquet that evening, the start time of which was brought forward by one hour.

With the ship secured to the mooring mast and only a duty crew on board to oversee refueling, Dr. Eckener, the passengers, and the rest of the crew drove off into town to make use of the remaining hours in Los Angeles. Some shopped; some fulfilled business appointments; some, like Dr. Megías, went on a tour of Hollywood and had themselves photographed with the stars. In Los Angeles's grandest hotel, the Ambassador, Eckener and his senior officers and passengers were accommodated in a style befitting world heroes. Eckener himself was installed, appropriately, in the Lindbergh Suite, where he chose to rest under guard behind closed doors. "Let no one disturb me," he ordered. "For no purpose, at no time, under no circumstances."

The Hearst party at the Ambassador started at five o'clock. It was a glittering affair. Two thousand guests had been invited: VIPs, celebrities, and film stars. But Dr. Eckener was ill at ease. His mind was on the final leg of the flight and the world record that was the *Graf*'s for the taking. The weather forecast was good, with favorable winds likely to assist the ship on a swift crossing of the American continent. The *Graf* was in perfect shape, and a painstaking examination of its structure and machinery revealed no flaws of any kind after the Pacific flight. Thirty-six thousand pieces of mail had already been stowed in the hold, and the passengers had been advised that they must be back on board by eleven sharp. Eckener was anxious to be away.

There was another component to his anxiety. Landing the *Graf* at Los Angeles had proved difficult, and he feared that the takeoff would prove even more so. An inversion works two ways, preventing an airship from coming down through its top layer or going up through its bottom layer. When Eckener finally got away from the banquet, he arrived at the ship to find Captain Flemming, the duty watch officer, in a state of grave concern. "Doctor," he said, "the ship is too heavy and won't rise."

This was a rare predicament in Eckener's experience. Calculating the amount of hydrogen and fuel that had been taken on board during the refueling and regassing of the ship, he concluded that there had been insufficient hydrogen available to replace all the gas that had been valved during the landing, and that further hydrogen had been lost during the afternoon when the gas cells heated up in the sun, causing the gas to expand and blow off through the automatic valves. As the gas cylinders at the airfield were now empty, it would be impossible to refill the cells, so the only way the ship could be weighed off was to lighten it by disembarking part of the crew—six men would have to travel on to Lakehurst by rail—and reducing fuel and water ballast to an absolute minimum. But even when this was done, the ship floated up only a few feet in the cool ground layer of air, and at once became heavy when it reached the warmer upper layer. There was only one option left: to take the ship up aerodynamically, like an airplane. This was a risky maneuver, but there was no alternative.

"All engines, flank speed!" Eckener ordered.

The engine telegraphs were set to full speed and the *Graf* began to move along the ground, gathering momentum, with the after gondola barely fifteen feet above the ground. Suddenly, dead ahead, Eckener saw red warning lights on top of the towers of a high-tension line running diagonally across the field at a height of at least sixty-five feet. If catastrophe was to be avoided, the ship *had* to climb over the wires. More elevator had to be applied to lift up the nose of the ship, but this depressed the tail. The lower fin and rudder hit the ground, ploughing a furrow. "What a sickly feeling," noted Rosendahl, "bouncing along in a craft not fitted with landing wheels. Overboard went even provisions from the galley in the effort to lighten up. And still she did not rise."

The crowd on the ground looked on aghast as the *Graf* careered toward the line of high-tension cables. Most of the passengers on board thought this was not only the end of the world flight, but the end of the world as well—"an overdraft," as Karl von Wiegand put it, "on the bank of good luck." Rosendahl recalled: "How intensely those danger signals burned that night as we raced towards them at ever-increasing speed. Would the ship never feel the dynamic effect and start climbing? The rate-of-climb meter must be stuck. And say, this ship is filled with hydrogen!" With barely three feet to spare, the control car just cleared the electricity line. But this wasn't the end of it, as Rosendahl, an experienced rigid airship pilot, well knew:

> The ship has a tail some 700 feet astern and below, and trigonometry suddenly stares me in the face with the fact that at an angle of 10 to 12 degrees in that length, the stern is quite some vertical distance below the wires. I don't blame the people on the ground for scattering like rabbits. Is Dr. Eckener never going to give the word to shift the elevators to lift the tail—yes, literally to hurdle the stern over the wires, with the bow pointed down towards the ground at fifty miles an hour? He nods. His son, Knut, spins the wheel. Down goes the bow even though we are not so terribly high off the ground. But up goes the stern. That is what counts. The telephone rings. A thoughtful officer in the darkness aft reports that the tail has cleared the wires. Reverse the controls and climb once more! She responds. Thank God that's over. And as those in the control car glanced about with sickly but happy relieved expressions, not a trace of California tan remained on any face. We had narrowly averted what might have been the greatest aerial catastrophe in history.

Leaving behind a trail of vegetables, cans, boxes, packs of tea, and cases of ginger ale, the *Graf Zeppelin* began to climb, a bedlam of car horns braying a farewell salute. It had been a very close-run thing. "After a tremendous strain I finally could relax," Eckener wrote, "but for a long time after my limbs felt like lead. For just imagine what could have happened!" There had been a general feeling that once the *Graf* reached America the greatest dangers of the flight were behind them. Eckener no longer shared this view. He now thought America was potentially a greater ordeal that even Siberia had been:

> I began this flight across the American continent with qualms such as I had never before experienced. Would I be able to overcome all the difficulties that might occur? The beginning of the journey had nearly been fatal because we had no water ballast in the ship. Now we had to make the whole flight practically without ballast, and with a minimum of fuel. I thought of the unpredictable weather in this region, with tropical heat in the deserts of Arizona and Texas, with sudden cold fronts and thunderstorm fronts from the north-west, with tornadoes and hurricanes which at this season are likely to roar in from the Caribbean. I was not yet familiar with continental summer weather conditions, for our flight across Siberia had taken place at such a high northern latitude that it was hardly comparable. We had to have plenty of luck if we were to arrive at Lakehurst.

An immediate damage report ascertained that the *Graf*'s lower fin had sustained only slight damage—a few girders bent—and the ship was in adequate structural order to proceed with the flight across America. In other respects, however, the ship was not in good order. Low on gas and virtually out of ballast, the *Graf* was dangerously short of the basic materials of aerostatic flight, the ingredients that controlled buoyancy and altitude. A direct course east across the high Sierras and the Rockies in this condition was out of the question. Eckener's only option was to head for the flatlands, where he could maintain a low altitude and thus conserve gas and ballast. The *Graf* therefore flew south through the night to San Diego, aiming to go around the southern end of the Rocky Mountains and then make a low-level passage to Yuma on the Arizona border. Dawn found the ship on the edge of the Arizona desert, in calm airs and visibility so breathtakingly clear that the few passengers who were up could see as far south as the Gulf of California and into Mexico, and as far north as the Colorado River emerging from its mountain gorges.

That morning there was a curious "deadness" on board, as Lady Hay put it. Most passengers slept late, and when they did get up they were quiet and listless. There was no water to wash or shave with, so the men did without and Lady Hay wiped her face with cream. Some of the passengers passed the time opening their mail, which contained pressed flowers, photographs, handkerchiefs, prayers, hymns, requests for autographs, and free rides. For that first morning of the America flight, at least, it seemed a reaction had set in, an impatience, a collective urge to return to normal life after weeks in the air. For the moment the planet passing by below was of secondary interest— except to Sir Hubert Wilkins, sitting as always in his window seat, tirelessly noting the details of the mosaic of the American West laid out before him: wild dogs scampering, eagles soaring, a dead white horse by a dry riverbed, deserted old mines in the foothills, cattle crowding around a watering hole, dusty trails to nowhere.

As the sun rose and the desert air warmed up, conditions grew more turbulent and the ship began to toss about. By noon the movement had become so violent that the ship was being lifted bodily six hundred to a thousand feet at a time by the rising air masses, then sucked back down the same distance by the downdrafts. The crockery on the lunch tables in the saloon began to jump about, and the fiddleboards had to be raised just as on board an ocean liner in heavy seas. Though Eckener was not actually airsick, the possibility was sufficiently pressing for him to make a mental note never again to fly a rigid airship over a desert by day in summer.

By evening the *Graf* had completed its long swing to the south across Arizona and New Mexico and reached the border city of El Paso, Texas, where this turbulent stretch of the flight—what Eckener called "our galloping horseback ride"—gave way to the calm airs over northeast Texas. All through that calm and beautiful night, the ship flew steadily on, crossing the Arkansas River in Oklahoma at dawn, heading for the Missouri at Kansas City, and on to Davenport, Iowa, and Chicago beyond. "For me," Eckener wrote, "our flight from the extreme southwest coast of California diagonally across the entire continent to New York was one of the most impressive experiences of my life." For Hubert Wilkins the flight was like a mighty drama, with the whole world as its stage. It wasn't just the huge variety of landscapes and views and regions, there was also the excitement on the ground when the dream machine passed overhead.

"But what we experienced in Chicago," Eckener wrote, "exceeded all our expectations and fantasies. What the Chicagoans produced in the way of noise-making and other signs of enthusiasm on our appearance probably set a record that can never be beaten." The big parks on the shores of Lake Michigan were packed with hundreds of thousands of people, the streets and roofs of America's second-biggest city thronged with humanity in their millions. In hospitals the patients tottered toward the windows of the wards while the doctors and nurses rushed for the roofs to look up at the *Graf* as it sailed slowly in at 5:25 P.M. and executed circles and figures of eight over the skyscrapers, the city squares, and the vast crowd in Soldier Field. Escorted by forty planes and a huge swarm of seagulls, it flew low enough for those on the ground to discern the faces of those in the air looking down at them through the gondola windows. Over all was the noise, much of it coming from the automobiles packed bumper to bumper in the worst traffic jam in Chicago's history—an uproar so deafening that even the radio commentator had difficulty making himself heard. Of all the wild welcomes in all the wild cities the *Graf* had flown over, this was the wildest. "*Fabelhaft,*" muttered Eckener, deeply moved. "Fabulous." Fifteen minutes after its first curving arrival over the city, the *Graf* was gone, swallowed up in the mists of the eastern horizon as it resumed its race to journey's end and the world circumnavigation record.

The *Graf* headed out across the great horizons of the corn belt of Illinois, bearing down toward the small town of Sterling, where rumor had it that the giant ship—"almost as long as the pasture is wide, and as wide as two windmills stacked on top of each other"—would fly over at ten the next morning. Everyone from miles around was going to be heading for Sterling at daybreak. At a little farmhouse fifteen miles out of town, the nine inhabitants were beside themselves with excitement at the prospect of the fabulous flying machine passing over their heads the next day. But when the time came to go, the grandmother refused to leave, and her eight-year-old grandson, John

McCormick, decided to stay and keep her company. "I don't want to see the Zeppelin anyway," he said, though there was nothing he wanted to see more.

He busied himself making sand castles in the yard, and time drifted slowly by. After a while he became uneasy. Something wasn't quite right. Suddenly he realized why. Years later he would recall: "We were alone, absolutely alone, and surrounded by a profound silence. The whole land, usually so full of sound and action, was empty and still. Even the animals were quiet. There was no wind, not the slightest breeze."

And then the little American farm boy heard what those distant Siberians in their wilderness settlements had heard, and soon he would see what they had seen:

> Into that remarkable silence there came from far away the smallest possible purring, strange and repetitive, gradually approaching, becoming louder—the unmistakable beating of powerful engines. I looked to the west and at first saw nothing. Then it was there, nosing down out of the clouds a half mile away, a gigantic, wondrous apparition moving slowly through the sky.
>
> "Grandma!" I screamed.
>
> She was out of the kitchen door in an instant. I pointed to the sky. The great dirigible was very low, moving ever so slowly above us. We saw every crease and contour from nose to fins. It was so low we could see people waving at us from the slanted windows of its passenger gondola.
>
> We stood entranced. Slowly, slowly the ship moved over us, beyond us, and at last was gone.
>
> We looked at each other, my grandmother and I, then silently walked to the front porch and let ourselves down on the steps. And we gazed at each other in triumph.

The boy was speechless. Not so the livestock in the barnyard and pasture. The dogs were barking madly, horses galloping, pigs squealing, chickens screaming.

"John," his grandmother said. "We have to keep it a secret. We mustn't tell the others what we saw. Because they'll be disappointed enough that they missed it. No one else will ever know. We'll just keep the Zeppelin to ourselves for ever and a day."

" 'I'll never tell,' I promised, and I never have until now."

Night fell as the *Graf Zeppelin* droned on over Lake Michigan en route to Detroit, and then across Lake Erie to Cleveland. By midnight they were over the American Goodyear-Zeppelin Company head-quarters in Akron, Ohio, and by crack of dawn they were over the skyscrapers and waterfront of New York, making for the Statue of Liberty, which marked the end of the American, or official, version of the around-the-world flight. "It was a solemn moment," wrote Lady Hay. "A solemn prayer went up in all our hearts in thanksgiving for the successful journey and safe return. My eyes and heart were full as I looked down upon New York, realising the immensity of what the Zep had accomplished."

Safely, swiftly, and efficiently, the *Graf Zeppelin* had flown sixty men and one woman, and, for part of the way, a cat, across two oceans and three continents, an around-the-world flight completed in the record flying time of twelve days and eleven minutes, in a total elapsed time (also a record) of twenty-one days, five hours, and thirty-five minutes. "We had circled the terrestrial sphere," reported an ecstatic Rosendahl. "A glorious adventure."

A crowd of some twenty-five thousand was at Lakehurst Naval Airship Station to see the *Graf* come in at the end its world flight. At 7:52 A.M. a cry went up as the great ship was sighted coming through the haze. At 8:06 A.M., as it maneuvered slowly over the landing place, the first handling line was dropped, and the *Graf* settled gently to the ground, nose first. The crowd in its excitement broke through the cordon and surrounded the ship, wildly cheering the first man off, Lieutenant Jack Richardson, who was immediately enveloped in the arms of his wife. No one else cared to follow him into the midst of this mob of well-wishers, and the ship was promptly walked into the depths of Lakehurst's huge airdock. Even so, Dr. Eckener was nearly mobbed as he made his way to the end-of-flight press conference, along with prominent passengers like Lady Hay. By now the first woman to fly around the world had finally succumbed to exhaustion and was too fatigued to give a formal interview, but she reassured the gathering: "I am the happiest girl in the world today." New Yorker Bill Leeds told a reporter that home for him meant a good bathtub full of warm water. He'd been around the entire world, he said, and seen only three bathtubs in three weeks.

"This trip," Eckener told the assembled officials and press, "has demonstrated the fact that we face the beginning of a new era of lighter-than-air transportation, and the people of the world will appreciate the rapid strides made by this branch of aeronautics—a progress which to my mind is second to none."

The *Graf Zeppelin*'s record of 21 days, 5 hours, and 35 minutes total elapsed time around the world beat Magellan's first-ever circumnavigation time by 1,103 days, 18 hours, and 25 minutes, and its flying time of 12 days and 11 minutes beat that of the U.S. Army around-the-world planes of 1924 by 3 days, 5 hours, and 52 minutes, and the 1928 circumnavigation record of Mears, Collyer, and Tailwind by 2 days, 21 hours, and 46 minutes.

The voyage set several other world records, including the fastest flight across the Atlantic, the fastest flight from New York to Paris, the fastest flight from Berlin to Tokyo, the longest nonstop flight ever made (Friedrichshafen to Tokyo, around seven thousand miles), the first nonstop flight across Siberia, the first nonstop crossing of the Pacific by air, and the first aerial crossing of the Pacific by a woman.

New York would not let Eckener and his passengers and crew creep away to rest. By radio he was requested by the New York police commissioner to prepare all on board for a triumphal entry into the city and a second ticker-tape parade up Broadway to City Hall in two years. "The enthusiasm this time was even greater than two years before," Eckener wrote, "and the number of telephone books ripped up was greater than ever before and broke all records. The enthusiasm of the New Yorkers matched the general enthusiasm of the American people."

To honor the success of the Hearst-Zeppelin around-the-world flight, President Herbert Hoover welcomed Hugo Eckener at the White House in a manner seldom accorded to a foreigner. Half the American government took time off to attend the ceremony. As Eckener was presented to him, the president remarked, "I thought the day of the great adventurers, like Columbus, Vasco da Gama, and Magellan, was in the past. Now I know such an adventurer is in my presence." Congratulating Eckener on his immense achievement, Hoover stressed that this was first and foremost a German triumph: "Its success has been due to the eminent scientific and engineering abilities of the German people, translated by your own skill and courage. You have given a most valuable service to aviation. You have lifted the spirits of men with renewed confidence in human progress."

Eckener's eyes dimmed. He had been greatly affected by his reception from the American people—even in Washington, where there had been no advance notice of his visit, the streets were lined with cheering crowds. In the government departments where he had business, the young women clerks cheered him down the corridors, just as they had cheered their own homespun hero, Charles Lindbergh, not long before.

"I am tired and quite weary," Eckener replied to the president, speaking in German and fidgeting nervously with his little yachting cap and the brass buttons of his old reefer jacket, "but immeasurably happy. The success of my trip is in large measure due to the help of the United States." His one profound regret, he went on, was that he was not able to take his record-breaking ship back to Germany himself.

Eckener was staying behind in the States for two weeks or so for strategic discussions with the president of the Goodyear-Zeppelin Corporation, Paul W. Litchfield, and government officials, shipping directors, and financial leaders regarding major plans for linking up the continents of the world by airship lines—particularly between Europe and the Americas and Far East. The world flight of the *Graf Zeppelin* had provided incontrovertible proof of the airship's capability as an intercontinental transport mode, and it was Eckener's hope that Goodyear-Zeppelin could pioneer the construction and operation of commercial airships in transoceanic service, financed in the United States but built and operated under German management—and ideally with safe American helium in their gas cells, not unsafe German hydrogen.

On September 4, 1929, the *Graf Zeppelin* under the command of Captain Lehmann finally returned home. The flight was unremarkable, except that one passenger was caught smoking a day or two before the completion of the around-the-world adventure. "The other passengers would like to have thrown the culprit overboard," Lehmann recalled. "I could not put him in irons, but the unanimous contempt of the other passengers during the rest of the voyage was punishment enough."

The *Graf* received a triumphal welcome on the completion of the German version of the around-the-world flight, having completed a total of 21,255 miles in a flying time of twelve days, twelve hours, and twenty minutes. It had failed to beat the flying-time record of the American version of the world flight by a little over twelve hours (though with a total elapsed time of twenty days, four hours, and fifteen minutes, it broke the American version of this record by one day, one hour, and forty minutes). Including the initial flight to Lakehurst and back, the *Graf Zeppelin* had flown a total of over thirty-one thousand miles on the world flight, or nearly six thousand miles more than the distance around the equator. "Such a record for such distance and payload," noted an optimistic Commander Rosendahl, "will not soon be broken."


The world flight had been brilliantly executed in both its planning and its operational stages. At first it appeared to have put the seal on the zeppelin concept. "Die Sensation der Weltfahrt ist," Max Geisenheyner observed, "dass es keine Sensation gibt." "The sensation of the world flight is that it provides no sensation." Though the *Graf Zeppelin* was basically a demonstration ship, it was superbly designed and constructed. Even so, it still had the defects inherent in the giant rigids of that time—vulnerability to weather masses and risk of hydrogen fire. The *Graf* got away with it on the world flight partly because it was a first-class aircraft, but above all because of the masterly expertise of the crew.

Inevitably, risks had been taken, especially flying such vast distances across little-known regions of the Earth. In a sense Eckener was pitting the dream machine against the planet. He succeeded, but only just. Siberia was a wild card: any hitch would have been fatal. Crossing the Stanovoy by the seat of their pants was touch and go: the slightest deviation in height and direction and they would have gone down.

Crossing the Pacific in wretched visibility was potentially hazardous but demonstrated not only the navigational skill of the officers, but also in this instance the virtue of the airship over the airplane—in those conditions an airplane crossing would have been impossible. Direst gamble of all was the takeoff from Los Angeles. They got away with it by inches, thanks entirely to the skill of Eckener. Otherwise there would have been no *Hindenburg* disaster, just a *Graf Zeppelin* catastrophe to end the zeppelin enterprise once and for all.

The German public did not see the world flight in this light, nor did rivals in Britain and America, nor the American public and big business. But the German government continued to remain skeptical, and progress toward a fully up-and-running commercial zeppelin service remained slow and uncertain. Then, less than two months after the *Graf*'s triumphal return to Germany, Wall Street went into free fall, and the entire global economy collapsed in the Great Crash of October 1929.

In the worldwide depression that followed, Germany was to suffer even more grievously than most. Industrial production was to plummet by half, and unemployment reached 6 million, with one in two men under thirty out of work. With hardship and hunger widespread, parliamentary government only survived the crash for six months, as the German people in their desperation turned to the extremist parties of the right and left, the Nazis and the Communists. Before long Hitler's Nazi Party had secured 37 percent of the vote in the Reichstag. And as the big banks closed, the nation plunged into bankruptcy.

## Chapter Six

# The Dream Becomes Reality

*The fight to conquer the air has ended. World traffic via airships has begun. It will spread out over all the seas and continents.*

CAPTAIN ERNST A. LEHMANN (1936)

T he *Graf Zeppelin* was not laid up after its marathon record-breaking flight. After more than twelve days in the air, the ship was still in perfect running order, and Eckener was determined to make maximum use of the remainder of the flying season by making short-haul promotional and publicity flights around Europe, with fare-paying passengers on board whenever possible. A number of these flights were local, for it was Eckener's aim to fly over every city, town, and village in Germany. It was the German people who had put up the money to build the *Graf*, he argued; therefore the German people had earned the right to the pleasure of seeing it fly over their heads.

Other flights in late 1929 were more ambitious. Several were over Switzerland and its wonderland of Alps and lakes, floating at the speed of a cyclist just a few hundred yards from the north faces of the Eiger and the Jungfrau and over their rugged glaciers, or down across the vineyards on the slopes of Lake Geneva's lovely shore. At two hundred marks per passenger, two hundred times the hourly wage of a qualified German worker, these joyrides were not cheap, but there was never any lack of takers. Other flights went west to Holland

and England, east to the Balkans, and south to Spain; in the summers that followed, to Budapest, Copenhagen, Helsinki, London, Moscow, Rome, Stockholm, and many other foreign capitals. In December 1929, at the end of an extraordinary year in zeppelin history, the *Graf* was finally laid up for its winter overhaul, having flown a total of seventy-three thousand miles.

Hugo Eckener now turned his mind to grander things. He had never lost sight of his great dream of an intercontinental commercial zeppelin air service. Every flight he made in the *Graf,* every speech he gave, every letter he wrote was designed to bring this ambition a step nearer. But it was a frustrating business. He had known from the outset that the *Graf Zeppelin* was too small and too slow to operate a regular, safe, and reliable service on the most profitable air route between Europe and the United States. The weather over the North Atlantic could be treacherous and unstable. Its violent thunderstorms, sudden squalls, and blanketing fogs could force an airship to divert on a roundabout route that could add a thousand miles to the flight. Bigger and more efficient super-zeppelins were needed to cope with the North Atlantic on a regular basis, but the German government dragged its feet over the possibility of funding the construction of such costly ships, and the economic crisis that followed the Great Crash seemed to rule out their construction altogether for the foreseeable future.

But the prospects were not entirely bleak. Shortly after the *Graf* was laid up, Eckener again picked up the threads of a venture he had explored a few years previously. The idea was not his own, though it conformed to his vision of a commercial transoceanic airship service. Back in 1920, before the first transatlantic zeppelin, LZ-126, had been built, let alone flown to the United States, Eckener had been approached by a wealthy Basque former sea captain named Tomas Rementeria, who had the notion of forming a fast airship link between Spain and Argentina. "No area in the world was more suitable for an airship line," he wrote to Eckener, "than the area from the Spanish coast, starting from Seville, through the trade winds and the belt of calms on the Equator to Argentina."

Eckener was inclined to agree. In terms of passenger transport, the South Atlantic was poorly provided for. No passenger planes could yet fly such huge distances across oceans, and fast, comfortable steamships operated virtually exclusively on the North Atlantic routes. Travel by sea between Europe and South America was as often as not by cargo boat, entailing irregular schedules, slow crossings, and hot and often uncomfortable accommodation. To those who could afford it, a zeppelin air service would offer a sensational alternative: fast, comfortable, reliable, and utterly memorable. In addition to Argentina, Brazil also offered a significant potential market, for a sizeable proportion of its population was of German descent.

In July 1921 Eckener set off for South America on a fact-finding mission paid for by the Basque sea captain. On the long sea voyage to Buenos Aires, he was able to observe at first hand the kind of wind and weather a commercial zeppelin could expect to encounter on flights to and from South America; he was convinced that a zeppelin service between Seville and Buenos Aires was perfectly feasible. Soon afterward, however, the political climate changed and the idea withered on the vine.

Seven years later, when the *Graf Zeppelin* was launched and its oceangoing capabilities sensationally proven by the world flight, the idea was reborn. At the end of 1929, with the *Graf* laid up for its winter refit, Eckener once again set off for South America. Once more he observed the South Atlantic weather patterns, especially the stormy squall fronts of the calm zone, or doldrums, and decided once and for all that the weather conditions along the route were entirely suitable for a scheduled airship service.

But there could be no such service without an airship hangar at the terminal point. Argentina was enthusiastic about an airship link with Europe but was reluctant to contribute to the cost of a hangar in Buenos Aires. Brazil was equally enthusiastic but was even more reluctant to commit to a hangar in Rio de Janeiro. Then Eckener had an idea:

> My own observations had taught me that in the real trade-wind zone between the 25th to 15th parallel of north latitude and 15th to 25th parallel of south latitude, the weather conditions are so uniform and almost entirely free of major disturbances that one could manage without an

airship shed and could leave the ship out at a mooring mast. Therefore we might choose Recife de Pernambuco [in northeast Brazil] as a permanent terminal and thence make the short journey on to Rio with only a brief landing there.

The governor of the state of Pernambuco, it turned out, was happy to build a landing field at Recife, complete with a mooring mast and a fuel and gas-cylinder depot for refuelling the *Graf*. For Recife, a relatively obscure seaport, to become the terminal airport for the world's first transatlantic air service would put it on the map in spectacular fashion. For much the same reason, the Spanish authorities agreed to provide similar facilities at Seville.

"At last," Eckener reported with relief, "the foundation was laid for a transatlantic Zeppelin service which was destined to be truly epoch-making in the history of aviation. . . . I intended to make the first flight a convincing demonstration in the eyes of the world."

This first voyage was to be the so-called triangular flight, from Seville to Recife and on to Rio, then from Rio via Recife to Lakehurst, and from there back to Seville. The total distance to be covered was more than eighteen thousand miles (not a great deal less than that of the world flight). By the middle of May 1930, following a feasibility flight from Friedrichshafen to Seville, the *Graf Zeppelin* was ready for its great voyage to the southern hemisphere. There was a crew of forty-three on board (insured for $360,000, or rather less than half the insurance value of the ship itself), and twenty-two passengers from seven European and South American nations, including four veterans of the world flight—Dr. Jerónimo Megías, the German newspaper reporter Dr. Gustav Kauder, and the two Hearst Press reporters, Lady Hay and Karl von Wiegand—along with senior representatives from the Lufthansa airline, the German air ministry, the U.S. Navy airship service, and interested parties from Spain, Brazil, and Argentina.

For the fare-paying passengers who were making the whole trip, the cost of a ticket was $6,500 (more than £35,000 in today's money). Once again, another major source of revenue was postage stamps. Thousands of letters and cards bearing special-issue zeppelin stamps printed in America were sent by philatelists all over the world to be postmarked on board the ship and posted off as valuable collectors' items. Altogether, the sale of these stamps raised $100,000 for the Zeppelin Company.

A little before five o'clock on the afternoon of May 18, 1930, Hugo Eckener entered the hangar at Friedrichshafen and gave the command for the ship to be weighed off and then undocked. With all the crew at their posts and the passengers cramming the saloon's flower-garlanded windows, the ship was walked out onto the landing field, and at the order "Up ship!" it floated upward amid a blizzard of dandelion down at the start of its first flight to the southern hemisphere, indeed the first nonstop flight from Europe to South America by any aircraft.

The first stage of the flight—past the Alps, over the Black Forest, down the Rhine, across Burgundy, speeding along the Rhône on the back of the mistral at 125 miles per hour, over Avignon and out into the Gulf of Lions and the blue Mediterranean as daylight faded—was idyllic. By the time the passengers assembled for breakfast at seven the next morning, the ship was approaching the southwest corner of Spain, cutting across the dry lands of Almeria and the vineyards of Malaga en route to their first staging post at Seville. The plan was to land there around five, when the air was cooler and less turbulent. Since they had time to spare, Eckener took the ship on a bonus pleasure cruise over North Africa before coming in to the Seville landing field at the appointed time in front of a huge crowd roaring its greetings.

The *Graf* rested on the stub mast for the night and in the morning took on more fuel and gas, along with a number of Spanish passengers, including the cousin of King Alfonso, the Infante Don Alfonso de Orleans. This brought the number of passengers to twenty-eight and the total on board to seventy-one, the greatest number ever carried on the *Graf*. After leaving Seville they flew over the Spanish harbor of Palos, at the mouth of the Rio Tinto, from which Christopher Columbus had sailed at the start of his voyage to America. Eckener had been dubbed "a modern Columbus" by President Hoover but felt he was more a pupil of Columbus, who "had many more setbacks to put up with than I." Looking down, Eckener reflected: "The Columbus statue at the mouth of the harbour looked up at us, we imagined, with shocked disbelief. He actually spent more days on his journey than we would spend hours. A new world of technology had arrived!"

The leg from the southwest tip of Spain to the northeast tip of Brazil was a long one. Ahead lay a vast stretch of ocean with only a few small islands—the Canaries and Cape Verde Islands on this side of the Atlantic, St. Paul's Rock and Fernando de Noronha on the other— to serve as navigational checkpoints. "We were now over the blue ocean," Eckener wrote, "and the ship flew on as softly and quietly as she always did over water. As far as the eye could see, a clear heaven spanned the sea."

Eckener set a course southwest toward Madeira, cruising for nine hours before a southerly wind, then made a heading for the Canaries when the wind veered west-southwest. "Now we were waiting the big sensation," reported Eckener, "the northeast trade wind, which, like a helpful spirit of the elements, was to take us in its arms and bear us at great speed to the south across twenty degrees of latitude—a good 1,600 miles—in constantly fair weather." The *Graf* was heading out into the broad Atlantic at sixty to seventy knots, and by three o'clock on the afternoon of May 20 it was over the Cape Verdes, where it dropped its first mailbag. By three the next morning it was near the fifth parallel of north latitude, having covered fifteen hundred miles in the last twenty hours.

The *Graf Zeppelin* now entered a critical zone, where the cool trade wind met the warm, moist air of the doldrums, generating a constant stationary front of heavy thunderstorms and squall fronts. "According to airship experts and meteorologists," noted Eckener, "this was the zone we could never pass through in a Zeppelin. We were extremely concerned as to how the ship would handle it." At four in the morning, charging blindly through the dark, moonless night, he ran straight into a heavy, rain-charged squall front:

> We could see nothing. We could only hear the rain lashing at the windows, and the elevator-man noticed the ship becoming heavy. After two or three minutes it became quieter, and we had apparently passed through the first barrier. Then in a short time we ran into a new barrier. The rain

drummed down once more, and by the ship's lights we saw grey tatters of cloud swirling past the windows. This time it lasted longer; there seemed no end to it. The water drove through the chinks and crevices of the windows and lay inches deep on the deck of the control car. Then from inside the ship it began to pour down through the canvas-covered ceiling. The ship became heavier and heavier, and I glanced anxiously at the elevator-man to see if he could hold her at her altitude.

Ten minutes later the *Graf* emerged through the cloudburst. Eckener estimated that some eight tons of rainwater had accumulated on the ship. He calculated that little more than half the ship's dynamic lift was needed to carry such a load of rain and found that the ship held up well on the elevators at an angle of four to five degrees. "This was a crucial discovery," he observed, "which lifted a great weight from our minds. We did not have to be afraid of tropical cloudbursts. If we navigated prudently, as we usually did, we could be sure of getting through the squall zone safely."

Four hours later the *Graf* crossed the equator for the first time, the first airship ever to have done so. The historic moment was celebrated with due ceremony. But instead of Neptune, God of the Sea, making an appearance as he traditionally did at sea, it was Aeolus, God of the Winds, looking extraordinarily like Hans von Schiller, who solemnly granted Dr. Eckener permission to fly his ship across the line.

Traveling on the *Graf Zeppelin* as the representative of the German air ministry was Lieutenant Commander Joachim Breithaupt, a comrade and colleague of Eckener's since the Great War, when he served as a naval zeppelin commander of distinction until he was shot down and made a prisoner of war. Breithaupt tried to remain objective, but watching Eckener at work over the South Atlantic, he could not conceal his admiration:

> The bridge is where Dr. Eckener can be found, seated or standing in his "historic" corner, hands buried in his trouser pockets, steadily gazing into the distance. He observes the passing of the clouds and the direction of the waves, contin-

uously keeping an eye on the numerous instruments informing him about the navigational status of his airship. Bent over the nautical chart he makes his decisions, based on his observations. And everybody knows perfectly well that they are correct. For here is a man able to master any critical situation with which fate may confront him. Trained by decades of experience in the building and piloting of airships, he is rightly renowned as the epitome of a pilot. Recently Lord Thomson, the English Minister for Aviation, called him "one of the most remarkable men he had ever met, a personality the like of which cannot be found in every generation." Crew and passengers have unlimited faith in such a man. Tirelessly he is concerned with the safety of the airship entrusted to his command, a concern that surpasses all other considerations. His own person is as nothing to him; all he knows is the cause and his work, to which he is devoted with all his soul.

By early afternoon, after flying more than thirteen hundred miles without sight of land or ship since leaving the Cape Verde Islands, the *Graf* arrived with impeccable accuracy at its next landmark, the hilly green islet of Fernando de Noronha and its "Finger of God" rock needle, three hundred miles off the northeast coast of Brazil. The passengers were thrilled to see their first patch of dry land for two days, and those on the island were no less thrilled to see the *Graf*. "Fernando de Noronha is a Brazilian penal colony," Eckener noted, "and we could see how its involuntary inhabitants stared up at the huge silver bird, shouting and waving with mass enthusiasm. Unexpectedly we had intruded on their isolation from the world like a supernatural miracle. With longing eyes they must have followed our flight until we vanished beneath the horizon."

In Recife, meanwhile, the excitement was mounting. Out at the airship field, former swampland on the edge of town, the activity was feverish. Though the gas-storage installation was finished on schedule, the mooring mast had been erected only a few days before. Trains were arriving from the interior packed with people eager to witness the first landing of an airship in South America. All the hotels in town were full, and the lines for tickets to the airship field grew ever longer. The demand for commemorative postage stamps was unprecedented, and mail poured in from all over the world containing money and self-addressed envelopes to be posted with the special-issue zeppelin stamps. Zeppelin fever and pro-German fervor went hand in hand.

When the *Graf Zeppelin* radioed that it was expecting to land at six o'clock that evening, a mass of people on foot and in cars, on trams and trains, hurried out to the field. Three hundred soldiers were assembled as ground crew, along with 240 policeman and 100 horsemen for crowd control, and seventy firemen in case of a blaze. As arrival time drew nearer, the grandstands began to fill with dignitaries and officials, including the state president, the governor, the president of the senate, the minister of finance, the minister of agriculture, the consuls of all the nations, and all the members of the local German colony.

From the top of the stub mast a group of excited workmen scoured the horizon for an approaching shape in the sky. The *Graf* was reported delayed by head winds, and when night fell and three searchlights were turned on, the atmosphere became even more expectant. Time passed, and the crowd continued to grow. Then, a little before eight, a young German by the name of Roland Lütjohann, who lived locally, reported:

> Suddenly a siren howled in the distance, and then a neighbouring factory joined in. There, off in the distance—was that a star or the Zeppelin? And then the ghostly ship drew over the field, vanished to the south, and reappeared in the west. With throttled motors, the ship hung in the air, and then the nose sank, the ropes were dropped, and the ground crew took hold. The *Graf Zeppelin* had landed in Pernambuco. The band played and the acclaim knew no bounds. Everyone rushed towards the colossus, crowding close together to see this *bicho,* this wonderful animal, at close range. The first passengers landed amid the loud applause of the spectators, whose enthusiasm exceeded all bounds when Commander Dr. Eckener and Captain Lehmann appeared in the grandstand.

This was, the state governor told Eckener, an "epochal event." Brazil was connected with Europe by air. The future was here. There was a big reception in town, a banquet, more speeches. "When a man achieves fame and success," Eckener later said, "what he needs most is a cast-iron stomach." Meanwhile, the complicated procedure of replenishing the ship with hydrogen and gaseous fuel continued night and day under the gaze of up-country folk, for whom the giant airship was something almost supernatural.

At two minutes before midnight on May 23, the *Graf* was off again, flying down to Rio, low along the white sand beach that stretched endlessly south of Recife, with the crashing surf rolling in from one side and the emerald forest on the other. On and on they flew, past tiny bays and river mouths and picturesque old colonial towns huddled along the shore, greeted here and there with fireworks and sirens, buffeted now and then by tropical rainstorms heavier than anything they had ever experienced, till finally, after nearly twenty-four enchanted hours in the air, "the finest part of an airship journey to South America," Eckener reckoned, they came late on the second night into Rio bay.

"The glamorous sea of light that was Rio de Janeiro, the most extravagantly illuminated city on earth, dazzled us," Eckener wrote. But he resisted the temptation to go down. The bay was unknown territory and was surrounded by high mountains. Instead he stood out to sea a little, with the engines running at low speed, and waited for daybreak. "The passengers slept on undisturbed," he wrote, "while the ship moved on absolutely steadily and almost noiselessly. When the sun rose towards 6 A.M. it flooded with its golden-red rays a landscape of such unprecedented beauty that we were silent with wonder."

By the time the *Graf* had landed at Rio's military airfield at Campo dos Affonsos, where it was held down by Brazilian troops, the sun was rising, and the gas cells were heating up fast. An hour and twenty minutes later, after the usual greetings had been exchanged between Dr. Eckener and the city fathers' welcoming party, the *Graf* took to the air again and by eight the next morning, May 26, was back on the mast at Recife.

Here they remained for two days while the ship was regassed and refueled, and Eckener sat in close discussion with Brazilian officials about ways of improving the facilities at the base. On the night of May 28 the *Graf* set off on the second leg of its three-leg flight, the first passenger airship flight from South to North America. So far the flight had gone impeccably. The *Graf Zeppelin*'s reputation as the most luxurious aircraft in the history of flight—and the most expensive mode of travel in the history of transport—remained undimmed.

Rounding the northeast tip of Brazil, Eckener set a direct course to Barbados. The plan had been to make a short intermediate landing in Cuba, partly for the interest of the Spanish passengers on board, partly in the hope that a goodwill visit by the cousin of the Spanish king might bring about closer relations between Spain and its former colony. But now the *Graf* began to pick up a stream of radio messages from the meteorological experts in Cuba, urging Eckener on no account to attempt a landing on the island. "A mass of cold air had forced its way down from Canada into the Caribbean," Eckener reported, "and was causing violent thunderstorms and squalls. The disturbances were especially severe over Cuba." There was nothing for it, he decided: the landing at Havana would have to be canceled.

By refusing to land the *Graf* in Cuba as scheduled, Eckener earned the wrath of a number of Spanish passengers who had paid big money for a ticket that promised a landing in Cuba and a flight over the Bahamas and Florida. Now they were going nowhere near any of these places but instead were going to fly over sea all the way to New Jersey. In vain Eckener tried to pacify them, explaining that it was for their safety that he had to change course and bypass Cuba, that the weather left him no choice. He returned to the control car grim-faced, Captain Flemming closing the door behind him.

"Those people back there are practically ready to tear me apart!" Eckener growled, jerking his thumb in the direction of the passenger lounge. "But I can't allow myself to be swayed by what they say or threaten. I've got to do what airmanship and navigation dictate as best."

He looked around at all the officers on the bridge. "Always remember this," he told them. "If you want to become a safe and successful Zeppelin commander, regardless of what it may cost you in popularity and prestige you *must* be able to say no. And once you say it, you have to be able to *stick* to it at the time. Don't forget, you can't command an airship and be a yes-man to the public at the same time."

Passenger goodwill soon returned, but not before Gustav Kauder, a reporter from the Ullstein publishing empire in Berlin, had radioed a sensational, untrue, and potentially damaging story that was published by the *New York Times* on June 1 under the headline WHY DID THE *GRAF ZEPPELIN* NOT GO TO HAVANA? The article contained lurid details of how a mutiny on board the zeppelin was brutally put down by the ship's officers armed with revolvers, and launched a vicious attack on Eckener for breaking his promise to land in Cuba, adding for good measure passenger complaints about the shortage of water, the no-smoking rule, and Flemming's grumpiness. "I admire Dr. Eckener as a technical man," confided one interviewee, "but not as a tour conductor." The story was picked up in the Spanish press, and the leading Madrid newspaper reported, "The flight of the *Graf Zeppelin* is a technical triumph, but a political disaster." Eckener was unmoved and unrepentant. His only response was to make sure that when the *Graf* eventually reached Lakehurst, Kauder found some other means of returning to Germany.

The *Graf* flew on. It was soon evident that the weather front that had barred its way to Cuba now barred its way to Lakehurst. The difference was that Eckener *had* to get through to Lakehurst. And that meant running headfirst into the storm. At Puerto Rico Eckener changed course more to the north, toward Cape Hatteras. At the same time the radio room began to pick up a series of urgent storm warnings from Lakehurst and Washington. Not long after midday, a towering blue-black wall of cloud appeared on the horizon. Hurtling along at ninety miles per hour on the back of a following wind, Eckener ran the *Graf* down the line of this black storm wall, looking for a point where he could break through to the west. But the wall extended for some 1,150 miles across fifteen degrees of latitude. Since there was no way around it, Eckener steered straight into it. He was never to forget what happened next:

> The airship was thrust upwards so violently that we felt
> as if we were being forced to our knees. Immediately the

bow plunged downward so fast that it felt as if the gondola floor was being jerked out from under our feet. At the same time the ship trembled in every part, and we wondered if the framework could stand the tremendous stress. As soon as she started pitching I set the telegraphs at half speed to decrease the forces acting on the ship; but the situation was still critical. In a raging turmoil of conflicting air masses we were driven up and down, back and forth.

During this drama the wind got up to forty-five miles an hour and shifted a full 180 degrees from southwest to northeast in a few seconds, while the temperature dropped from seventy-two to fifty-seven degrees and continued to fall till it reached forty-two degrees. When the *Graf* was through and the air grew calmer, Eckener told Karl von Wiegand, "This was the wickedest squall I have ever experienced, and I don't believe there could be a worse one. But you can see how the ship came through. We can fly into *any* kind of weather with complete confidence."

As soon as the *Graf* was safely in the hangar at Lakehurst early on the morning of May 31, Eckener was once again making plans. "An important and interesting journey had come to an end," he wrote of the South American section of the triangular flight. "My plan was to organise a regular Zeppelin service to South America. I was now entirely certain, this could and would be carried out as soon as some necessary arrangements and improvements had been made at the base in Recife."

Taking advantage of the two-day stopover at Lakehurst, he had further discussions in New York with interested American businessmen about the possibility of founding a German-American zeppelin airline company. On the night of June 2 the *Graf* took off for the return flight to Europe, flying so low on the by-now obligatory circuit of New York that two of the city's tallest skyscrapers, the Woolworth Tower and the Singer Building, loomed 150 feet above the ship. "I headed for home well satisfied," Eckener noted.

The flight across the North Atlantic to Seville via the Azores was uneventful, and in spite of incessant rain squalls and shifts in wind speed and direction, it proved possible to navigate with pinpoint accuracy over the featureless ocean using a refined technique for wind and drift measurements. After thirty-three hours over the open sea, the first of the Azores Islands rose ahead of them at precisely the calculated time and in exactly the calculated place.

At a little after 3:30 P.M. on June 4, after a flight of thirty-nine hundred miles in the fast time of sixty-one hours, twenty-four minutes, the *Graf* reached Seville by way of Lisbon and Cadiz, to be greeted by a vast crowd. Twenty minutes later the ship had gone. With the weather worsening over southern Spain and everyone weary after three weeks of circling half the globe, Eckener was in no mood for the grand banquet the city fathers had planned.

His preferred route was via the Straits of Gibraltar and up the Mediterranean to the Rhône at Marseilles. But soon after passing Lyon at the junctions of the Rhône and Saône Rivers, the radio room reported strong atmospheric disturbances and electrical discharges. Eckener calculated that a thunderstorm was probably developing in the Saône Valley up ahead, but as they were now flying blind in cloud they could not see it. There were two options: turn back and wait for the weather to clear, or carry on. Eckener decided to carry on. They continued up the Saône and reached the vicinity of Bourg-en-Bresse.

We flew on across the Saône and into a cloud formation whose previous developmental processes and present make-up were unknown to us—a thoroughly disagreeable sensation and—I admit—a foolish thing to do. The atmosphere soon became more turbulent and unstable, and the ship began to pitch and bump. But these were preliminaries which we were familiar with and which did not alarm me.

Suddenly, however, an unprecedented cloudburst poured down on the ship, more and more violently from second to second. Even in the rain squalls of the belt of calms we had never experienced anything of the kind. And then the huge raindrops began to change to hail, with pieces of ice the size *hail storm*

of walnuts! They beat on the taut outer cover of the ship as on a drum. It was more than the ship could carry! She began to sink in spite of the elevator man's energetic efforts to hold her at the flight altitude. From 1,000 feet above the valley floor we fell to 650, to 500, to a bare 300 feet. At times the valley gleamed faintly below, covered with a white mantle of hail, and it drew closer and closer, although the ship, flying at 12 degrees up angle, was developing her maximum dynamic lift.

Flemming had the watch. "Doctor, shouldn't we stop the engines?" he called out in horror.

"No!" cried Eckener, aware that the only way out of impending catastrophe was to minimize the impact, not by floating down aerostatically, but by driving the ship out of trouble aerodynamically, like an airplane. "We need them now more than ever! Set them on flank speed! If we pile up, it will be all the same whether we hit the ground at fifty miles per hour or sixty-five."

As the passengers sat silent and anxious in their cabins, the *Graf* sank to below two hundred feet above the ground, and the altimeter showed it was still falling. The ship was twenty-two thousand pounds heavy, and there were only two bags of water ballast left, weighing a mere nine hundred pounds. In this direst of situations, Eckener decided the only action he could take was to release the last of the precious ballast, even though it was insufficient to bring the ship back to equilibrium. He was just leaning across to Flemming to give the order when there was a shout from the other side of the control cabin. "You don't have to!" the elevator man cried. "I can hold the ship up!"

Eckener could hardly believe it. The ship was holding its height on the elevators. Then, very slowly, it began to climb. Soon they were emerging out of the nightmare of the hailstorm. Later Eckener found that the hailstones had made more than fifty holes in the ship's outer cover. It was the impact of the hail as well as the weight of the rain that had caused the *Graf* to sink. An airplane caught in the same storm had gone down between Geneva and Lyon with the loss of all on board. Among the passengers, relief was tinged with unease. Eckener himself was utterly shattered, "exhausted," he admitted later, "by the unbearable tension of the two or three minutes that made the difference between life and death."

Three hours later a jubilant home crowd welcomed the *Graf Zeppelin* back to Friedrichshafen. Eckener, however, was hardly in a mood for jubilation. "Yes, we have come back," he told Countess von Brandenstein-Zeppelin when she congratulated him as he climbed down from the ship. "But we came within a hair's breadth of ending everything—and would have if we luckily hadn't kept our nerve."

But there was much to be thankful for. The *Graf* had flown a total of 18,488 miles in 298 hours, 32 minutes (just under twelve and a half days' flying time, nineteen days including stopovers), at an average speed of sixty-two miles an hour. The ship's frame had stood up to the severest weather without a single hitch, its engines to constant running without a single breakdown. In his postflight report, Lieutenant Commander Joachim Breithaupt of the German air ministry was effusive in his praise of both the *Graf* and its personnel: "Confidence in the ingenious construction of the Zeppelin was unfaltering. The skilful piloting of the ship excited the general admiration of the spectators on land and on board. The mere appearance of Dr. Eckener instilled confidence in the passengers, and he knew how to inspire confidence in his crew, too." Captain Lehmann commented, "In practical results the triangular flight was of great significance, for it was decisive in the formation of the first transatlantic airship line."

Eckener was now ready to go ahead with the organization of a regular commercial zeppelin service to South America, just as soon as the landing ground at Recife had been improved, a proper intermediate base established at Seville, and an agency set up in Brazil to handle publicity and travel arrangements and deal with officials from the Brazilian post office and customs, since revenue from mail and cargo would be crucial if the service was to be profitable.

All this would take time to arrange, and no further flights to South America were planned until late summer of the following year. Much of the rest of the summer of 1930 was taken up with "circus flights" around Germany, and two rather longer flights to Scandinavia, Iceland, and Moscow. In the autumn the *Graf Zeppelin* was taken into its hangar for its winter layover and refit, having completed no fewer than 130 flights in its short life.

During the layover Joachim Breithaupt produced his end-of-term report. In his view, the future for rigids looked interesting, not to say rosy:

> Trans-oceanic services by aeroplane are still a long way off. Only the large airship with its huge range is suitable for bridging the vast ocean routes where there are no islands. The airship's superiority lies, above all, in its capability of carrying payloads over large distances at economic speeds and with static lifting powers. It is unusable for bulk cargoes. Its domain is the transport of people and high-value articles, such as mail, valuables and samples of merchandise, where time is of the essence. The airship cannot compete with overland train, plane and car services, but it may come into its own in geographically difficult areas such as mountain ranges, swamps, frozen wastes and deserts, where the establishment of railways, roads or landing strips for planes is impossible or would entail huge expense. Unlike the aeroplane the airship does not need to carry a huge weight in fuel, it can fly in fog and at night, cover long distances without stopping and fly on detours if meteorological conditions require.

There was a lot of interest in long-distance airship traffic in a number of countries, Breithaupt pointed out. A regular South America service would appear to be the most promising option initially, and the Spanish government was pursuing this. A consortium of American bankers and shipping companies were about to set up the Pacific Zeppelin Transport Company, offering a thirty-six-hour service between California cities and Hawaii, with a later extension to the Philippines and Japan. The American Departments of Trade, Marine, and War were also interested in airship deployment for the surveillance of mercantile shipping and navy warships, and airship ports were being planned in Los Angeles, San Francisco, and San Diego, while a site for a landing mast was being chosen in Honolulu. The Soviet Union was also exploring the possibility of long-range airship operations in remote, undeveloped regions such as northern Siberia, while Britain was proposing to use airships to link the far-flung outposts of its empire. But, Breithaupt warned, "the public must be convinced that the airship is a safe, regular and comparably punctual mode of transport."

There were at this point only four rigid airships in existence in the world. Two of these—the reparations ship LZ-126 (now the U.S. Navy airship *Los Angeles*) and the LZ-127 *Graf Zeppelin*—were German zeppelins. The other two were British rigids built as part of the British Imperial Airship Programme to link the major cities of the empire by air. One of these, the so-called capitalist ship, R-100, built by private enterprise, had already made a successful proving flight to Canada and back. The other, the so-called socialist ship, R-101, built by the state, was due to make a proving flight to India shortly after the *Graf Zeppelin* was put into its hangar for the winter.

Both British ships were bigger than any airship built so far, with a gas capacity a third more than the *Graf*'s and accommodation for up to a hundred passengers. But while the R-100 was an engineering triumph and the simplest rigid ever built, the R-101 was the most complicated ever built, containing a plethora of newfangled, half-developed technological innovations. Overweight and underpowered, unable to fly high, fast, or level enough, the R-101 crashed into a hill near Beauvais in northern France shortly after the start of its maiden flight to India on October 5, 1930. The resulting hydrogen fire killed forty-eight of the fifty-four men on board, including the air minister, Lord Thomson, and most of the leading figures of the British airship service.

In Britain the population plunged into mourning. The state funeral for the victims, with tens of thousands lining the London streets, was attended by Hugo Eckener and Hans von Schiller, representing the German airship service, and at the court of inquiry that followed, Eckener was invited to give expert evidence. In his view, the probable reason for the disaster was a large tear in the outer cover of the airship caused by severe turbulence over the coast of France. This in turn probably led to a sudden deflation of the forward gas cells, making the ship extremely heavy in the bow. Flying very low and very bow-heavy, the R-101 was then probably forced down by a violent downdraft it no longer had any means of resisting. Eckener's opinion accorded with the official finding of the committee.

The ship and most of the men on board might have survived the crash if it had not been inflated with hydrogen and had not caught fire, possibly as a result of the calcium navigation flares in the control car igniting by contact with the rain pouring through the open window. Whatever the precise cause of the disaster, the British public turned against the big airships, and all future development was stopped. The successful R-100 was sold for scrap for less than six hundred pounds.

It was Eckener's belief that Lord Thomson was the prime cause of the tragedy. The events leading up to the maiden flight of the R-101 had departed totally from the iron rule he himself had imposed on all zeppelin operations: namely, that the safety of the ship had to take precedence over all other considerations. The R-101 was an experimental ship that had failed to meet its performance requirements. Its lift was barely enough for a long-distance flight to the tropics, it had performed badly in its early trials, it had never even done high-speed trials or a forty-eight-hour endurance flight, its certificate of airworthiness was a fix, and it had never flown in bad weather, certainly not in the strong, gusty headwinds and driving rain forecast for the night of its departure. Incredibly, because of the high temperatures in Karachi during most months of the year, R-101 would rarely have had enough lift to enable it to return to Britain anyway. And yet the air minister, who had hopes of becoming viceroy of India and reckoned his triumphal arrival in the subcontinent on board the giant airship would enhance his chances, insisted that the flight must go ahead, and the ship's captain, Flight Lieutenant H. Carmichael Irwin, had no power to countermand him.

The R-101, Thomson had once said, was as safe as houses—except for the millionth chance. He had taken that chance, at the same time taking out extra insurance for himself and his valet and loading the already overloaded ship with a six-hundred-foot-long blue carpet, crates of champagne, barrels of beer, and boxes of silverware for state banquets, together with his own personal baggage, which weighed more than a ton. And so, on an exceptionally wild night, the ship staggered low over the Channel and collided with the first rising ground it came to, incinerating the minister, his valet, and just about everyone else on board in the ensuing conflagration.

The loss of the R-101 confirmed the worst fears of critics of the whole rigid airship concept. One of these was a British marine designer and shipbuilder with the appropriate name of E. F. Spanner. "My own opinion about rigid airships," he announced even before the R-101 had gone down, "is that they are, have always been, and always will be utterly unable to justify themselves for either military, naval or commercial purposes." They were, he claimed, unsafe, inoperable, unaffordable, uncommercial. Their materials were fragile and their structure vulnerable to bad weather. They were difficult to take off and land in even moderate winds, and it was virtually impossible to make intermediate landings in an emergency. What did the passenger airship business actually offer, he asked. "Simply the prospect of developing huge aircraft which in fine weather would carry a very few passengers a long distance with a problematical saving in time. The fares would be too high to be of interest to other than millionaires or government officials travelling at the public expense. The taxpayer has been forced to subscribe to the construction of a super-Pullman in which he will never be able to afford to ride. I am convinced there is no money at all in rigids."

Spanner was not alone. Even Charles Lindbergh, pioneer conqueror of the Atlantic in his plane *The Spirit of St. Louis,* was nonplussed when he first went on board the *Graf Zeppelin.* "The ship seemed wonderfully designed and built," he reported, "with comfortable cabins and a sumptuous saloon. But only forty passengers for such an enormous aircraft? I can see no future for the airship. It is too slow, it has only half the speed of an airplane. Between the steamer and the airplane there is no niche for the rigid airship."

Airship leaders like Eckener in Germany and Rosendahl in America disagreed, but the fact remained that with Britain's departure from the field, only Germany and (for the moment) America were left in the rigid airship business. The Germans had an unsurpassed depth of rigid design and construction experience and operational expertise, thanks in large part to the zeppelin operations in the Great War. To date they had designed 127 zeppelins and built and flown 117 of them. By comparison, the British had built sixteen rigids, America would build three, and the French and Italians would never build any. Above all, the Germans had Dr. Eckener. Turning his back on the failures of others, Eckener returned to his vision of an airship future. With the coming of spring he had yet another great zeppelin adventure to prepare for.

The idea of exploring the unmapped wastes of the Arctic by air was not new. In 1897 Salomon Andrée and two fellow Swedes had attempted to reach the North Pole by balloon but perished in the attempt. Ten years later an American, Walter Wellman, had tried it by airship but failed. In 1910 Count Zeppelin himself had sailed on a seaborne expedition to Spitzbergen to investigate the possibility of exploring the Arctic by zeppelin—an ideal vehicle, he reckoned, with which to solve one of the great geographical mysteries and determine whether there was dry land or open sea beneath the polar ice, though he was never to see the idea through. In the summer of 1926, two years before the launch of the *Graf Zeppelin*, the legendary Norwegian polar explorer Roald Amundsen, the millionaire American polar explorer Lincoln Ellsworth, and the Italian airshipman General Umberto Nobile successfully made the first aerial crossing of the North Pole in the small semirigid airship *Norge*. In the summer of 1928, shortly before the *Graf*'s first flight to America, Nobile attempted to reach the North Pole a second time, a venture that ended in catastrophe when the airship crashed on the return leg, killing eight men. Nobile and the rest of his crew were marooned on the ice, and Amundsen lost his life when his search plane disappeared without a trace. Though he was eventually rescued, Nobile was blamed for the disaster and left Italy in ignominy to continue airship work in virtual exile in Russia.

The *Italia*'s crash did not diminish interest in Arctic exploration by airship. Toward the end of 1928, when the world became aware of the *Graf Zeppelin*'s potential as a long-range passenger aircraft, Hugo Eckener was approached by the veteran Norwegian Polar explorer Fritjof Nansen. Nansen had recently founded an organization called the International Association for Exploring the Arctic by Means of Airships (Aeroarctic for short) and was interested in the possibility of using the *Graf Zeppelin*. Though Eckener agreed that the *Graf* was probably ideal for the purpose, he was too preoccupied with the around-the-world venture to fit such a complex and demanding project into his program. Then, in May 1930, shortly after the *Graf*'s triangular American flight, Nansen died, and Aeroarctic invited Eckener to be its new president.

Coincidentally, on the Lakehurst-Seville leg of the triangular flight, the polar explorer and aviator Sir Hubert Wilkins had buttonholed Eckener with an amazing proposal. He had formed the notion of reaching the North Pole by submarine, then boring through the ice to the surface with an ingenious ice auger. "Why don't we rendezvous at the North Pole?" he suggested. "Me in my submarine and you in your Zeppelin?" Though the plan seemed wildly improbable, Eckener, perhaps to his own surprise, found himself replying, "Why not?" A month or so later, in July 1930, he took the *Graf* on a three-day flight to Norway and Spitzbergen to see how it handled in northerly climes, returning via the Orkneys and the east coast of Scotland. This was followed shortly by another three-day flight, to Iceland. There were no obvious technical problems. The next question was money.

Wilkins took the idea to William Randolph Hearst, who had been well pleased with the *Graf Zeppelin*'s world flight. He was as intrigued by Wilkins's proposal as Eckener had been and offered a conditional contract in which the Zeppelin Company would receive $150,000 for reporting rights if the airship and the submarine succeeded in meeting at the North Pole and exchanging passengers and mail. The sum would be reduced to $30,000 if they merely met somewhere in the Arctic. Ultimately Hearst never paid a cent, because Wilkins didn't get anywhere near the North Pole. With some difficulty he managed to obtain an obsolete submarine from the U.S. Navy, but it broke down several times on its way to Norway and eventually had to be scuttled in Bergen Fjord.

Eckener devised another scheme, involving a rendezvous between an airship and a submarine in polar waters. Through the intermediary of the Soviet government, Eckener arranged for a meeting and exchange of mail between the *Graf Zeppelin* and the large Russian ice-breaker *Malygin*, which was shortly setting off on a scientific expedition to Franz Josef Land. Stamp collectors around the world were alerted and before long had sent fifty thousand items of mail, weighing a total of 650 pounds, to be carried on the *Graf*. A further 270 pounds of mail would be carried on the *Malygin*. The stamps paid for all the

Zeppelin Company's major expenses of the expedition. The Aero-arctic Society, of which Eckener had become president, and the Ullstein publishing empire in Berlin, which took over the reporting rights from Hearst, paid for the rest.

This in itself was an achievement, for in Germany the depression had hit rock bottom. The four biggest banks had gone bust, the government had no funds to continue reparation payments, and more than 6 million people were unemployed. Even so, a patriotic appeal to German manufacturers to donate supplies and equipment free of charge yielded an avalanche of goods, from dried fish, biscuits, and Rhine wine to sleds, storm lamps, harpoons, and menthol-flavored imitation cigarettes.

Only one obstacle proved insuperable: flight insurance. The route proposed by Aeroarctic went from Leningrad to Kamchatka at the extreme eastern end of Siberia via Archangel, New Land (Novaya Zemlya), the Taymyr Peninsula, Northern Land (Severnaya Zemlya), and the North Pole. This was perfectly feasible in terms of fuel and flying conditions, but the very mention of the words "North Pole" caused the insurance companies to recoil in horror. A compromise, radically changing the remit of the enterprise, was reached between the Zeppelin Company and the insurance companies. It was meant to be kept a secret but was quickly found out by twenty-six-year-old Arthur Koestler, the only reporter attached to the expedition. Koestler, who was working for Ullstein, was an unusual young man, a Hungarian-born German Jew who was a naturalized Palestinian, a member of the Society of Friends of the Soviet Union, and a Zionist, who was soon to be a card-carrying member of the German Communist Party and before long a British citizen destined to achieve distinction as the author of anti-Communist works such as *Darkness at Noon* (1941).

"Up to the 80th degree of latitude," Koestler recalled, "the premiums mounted in arithmetical progression; from the 80th degree upwards they rose in geometrical progression. After some haggling with the insurance men, the 82nd degree was secretly agreed upon as the northernmost limit of our itinerary. During the flight, Eckener kept strictly to the letter of the agreement, to the despair of the other members of the expedition, hugging the fateful 82nd as if he were skirting a wall."

Not that the Pole mattered all that much; it was more a symbolic geographical totem than a patch of *terra incognita* to be explored from the air. The true interests of the zeppelin's Arctic journey lay elsewhere. Essentially there were two broad objectives of the enterprise. The first, though officially subsidiary, aim, was to test the zeppelin's capabilities in polar conditions, and incidentally to reap the benefits of the massive publicity that would be generated if the venture were a success. The second, officially principal, aim, was the scientific and geographical exploration of vast tracts of the Arctic from the vantage point of a low-flying giant airship.

One important part of this scientific program was to measure variations in the Earth's magnetic field in high latitudes, using a sensitive double compass and various magnetometers housed in a converted cabin at the rear of the gondola. Another involved taking high-altitude meteorological readings using radiosondes, miniature radio transmitters carried up into the atmosphere by balloons released from the *Graf* to a height of fourteen thousand feet as part of a program to produce a weather profile of the planet. Finally, a complete geophotographic survey was to be undertaken over a huge range of the high Arctic to the north of Russia, using a special panoramic camera that automatically took nine photographs every few seconds. A comparable survey by a conventional land-and-sea expedition would take years to complete. To these two aims Arthur Koestler attempted to add a third. "A few days before the start," he wrote, "I had an inspiration which made me jump up from my desk and run, unannounced, straight to the head of the firm, Dr. Franz Ullstein."

The premise behind Koestler's idea was his understanding that anyone who planted a flag on a hitherto uncharted island or territory automatically staked a claim to that territory on behalf of the nation represented by the flag. "The idea," he wrote, "was, simply, to establish a colony of the future Jewish State in the Arctic." Since he had a Palestinian passport, all he had to do, he reckoned, was drop a weighted Zionist flag on an unknown island and lay claim to it as a colony for a future state of Israel. Dr. Ullstein, who was gifted with a great sense of humor, considered the plan. "Not a bad idea," he said. "As ideas go." Then he called in a couple of advisers. The idea was dropped only when an expert in international law pointed out that all

Arctic lands in the territory over which the *Graf* would be flying belonged automatically to Russia, regardless of who discovered them.

To accommodate all the scientific equipment and five tons of survival gear in case of a forced landing on the ice—twenty-three sleds, twelve tents, sleeping bags, emergency rations to last nine months, cooking stoves, hunting and fishing gear—the *Graf* had to undergo extensive modification. The usual passenger comforts were removed, cabins were taken over as research and observation quarters and packed with instruments, and bunks were installed along the keel. Since this was an expedition and not a pleasure cruise, officers and scientists alike would have to eat off cardboard plates and sweep out their quarters themselves, though even in the depths of the unexplored polar wilderness they would be expected to wear a collar and tie at all times.

To save weight the crew of the *Graf* was scaled down to thirty-one, including a Russian radio operator to communicate with the Soviet ground stations. The expedition was made up of twelve scientists from four countries (Germany, Russia, Sweden, and the United States), a reporter, a news photographer, and a film cameraman (world-flight veteran Robert Hartmann). There were two leaders—Dr. Eckener, in command of the ship, and Professor Samoilowich (a Russian scientist who in 1928 had led the rescue of the *Italia* survivors by the Russian icebreaker *Krassin*), in charge of the scientists.

"There was little friendly feeling on board," Arthur Koestler noted. "Partly this may have been due to the fact that the German professors were either Nazi or reactionary to the marrow, and they and the Russians displayed a mutual distrust veiled by stiff academic courtesy. But it may be that the well-known psychological influence of the Arctic landscape was asserting itself—the unbearable feeling of solitude which befalls man when he is exposed to the influence of another, prehuman geological age—an experience of cosmic rejection."

Before setting off on his great flight to the Far North, Eckener made two preliminary flights. The first, in April 1931, was a goodwill flight to Egypt, where the Zeppelin Company hoped to establish an intermediate airship base in the event that they could organize a commercial airship service to the Dutch East Indies. The second, in July, was another flight to Iceland, a shakedown sortie prior to the Arctic venture proper later that month. Finally, on July 24, the *Graf Zeppelin* took off from Friedrichshafen at the start of its Arctic flight. Cutting across Germany to Berlin, it circled for an hour over the ecstatic crowds in the capital before landing at the nearby airship base of Staaken in the early evening to take on extra fuel.

Berlin was Koestler's home town, and as everyone was free for the evening, he took the two Americans on the *Graf,* the polar explorer Lincoln Ellsworth and Commander Edward Smith of the U.S. Coastguard, to see the famous nightlife of the city, clad in the only clothing they had, their clumsy padded polar suits. "Berlin was in the throes of the Zeppelin fever," Koestler recalled. "We were recognised in every *Lokal* and attentions were not lacking. Taxi-drivers refused to accept pay, night club proprietors regaled us with free champagne, the ladies at the bar swooned by just glancing at us. It was a wonderful feeling to be a hero." Out at Staaken tens of thousands of Berliners poured onto the field to see the mighty *Graf Zeppelin* on the verge of perhaps its most hazardous adventure.

Just after five o'clock the next morning, the *Graf* took off for Leningrad via the Baltic and the Gulf of Finland. A large banner greeted the ship when, escorted by five Soviet military airplanes, it landed at the Leningrad field at the end of the day: WELCOME TO THE RECKLESS HEROES OF THE ARCTIC! It was a festive night. The Red Army Choir sang hearty revolutionary songs, a sumptuous banquet was laid out, with abundant champagne and half a dozen kinds of caviar. The German ambassador made a speech, followed by the chairman of the Leningrad soviet, then the president of the Russian Academy, then Dr. Eckener.

"The banquet broke up in the small hours," recalled Koestler:

> when the celebrated white night of the Neva began to glow with the approach of day. As we made our way through the milky mist on the airfield, past the blinking torches of the sentries, to our ship, I felt this had been one of the most wonderful experiences of my life, a sensation of complete fulfilment. Reflectors had been mounted near the ship,

bathing its hull in a violet, phosphorescent hue; attached to its mast, it seemed to swim through the drifting gusts of mist like a gentle prehistoric monster. We crept into our sleeping bags, listening to the sound of the Russian songs through the fog.

The ship had been refueled and now had enough fuel for 105 hours' nonstop flying on all five engines, or 135 hours on four engines. Generous quantities of caviar had also been put on board, a parting gift from the Russian government. Shortly after nine on the morning of July 26, amid enthusiastic cheers from the crowd, the *Graf* took off and headed across the primeval forests of the Karelian Soviet Republic toward the Arctic Circle and regions of ice and water never before seen by man from the air. Koestler wrote, "Lake Ladoga lay behind us, the taiga opened its green arms and enclosed the whole horizon in its embrace. The virgin forest of firs moves past in majestic monotony. For hours on end we can detect no human being from horizon to horizon, no animal, no house, no sign that a living being has ever penetrated into the heart of this green darkness."

The *Graf*'s route took them from Karelia and over Archangel and the Kola Peninsula out into the Barents Sea, and by 8 P.M. Central European Time they were over the White Sea and crossing the Arctic Circle, an event celebrated with a dinner of ham, sausage, cheese, cake, and wine. Here Eckener received warnings that bad weather was moving in from the east and decided on a "right-about" route to Franz Josef Land and thence east to Severnaya Zemlya, rather than a "left-about" route northeast to Severnaya Zemlya direct.

To his left Eckener could see squall clouds above the Kola Peninsula, and a threatening blue-black wall of cloud dead ahead across the Arctic entrance of the Barents Sea. "It was as if the Polar Sea were erecting a belt of fortifications against us," he noted. "Abandon hope all ye who enter here!" The temperature had been up to seventy-five degrees that morning. Now it fell to fifty, and cold rain lashed at the windows of the control car. The ship pitched and bumped as it entered the cloud wall and ran into a strong head wind, so it made slow progress toward Franz Josef Land. By midnight they had just cleared the European landmass. Arthur Koestler sent a radio dispatch to his office in Berlin:

*midnight centropatime stop fog lifted for a short while could just catch glimpse of lonely lighthouse on Cape Kanin comma where eight men hold this extreme outpost of civilisation under conditions of unimaginable hardship stop now the good earth is behind us comma are flying across the Barents Sea with course set on distant Franz Josef Land to keep our polar rendezvous with Soviet icebreaker Malygin stop the local time is 2 a.m. time for bed but who wants bed comma arctic looks like an infinite desert in milky shimmer of ghostly polar twilight stop strong northwesterly wind lashes gondola floating veils and rags and tatters of white mist give land-scape absolutely fantastic character everybody wildly elated stop end*

The crossing of Siberia on the world flight had not prepared Hugo Eckener for the miracle of the world above the Arctic Circle:

> I had never seen anything comparable in the way of light, reflection and colour phenomena to be found here over the Polar Sea. The wonderful clearness and sharpness of the air and the mingling of air masses of different temper-atures produced constant mirages, which we watched with continual satisfaction. How often we observed ice-fields or blue channels of water or rough sea, only to realise finally that it was just a weird illumination from clouds or mist at a great distance! A strange experience: to be floating peace-fully above an ocean which had seemed unfriendly and treacherous in our imagination, and which now revealed itself in brilliant light and colour and beauty.

The farther north the ship flew, the more magical became the world below it. A little after noon the next day, July 27, at about seventy-eight degrees north latitude, there appeared on the horizon the edge of the ice field, and then in the distance the glaciers and snowy mountains of Franz Josef Land. Eckener was transfixed: "Whoever has not seen a polar landscape like Franz Josef Land has not known anything of the most beautiful thing which this earth has to offer our eyes and our souls."

At three in the afternoon the *Graf* crossed the seventy-eighth parallel, and the fog vanished to reveal a leaden sea spattered with drift ice, which before long merged into pack ice. An hour later they sighted Cape Flora on the southernmost island of the Franz Josef group. All this time the *Graf* had been flying through eternal day, for in this high latitude in summer there was no night, only a dipping of the sun toward the horizon. As they approached Cape Flora and the sun sank to its lowest point in the sky, the entire landscape was suddenly transformed into miracle ground. Koestler wrote:

> Around Cape Flora there was a stretch of open sea, and the colour of the water was black. Onto this black surface the red glacier poured its reflection like a burning glow of lava. It was all too spectacular to be beautiful; but it was certainly the most startling sight that I have seen. Yet this fantastic display caused no surge of elation—rather a feeling of awe and oppression; in the heavy silence which dated from the last Ice Age, the faint hum of our engines swelled to a roaring blasphemy. The empty immensity indicated that we were trespassers, definitely not wanted here.

He was relieved when for the first time he saw living beings in that dead and frozen waste—a family of polar bears drifting along on an ice floe, the male standing on his hind legs, shaking his head in remonstrance at the intrusion of the zeppelin into that still world.

For several hours the *Graf* had been in radio contact with the *Malygin,* which was waiting off Hooker Island in the Franz Josef group. On board the Russian icebreaker was General Umberto Nobile. On board the *Graf* was Lincoln Ellsworth, who had been with him on his first polar flight. Their reunion would add a tragic poignancy to the rendezvous.

The *Graf* passed more islands—Prince George Land, McClintock Land—then nosed into the so-called Quiet Sound. And there, exactly on the eighty-second parallel, which was the zeppelin's agreed northern limit, was the *Malygin*, hidden away in the deepest inlet of the sound beneath the daunting cliffs of Hooker Island, dressed overall with flags and pennants and hooting for joy on its siren.

The *Graf* came in, did a few slow turns overhead, and exchanged greetings by radio. Eckener confirmed he intended to land on the water near the ship. The engines were stopped, gas was vented, and slowly the *Graf* began to sink. At three hundred feet, two canvas buckets on lines were thrown into the water to act as sea anchors. Lower still, a hosepipe was let down into the sea, and water was pumped through it into the ship to make it heavier and obviate the need to valve more of the precious gas. Two hundred yards from the *Malygin*—the closest Eckener dared get without running a risk of sparks from the icebreaker's smokestack igniting the airship's hydrogen—the *Graf* came to rest on the sea, riding gently on the gondola's pneumatic buffer in a state of delicate equilibrium. A sea anchor resembling a parachute was thrown out, and the forward and after gondolas were ballasted with water, so the ship lay steady with its bow pointing into a light wind. It was about 5:30 P.M. on July 27, 1931.

A rubber inflatable was ready to launch from the *Graf*, but before they could lower it into the sea, a tender from the *Malygin* came up alongside, packed with excited, weather-beaten men clad in furs. Chaos and confusion reigned. The door of the gondola was blocked with large mailbags containing the fifty thousand letters and cards. For the entire flight two men had been busy day and night inside the *Graf*'s own flying post office, a bright red polar survival tent, stamping the mail with the zeppelin's special rubber stamp. The value of the mail was fifty thousand dollars, half of which went to the German post office and half toward the cost of the Arctic flight.

Unable to enter through the gondola door, the men from the *Malygin* grabbed the handling rails and shouted greetings in Russian through the saloon windows. One of the fur-clad men was General Nobile. He was shouting for his old comrade Lincoln Ellsworth. Looking at the disgraced airship commander, someone on the *Graf* muttered: "God, how the man has aged!" The improbable meeting of these two figures of polar airship history, Ellsworth and Nobile, in the midst of the Arctic wilderness, was rather like that of Stanley and Livingstone in Darkest Africa—and their words of greeting almost as anticlimactically banal.

"Hello," said Ellsworth. "How do you do?"

There was no opportunity to say more, even if either of the men, both deeply moved by the occasion, could have thought of anything more to say. Pieces of drift ice, some of them big, were beginning to float by not far from the ship's fragile gondola. Suddenly there was a roar from Eckener: "Geht schnell achtern und holt die Postsäcke! Wir haben keine Zeit zu verlieren!" "Hurry up and grab the postbags! We've no time to lose!"

Zeppelin crewmen came running from the bridge. The mailbags were hastily transferred between the *Graf Zeppelin*'s door and the *Malygin*'s tender, and the door slammed shut. The sea anchors were hauled in, ballast water pumped out from fore and aft; the watch officers and helmsmen were at their flight posts on the bridge. Nobile had been hoping to fly on the *Graf* for the rest of its Arctic cruise as Eckener's guest. Eckener had scant respect for Nobile as an airship commander; he blamed the *Italia* disaster on his tendency to panic in a crisis. But he would gladly have had him on board, out of harm's way at the back of the control room. As it was, a crestfallen Nobile was now receding rapidly from view, along with his comrades from the *Malygin*. "The whole adventurous rendezvous had lasted exactly thirteen minutes," reported Koestler. "As the bay began to veer out of sight, the *Malygin*'s whistle broke into a long, plaintive howl, like an abandoned bride."

It was Moscow and Havana all over again, and the recriminations were bitter. A German reporter on board the *Malygin* filed a report for a major German newspaper complaining that Eckener and his crew had behaved with gross lack of consideration for the men of the icebreaker. It seemed that a historic event in Arctic exploration had been shortchanged. But if Eckener had been brusque, even rude, he had also been correct. He had noticed something that the men from the *Malygin* had not: the *Graf* was beginning to drag its sea anchor in the light wind and was rapidly sidling toward an area full of big chunks of drift ice, any one of which could have punctured the flotation gear or the gondola and endangered the ship. Hence the emergency takeoff.

A rendezvous had been made, however, and in Eckener's view the incident had demonstrated the airship's potential, with its unique capability of coming down on the open sea or level ice, as a flying laboratory in polar exploration. When he came into the saloon from the flight deck once they were safely airborne, he was given a standing ovation.

For the rest of the day the *Graf* tacked over Franz Josef Land, usually at a height of three thousand feet, sometimes at slow-ahead, sometimes stopped dead in the air, while the expeditionaries proceeded with the first-ever geophotographic survey of the vast archipelago below, remapping the islands, discovering six new ones, erasing two old ones, redrawing the outlines of a dozen others. By midnight the ship had reached the most northerly point of Franz Josef Land. The work was done, the weather was perfect, and the North Pole was only a few hours' flying time away. "Sure enough," Arthur Koestler lamented, "we veered round through 90 degrees, setting course due east. The insurance companies had asserted themselves over 'The Reckless Heroes of the Arctic.' How right Karl Marx was after all!"

By seven o'clock next morning, July 28, they were over Severnaya Zemlya, the second objective of the expedition. Only a segment of its east coast had been mapped; the remainder was a blank on the map. For six hours the *Graf* explored from a height of four thousand feet, discovering that Severnaya Zemlya consisted of two islands, not one, and that it was the most sublimely grandiose polar landscape they had ever set eyes upon.

Polar exploration on the *Graf* was a far cry from the hardship and suffering experienced by traditional explorers down amid the frozen hell of the sea and land. No lung-bursting slog with sleds here, no overwintering in an ice hole subsisting on blubber, no frostbite, starvation, despair. The men of the *Graf Zeppelin* arctic expedition slept in warm beds all night, sat around in chairs all day, went about in pullovers in a temperature that never fell below five degrees centigrade, and above all ate well, for even on an expedition the *Graf*'s chef never let standards sink too low. Yet for all their full bellies and life of sybaritic ease, the expeditionaries on the *Graf* could achieve more in five minutes, in terms of geographical discovery, than the old-timers down below could achieve in five months.

Crossing Northern Land, the ship reached Cape Chelyuskin on the Taymyr Peninsula, the most northerly point of Asia, then flew southwest across the Taymyr, the third objective of the expedition: "a God-forsaken wilderness," Koestler called it, traversed by only one explorer in the last fifty years, where occasional herds of reindeer fled headlong at the approach of the *Graf*. During the course of the flight over the peninsula, it was discovered that Lake Taymyr was a great deal longer than existing maps showed, the adjacent mountains much higher.

On the fourth morning, crossing the Taymyr's western coast after a three-hundred-mile flight across this wasteland, the *Graf* passed over the remote weather station at Dickson Haven in the mouth of the mighty Yenisey, the most northerly weather station in the Eurasian continent. To boost the morale of the beleaguered inhabitants, they made a parachute drop of strawberries and flowers, loaves of bread, a large sausage, and a packet of newspapers only three days old. Then they headed north once more, crossing the Kara Sea en route to Novaya Zemlya, the fourth and last objective of the expedition, a long, narrow island stretching north to south from the seventieth to the seventy-seventh meridian. A world of glaciers remorselessly grinding down to the sea, at times it was more savagely beautiful even than Northern Land and, for a while, no less lonely.

Since reaching Northern Land the *Graf* had been flying through a radio blind spot, and though it could pick up stations from as far away as Japan, it could send none. Then suddenly, over Novaya Zemlya, they established radio communication with a steamer off Spitzbergen and soon afterward with stations in continental Europe.

"The spell was broken," Koestler noted wistfully, "the adventure drawing to its close. I took a last long look at the sparkling glaciers, the icebergs floating on the tranquil sea; then said farewell to the arctic nirvana and surrendered to my typewriter." For him the flight had been a majestic experience. "No lesser adjective," he concluded, "would fit both the landscape over which we hovered during four indistinguishable days and nights of midnight sun, and the airship which carried us—a monster of supreme beauty.... It had all the charm and quiet excitement comparable to a journey on the last sailing ship in an era of speedboats."

Twenty-four hours later, at five o'clock on July 30, 1931, the *Graf Zeppelin* landed in Tempelhof, Berlin, flying down through the blazing sun with its complement of human beings exhausted by the sleepless nights and the sheer profusion and brilliance of their polar impressions, to be greeted by a crowd of several hundred thousand singing the German national anthem.

The leading members of the expedition were dragged in front of a microphone to address the multitude. First was Professor Samoilowich. In a nonstop flight of five days and four nights, he told them, they had carried out a geophotographic survey of the Arctic landmass between the 40th and 110th degrees of longitude east, as well as accomplishing valuable observations in polar meteorology and Earth magnetism, work that would have taken a sea-and-land expedition two or three years to accomplish, and without producing such reliable results. The *Graf*'s cruise marked the end of the romantic era of Arctic exploration and the beginning of the scientific era.

When it was Eckener's turn to speak, he did so with his own long-term agenda in mind. He had taken part in the expedition not so much to further the cause of science as to publicize zeppelin travel over any part of the planet and, in the process, to learn more about weather conditions in the Far North. His aim was to reassure rather than dismay, to normalize rather than sensationalize. The dangers of the Arctic were a myth as far as airships were concerned, he told the crowd, to the disappointment of many. They had made their trip in the clearest sunshine, with all kinds of good things to eat and drink. In his opinion, such excursions would enjoy great popularity in the future. "In the centre of the Arctic Ocean," he would observe later, "airship navigation is no more difficult or dangerous than in the temperate zone, perhaps even less difficult."

The airship's advantages as a flying aerial platform for science and exploration were indeed unique, but no more great airships would follow the *Graf Zeppelin*'s lead into the Arctic. The catastrophe of the

*Italia* had discredited them as polar vehicles, and future explorers would turn instead to cheaper, faster airplanes.

Before dawn on July 31 the *Graf Zeppelin* reached its home base at Friedrichshafen, 145 hours, 26 minutes, and 13,039 kilometers after it had taken off from there the previous week. So ended the last spectacular proving flight the *Graf* would ever make. Its destiny now lay where its commander had always intended—in scheduled commercial air services between continents. The adventures were over, the routine of transoceanic flying by passenger airship was about to begin. The promise, it seemed, was at long last about to be fulfilled.

On August 18, less than three weeks after returning from the Arctic voyage, the *Graf* was in the air again, this time on a three-day flight to Great Britain. After circling low over London, Eckener landed at Hanworth Air Park on the western outskirts of the city before a huge crowd, later taking off for a circumnavigation of Britain watched by tens of thousands of enthralled Britishers.

Little more than a week later, the *Graf* was again in the air, on the first of three scheduled advertised flights carrying passengers and mail to South America. For those first scheduled transatlantic air passengers in history, the experience was wilder than their wildest dreams. Everywhere the *Graf* was greeted like the miraculous vision it was. Turbaned, horse-borne tribesmen of the Spanish Sahara gleefully loosed off their antique muskets at it. The great four-masted grain ships beating up from Australia under full sail dressed overall for it. The convicts of Fernando de Noronha once again jumped up and down in the surf in ecstasy over it. And as it crossed the jungle coast of Brazil, the tropic birds swarmed up like giant dragonflies toward it, the dogs howled, the brown-skinned girls waved, and the children in shrill voices screamed their greeting: "Conde Sep-pel-liiiin!"

The flights ended at Recife, where passengers for Rio transferred to airplanes of the German Condor Line for forward travel to airports in southern Brazil, Uruguay, and Argentina. These flights were successful enough, both operationally and, to a limited extent, financially, for the Zeppelin Company to expand its South America service for the following year.

Back at home with his wife in the quiet of the year's end, Hugo Eckener scribbled in his private manuscript book his own overview of the point he and his dream machine had reached in their long adventure together:

> The *Graf Zeppelin* has ended the third year of its flying career. At the beginning of October 1928 it set off on its first American flight, which was to bring it to the attention of the world. Since then it has flown more than 300,000 kilometres—or more than eight times round the world—on 222 different flights, in all kinds of weather, at the Pole as well as in the tropics—and is still as operational as it was at the beginning of its career.
>
> Currently the *Graf Zeppelin* is making a series of South America flights which raise the possibility of a scheduled airship service in the southern hemisphere. These first flights have been a complete success. We have been able to carry mail and passengers from Friedrichshafen to Brazil in eighty hours, from Berlin in eighty hours, and back against the north-east trade winds in eighty-one hours.
>
> I am quite sure that in the eyes of the world the efficiency and reliability of the Zeppelin airship for transoceanic travel have in large measure been proven. We have observed this all over the world. The conviction is so strong that people no longer get particularly excited about great Zeppelin flights, they are more interested in their punctuality.

The zeppelin was also potentially profitable, he went on. Only 15 percent of its income came from state grants, the rest from earned revenue—75 percent of this from abroad. "So we say this: the *Graf Zeppelin* is a form of transport that brings in foreign exchange, and this foreign exchange is worth quite a few millions." In short, zeppelin travel worked, was widely seen to work, and was reasonably profitable.

At this point, as Eckener was well aware, the zeppelin had little competition as a means of intercontinental transportation. Ships were much slower: it took a passenger ship up to three weeks to sail from Germany to Brazil, whereas the *Graf Zeppelin* took only three days or so. As for planes, though they were catching up and were faster and more capable of handling moderately adverse weather than the zeppelin, they remained a lot less comfortable, a lot more conducive to airsickness, and in the early days were more prone to accidents. In any case, they did not yet have the range to fly across a wide expanse of ocean. Unlike the zeppelin, which was an intercontinental aircraft, suited to long-haul flying over water, the plane was still a largely continental aircraft, suited to flying over land, proceeding in hops from one landing field to another.

All this would change before long. Not much more than six weeks after the end of the *Graf*'s world flight, for example, the huge Dornier Do-X flying boat—by far the biggest plane in existence, with twelve engines, a 157-foot wingspan, and a dining room–cum–dancing salon nearly sixty feet long—made its first trials from Friedrichshafen. On October 21, 1929, the Do-X carried a record 169 people (double its normal complement and nearly three times the usual number on board the *Graf*), including ten crew and nine stowaways (another aviation record), on a one-hour flight over Lake Constance. On August 5, 1931, five days after the *Graf*'s return from its Arctic flight, the Do-X arrived in New York after a hazardous, eventful, and roundabout flight from Friedrichshafen via the South Atlantic that had taken a total of nine months and entailed a large number of lengthy intermediate landings. Like most of the giant planes of this era, the Do-X was an overambitious freak and never went into service. But it was clear that the airplane was snapping at the zeppelin's tail as a long-distance load carrier and would one day develop the technology to match it.

That winter, while the *Graf* lay in its hangar undergoing a total overhaul, Hugo Eckener was out and about doing his best to help create a worldwide zeppelin airline network. A key move in that grand strategy was the foundation of the German-American Zeppelin Company, and in March 1932 Eckener went to Akron, Ohio, to participate in the formal setup of the new company, of which Paul Litchfield, president of the Goodyear Company and a staunch supporter of the zeppelin cause in America, was made general manager. The establishment of this organization was a personal coup for Eckener, providing him with a launchpad for a new zeppelin initiative and support for the next phase of his plan to develop airship communications throughout the world. In this regard the major colonial empires, especially the British, French, and Dutch, provided an obvious potential market, with extensive territories spanning virtually the whole of the globe, many of them best reached along transoceanic routes suitable for long-haul airship flying.

Meanwhile, the popularity of the *Graf Zeppelin*'s scheduled service to South America continued. With Eckener more and more preoccupied with Zeppelin Company business and the grander zeppelin plan worldwide, the command of some of these flights was increasingly delegated to Captains Lehmann, Flemming, and von Schiller. Though the experience of flying down to Brazil remained unforgettable, so routine did the flights become in an operational sense that untoward incidents were few and far between, though they did occur. On one occasion when the *Graf* was landing at Rio, the Brazilian troops acting as ground handlers let go of the aft engine car in order to pose for a group photograph, with the result that the stern of the ship rose a hundred feet into the air while the control car remained firmly resting on the ground.

On a later occasion the *Graf* was seriously delayed off Recife when revolution broke out in Pernambuco just as the airship was due to come in. There was no alternative but to hold off out to sea till the fighting around the mooring mast died down, by which time the *Graf* had been aloft and unrefueled for a full 118 hours, 40 minutes (nearly five days).

But it was the vagaries of weather that usually produced the most serious crises. One night when the *Graf* was approaching Recife in a tropical cloudburst, the elevator steersman lost his footing in the floodwater slopping around the control car floor and slipped, losing his grip on the elevator wheel, so that it spun loose and put the ship, already low and heavy with the weight of the rainwater on its outer cover, in a dive toward the sea. Just in time, a bystander rushed forward, grabbed the wheel, and brought the bow up before the ship fell into the wild black waters of the stormy ocean.

Another time the *Graf,* under the command of Captain von Schiller, was nearly lost when it was slammed down half a mile short of the Recife landing mast by a tropical rainstorm, hitting the ground so heavily that the lower fin and rudder were badly damaged and several palm trees and the smoking chimney of a peasant's hut were found sticking up inside the hydrogen-filled hull. It was a mechanic from the aft engine car who saved the day. Realizing the danger, he leapt from the car, dashed across to the peasant's hut, burst through the door, and without so much as an *Entschuldigung* grabbed the coffee pot bubbling on the burning wood fire and, to the astonishment of the hut's inhabitant, emptied the contents in a flash over the fire and put it out, thereby saving the world's most famous aircraft and all the human beings in or near it, including the peasant farmer himself, from a spectacular demise.

Dr. Eckener was not amused. "It is absolutely necessary to *know* an operation will be successful before proceeding," he railed at von Schiller on his return to Friedrichshafen. "If a disaster occurred the whole airship industry could be destroyed."

Hugo Eckener spent Christmas of 1932 quietly at home in Friedrichshafen with his wife and family. It had been a satisfactory year in some respects, a frustrating one in others. A little over a year ago, work had started on the design of a brand-new super-zeppelin, reference number LZ-129, intended to do on the service to North America what the *Graf Zeppelin* was doing on the service to South America. But progress on the new ship had been painfully slow. Germany was in the depths of a depression, and as government funding ran out, work on the new ship, still at the drawing-board stage, came to a virtual standstill. But it was a beginning, Eckener felt, an affirmation of his determination to realize his dream of fast, reliable intercontinental airship travel.

Shortly after Christmas, Eckener traveled down to Marseilles to catch a fast cargo boat to Port Said on the first leg of a voyage to the Dutch East Indies. Traveling with him was his daughter Lotte, a photographer. They had a few days to wait at Port Said before their ship to the Indies came in, and Eckener used the time to make some contacts in Cairo, including the British High Commissioner, Egyptian government departments, and King Fuad himself, for he saw the Egyptian capital as a promising intermediate stop on the proposed New York–Seville–East Indies zeppelin route.

The onward voyage from Port Said took nearly two weeks, and Eckener spent much of the time studying the set of the weather en route. Based with Lotte in the house of a friend in Batavia on the island of Java, he continued his research, and by and large the results seemed promising. So he was in a relaxed and optimistic vein when one morning toward the end of his stay the house servant brought him a copy of the daily paper. When he opened it he saw an item of news that was to turn virtually every aspect of his life and work upside down. Lotte, seeing his blankly staring, painfully contorted face, spoke to him with some concern. "What's the matter, Father? Are you ill?"

Eckener shook his head. His eyes looked weary. "No, there's nothing the matter with me," he replied. "But Germany . . ." He passed the newspaper across to her. The government had resigned, and on January 30, 1933, Adolf Hitler had been made chancellor.

"That man—Chancellor of Germany," Eckener muttered in disbelieving disgust. "Hindenburg was not strong enough to hold him down. And they think that Hitler is going to rescue Germany from want and oppression—Hitler!"

Never had Eckener gone home in a mood of such outrage and despair. At the British port and colony of Aden he went ashore for a brief visit to investigate the prospects of establishing another intermediate zeppelin base there. Then he caught a passenger ship to Genoa and the night train to Friedrichshafen. Even in the short time he had been away, Germany had changed. A few years previously, following his first transatlantic flight in the ZR-3 (*Los Angeles*), Eckener had given an address to the students at the University of Prague. "The man who preaches force to Germany," he told them, "preaches Germany's destruction." That man was now in place. The rest, he felt sure, would follow.

Eckener had been well aware of his own standing in government and public eyes. Though the German people had adored him and his zeppelin from the start, the government had been an uphill struggle. Gradually public opinion and the palpable success of the *Graf Zeppelin* as a commercial aircraft and symbol of German workmanship and know-how began to win over the Weimar government, and it began to support the zeppelin cause to the best of its limited ability in those bankrupt days. "The Zeppelin concept, the Zeppelin dream, was a very interesting episode in the history of German spiritual development," Eckener was to reflect. "Unfortunately this dream was short-lived, and it was suddenly interrupted by the folly of a criminal madman."


The Assumption of Power, as the Nazi takeover came to be known, was a revolution of the most extreme sort—"a political earthquake," Eckener called it, "fraught with consequences." Hitler offered the German people bread, work, security, pride, a return to greatness. For many, this was irresistible. Only initiates and political clairvoyants in the early days perceived the hidden agenda: hegemony over Europe, coercion, terror, conquest, genocide. Hugo Eckener was one of the clairvoyants.

Like most people throughout the length and breadth of the Reich, he tried to assess the consequences and take stock. "What attitude would the new regime take towards the Zeppelin concept?" he asked himself. "This was the question which interested me most of all and which disturbed me somewhat, for I was fully aware already that I was not liked at all by the new heads of the government."

For most of his life Hugo Eckener had been a man of the center, a democrat, a humanist, a man brought up, in the very broadest sense, on Christian principles. Throughout the world he was a symbol of reawakened German prestige and achievement. "Who is the best-known personality on earth?" the Italian newspaper *Corriere della Sera* asked its readers. "Hugo Eckener" was the majority vote. In vain the Nazis had sought Eckener's support during their climb to power. He had left them in no doubt where he stood. Asked if he would make the zeppelin hangar at Friedrichshafen available for a Nazi rally to be addressed by Hitler, he said no.

Asked if he would make a political broadcast in support of the moderate anti-Nazi German chancellor Heinrich Brüning, he said yes. Eckener's 1931 address to the German people was more than just a party political broadcast; it was an affirmation of his conviction of the preciousness of civilized values, and a warning against letting the forces of darkness prevail. He spoke of the depression that was plunging the country into poverty and despair and exhorted all Germans who loved their country to rally behind the Brüning government in the fight against the economic and political crisis that threatened the nation.

"Danger rises from our unrest," he warned. "We are preparing, by our lack of unity and by our political differences, a fertile field for the growth of every kind of demagoguery." Though he did not mention the National Socialists by name, he had them in his sights when he warned against political movements and philosophies driven by hate and revenge. "We must consider it the mission of the German people," he ended with a heartfelt plea, "to bring about the return of righteousness and reason to politics."

The Nazis publicly vilified Eckener for his broadcast, insulted him in their newspapers, ridiculed him in cartoons as a man on the make, a corrupt has-been who would say anything for a backhander. The conservatives and democrats saw him in a different light. Desperate to find a strong and popular figure who could credibly head a last-ditch stand against the Nazi landslide, the leaders of the Central Party and the Social Democrats approached Eckener in the spring of 1932 and asked if he would consider running as their candidate for the forthcoming presidential elections in place of the frail, aging Field Marshal von Hindenburg, now in his mid-eighties and judged far too conciliatory in his dealings with Hitler. The idea that a zeppelin commander could become president of Germany was not as far-fetched as it might seem. A Berlin banker said of Eckener at that time, "I knew all the leading political and commercial leaders of Germany in the early 1930s. Nowhere on the national scene was there a man so competent to assume the leadership of the government as was Hugo Eckener."

"Gentlemen," Eckener replied, "I am flattered by your offer and I appreciate your backing, but, as you know, my life's work is the Zeppelin and I still have much to do with it. I have no desire to enter politics." He would stand for president, he said, only if Hindenburg decided not to run for reelection. As it happened, Hindenburg stood again and became president a second time, though the press continued to speculate on the possibility that Eckener might be the man to succeed him when he finally departed the scene. "Who comes after Hindenburg—Hitler or Dr. Eckener?" asked the front page of *Neues*

*Deutschland* on January 1, 1933. But on January 30, a fateful day for Germany and the world, Hindenburg appointed ex–Lance Corporal Adolf Hitler as chancellor of the Reich. And so the Nazi Revolution began.

Hitler's assumption of power so disgusted Eckener that, unlike most cautiously sensible Germans of liberal persuasion, he was not prepared to keep his mouth shut. His sense of moral outrage was stronger than his instinct for personal survival. "I am ashamed of my countrymen," he would say both in public and in private, "that they allowed themselves to be hoodwinked and victimised by this conscienceless rabble-rouser who's been promising everything to everybody." He would add, "My birthplace was Flensburg. It used to belong to Denmark. I'm going to call myself a Dane."

The clearer the real nature of the Nazi regime became, the more Eckener spoke up against it. Sitting with an Austrian guest in a public park in Friedrichshafen, his voice could be heard booming between the trees for all to hear: "You're forgetting, my dear Count, that Germany is now a nation governed by criminals!" Once, in the lobby of the fashionable Hotel Bristol in Berlin, he took umbrage at the uniformed Nazis having coffee there and growled in a voice so loud that everyone could hear: "Look at those gangsters. They would have locked me up long ago if they had any guts!" Asked by a group of foreign journalists whether he proposed to give the Nazi salute, he replied mockingly, "When I get up in the morning I don't say 'Heil Hitler!' to my wife, I say 'Good morning.'"

"My father never attempted to hide his contempt for the 'Brown Dictator,'" his daughter Lotte recalled. "We were always worried that 'something might happen.'" Before long it did. At the beginning of June 1933 Eckener received word that Rudolf Diels, the chief of the state secret police office (the future Gestapo), would like to meet him.

Say, dinner? Say, the Hotel Esplanade, Berlin? There was some polite small talk to get through, cocktails to order, a look at the menu. Then Diels got to the point. There had been complaints, he said. Many of them. Dr. Eckener had been overheard making a number of remarks about the Nazi Party and its Führer. Dr. Eckener should watch his step. The secret police had a dossier on him. "We don't expect you to become a member of the Party," Diels said. "But it would be in your best interest to stop your remarks and to retract those that you've already made."

Diels was polite, courteous, affably menacing. Eckener looked at him, glanced at his watch, stood up, apologized for his precipitate departure, and explained: "I've got a Zeppelin to catch. I've got to get back to Friedrichshafen for a flight to Brazil. I'll think it over." So saying, he turned on his heel and left to catch the June 3 flight to Recife on board the *Graf Zeppelin*.

That summer Eckener met Hitler face to face. Eckener was on holiday with his wife and daughter at Hintersee in the Bavarian Alps near Hitler's summer retreat at Berchtesgaden, and by coincidence Hitler turned up at Eckener's hotel. When his arrival was announced, a disgruntled Eckener muttered an old Bavarian homily to himself: "Gehe nicht zu deinem Ferscht, wenn du nicht gerufen werscht." "Don't toddle along if you haven't had the call." But the landlord advised Hitler of the presence of another distinguished visitor, and Hitler sent a message for Eckener to come and see him.

They met in the coffee garden. It was an embarrassing encounter, which Lotte and her mother observed nervously from behind a curtain inside. "They were terribly standoffish, the two of them," Lotte recalled. "Hitler was standing. He didn't offer my father a chair. The table between them was like a chasm across which neither of them intended to get even a hairsbreadth closer to each other." Eckener found himself in front of a man who, he thought, looked like a low-grade civil servant who didn't know what to say to his boss and so just gushed words in an excited, animated manner while managing to convey absolutely nothing of consequence. He thought Hitler was talking simply for the sake of not staying silent, and he perceived a glint of rage in the Führer's eyes, perhaps because of his awareness of the poor showing he was making. After a few agonizing minutes, they parted, never to meet again.

Dr. Hugo Eckener was the kind of man the new Führer might be expected to silence or even liquidate. Yet Eckener remained free to go about his business while others were being pulled off the streets and taken from their homes. "I'm beginning to think," he confided to his wife, Johanna, "that they feel I'm more valuable to them alive. They know the propaganda value of having German airships flying the world's air routes. They also know I enjoy many overseas friendships, particularly in America, and that I can succeed in obtaining foreign co-operation and support whereas they cannot."

But perhaps there was another reason, unknown to Eckener at the time and revealed to him only years later by a doctor who had tended Hindenburg when he lay dying. Shortly before his death, the doctor said, Hindenburg told him that it was he who had protected Eckener from the Nazis and so saved his life. Shortly after Hitler assumed power, it seems, Hindenburg took Hitler aside. He was well aware of plans to do away with Eckener but insisted that he should be left alone. "I want you to promise me," he said, "that you keep your hands off that man. You're to leave Hugo Eckener alone!" Hindenburg had been Hitler's hero in the Great War, and it was Hindenburg who had made him chancellor of the Reich. It appears this may have been one promise the Führer kept.

So, for the moment, Eckener continued to fly his zeppelin to South America and to plan for the day when he could build the super-zeppelins of his dreams and fly them all over the world.


In 1933 there had been nine more passenger flights to Brazil and back. On the eighth of these the president of Brazil, Getulio Vargas, and several of his ministers flew as guests from Recife to Rio, an experience reassuring enough to persuade the government to sanction the construction of a full-fledged airship base at Santa Cruz de Sepetiba, forty miles from Rio, with hangar, traveling mooring mast, hotel for passengers, and quarters for crew. Completion was scheduled for 1935.

The last flight of the 1933 season was another triangular voyage. The directors of the Chicago World's Fair had invited the *Graf* to make an appearance over the city as a kind of deus ex machina to cap the celebrations. The flight started from Rio on October 19 and, after an uneventful cruise along Brazil's beautiful Atlantic coastline and a refueling stop in Recife, continued north over the mouth of the Amazon and the notorious French penal colony of Devil's Island to Trinidad and the Antilles, thence to Florida, where it moored briefly at the U.S. Navy airship mast at Opa-Locka, near Miami.

Zeppelin fever still raged in America, and tens of thousands of people had driven out to the landing field to watch the great ship come in. But a lot had happened in the three years since the *Graf* had last visited the United States, not least the advent of Adolf Hitler. So though there was still generous appreciation at the arrival of the airship, there were growing reservations about the nation, or at any rate the regime, whence it came. These grew all the more entrenched when the *Graf* tied up at the stub mast and the huge crowd could take a clear look at it. Emblazoned on the right-hand side of the tail was a huge black swastika set inside a white circle on a bloodred background, the symbol of Adolf Hitler's Nazi Party.

There were many in the crowd who wondered at this. Was the *Graf Zeppelin* now a Nazi ship, an international propaganda machine? Had Dr. Eckener become a Nazi, or had his crew?

"Why are you carrying the swastika?" Eckener was asked.

"Because it's the law!" he replied testily.

The swastikas on the *Graf* had been the occasion of a further altercation between Eckener and the Nazi regime. German aircraft were required to carry the swastika only on the tail plane, but Josef Goebbels, the propaganda minister, could not resist the opportunity offered by the huge bulk of the *Graf Zeppelin* and had ordered that huge swastikas over a hundred feet high be painted on the side of the ship, running all the way from top to bottom. Eckener refused pointblank. The *Graf* would look ridiculous emblazoned like that, he said, and might be negatively received abroad, particularly in the United States. The swastikas, he insisted, should go only where they were on other German aircraft—on the fin. He won the day but was now viewed with even greater hostility by the Nazi elite. The feeling was mutual. "Is that disgusting flag already out?" Eckener would growl at takeoff after the order came through that henceforth the *Graf* should fly the Nazi flag at the start of each flight.

On the morning of October 26, the *Graf* arrived in Chicago, where it did a brief circuit over the city (carefully flying on a clockwise course so that the swastika on its tail was not visible from the center of the city). It was here that Eckener began to perceive how differently the *Graf* was now regarded by some Americans. He was advised by the police not to keep the ship on the landing field too long. "We've had tips that your airship may be sabotaged," they warned him. "People don't like Nazi airships around here." The police cordon round the ship was so heavy that not even the passengers could get near it. That evening, when Eckener and the German ambassador were the guests at a celebratory banquet organized by the German-American Clubs of Chicago, they were greeted with applause and cheers by all, and with the Nazi salute by some. The ambassador returned the salute. Hugo Eckener, staring straight ahead, did not.

On October 28 the *Graf* began its return flight to Europe with a full complement of passengers on board, flying over the White House to pay respects to President Roosevelt and finally arriving back in Friedrichshafen via Seville early on the morning of November 2, 1933. Eckener's experiences in America had greatly disturbed him. He told family and friends afterward:

> On every other arrival in the States we've been greeted like heroes and our craft admired, respected, even loved. This time we weren't wanted. We have Hitler to thank for this. Always, up to now, the *Graf Zeppelin* has symbolised international friendship, goodwill and commerce. Now, with that cursed swastika on the tail, it's been perverted to a propaganda vehicle for Goebbels and that damned Ministry of Propaganda of his. Everything we've worked for is being subverted and destroyed.

By now the Nazi creed had begun to win over some of the *Graf*'s crew, generally the younger and newer members, though such was their deep regard for Eckener that none took objection to his occasional anti-Nazi outbursts in the control room. "Pay no attention to Dr. Eckener," they would say. "He's an airshipman, not a politician. He just doesn't understand what's going on in the world today."

In 1934 the *Graf* was advertised to fly to South America every fourteen days. It finally made twelve trips, including one to Buenos Aires, an unsuccessful attempt on Eckener's part to extend the service to Argentina on a regular basis. Perhaps fortunately, Eckener was in Buenos Aires on June 30, the infamous Night of the Long Knives, when the Nazis shot or incarcerated many of Germany's leading opposition figures. A further sixteen South American flights were scheduled for 1935, along with several pioneering airmail flights from Brazil to the Gambia in British West Africa.

Hitler's ascension to power had occurred barely three months after the *Graf*'s final flight of the 1932 season, when Eckener was busy planning the coming season's schedule and looking for funds for the construction of one or more super-zeppelins to add to his fleet of one. Ironically, the same economic collapse in Germany that had thwarted Eckener's plans helped bring Hitler to power, and it was the advent of Hitler, whom Eckener loathed, that was to bring about a dramatic revival in the zeppelin's fortunes and eventually its no less dramatic and absolute demise.

## Chapter Seven

# The End of the Dream

*They mark our passage as a race of men,*
*Earth will not see such ships as these again.*
JOHN MASEFIELD, "SHIPS"

Anyone in the summer of 1935 who paid their fifty pfennigs and joined the line of locals, holidaymakers, brownshirted SA men, and hearty "Strength through Joy" hikers from the Nazi Labor Organization waiting their turn to enter the huge hangar in Friedrichshafen—where the *Graf Zeppelin*'s sister ship, the as-yet-unnamed LZ-129, was being constructed—would have been in for a shock.

Shuffling through a small door, they would have entered a world where everyday standards of size and shape no longer applied, a vast hall of technological fantasy, as hushed and huge as a great cathedral, with steel arches reaching upward to a vaulted roof 164 feet above the floor, and almost the whole of this vast void filled with a structure so intricate and monumental as to defy comprehension.

Beneath this awesome structure, the skeleton of a flying machine over eight hundred feet long, a line of people stopped and stared, marveling at the lacelike filigree of the latitudinal Duralumin girders, miles of them, the beautiful flowing curves of the longitudinal girders, and the whole empty void of this monstrous silvery spider's-web skeleton of the biggest, most advanced, and most luxurious zeppelin yet built, the last word in lighter-than-air transportation, LZ-129.

With a mass of 242 tons, this behemoth of metal and fabric would soon float off the ground laden with fuel, ballast, equipment, furnishings, freight, mail, a hundred or so human beings and their baggage, and all the water, wine, gin, pâté, capon, aspirin, and shoe polish they would need for the two-and-a-half-day crossing to the United States of America.

It had been a long struggle for Dr. Eckener and his colleagues to get this far. The first breakthrough came following the triumphant success of the *Graf Zeppelin's* world flight in 1929, but until now there had been no possibility of building a big new ship because there was no construction shed large enough to build it in. Now the German government and the state of Württemberg had agreed to provide funds to build a new shed next to the old *Graf Zeppelin* shed at Friedrichshafen, the dimensions of which were sufficient to accommodate a new generation of giant zeppelin airliners.

The first new design on the drawing board, factory number LZ-128, was for a ship built on the same basic principles as its predecessor, LZ-127, but bigger in most respects, with a hydrogen capacity of 5,307,000 cubic feet (a third more than the *Graf*), a length of 761 feet, and accommodation for thirty to thirty-four passengers, housed not in an appended gondola but inside the hull of the ship.

The R-101 disaster in October 1930 put the kibosh on the LZ-128 before it had proceeded beyond the drawing board. Whatever the causes of the crash that destroyed the British rigid on its maiden flight to India, the deaths of most of the people on board were caused by the hydrogen fire that followed the ship's relatively gentle impact with the ground. The lesson for the Zeppelin Company was obvious. The next zeppelin airship would have to be designed to be inflated with inert, nonflammable helium. Since helium has only 93 percent the lift of hydrogen, it followed that the next ship would have to have substantially greater dimensions to accommodate the increased gas capacity necessary to provide the same lift as the canceled LZ-128.

In the autumn of 1930, as the *Graf Zeppelin* was completing its first series of commercial flights to South America, the Zeppelin Company design team set to work on drawings for an ambitious new super-zeppelin, LZ-129. The final drawings envisaged the ship as only about 30 feet longer than the *Graf,* at just under 804 feet, but with the diameter increased to over 135 feet, giving it a fatter and more aero-dynamically efficient hull that contained more gas in relation to weight—7,062,100 cubic feet, to be precise, more than double that of the *Graf*—and offered greater resistance to bending forces. Almost as big as the biggest ocean liner afloat, the new ship, to be christened *Hindenburg,* would be the grandest and most magnificent flying machine the world had ever seen.

Though neither Hitler nor Goering had any time for the zeppelin, nor the slightest desire to fly in one, they both saw its value as a spectacular propaganda medium and a soaring symbol of Nazi hegemony at home and German reawakening abroad. In the summer of 1934 Eckener was asked by Goebbels, almost in passing, how he was coming along with the new ship, and whether he had raised the money to finish it. Greatly surprised by this unexpected show of interest, Eckener replied that he was still some half a million marks short, whereupon Goebbels coolly rejoined, "Is that all? Why, that's a mere bagatelle! I'll approach some big industrialist and suggest they contribute what you need."

Stung to rivalry by Goebbels's offer, Hermann Goering, the air minister, intervened with a proposal of his own. To guarantee funding for further zeppelin development, he suggested that from March 1935 the air ministry should take control of the enterprise by setting up a new company, the Deutsche Zeppelin Reederei (German Zeppelin Airline Company), with a capital of 9 million marks (2.2 million dollars), half of which was to be contributed by the German state airline, Lufthansa.

There would be changes. From now on the Zeppelin Company would be solely concerned with airship construction and development in Friedrichshafen, while the Reederei would take over all flight operations from headquarters in Frankfurt. Ernst Lehmann was put in charge of the Reederei as joint manager alongside an ex–wartime navy flyer and future chief of the German air force in the Netherlands,

Friedrich Christiansen. Eckener was made chairman of the board, a vague appointment that left his eminent name on the letterhead but effectively removed him from direct executive control of Zeppelin commercial affairs and flight operations, though he remained as head of the Luftschiffbau Zeppelin construction company. The zeppelin had been saved in return for the head of its chief executive and guiding light, Hugo Eckener—or so it seemed.

Eckener's first thought was to go quietly and retire. He was sixty-six, and the last ten strenuous years had taken their toll. But the more he thought about it, the more he was convinced that to turn his back on the work and passion of his life would be a total abrogation of his responsibilities. Finally he made his decision: "I would remain in commercial operations in the interest of the enterprise for which I had formerly been responsible," he declared, "even if I were only a 'fifth wheel.' I would personally intervene in the enterprise as its responsible head whenever or wherever it would seem to me desirable, even if this resulted in conflicts of authority."

So the work on the LZ-129 resumed after three years in limbo. Chief of the design team was once again Ludwig Dürr, who had been with the zeppelin enterprise since 1899. In charge of structural design was Arthur Foerster. Other engineers supervised specific divisions, including power plants, fuel and electrical systems, radio installation, crew and passenger quarters, and so on. Head of construction was Dr. Eckener's son, Knut.

Though the hull was basically of conventional zeppelin design—evolved, tried, and tested over more than a quarter of a century—the scale and intricacy of the structure never failed to impress. Fifteen transverse main rings consisting of thirty-six-sided girderwork polygons divided the hull into sixteen compartments to contain the lifting-gas cells; thirty-six triangular longitudinal girders totalling thirteen miles in length ran from one end of the hull to the other to tie the main rings together; between each main ring, two intermediate rings reduced the bending stresses in the longitudinals. All this was enclosed by an outer cover of huge cotton panels totalling 367,000 square feet in area, aluminum doped to reflect the sun's rays.

The ship's fins alone were 135 feet high, nearly 100 feet long, and 50 feet broad. They were 11 feet thick at the base, so roomy that the lower one was fitted out as a manned auxiliary steering station in the event of a breakdown in the main steering system in the control car. The control car itself was carried well forward beneath the ship, and four streamlined engine cars, each housing a specially designed 1,320-horsepower Daimler-Benz diesel engine—a lot safer than petrol—were slung in pairs aft and amidships. On both sides of the keel that ran along the bottom of the ship from bow to stern were crew's quarters, freight rooms, and fuel-oil and water-ballast tanks. The pièce de résistance of this extraordinary colossus was the lavish and expansive passenger accommodation housed inside the lower hull a little forward of amidships.

Two severe setbacks befell the enterprise. At the end of 1935, the United States, then the world's only substantial provider of helium, a by-product of the Texas oil and gas wells, refused to make helium available for the new ship. The reason was not, as has often been assumed, because of the Nazi rise to power in Germany, but because the Helium Control Act of 1927 reserved to the U.S. government all the helium produced in the country, prohibiting its export. Eckener had assumed that a joint German-American airship company would be granted access to American helium, but the worldwide economic depression made it impossible for the U.S. authorities to bend their own law and release a precious raw material to a foreign concern.

In addition, the Americans had recently suffered catastrophic accidents to their navy's finest airships, the *Akron* and the *Macon*, both intended for long-range missions at sea and both inflated with helium. The *Akron*, the first to see service, was a splendid airship capable of carrying up to 270 people (a record) and five fighter aircraft a distance of ten thousand miles without refueling. In April 1933 it flew into a storm off New Jersey and was forced down into the sea with the loss of all but three of the seventy-six men on board. In February 1935 the *Akron*'s sister ship, the *Macon*, ran into severe turbulence while taking part in naval maneuvers over the Pacific and had to crash-land off the coast of California when the tail structure began to break up. Though only two of the eighty-three crewmen lost their lives, the disaster ended America's interwar experiment with rigid airships. The public turned against them on the grounds that they were dangerous, the navy on the grounds that they were useless. Only Germany was left to continue its pursuit of the zeppelin dream.

But if helium had not saved America's airships, at least it had spared them the nightmare of fire, and the prospect of operating a zeppelin airline with hydrogen-inflated airships was not a happy one for the Germans. But it was too late to change the ship's design and structure. Like it or not, the *Hindenburg*'s sixteen huge gas cells—not made of gold-beater's skin but of two layers of lightweight cotton with gastight film in between—would have to be inflated with hydrogen.

Shortly after this setback came another. Since the *Hindenburg* was intended primarily for the North America route, it was crucial that the U.S. government give its permission for the ship to make use of the hangar at the Lakehurst Naval Air Station, the only terminal available for the zeppelin transatlantic service in the United States. It was a bitter blow when Eckener was told that Lakehurst could not be made available for enterprises of a purely commercial nature. "Only the President of the United States could permit an exception," said the official letter, "in case he should determine the flights were experimental in character."

This setback was infinitely graver than the helium one had been. Refused helium, the *Hindenburg* could still fly on hydrogen; refused Lakehurst, it could not fly to America and back, the principal reason for its existence. There were only two men in the world who could hope to resolve this crisis: the president of the United States and the man who might have been president of Germany. At the end of February 1936, therefore, little more than a week before the *Hindenburg*'s first test flight, Eckener arrived in Washington to seek an audience with President Roosevelt.

The situation was fraught. Germany was becoming a great power again, and Eckener thought he detected a cooling of attitudes to all things German in America, a reaction to the growing militancy and extremism of the Nazi regime. When the German ambassador in Washington applied on Eckener's behalf for an audience with the president, it was denied on the grounds that the use of a U.S. Navy facility by a foreign business organization was clearly against the law and was not negotiable. For several days Eckener sat around in his hotel hoping for a change of heart on the president's part, growing more depressed by the hour. Then he had a most unlikely visitor: Bill Leeds, the young multimillionaire whose phonograph had so riled him on the world flight but who had remained a staunch zeppelin supporter. Leeds's father, it so happened, was a great friend of Roosevelt's. Leeds said he would see what he could do.

"The next day at noon," Eckener recalled, "he came to me from the White House and announced, 'The President will see you tomorrow at five o'clock.'"

Eckener had been received at the White House several times before, twice by President Coolidge in 1924 and 1928 and once by President Hoover in 1929, after the world flight. But President Roosevelt made the most favorable impression.

"He received me seated," Eckener wrote, "being condemned by his crippled state to sit permanently behind his big desk, with customary remarks—'Hello, Dr. Eckener! How are you? I'm glad to meet you personally!'—but spoken with such warmth and in such a sympathetic tone of voice that they seemed to come straight from the heart. After complimenting me on the flights of the *Graf Zeppelin* he suddenly came straight to the point."

"Well, you want to make regularly scheduled flights over the North Atlantic?"

"Yes, Mr. President," replied Eckener, "I would like to."

"I must tell you frankly," Roosevelt said, 'I don't believe you can do it."

"I believe we certainly can," said Eckener. "I am certain we can do it."

"I am very doubtful, Dr. Eckener. I'm an old sailor, and I know how the North Atlantic can be in bad weather."

"I am well aware of the treacherous weather of the North Atlantic, Mr. President. We can handle it."

"Well, what can I do to help you?"

"I would like to ask you to make the Lakehurst hangar available to us again for the ten flights."

Roosevelt thought for a second or two, studying Eckener's face, considering his verdict. "Good, you shall have it!" he said finally.

"The question interests me. Go tomorrow to the secretary of the navy and discuss it with him further. I'll be glad to help in any way I can. Good luck!"

Eckener would meet Roosevelt on three more occasions during the next two years. The president kept his word and remained pro-Eckener and pro-zeppelin for as long as the political climate allowed. Eckener returned to Friedrichshafen a very surprised and relieved man. The zeppelin enterprise had been saved at the eleventh hour, thanks to the good will of the American president, the continuing interest of the U.S. Navy in the transatlantic airship experiment, and the timely intervention of Bill Leeds.

The first trial flight of the new ship took place on March 4, 1936. Later Goebbels asked Eckener if he would consider changing the name from *Hindenburg* to *Hitler*. Eckener politely but firmly refused. Not that Hitler objected to this apparent slight, for he regarded zeppelins with ill-concealed anxiety, declined to fly in one, and was unwilling to have his name associated with one in case it blew up or crashed. "The whole thing always seems to me like an inventor who claims to have discovered a cheap new kind of floor covering which looks marvellous, shines forever, and never wears out," he once said. "But he adds that there is one disadvantage. It must not be walked on with nailed shoes and nothing hard must ever be dropped on it because, unfortunately, it's made of high explosive."

A few days later Goebbels ordered the *Graf Zeppelin* and the newly completed *Hindenburg* to undertake a three-day propaganda flight across the length and breadth of the Reich to drum up support for a referendum on Hitler's occupation of the Rhineland, which had taken place on March 7. Eckener was appalled: "Apart from my political convictions, I considered this misuse of the airships in bad taste, a sort of sacrilege, and I refused to participate myself." But he was in no position to stop the flights, which were due to start on March 26.

As the new head of Zeppelin operations, Captain Lehmann was under a direct obligation to fulfill the Nazi minister's wishes. This was not as onerous for him as it would have been for Eckener, for though Lehmann was not a Nazi Party member, he was less unsympathetic to the cause. Anxious to please his new masters, Lehmann rushed the

*Hindenburg* out of its hangar in spite of gusty crosswinds, with the result that the tail tore away from the handlers and smashed into the ground, damaging the lower fin.

Eckener was beside himself. "Wie können Sie das Schiff für diese Scheissfahrt riskieren!" he roared at this most senior of airship commanders. "How could you risk the ship for a shit [literally] flight like this!" He went on: "You had the best excuse in the world to postpone this idiotic flight. Instead, you risk the ship merely to avoid annoying Herr Goebbels. Do you call this showing a sense of responsibility towards our enterprise? What are you trying to do? Wreck us? Have you lost your senses? Are you afraid of Goebbels?"

Lehmann told him that the fin could be temporarily patched up in a couple of hours and the flight carried through. He reminded Eckener that he had received direct orders from the government to proceed with the flight, and he had no alternative but to carry out those orders.

"So that is your only concern," Eckener replied bitterly. "To take off quickly on this mad flight and drop election pamphlets for Herr Goebbels? Goebbels! Idiotic Propaganda Ministry! Ridiculous mission! The fact that we have to take off for Rio in four days and have made no flights to test the engines apparently means nothing to you?" The *Hindenburg*'s first transatlantic flight was scheduled for March 31. The normal twelve-hour engine test flight at full power had not yet been made, and because of the three days taken up with the propaganda flight, there would no be no time to make it.

An official from the propaganda ministry, who was on the *Hindenburg* to supervise the propaganda aspects of the flight, overheard Eckener's angry exchange with Lehmann. The consequences were soon to come.

From March 26 to 29 the *Hindenburg* and *Graf Zeppelin*, emblazoned with huge swastikas on their tail fins, flew over almost every town and city of the Reich as part of a Nazi program to persuade every German to vote in favor of Hitler's reoccupation of the Rhineland. Millions of leaflets were dropped from the stern of the *Hindenburg*, and all 104 people on board voted for the Führer and his policies. Eckener declined to take part.

At his first press conference following the propaganda flights, Goebbels announced to the assembled reporters, "Dr. Eckener has alienated himself from the nation. In the future his name may no longer be mentioned in the newspapers, nor may his picture be further used." Hugo Eckener, the people's hero, had become a nonperson in his own country.

At the time of Goebbels's announcement, Eckener was on board the *Hindenburg* on its first intercontinental flight, making his way to Rio, where the big new airship port at Santa Cruz de Sepetiba was now in operation. The ship was a revelation, everything that Eckener had dreamed of, everything the specifications had led him to expect. The flight was a joy, and he found himself in as good a humor as all the passengers on board. This faded a little, however, when one of the engines came to a dead stop with a violent jerk midocean after the ship had passed the Cape Verde Islands. The damage was so severe—wrist-pin breakage—that it could be mended only in Rio. Three good engines and a following trade wind kept the ship's speed up, and the flight continued.

Then a reporter for a major British newspaper approached Eckener. "I have just received a radio message from my paper," the reporter explained, "asking me to enquire the reason for the declaration of banishment which Dr. Goebbels has imposed on you. I would like to send five hundred words on this."

Eckener was dumbfounded. He would gladly have given the reporter a story, he said, but he knew absolutely nothing about it. None of the German journalists on board knew anything about it either, since their editors back home were forbidden to mention Eckener's name to anyone, including their own reporters. After some hours a representative of a Berlin paper was able to extract from his office a mysteriously worded snippet to the effect that "Lotte's father is seriously ill." Eckener had to complete the rest of the journey "seriously ill," without any idea what illness he was suffering from. He later learned that he would be allowed to return to Germany but that his citizenship would be taken away from him.

In Rio the *Hindenburg*'s damaged engine was repaired as best as could be, though as a precaution it was run only at half power on the return flight. This was trouble-free until the ship reached the Cape

Verde Islands again. Here they had to buck a strong northeast trade wind set nearly dead against them, and at this point another engine failed for the same reason as the first. The worry now was that if two engines had failed for the same reason, the remaining two might do the same. The only solution was to cut power by half, with the prospect of flying against the wind for up to forty-five hours over a distance of fourteen hundred miles at a ground speed of only thirty-two miles per hour.

"The situation was really critical," Eckener wrote. "Beneath us the open sea, to starboard the wastes of Africa, and seventy-five people in the ship. A very, very serious situation. I confess that I have hardly ever experienced so much mental torture as in these hours of vacillation and complexity."

The options were few. If he ran the remaining engines at full power, they would probably all fail, and the ship would drift out of control like a colossal free balloon to eventual destruction. He could turn the ship around and run before the wind to Recife, but it was doubtful if the engines could be repaired there, and the *Hindenburg* would be stranded on the mast without a sheltering hangar. Another option was to head for the African coast, so that in the event that another engine failed the ship could be set down on dry land in the desert. At least the passengers could be saved, though the ship would be lost. The final option was to try to escape from the northeast trade wind by climbing above it, and with luck find the more westerly counter–trade wind. This was usually only found at over five thousand feet, which was some way above the *Hindenburg*'s pressure height.

Luck was with them. "We climbed to 2,600, 3,000, 3,300," Eckener wrote. "Still the same northeast trade wind. We rose to 3,600 and who can describe our joy as we came upon a northwest wind here which permitted us to make a speed of 80–87 miles per hour towards Gibraltar, so that we came home on three legs. We were lucky, but so was Dr. Goebbels, who had prevented the thorough engine trial."

On April 10, after a marathon flight of just under 104 hours, the *Hindenburg* returned to its giant hangar at Löwenthal on the edge of Friedrichshafen, and while all four engines were being overhauled by Daimler-Benz, Eckener set off for Berlin to discover where he stood with the Nazi hierarchy and of what he was accused. His first port of call was the air ministry, where the secretary of state, Field Marshal Erhard Milch, who had always been friendly to him, advised him that the air minister, Hermann Goering, wanted a word with him.

Goering, as airman to airman, was courteous and genial. But as Nazi to anti-Nazi, he was uncompromising. He made no mention of the rude remarks Eckener had made about Goebbels at the time of the propaganda flights, partly because he himself had no time for Goebbels, either, and partly because he was well aware that on technical and operational grounds Eckener was right to have opposed the flights. But Eckener had refused to voice his support for the occupation of the Rhineland and had made fun of the Hitler salute in front of the foreign press. Worse, it was understood that he had wanted to succeed Hindenburg as Germany's president. Eckener began to form the impression that the Nazi hierarchy, Hitler above all, viewed him, because of his great popularity among the German people and his outspoken anti-Nazi views, as a potential focus or even leader of opposition to the Nazi government. Since it would be politically maladroit to have him shot or locked up in a concentration camp, the next best thing would be to pretend he did not exist by slapping a permanent press embargo on any mention of his name or any facts regarding him. Eckener could try writing a letter of apology to Goebbels, Goering suggested, explaining his technical worries about the *Hindenburg*. Meanwhile, he himself would have a word with Hitler about having the banishment order lifted.

On the way out of the air ministry, Eckener met the general in charge of the technical department that dealt with engines. "You were right about the *Hindenburg* engine test business," he told Eckener. "I would have done the same myself."

Several years were to pass before Eckener's name could be mentioned in public again in Germany. In despair, he considered seeking political asylum abroad. But he chose to stick it out, hoping he might still advance the zeppelin cause in spite of the revulsion he felt for the new masters of the Reich.

The date for the *Hindenburg*'s first scheduled passenger flight to the United States was set for Wednesday, May 6, 1936. For this historic event a bevy of international celebrities gathered at the Kurgarten Hotel in Friedrichshafen, among them old zeppelin hands like Lady

Grace Hay, her colleague Karl von Wiegand, and Sir Hubert Wilkins and his wife. Others included the best-selling crime writer Leslie Charteris and his wife, the governor of Bavaria, the president of the Junkers Aircraft Works, and the head of German Railways.

After an early dinner the fifty passengers were taken by bus to Löwenthal. It was dusk now, and the great hangar loomed hugely in the darkening sky. The enormous doors had already been slid open, revealing the *Hindenburg*'s colossal silver nose and beneath it a crowd of swarming human figures, dwarfed by the breathtaking proportions of the great airship now being prepared for flight.

Embarking on the *Hindenburg* was more like boarding an ocean liner than an airplane. First the passengers went through passport and customs control, then a double security check, where they were obliged to hand over any matches and lighters, along with their cameras, since photography from the air was prohibited by the governments of the countries over which they would be flying. Then they clambered on board the ship by means of two small retractable aluminum stairways lowered from the hull below the passenger quarters. These gave access to B deck, in the lower part of the hull, where the ship's public rooms were situated. Another set of stairs led up to A deck, where twenty-five double cabins opened off a series of passageways. Here the passengers deposited their hand luggage before proceeding to the hundred-foot-long promenades back on B deck, with six large Plexiglass windows on each side, slanting outward at forty-five degrees, and usually open since there was no draft, even at an air speed of eighty knots. Chatting excitedly among themselves or with family and friends on the ground below, the passengers waited with keen anticipation for the moment of takeoff.

At a quarter past nine, word was given that the ship was ready, and the band began to play: first a sentimental little German song of farewell, "Muss ich denn zum Städele hinaus?" ("Must I Leave the Hometown I Love?"), followed by the national anthem, "Deutschland über Alles," and after that "The Stars and Stripes Forever." Then Captain Lehmann, the ship's commander, shouted the order, "*Zeppelin marsch!*" and slowly the great ship was hauled out of the hangar into the full moonlight, revealing to the crowd first the nose, then the control car, with the name *Hindenburg* in bright red Gothic script above it, then the promenades with the passengers calling and waving through the windows, and then, emblazoned on the sides amidships, the interlocking rings of the logo of the Olympic Games, due to start in Berlin in a few weeks' time, followed by the international registration number, D-LZ-129, the rear engine cars, and finally the massive tail fins emblazoned with swastikas. The *Hindenburg* was just seventy-nine feet shorter than the *Titanic*; from fin tip to fin tip it was as high as a thirteen-story building; inside was a quantity of hydrogen equal to the volume of three hundred average American homes.

Lehmann leaned out of a control-car window. "*Schiff hoch!*" he ordered. "*Up ship!*"

The handling lines were cast off, the ground crew gave an upward shove on the control-car handling rails, a few tons of ballast water were released, and the flight began. Soon the four powerful diesel engines started up, barely audible from the passenger accommodation, and the ship began to move forward and gain height as it gathered speed. There was no noise, no vibration, no pitching and tossing, just a feeling of smoothness and solidity. So quiet and steady was the *Hindenburg* at takeoff that on later flights passengers still in their cabins, unaware that the ship had left the ground, would summon the steward and demand: "Steward, when are we leaving? It's half past twelve." The steward would reply, "Madam, we left two hours ago."

Many passengers stayed by the promenade windows as night fell and the *Hindenburg* headed north across Germany to the Dutch coast and the English Channel. It was a clear night, and the countryside was silvered with the light of the full moon, punctuated here and there with the lights of a town or farm or *Schloss*. Gradually the passengers drifted away from the mesmerizing windows to explore the public rooms of this flying hotel or to unpack and settle into their cabins.

The cabins on the *Hindenburg*, colored light blue, gray, or beige, were barely bigger than those on the *Graf Zeppelin*. As on the *Graf*, the two berths were arranged one above the other. Unlike the *Graf*'s, however, the cabins on the *Hindenburg* were situated within the interior of the ship and had no windows. A folding washbasin provided hot and cold running water, and ventilation and heating were available. There was a folding writing table and a shallow wardrobe, but no drawers, so most clothes had to be kept in suitcases.

It was the public rooms that got the most acclaim. Even though the living space on the *Hindenburg* occupied only 1 percent of the volume of the ship, no aircraft before or since provided such spacious accommodation. Unlike the *Graf Zeppelin,* the design and decor was ultra contemporary: cool, uncluttered, almost Bauhaus. The grandest rooms were on A deck outboard of the passenger cabins: lounge and reading room to starboard, dining room to port. Here on the first evening, the passengers, who had eaten dinner already, were offered a simple cold buffet of sandwiches, wine, and beer, after which most chose to retire for the night. A handful of merry late-nighters chose to avail themselves of the facilities of the smoking room and its bar down on B deck.

The smoking room, an unusual feature on a vessel inflated with over 7 million cubic feet of hydrogen, was a response to the endless complaints of smokers on the strictly no-smoking *Graf.* Safeguards were strict. The room was pressurized and sealed with an air-lock door. The furniture and walls were of fire-resistant leather, the floor of fire-resistant peachwood. Since matches and lighters had been confiscated on embarkation, the bar steward alone was responsible for lighting every cigarette and cigar, using a car cigarette lighter for the purpose, and checking that passengers were using the automatic self-sealing ashtrays properly and were not still smoking when they left the room. The smoking room was a popular venue, a world of its own detached from the rest of the ship, decorated with murals portraying the history of lighter-than-air flight, from the first Montgolfier to the present-day *Graf Zeppelin,* and with windows looking down on the world and a bar offering a choice of cocktails that included Martinis, Manhattans, and a knockout Zeppelin house special (ingredients unknown) called the Maybach 12, after the powerful zeppelin petrol engine of that name. Conveniently, B deck also housed four toilets and a gents' urinal, as well as another facility never seen on an airship before: a shower room.

After breakfast the next morning the passengers were handed the shipboard rules and regulations drawn up by the Reederei. Times: breakfast, 8 to 10 A.M.; lunch from 12 noon onward; afternoon tea, 4 P.M.; dinner at 7; public rooms closed at 11; smoking room and bar open till 3 A.M. Services: ship's doctor available free, books available from library, personal telegrams via ship's radio room. Rules: no smoking except in the smoking room, no throwing things out of the windows, no photos allowed inside territorial three-mile limits.

The day was free to spend as they chose. Few were ever bored. Some were happy just to look out the promenade windows at the clouds and at the waves sliding past below at a distance of little more than three-quarters of the ship's length. A few attended Mass held by Father Paul Schulte, the "Flying Priest," in a makeshift chapel on one of the promenades, complete with portable altar, flowers, and unlit candles—the first Mass ever celebrated in the air.

Others availed themselves of the remarkable facilities on board. Flying on the *Hindenburg* was strictly for the well-heeled. The fare was $400 one way, equivalent to the cost of an automobile, or $720 return (first-class on the *Queen Mary,* the fastest and most luxurious of the transatlantic liners, cost rather more). Nothing but the best would do for such a clientele, and this the *Hindenburg* provided to a degree unrivaled by any airliner before or since.

The passenger space on the starboard side of A deck consisted of a thirty-four-foot-long lounge and a sixteen-foot-long writing room. The lounge was popular with those who wanted to curl up in a chair with a book, take a nap, or chat with fellow passengers. On the wall was an enormous Mercator projection map of the world bearing pictures of the ships and the voyages of Columbus, Vasco da Gama, Magellan, and Cook, the luxury North Atlantic liners *Bremen* and *Europa,* the Atlantic flight of LZ-126 (later *Los Angeles*), the world flight of the *Graf Zeppelin,* and the *Graf's* passage to South America. The lounge boasted a leather-covered aluminum baby piano weighing only 397 pounds, soon to be put to good use for the entertainment of all on board.

The reading and writing room had restful gray walls, paintings depicting the story of mail services through the ages, from Eskimo dog sled to *Graf Zeppelin* airship, together with a small library and writing tables where journalists like Lady Hay clattered out copy on their typewriters and other passengers busied themselves scribbling mounds of postcards, which could be dispatched by pneumatic tube straight to the mail room above the control car for franking with a *Hindenburg* stamp.

On the port side of the same deck was the elegant and very modern dining room, measuring fifty feet by fifteen, flanked by a promenade with sloping windows, providing seating for thirty-four passengers per sitting at eleven tables of special lightweight aluminum (like the chairs) and partially enclosed by inner walls of cotton fabric decorated with paintings of airship travel.

To dine in this flying restaurant was an incomparable experience. At tables laid with crisp white linen, fresh-cut flowers, fine silver, and special *Hindenburg* ivory porcelain, the passengers, along with the commander and senior officers and Dr. Eckener, who distributed themselves around the tables, were served hearty gourmet meals of mainly German or French provenance (fattened duckling Bavarian style or venison cutlets Beauval), with German white wines or a small choice of French red, prepared by the chef and his five assistants in the all-electric galley on B deck below and sent up by dumbwaiter to the serving pantry next to the dining room.

Any passengers who felt they had time on their hands could go on a guided tour of the extraordinary ship, working their way along the keel—a triangular girder the height of a man with a narrow catwalk at the bottom—all the way from the nose cone to the tail fin via the control car. In wonderment they stopped to view the sixteen towering translucent gas cells, lovingly tended by their three duty riggers; the big Duralumin tanks containing diesel fuel, fresh water, and ballast water; the freight rooms big enough to hold an airplane with wings disassembled; the spares stowage, complete with an entire Daimler-Benz diesel engine and spare propeller; the three storerooms that housed two and a quarter tons of food and provisions, including 440 pounds of meat and poultry, 220 pounds of fish, 330 of sausage and cold cuts, 220 of butter, cheese, and marmalade, 40 gallons of milk, 250 bottles of wine, and an unspecified number of bottles of spirits.

For some passengers, the *Hindenburg*'s nerve center—the control car with its bridge, navigation room, and radio room, located in the hull immediately above—was the most fascinating part of the ship's working innards. The bridge in essentials was not greatly different from that of the *Graf,* with the elevator wheel on the port side, the rudder wheel up front, gas board, ballast board, and engine room telegraph at hand. Though it looked sparsely simple to the average passenger, any attempt to explain the physical principles of airship flying and the techniques of transoceanic navigation—dynamic and static lift, pressure-pattern flying, drift triangles, Echolot soundings, and all the other tricks of the trade—quickly produced blank looks and puzzled frowns. The radio room was rather more accessible for the lay traveler, for this was where passengers' telegram messages came and went (most of them to and from Lady Hay), though the room's main function was to communicate by telegraph and telephone radio links with shore stations and ships at sea to gather meteorological data essential for navigation and the avoidance of storms.

For those who felt they could brave it, the visit to the engine cars slung outboard of the hull was the most dramatic, even unnerving, part of the tour. United Press correspondent Webb Miller was taken to the engine ladder by Lehmann, who was in an impish mood. To show how tough the ship's outer cover was, he leapt off the catwalk and gleefully bounced up and down on the fabric like a boy on a trampoline. At the shipboard end of the flimsy engine ladder, which had no guard rail and was lashed by an eighty-mile-per-hour slipstream, Lehmann showed Miller how to descend without being swept to his death by crooking his elbow around the ladder's windward edge. Though Miller was wearing a protective padded helmet, like the duty mechanic, he found the engine noise deafening, "as if we were being shot through the air inside a huge artillery shell with open windows."

For Dr. Eckener, this flight was what he had been striving toward for the last three decades of his life. Though he was not the ship's commander and appeared to be traveling in a purely honorary capacity, his gentlemanly courtesy and infectious good cheer captivated all on board, and he seemed to be tireless, indeed sleepless, in his determination to savor every minute of the experience of flying to New York on this fabulous aerial liner of his dreams. He was not in command, but the *Hindenburg* was his ship.

The sense of safety and security seemed universal. Even in high winds the ship rode through the sky as steady as a rock. At lunchtime on Thursday, when Eckener was sitting at the head of one table and Lehmann at the head of another, they ran into a storm. Rain and hail lashed the ship, the flower vases on the tables trembled a little, and the *Hindenburg* rolled slightly—and that was all.

So steady was the ship in flight that there was scarcely a ripple on the surface of a glass of water, and a pen or pencil could be stood on end on a table. When reporter Louis Lochner was taken to the so-called seaman's rest, a lookout in the very point of the ship's bow, he found there was not the slightest trace of engine vibration and noted in his log, "You feel as though you are carried in the arms of angels." As for the noise, it was barely perceptible, the faint drone of the engines never measuring more than sixty-one decibels, compared with an ocean liner at sixty-eight decibels and the New York subway at one hundred. "The *Hindenburg*," the American engineer Preston Bassett concluded, "is the quietest form of transportation now available."

On the last night many passengers were restless and sat up late. At half past three in the morning some of them remained up in anticipation of their first sight of the New World from the air, among them Lady Hay, still typing her copy. At four Captain Lehmann and Dr. Eckener, dressed as always in leather jacket and white scarf, came into the passenger area for coffee. Just after five, as day was beginning to break, the *Hindenburg* arrived over New York, a vast sea of light from which issued a great cacophony of welcoming sirens and hooters, made a low pass over the Empire State Building, Manhattan Bridge, Brooklyn Bridge, and the Statue of Liberty, then headed inland to Lakehurst.

At 6:10 on the morning of Saturday, May 9, 1936, gloriously lit by the red rising sun, LZ-129 *Hindenburg* locked on to the Lakehurst mast at the end of the first-ever commercial passenger airline flight to North America, completed in the record time of sixty-one and a half hours, or about two and a half days.

Though Lehmann was the ship's commander, it was Eckener the press and newsreel men wanted to talk to, for it was not often that world-famous nonpersons arrived in America in such spectacular fashion. Was it true, they clamored, that Hitler had ordered his banishment from the German public and media? Eckener smiled, evaded the question, muttered about the record-breaking flight. He eased up when asked about his forthcoming meeting with President Roosevelt. It was Roosevelt, Eckener acknowledged, who had made the new

transatlantic airship service possible. Work would soon begin
American commercial airship port to complement the new F
Main intercontinental airship port in Frankfurt, where the *Hinden-*
*burg* would be based on its return to Europe. LZ-130, a sister ship to
the *Hindenburg*, was already being built at Friedrichshafen and was
due to be completed by September 1937, and two even larger ships to
take up to eighty or a hundred passengers were in the planning stage.
That was just the beginning. The Zeppelin Company was considering
a ten-year plan that would see the construction of thirty-six or forty
super-zeppelins operating a worldwide service by 1945.

Nonperson or not, Eckener was a contented man. It seemed his
life's work had not been in vain.


The *Hindenburg* completed ten scheduled round trips between Germany and America in 1936, and seven nonstop flights to Rio de
Janeiro. At the same time, the *Graf Zeppelin* made thirteen flights to
Rio and back, including an airmail shuttle flight from Brazil to and
from the Gambia. To crown a triumphal season, Eckener planned one
final public-relations extravaganza: the so-called Millionaires' Flight
at the conclusion of the last flight of the year. He invited seventy-two
of the most wealthy, powerful, and influential men in America—
among them Nelson Rockefeller, the chairman of the Chase Manhattan Bank, and a number of congressmen—for a joyride on the
*Hindenburg* over New England in all the flaming colors of fall. Flying
with them was NBC radio commentator John B. Kennedy, broadcast-
ing live from the ship as it headed north. "We've got enough notables
on board," he informed his listeners, "to make the *Who's Who* say
what's what."

The VIPs were impressed with the food, the view, the ship, the
facilities, the sense of space, solidity, security, the sheer fun and nov-
elty of it all. Never had Captain Max Pruss's dictum, "If you want to
travel quickly, take an aeroplane; if you want to travel comfortably,
take an airship," been more impressively demonstrated. After ten
supremely memorable hours in the air, the influential political, industrial, and business leaders of America were returned to terra firma as
gently as a goose-feather fall. For Hugo Eckener things had never

looked so bright. The Millionaires' Flight would soon lead to the founding of the American Zeppelin Corporation (a subsidiary of Goodyear), with plans to operate four airships on the transatlantic service, two under the German flag and two under the American.

And so the 1936 flying season closed. In its first year of operations, the *Hindenburg* had flown sixteen hundred transatlantic passengers and logged over three thousand hours in the air. Its average flight time from the coast of Europe to the coast of America was fifty-nine hours, forty-seven hours in the opposite direction. On the westbound flight the ship averaged nearly 83 percent capacity, on the eastbound flight nearly 107 percent capacity, with some passengers accommodated in cabins in the officers' quarters along the keel.

No wonder Eckener described the financial results of the first year's operations as an "agreeable surprise." Each transatlantic flight of the *Hindenburg* cost twenty-eight thousand dollars, including salaries, depreciation, insurance, and terminal charges. Passenger fares brought in twenty thousand dollars per trip, and airmail and express freight charges made up the balance. "It was not difficult to prove," noted Eckener, "that a weekly service with two ships would make a profit."

For its part, the *Graf Zeppelin* had now made nearly 590 flights in eight years, including over 140 ocean crossings, flown nearly a million miles, been airborne for more than seventeen thousand hours, carried thirty-four thousand people, more than thirteen thousand of them fare-paying passengers, as well as nearly seventy tons of mail and freight, for the most part without a hitch and without any passenger receiving so much as a bruised finger. Recently the *Graf* had been declared fit for a further three years' flying by the air-board inspectors.

These were now the only two rigid airships in the world still flying operationally.

During the early months of 1937, the *Hindenburg* and the *Graf Zeppelin* underwent complete overhauls in preparation for a busy new flying season starting in late spring. Nine extra cabins were inserted into the *Hindenburg* on B deck, increasing the passenger capacity to seventy. Meanwhile, its sister ship, LZ-130, was nearing completion and was advertised to depart for Rio on its maiden voyage on October 27, 1937.

On March 6 the *Hindenburg* set off on a round trip to Rio de Janeiro with Captain Max Pruss in command and Dr. Eckener on board as guest of honor at the ceremonial opening of the new airship terminal at Santa Cruz de Sepetiba. Following the *Hindenburg*'s return, all efforts were concentrated on preparing the ship for the forthcoming North Atlantic season, comprising eighteen round trips to Lakehurst and back between May and November. The American Zeppelin Transport Company would be acting as general agents for the Deutsche Zeppelin Reederei, owners and operators of the *Hindenburg,* and the Hamburg American–North German Lloyd shipping organization acted as the general passenger agents.

At this point there was no other aircraft in the world that could undertake this service. Though the *Graf Zeppelin* was well capable of crossing the Atlantic, as a commercial passenger aircraft it would have been unreliable and unprofitable on that route. As for airplanes, though Pan American Airways were to open a restricted, island-hopping passenger service across the Pacific toward the end of the year, using their Martin 130 flying boat "China Clipper," no plane yet existed that could fly fare-paying passengers across the North Atlantic. But the situation was changing.

Though long-distance airplane flights were still hazardous undertakings in the first part of the 1930s, international air races and continuing research had been improving performances constantly, and long-distance records were regularly being broken. In 1930 Amy Johnson had flown from England to Australia in nineteen days. In 1931 Wiley Post and Harold Gatty broke the *Graf Zeppelin*'s 1929 record by flying around the world in eight days, fifteen hours, fifty-one minutes total lapsed time (a little more than 106 hours actual flying time). In 1933 Wiley Post improved on this achievement with the first solo circumnavigation of the world, in seven days, eighteen hours, nineteen minutes, a record soon to be shattered when the reclusive millionaire aviator Howard Hughes, who already held the world airspeed record and the record for the fastest air crossing of the United States, flew around the world with a crew of four in a twin-engine

Lockheed in the phenomenal time of three days, nineteen hours, fourteen minutes, never departing from his schedule by more than a few minutes. Before long, astonishing performances were becoming almost routine, even accidental, like the solo transatlantic flight of Douglas "Wrong Way" Corrigan, who greeted his well-wishers on landing in Ireland after a west-east Atlantic crossing from New York with the immortal words: "Guess I made a mistake, I meant to fly to California." Height and speed records also continued to be broken. In 1933 two British biplanes flew over Mount Everest for the first time, at a height of nearly thirty thousand feet, and within five years the airplane altitude record had gone up to over fifty-six thousand feet, while by the end of the decade the airspeed record was set at almost 470 miles per hour (by a German Messerschmitt Me 109R prop fighter plane).

Improvements in aircraft performances were mirrored by a steady expansion of commercial airplane operations. In 1930 the first regular coast-to-coast service began operations in the United States, with an overnight stop in Kansas City. In 1932 a regular London-to-Capetown passenger service began. In 1933 Charles Lindbergh completed a twenty-nine-thousand-mile air tour to survey world air routes. In 1934 an airplane airmail service from England to Australia was opened, followed the next year by the first Pacific airmail service between San Francisco and Manila.

Airplane design was advancing just as rapidly. In 1933 the first "modern type" airliner, the low-wing, all-metal, monocoque Boeing 247, made its appearance, followed in 1935 by the Douglas DC-3, the most famous and successful airliner in history, which would soon be carrying the bulk of all American domestic air traffic. Even before the *Hindenburg*'s maiden flight, the first four-engine all-metal monoplanes were being developed, the prototypes of the civil airliners and strategic bombers of the future, starting with the Junkers Ju 90 transport and followed by the B-17 Flying Fortress, the legendary U.S. Air Force long-range bomber, which first flew in 1935.

In 1937, when the *Hindenburg* and the *Graf Zeppelin* still proposed to ply the North and South Atlantic routes, and the Cunarder *Queen Mary* was breaking the Atlantic sea-crossing record with a time of three days, twenty hours, forty-two minutes, Imperial Airways, in association with Qantas, was starting an island-hopping passenger service across the Pacific between San Francisco and Hong Kong. Only the North Atlantic was still beyond the capability of a passenger airplane, for no plane could yet fly two thousand miles without refueling. The giant zeppelins alone could operate this service, though airplanes that could match them in range (though never in comfort) were already on the drawing board. By 1938 the British Vickers Wellesley bomber would achieve a straight-line nonstop distance record of 7,158 miles, even farther than the *Graf Zeppelin*'s nonstop flight from Friedrichshafen to Tokyo on the world flight, while a four-engined German Focke-Wulf 200 Condor landplane would fly nonstop from Berlin to New York in under twenty hours. The following year a Boeing 314 flying boat "Dixie Clipper" would make the first commercial passenger flight across an ocean nonstop, carrying airmail from New York to Spain and England, and the first jet plane would be successfully flown in Germany. Airplanes had all but caught up. They flew faster and farther and higher by the minute. They crashed frequently for all sorts of reasons, but they were irrepressible and everywhere. There were tens of thousands of them, but still only two commercial rigid airships.

Dr. Eckener, like his mentor Count Zeppelin before him, was perfectly aware that the plane would one day overtake the zeppelin as a transoceanic passenger aircraft. He hoped that meanwhile the zeppelin would continue to have its day, occupying the niche between the ocean liner of the present and the airliner of the future. But that, in a decade in which technological advances had brought the world to the brink of the age of the jet plane, the atom bomb, and the electronic computer, would depend on circumstances beyond Eckener's control.

The *Hindenburg*'s first westward crossing of the 1937 season was due to start on May 3 from the Rhine-Main World Airport at Frankfurt, the new European terminus for the next generation of giant passenger zeppelins. Unlike the eastward crossing that would follow, which was completely sold out with passengers anxious to see the coronation of King George VI in London, only thirty-six of the seventy berths on the flight to Lakehurst were occupied. However, in addition to the normal crew of forty, there were twenty-one extra Zeppelin employees on board, including Dr. Rüdiger, the first regular in-flight doctor, Emilie Imhof, the first airship stewardess, and a number of young airshipmen undergoing training prior to joining the LZ-130. The number of people on board thus totalled ninety-seven. In addition, there were two dogs and the usual mail and freight.

In command of the ship for the first time was Captain Max Pruss, with two other captains, Albert Sammt (first officer) and Heinrich Bauer (second officer), as watch officers. Flying as observers were Captain Ernst Lehmann, the director of the Deutsche Zeppelin Reederei, and Captain Anton Wittemann, soon to take over command of the *Graf Zeppelin*. Lehmann was quiet and withdrawn, not at all his usual jaunty, confident self; he was in mourning for his little son, who had died of pneumonia a few weeks previously. There was also another cause for reflection. The German embassy in Washington had received a letter from a Kathie Rauch of Milwaukee, in which she wrote, "Please inform the Zeppelin company in Frankfurt-am-Main that they should open and search all mail before it is put on board prior to every flight of the Zeppelin *Hindenburg*. The Zeppelin is going to be destroyed by a time bomb during its flight to another country." They had received quite a few letters like that over the years, more since the Nazis came to power. Nuts, self-publicists, subversives. But you never know. . . .

At 8 P.M. on May 3, 1937, the *Hindenburg* took off in perfect weather, taking the northern route across the Atlantic past the southern tip of Greenland. The ship was slowed down by persistent head winds blowing at speeds of up to fifty miles per hour, but everyone on board was struck by the steadiness of the ship. When a passenger told Lehmann that he had been in three air crashes, Lehmann reassured him, "You don't need to worry, my friend, Zeppelins never have accidents." In the winter refit, everything had been done to make the ship fireproof. To eliminate the possibility of sparks that could ignite the 7 million cubic feet of hydrogen, the catwalks and ladders that gave access to the gas cells had been rubber-coated, the riggers wore asbestos suits with no buttons or other metal components, and the engines required no ignition to start them. Every single member of the crew from Lehmann down had absolute faith in the safety of the *Hindenburg*. It was not an issue.

By the afternoon of May 5, the North American coast was in sight near Newfoundland, and by noon on the following day, the *Hindenburg* was over Boston; by three in the afternoon it was over New York, passing so close to the top of the Empire State Building (planned to serve as a zeppelin mooring mast in the near future) that the passengers could wave at the people down below waving at them. By a quarter past four it had appeared above the landing field at Lakehurst.

Originally the arrival had been scheduled for six o'clock that morning, but because of the delay due to the winds, it had been rescheduled for six that evening. Pruss therefore held the ship off to the southeast, cruising slowly along the coast and circling till the ground crews and customs and immigration officials were assembled. Meanwhile, a weather front accompanied by rain and thunderstorms was approaching from the west. Tucked in behind this front, the *Hindenburg* came in for the landing at six, but heavy rain was falling and a thunderstorm still lingered in the vicinity, so the naval station radioed the ship:

CONDITIONS STILL UNSETTLED x RECOMMEND DELAY LANDING UNTIL FURTHER WORD FROM STATION.

At 6:12 and 6:22 two more radio messages were sent while the *Hindenburg* was making a slow course in the direction of Atlantic City. The first reported improved conditions and ground crew in position; the second read: "Recommend landing now." But still Pruss held off.

At 7 P.M. the air station sent a reassuring weather report: "Overcast, moderate rain, diminishing lightning in west, ceiling 2,000 feet, improving visibility, surface winds west-southwest, 4 knots, gusts under 10 knots, surface temperature sixty-one, pressure twenty-nine seventy."

Eight minutes later, with daylight fading and conditions optimal, Commander Rosendahl, America's senior airshipman and veteran of the *Graf*'s world flight, now station commandant in charge of landing operations, sent a final, rather more urgent signal:

CONDITIONS DEFINITELY IMPROVED x RECOMMEND EARLIEST POSSIBLE LANDING.

After a few minutes a shout of "There she is!" went up as the great ship came into view and made a pass over the base at a height of five to six hundred feet to check conditions at ground level. Passengers had already been advised that landing was imminent, their cigarette lighters had been returned to them, their beds had been stripped and the sheets piled in the corridors. They settled their bar bills and checked their passports and customs declarations.

After making a circle around the field—a fairly tight circle, for Pruss was in a hurry to land while the weather was still stable—the *Hindenburg* came back over Lakehurst, heading into the wind with its two front lights on, then weighed off to check trim and equilibrium, valving hydrogen from its forward gas cells for thirty-five seconds and dropping thirty-five hundred pounds of water ballast from tanks near the tail. When the elevator man reported that the ship was still tail-heavy, six men were sent forward to the bow to help balance it. Then the ship descended slowly to about two hundred feet, inching forward toward the landing mast and backing down on its engines until it was virtually hovering above the landing party. At 7:21 the manila landing ropes were dropped to the ground. They were seized by the landing crew for the first stage of the landing procedure, while from the nose was lowered the steel mooring cable by which the *Hindenburg* was to be winched to the mooring mast.

Though the atmosphere was still electrically charged, the weather was continuing to improve. The thunderstorm had moved out of the area, there was only a slight drizzle, very light wind, and cloud cover that shaded the light of the setting sun. On the ship the officers and crew were at their landing stations, and most of the passengers were crowded along the starboard promenade and lounge and reading room, watching the landing operation and trying to spot friends and relatives in the viewing enclosure down on the ground. Their baggage was lined up in the passageways near the gangway in readiness for immediate unloading after landing.

At this point radio reporter Herbert Morrison from station WLS in Chicago began recording a commentary on the *Hindenburg*'s arrival. "Well, here it comes, ladies and gentlemen," he reported, "and what a sight it is, a thrilling one, a marvellous sight." It looked like another routine landing of the *Hindenburg,* with not a single celebrity on the ship to interview this time. On previous flights there had been film stars like Douglas Fairbanks to talk to, or sporting heroes like the German world heavyweight boxing champion Max Schmeling, or glamorous women like Lady Grace Hay-Drummond-Hay, the first woman to fly around the world. Well, he would do his best. "The sun is striking the windows of the observation deck on the eastward side," he continued, "and sparkling like glittering jewels against a background of black velvet."

Commander Rosendahl was out on the field, watching the landing with an approving professional eye. The *Hindenburg,* he thought, looked just like "a populated cloud." It was arriving in perfectly normal condition after a skillful and perfectly normal approach and was being landed in a perfectly normal way. The ship was weighed off and steady. The port and starboard bow lines had been dropped and secured, the mooring cable was being lowered. The inaugural North Atlantic flight for 1937 was two hundred feet and a few minutes away from its conclusion. Radio Officer Willy Speck sent a last signal to the *Graf Zeppelin,* which was over the South Atlantic on a return flight from Rio, to report that the *Hindenburg* had landed safely. The column of customs, immigration, and health officials was setting off from the mooring mast in the direction of the ship. The time was 7:25 P.M. Eastern Daylight Time. "Suddenly there occurred a remarkable stillness," recalled passenger Leonhard Adelt, a German journalist. "The motors were silent and it seemed as if the whole world was holding its breath. One heard no command, no call, no cry."

"The passengers are looking out of the windows waving," Herbert Morrison observed. "It's practically standing still now. They've dropped ropes out of the nose of the ship, and they've been taken ahold of on the ship by a number of men. The vast motors of the ship are just holding it, just enough to keep it from . . ." Morrison stopped talking.

Looking up at the motionless ship, the navy man in charge of the port-bow-line handling party noticed that the outer cover aft of the after port engine was beginning to flutter. It couldn't be caused by the slipstream or the propeller, he reckoned, for the ship was barely moving and the port engine was at idle, and in any case the flapping fabric was too high up. To him it looked more as if escaping gas was forcing its way up and out. From the top of the mooring mast three hundred yards or so from the ship, another navy man saw the same phenomenon: "The fabric behind the rear port engine was very loose and fluttering. It extended rearward and upward from that engine to a quarter of the way to the tail." Inside the ship, Chief Engineer Rudolf Sauter, who was in the auxiliary steering station in the lower fin, was puzzled to see that the third gas cell from the stern had risen very high and had apparently lost much of its gas.

Standing outside the main gate of the air station with his wife and son, bystander Mark Heald, an academic, had spotted something else—a dim blue flame, a form of static electrical discharge known as St. Elmo's Fire, flickering along the ship's backbone from about a quarter of the way back from the bow all the way to the tail. "Oh, heavens," he said to his wife, "the thing is afire." "Where?" she asked. "Up along the top ridge," he replied.

At almost exactly the same time, a member of the ground crew who was standing right under the ship saw a small spark, "like static electricity," that danced along the bottom of the hull. "Look!" he said to the man next to him. This was all there was time to say, for within a second or two a bright light suddenly flared up in the vent shaft between the two gas cells immediately forward of the upper tail fin. Then a brilliant flame shot out of the top of the ship.

Helmut Lau, a rigger, was on a ladder inside the *Hindenburg*'s skeletal hull not far from the lower vertical tail fin when he saw the start of the fire. "Suddenly I saw a bright reflection on the front wall of cell four," he would later testify. "At first I didn't see any flames, just a reflection through and inside the cell. In a flash the cell disappeared in the fire. Then I saw cells three and five go up." From his position there was no obvious cause of the fire. Three other crew members were at their posts in the tail, but none was aware of anything amiss before the fire broke out. Rudolf Sauter also saw the light in cell four. Within an instant all the hydrogen in cell four was ablaze, followed by the gas cells next to it.

The awful significance of this event was immediately apparent to Commander Rosendahl: "At 7:25, or just four minutes after the landing rope had been dropped, I saw a burst of flame on top of the ship just forward of where the upper vertical fin attached to the hull. It was a brilliant burst of flame resembling a flower opening rapidly into bloom. I knew at once the ship was doomed."

For a second or two the flower of flame hung on the top of the ship. Nothing could stop the spread of the initial flame igniting the 7 million cubic feet of hydrogen that kept the giant zeppelin in the air. There was a muffled report—"like the noise you hear when you turn a kitchen gas flame on or off," Lau recalled, though to others on the ground it sounded like thunder or a gun—and the flames spread swiftly through the after quarter of the ship. The four men in the stern huddled in the lower fin to escape the flames as the burning stern sank toward the ground. In the forward port engine car, mechanic Eugen Bentele felt a powerful shock run through the ship. When he looked down he saw a fiery glow lighting up the landing field and knew at once that the ship was lost.

So routine did the press corps deem the *Hindenburg*'s arrival that evening that one blasé newsman from the *Lakewood Times* was on the phone to his night editor with his back to the ship as it hovered over the field. Then he saw a flash reflected in the window of the phone booth and felt the booth tremble. He looked out and then shouted into the phone, "My God, the whole damn thing blew up!"

For a couple of seconds radio reporter Herbert Morrison remained too shocked to speak. Then, encouraged by his gesticulating recording engineer Charlie Nehlen, he attempted to describe the nightmare so rapidly unfolding before him. "Oh, oh, oh! . . ." he gasped into his microphone. "It's burst into flames . . . get this, Charlie, get this, Charlie. . . . It's flashing—flashing! It's flashing terrible! Get out of the way, please, oh, my, this is terrible, oh my. . . . Get out of the way, please! It is burning. . . . Oh! This is one of the worst . . . Oh! It's a terrific sight. . . . Oh! . . ."

Until the explosion, no one in the control car or the passenger quarters was aware that anything was amiss. In the control room the commander, Captain Pruss, was standing beside the rudder man Kurt Schoenherr, with Lehmann as observer on his right and Bauer, the second officer, on his left, in charge of the ballast board. Behind Bauer stood Sammt, the first officer, next to the elevator man Eduard Boetius, and in the center was Anton Witteman. All five officers were qualified rigid airship commanders; only von Schiller among the roster of serving zeppelin commanders was not with them. A shudder ran through the ship, like a mooring line breaking. "What is it?" Pruss asked. They looked out the windows, but they had no view aft. Then suddenly, in the glass of the hangar windows, they saw the reflection of the red glow of a fire. From the radio room at the rear of the control car came a yell from the radio officer, Willy Speck: "The ship's burning!" Then they saw the ground crews running and heard people shouting and screaming and the scrunch of metal.

Everything was happening in fractions of seconds, and there was little chance to coordinate any action, let alone save the ship. The ground crews and the customs and immigration officers, 250 men in all, ran for their lives from the falling inferno, but one of them, a civilian handler, stumbled, and before he could get to his feet the white-hot wreck had crashed on top of him. Friends, relatives, newsmen, airport officials, and spectators stared frozen and incredulous as the fire raced through the whole length of the ship. Towering clouds of flame and smoke from the burning hydrogen and fuel oil soared high in the sky as the stern settled to the ground.

"It is burning, bursting into flames!" cried Morrison, "and it's falling on the mooring mast and all the folks we . . ." He began to sob. "This is terrible . . . This is one of the worst catastrophes in the world . . ."

Some spectators crouched to the ground as if ducking shellfire, others turned and fled. Filming the whole disaster from beginning to end in a kind of hypnotized daze, a motion-picture news cameraman kept repeating like a mantra, "Oh my God, oh my God, oh my God."

As the stern quarter settled on the ground, breaking the ship's back, the four men in the lower fin made a break for it, escaping with relatively minor injuries. The remaining three-quarters of the dying airship, in the moments before its gas cells were consumed, was still buoyant enough to shoot up to a height of five hundred feet and an angle of forty-five degrees, sending the passengers sliding and tumbling down the promenade decks and piling up against a bulkhead in utter confusion.

"In the gondola," recalled Second Officer Bauer, "there was an oppressive calm. Some crewmen were groaning, others fell to the floor, and everyone attempted to hold on to something as the pitch became steeper."

Then a white-hot flame shot up the central axial corridor inside the hull, rapidly igniting one gas cell after the other, traveling so fast that it shot through the nose of the ship like a flame from a colossal blowtorch. There were twelve crew members in the bow, including the men manning the anchor chain and the six who had been ordered forward to help weigh off the ship. One by one they lost their grip in the searing heat and plummeted down into that giant tunnel of white fire, till only three were left. Miraculously they survived, even after the rest of the forward part of the ship was enveloped in fire.

The bow of the ship now hung momentarily in the air. Captain Pruss and his officers made an instant and critical decision, "one of the outstanding events in the whole disaster," in Rosendahl's opinion. Normal airship practice would dictate that to slow the rate of the ship's descent and minimize its impact with the ground, they should release water ballast. They decided that the ballast would stay, so the forward part of the ship would come down heavy and fast to give passengers and crew the maximum possible time to get out before the ship was consumed.

For the ninety-six human beings on board, there was no time for warning or aid. "The flames blew in, long tongues of flame, bright red and very beautiful," calmly noted passenger Margaret Mather, a fifty-nine-year-old New Yorker who lived in Rome. She heard a man scream in German, "Es ist das Ende!" (It's the end!), and fling himself out of a window. She recalled: "I sat just where I had fallen, holding the lapels of my coat over my face, feeling the flames light on my back, my hat, my hair, trying to beat them out, watching the horrified faces of my companions as they leaped up and down. . . . It was like a scene from a medieval picture of hell."

Escape from this inferno seemed impossible. Some of those who were still in their cabins or at their posts of duty would have been incinerated before they had registered what was happening. More passengers would have survived if the wind had been from a different direction, or if they had assembled on the port side of the ship rather than the starboard, for the wind at this moment was blowing directly onto the ship's port beam and driving the flames to starboard.

Miraculously, many people did survive. No one had more than a few seconds in which to find a way out of the horror. Some, hearing shouts from the ground to jump, hurled themselves through the promenade windows and were rushed away to safety by members of the ground crew, who had run back to the burning ship even before it had hit the ground. Not all the jumping passengers were lucky. George Grant, a British shipping man, landed from a window without a burn or a scratch and was then hit in the middle of his back and severely injured by another falling passenger.

The fit and agile stood the best chance of escaping the fire. Joseph Späh, stage name Ben Dova, a German vaudeville acrobat resident in the States, was sitting in the dining room on the port side of the ship when he suddenly found himself ringed with fire. He dashed to a promenade window but was unable to open it. In a frenzy he smashed the glass with his amateur movie camera, climbed out along with two other men, and clung to the outside of the ship. The forward part of the *Hindenburg* was still pointing steeply into the air—too high for the men to jump and survive. Unable to hold on, first one and then the other of the two men let go and fell to their deaths, spread-eagled and kicking all the way down. Späh clung on despite the heat. All around he could hear the screams of people who were being torched alive. Then the ship began to sink, and when he was about forty feet above the ground, Späh let go. He fractured a heel as he landed but was able to hobble out of the way of the burning wreck as it came crashing down.

Until now the men in the control room had remained at their posts. But as the forward section of the ship, and with it the control room and passenger quarters, sank to the ground, Captain Lehmann called out: "Everyone to a window!" Then, as the car's rubber landing tire touched the ground, Captain Pruss gave his last order: "Everybody out NOW!"

Seven of the twelve men in the control car leapt through the windows. All survived. Then the ship bounced back into the air on the landing tire, leaving five men—Pruss, Lehmann, Sammt, Franz Herzog, and Speck—still in the car. Slowly the car came down again, and the five hurled themselves out of the windows. Pruss and Sammt jumped from a height of fifteen feet. Sammt landed on all fours and saw Pruss disappear in a wall of flame. He picked himself up, but almost immediately the ship's red-hot skeleton fell all around him. It was so hot he had to lie down on the ground, though that too was burning. Then suddenly the pall of fire lifted, and he found himself surrounded by a tangle of smoldering girders and wires. He stood and began to pick his way through the web of scalding metal with his bare hands. Then he was through. He ran twenty yards then flung himself on the wet grass and rolled in the sand. His Zeppelin officer's hat was still on his head, but his uniform was scorched. He stood up and looked around. Twenty yards away he saw Pruss. His head and hair were badly burned, and he was moaning.

"Pruss?" Sammt shouted. "Is it you?"

"Ja," Pruss groaned.

"*Donnerwetter*, what a sight you are," said Sammt.

Pruss had done his duty as captain of his ship and was nearly to pay for it with his life. His hair and uniform in flames, he had stopped to pick up the limp, smoldering body of Radio Operator Willy Speck, and he carried him out of the furnace. When a rescuer rushed up, Pruss handed him his wallet, watch, and rings, mumbling incoherently, then suddenly shouted, "The passengers!" and rushed back into the burning wreck. Several times he was seen to enter the cauldron that had been his ship, searching for the human beings who had been entrusted to his care. Finally, as he was about to enter the wreckage yet again, three American sailors managed to restrain him and pull him, protesting loudly, to an ambulance.

Even as the fiery remains of the *Hindenburg* were crashing to Earth, the voice of Chief Boatswain's Mate Fred Tobin, a survivor of the 1925 *Shenandoah* disaster who was in charge of the U.S. Navy handling crew, could be heard rallying his team. "Navy men, stand fast!" he yelled. "There are people inside that ship and we've got to get them out!"

Tobin's men rushed forward as human figures emerged out of the inferno. Some ran, some staggered, some crawled; some were in flames, some naked and black or waxy white from the fire. The flames devouring one man were so hot it was ten minutes before rescuers could get near his charred body. Others were unharmed. Margaret Mather was still sitting where she had fallen in the observation promenade when the ship hit the ground. The next thing she knew, several ground crew were beckoning her through the window. "Come out, lady!" they cried. "As though led by a guardian angel," Rosendahl reported, "she left the ship by the regular hatchway with the calmness of a somnambulist, receiving only minor burns." One man strolled out of the midst of the flames as nonchalantly as if he were going off to the golf club; amazingly, he was completely unharmed. It helped that the ground was sandy and rain-sodden. The American Nelson Morris, an experienced airship traveler—he was the forlorn would-be passenger who was left behind at the start of the *Graf Zeppelin*'s world flight—jumped through a window on the starboard side, snapped the red-hot structural members about him with his bare hands as though they were twigs, and fought his way clear of the wreckage, sustaining only minor burns.

The most spectacular escape was by the most junior crew member. Werner Franz, a fourteen-year-old cabin boy, was washing up in the officers' mess when he felt a great jerk go through the ship, and all the plates fell out of the cabinet. He ran toward the gangway but lost his footing as the ship tilted. Trapped in the fire and barely able to breathe, he began to lose consciousness. Then a water tank burst over his head, drenching him from head to foot and reviving him. He managed to drop to the ground through a hatch at the bottom of the hull, then work his way out through the twisted girders into the open air, suffering only minor burns thanks to his sopping wet clothes. Three of the four cooks also jumped and lived.

Mechanic Eugen Bentele, eight weeks married, had ridden the ship all the way down inside the forward port engine and was thrown clear by the impact, which broke four of his ribs and knocked him unconscious. "When I came to," he recalled, "I was lying next to the propeller and I ran away from the side of the burning ship. About two hundred metres from the ship I was outside the range of the intense waves of heat. I stopped and turned round. In front of me lay the wreck of our beautiful and proud ship. In the mid-section the framework had melted and at the prow and stern warped aluminum rings and supports still showed the outline of the hull and above it hung black smoke from the burning fuel and oil."

Captain Lehmann, the world's most experienced and long-serving rigid airship commander still in service, walked out of the flaming wreckage, burning like a torch but still clear-headed. A sailor and the press representative of the Zeppelin Reederei ran toward him and beat out the flames with their hands. "Hello, again," said Lehmann, in shock but in control. "I can't believe it. How many of my passengers and crew are saved?" His back was burned as if by an acetylene torch from his head to the bottom of his spine. He stumbled, and the two men took him by the arm and led him away, muttering repeatedly, "I can't understand it, I can't understand it." His burns were so extensive it seemed unlikely he could survive.

Then the *Hindenburg* was finally and totally consumed by fire. "As I stood off to one side," Commander Rosendahl would recall, "spellbound by this most unexpected tragedy, I saw the flames eat rapidly along the fabric sides of the hull, greedily devouring the illustrious name 'Hindenburg' letter by letter. Within less than a minute from the first appearance of the fire, the ship had settled, not crashed, to the ground and lay there writhing and crackling from the hottest flame man knows."

Radio reporter Herbert Morrison struggled to find words to encompass what he was witnessing, his voice racked with emotion, near to breakdown. "This is terrible . . . Oh, the humanity and all the passengers . . . a mass of flaming wreckage. Honestly, I can hardly breathe . . . I'm going to step inside where I can't see it . . . It's terrible . . . I—I—folks, I'm going to have to stop for a moment because I've lost my voice. This is the worst thing I've ever witnessed . . ."

From the first sighting of the fire to the final destruction of the ship, just thirty-four seconds had passed.


Emergency services were swiftly on the scene. The small infirmary at the naval station was packed. "Its rooms swarmed with excited people like an ant heap," recalled Leonhard Adelt. "In the corridors, on tables, stretchers and chairs lay the seriously wounded. An ambulance orderly with a morphine syringe the size of a bicycle pump ran about and wanted to give everyone an injection." Among the injured waiting for an ambulance was Ernst Lehmann. Every so often he dabbed his appalling burns with picric acid. There was a smell of burnt flesh everywhere.

By midnight the intense heat had died down and a guard had been placed around the still-smoldering wreck of the *Hindenburg*. Lakehurst Naval Station was a hushed and sad place now. The survivors had been taken to various hospitals in the area, and the bodies of the dead were laid out in an improvised morgue inside the press room in the airship hangar awaiting the painful task of identification. As soon as he heard the news, President Roosevelt sent a message of condolence to Reich Chancellor Hitler. To the U.S. secretary of the navy came a cable from Goering: "The unreserved help of the American airmen in coming to the rescue of their German comrades is beautiful proof of the spirit which links the airmen of all nations."

Once the tangled skeleton of the *Hindenburg* had grown cold, a search party rummaged through it but found little to salvage. Most of the freight and mail had been destroyed, and only 133 letters were fit for delivery. Among the few personal effects that could be retrieved was a Luger pistol, one shell of which had mysteriously been fired.

Meanwhile, a vast traffic jam blocked the road from New York to Lakehurst as tens of thousands of people drove out to see the scene of the most spectacular disaster the media had ever presented to them.


Hugo Eckener was in Graz, Austria, where he was due to address the local flying club, of which he was an honorary member. During the day he had visited a local sculptor who showed him his latest work—a representation of the broken figure of Icarus, the mythological hero who had made himself wings, flown too close to the sun, and crashed to his death. Eckener was not a man inclined to paranormal sensitivities, but when he looked at the sculpture he was seized with an unaccountable feeling of dread and unease so disturbing that he became anxious to leave the studio as soon as he could.

After the talk that evening, Eckener had dinner and a few drinks, then retired to his hotel room for the night. Between one and two o'clock in the morning (8 to 9 P.M. Lakehurst time) he was awakened by the ringing of his bedside phone. On the line was the *New York Times* correspondent in Berlin. "Herr Eckener," said the newspaperman gravely, "I felt it necessary to inform you at once that I have just received a message from my office in New York, according to which the airship *Hindenburg* exploded this evening at seven P.M. above the airfield at Lakehurst. You will hardly be able to comment on this, for I still know nothing more about it."

The dark hours of that night were the bleakest Eckener had ever spent. Pacing up and down his room, agonized and racked in thought, he pondered the cause of this calamity. How could it have happened? If the ship had exploded above the landing field, that suggested sabotage was the most likely cause; there had been enough threats, heaven knows. He had hinted as much to the reporter in Berlin.

At seven in the morning the phone rang again. It was the air ministry in Berlin, confirming that the *Hindenburg* had been destroyed while landing at Lakehurst and requesting that Eckener proceed immediately to Vienna, where a special plane would fly him to Berlin. Reporters were waiting outside the hotel when he emerged, accompanied by his old airship colleague and Nazi-appointed minder Lieutenant Colonel Joachim Breithaupt, who was there to keep him out of trouble. Perhaps it was sabotage, Eckener told the reporters, but it was too early to say. In Berlin he had a brief meeting with Goering and air ministry officials. Goering told him he'd never thought much of airships, but it was a matter of sitting it out now. As a matter of extreme urgency, Eckener was told, he should proceed to Lakehurst at once as head of a six-man German investigation commission to help determine the circumstances of the loss of the *Hindenburg* and to cooperate with the American accident board investigation that was already under way at the crash site. But first he would be required to make a broadcast to the German nation, and then an English-language broadcast to the United States and Great Britain denying any suggestion that the *Hindenburg* might have been the victim of an act of anti-Nazi sabotage. Eckener made the broadcasts and the next morning was flown to Cherbourg to catch a ship to New York with nothing but the clothes he was wearing. He set sail for America in a state of shock and sadness—and guilt. "I deeply regret," he wrote to his wife, "that I was persuaded to allow the use of hydrogen when the *Hindenburg*, after all, had been designed for the use of helium."

◆  ◆  ◆

Meanwhile, the *Graf Zeppelin* was making good speed over the Canary Islands on its return flight from Rio. Captain Hans von Schiller, the ship's commander, was having an early breakfast in the saloon when the door opened and the radio officer, looking shocked and chalk-faced, frantically beckoned to him to come over. Von Schiller followed him to the radio room and was handed an incoming dispatch. It read: "Report received *Hindenburg* exploded, all passengers and crew dead."

Von Schiller was incredulous. Only last night he had received a report from the *Hindenburg* itself announcing the ship's safe arrival. Then he was handed another message: "*Hindenburg* report unfortunately confirmed." He was aghast. Many of the officers on the *Hindenburg* were his colleagues and friends; he had known some of them for the whole of his airship career.

It was not until the *Graf Zeppelin* was approaching Friedrichshafen that von Schiller informed the crew of the disaster, and not until after it had landed that he personally broke the news to the passengers assembled in the lounge. Friedrichshafen that day was a town in shock and mourning. None knew, though some suspected, that this was the end of passenger flights by zeppelins or rigid airships.

Von Schiller's next urgent duty was to make contact with Eckener. He finally managed to reach him by phone as he was about to board the ship at Cherbourg. Von Schiller reported that he had brought the *Graf Zeppelin* home safely and was due to take her back to Brazil in three days' time, if that was in order. "Captain von Schiller," Eckener replied, "until we know what made the *Hindenburg* burn, we must ground your ship. The flight must be cancelled."


The morning after the disaster, Commander Rosendahl had gone to visit his friend and colleague Captain Lehmann in the hospital. Though badly burned, Lehmann did not seem to be in excessive pain. He was aware that he could not survive his injuries but remained composed and uncomplaining, though sick at heart. Together the two old hands went over every possible cause of the disaster, from static electricity to a propeller fragment puncturing a gas cell. But nothing seemed to add up. "No, no," sighed the dying commander, slowly shaking his head. "It must have been an infernal machine." In other words, an explosive device, an act of sabotage. Captain Pruss, himself in critical condition with severe facial burns, thought the same, as did every surviving crew member.

Later that day Ernst Lehmann died of his burns. His passing moved Charles Rosendahl greatly. The two men had been friends for fourteen years. "Dapper, polished, suave, conversant with world affairs, a talented linguist," Rosendahl wrote, "his whole existence was bound up in a great ideal—the perfection of the Zeppelin principle. To this ideal he gave of his courage, ability, integrity, and finally, his life."

That night Willy Speck, too, died of his injuries, bringing the total number of dead to thirty-six—thirteen passengers out of the thirty-six on board, twenty-two (including the first airship stewardess, Emilie Imhof) of the sixty-one crew members, and one civilian member of the ground crew. Nearly two-thirds of those on board had survived. These included the commander, Captain Pruss, who was badly burned but would also pull through after endless skin grafts and many months of hospitalization; zeppelin captains Sammt (also burned and hospitalized), Bauer, and Witteman; and the ship's medic, Dr. Rüdiger.

The *Hindenburg* was not the greatest airship disaster in history: seventy-two lives had been lost on the *Akron,* and forty-eight on the R-101. But it was the greatest media airship disaster. The shocking photos of the ship's catastrophic demise were wired to newspapers around the world and filled the front pages of the American morning papers. By afternoon the harrowing newsreel images were being screened to stunned, sometimes hysterical audiences in cinemas around the country, and Herbert Morrison's shattering commentary was being broadcast nationwide by NBC.

The *Hindenburg* disaster marked the first passenger fatalities in commercial zeppelin operations since their beginning in 1910. Previously they had made twenty-three hundred flights and flown more than fifty thousand passengers with a blameless safety record.

◆　◆　◆

On May 11, the day after the U.S. government's public inquiry into the disaster had opened in the press room–cum-morgue in the Lakehurst hangar, the coffins of the twenty-eight European victims were given a ceremonial Nazi send-off from the New York docks before a crowd of ten thousand people. Then, with solemn pomp, the coffins were carried on board the SS *Hamburg*. Ernst Lehmann's coffin was given a hero's salute by the liner's captain.

On the same day, Dr. Eckener and his team arrived in New York and proceeded to Lakehurst. There, as always, he stayed as an honored guest at the home of his friend and fellow airship commander Charles Rosendahl, who was a member of the American investigation team. "Now Lakehurst was dead," Eckener mourned:

> The ground crew had been transferred, the few remaining stood by in their barracks, idle and dejected. In hospitals round about lay the passengers and crew of the ship. Captain Lehmann had died of his burns and Captains Sammt and Pruss hovered between life and death. Stretched out across the centre of the field lay the blackened framework of the *Hindenburg,* a disorderly tangle of girders, wires, and crumpled sheet metal. It appeared to me the hopeless end of a great dream, a kind of end of the world, a mournful symbol of what I expected to be the final outcome for Germany.

Eckener and his investigation team, which included the *Hindenburg*'s designer, Dr. Dürr, and Joachim Breithaupt, arrived on the fourth day of the hearings, during which they testified as witnesses. They later conducted their own investigations and released their own report of their findings. Between them the joint American and German investigations heard evidence from eyewitnesses and expert witnesses regarding the sequence of events and their possible interpretation. The inquiries were painstaking, thorough, and cautious, but no certain cause for the disaster was found.

"The investigation followed two courses," Eckener wrote. "Is an act of sabotage demonstrable or probable? Or is electrostatic ignition demonstrable or probable? Dozens of witnesses were questioned on these points, from the crew and from the crowd of spectators surrounding the landing field." In the end both investigations decided against sabotage, on the grounds that absolutely no evidence for it could be found.

Dr. Eckener and Professor Dieckmann, an expert on electrostatics and atmospheric electricity, thought the disaster was caused by leaking hydrogen being ignited by static electricity. Three factors suggested this. First, the ship was landing in thunderstorm conditions, where marked differences in electrical potential were prevalent, providing an opportunity for electrostatic ignition. Second, three people had seen a hydrogen flame on top of the ship near the tail, which indicated that pure hydrogen had escaped to the top of the ship. Third, during the landing the ship remained stern-heavy despite continuous release of ballast and the dispatch of six men to the bow, which indicated that gas had escaped from that part of the ship.

Eckener had examined the wreckage of the *Hindenburg* with Dr. Dürr. Though there was little left to provide clues, he had managed to locate some of the tension gauges that measured the tension in the bracing wires. These registered a high degree of tension, indicating that the hull had been subject to considerable stresses during the course of the landing. It was Eckener's belief that the final tight turn made by the *Hindenburg* as it came in to land had put excessive stress on the hull, causing a bracing wire to snap and tear gas cell four or five, resulting in a lethally flammable mixture of leaking hydrogen and air collecting high up inside the upper fin and beneath the outer cover aft.

As for the static discharge, it was Professor Dieckmann's view that once the *Hindenburg* had dropped its landing lines to the ground the static charges on the ship and on the ground would have been equalized, with the ship discharging electricity—St. Elmo's Fire—into the atmosphere, in the process igniting the leaking hydrogen. No evidence was produced at the inquiry that anyone had actually seen St. Elmo's Fire at the time of the disaster, so the hypothesis that this was the cause of the hydrogen catching fire remained likely but unproven.

Unknown to the investigators, however, the bystander Mark Heald did indeed see St. Elmo's Fire flicker across the spine of the ship, followed by an initial burst of flame. If Heald had given evidence at the inquiry, the commission's findings would almost certainly have been conclusive.

The German report included a guarded rider that "the possibility of deliberate destruction must be admitted in view of the fact that no other originating cause can be proven." It would have been easy enough to hide a nonmetal incendiary device next to a gas cell—an ordinary photographic flashbulb would have been sufficient to blow up the ship—and this would have produced precisely the effects that were observed when the *Hindenburg* exploded, destroying all evidence of sabotage in the process. Captain Pruss, who was too ill to give evidence at the inquiry, became increasingly convinced that sabotage was the only feasible explanation and pointed out that the instruments in the control car up to the time of the fire gave no indication of leaks in any of the gas cells. Most of the surviving crew members agreed with him, as did Dr. Dürr and Commander Rosendahl, who thought it possible that a device might have been preset to go off at 7:25 P.M., in the belief that the ship would have kept to its schedule and landed many hours before and thus be riding at the mast virtually empty of passengers and crew, saboteur included, when it exploded.

Many years later the sabotage theory was explored more exhaustively by two American journalists, first A. A. Hoehling and later Michael M. Mooney, working independently of each other. Both concluded that the likely saboteur was a twenty-three-year-old crew member named Eric Spehl, a shy loner with anti-Nazi connections who, as a rigger, had free access to the ship's gas cells. But of course there was no proof, nor was Spehl available for questioning, for he had died in the blowtorch fire in the *Hindenburg*'s bow. Sixty years were to pass before startling new evidence revealed the possibly true cause of the disaster.

One thing was clear. Never again could hydrogen be used to inflate a commercial airship. That meant that either the Americans released helium for the LZ-130, now approaching completion, or the zeppelin dream perished. "No matter what the circumstances," Eckener wrote to his wife, "we must get helium." Before returning to Germany, he proceeded to Washington to try to persuade Congress to release helium for the new zeppelin. Public opinion in America was with him, and the U.S. government saw fit to permit the export of helium to Germany provided it was for nonmilitary use. Eckener returned home convinced that at the last gasp he had rescued the zeppelin cause from tragic oblivion.

But helium would not save the *Graf Zeppelin*. The ban on any future flights using hydrogen spelled the death knell for this old workhorse. One of the most successful and beloved passenger aircraft in history, the *Graf* would make no more intercontinental flights. On July 19 it was flown to Frankfurt, hung up in a hangar and deflated, then opened to the public as a local tourist attraction. For fifty pfennigs you could peep through the windows into the passengers' cabins, and for one mark you could walk along the keel to the control car and out through the door.

The *Hindenburg*'s sister ship, LZ-130, which came to be known as *Graf Zeppelin II*, was modified so that it could be inflated with helium. The existing cabins, designed for seventy-two passengers, had to be removed and replaced by accommodation for only forty. Since helium was expensive then, a water-recovery system had to be built into the ship so that it could be flown with a minimum valving of precious gas.

Deliveries of helium for the LZ-130 began to arrive from America at the end of 1937. Then, on March 12, 1938, German troops marched into Austria. The political climate in Europe and America was galvanized at a stroke; Hitler, it was now widely believed, intended to go to war. One immediate result was the cessation of exports of helium to Germany. Dr. Eckener left for America immediately to lobby President Roosevelt. It was not a comfortable visit. The helium issue was being hotly debated in the American press. "Dr. Eckener, we like you and your Zeppelin, and would be glad to give you helium," declared a paper in St. Louis, "but you will understand that we cannot give helium to a liar, thief and murderer like Hitler." Roosevelt declined to see Eckener and referred him to the secretary of the interior, Harold Ickes, who had personally ordered the helium export ban.

"Mr. Ickes received me in a frame of mind which expressed hostility," Eckener wrote. "When I asked why he had abruptly interrupted the promised delivery of helium, he replied briefly and succinctly, 'Because your Hitler is preparing for war.... With a helium-filled ship you could fly over London and drop bombs.'" In vain Eckener denied that Zeppelins could play any part in a modern war. In the end he lost patience. "Mr. Secretary," he said, rising to his feet, "I believe there is no purpose in continuing the conversation." With that he left.

It was, Eckener realized, the end of the zeppelin service—and the end of his life's work. "I had to ask myself whether everything we had striven for and achieved in the last ten or twelve years might not have been in vain. Since we could not fly without American helium, I was forced to conclude that the Zeppelin enterprise had been driven to its death by Hitler."

Goering's air ministry agreed to the LZ-130 being inflated with hydrogen, on condition that it was used only for training and propaganda flights. When Lady Hay-Drummond-Hay wrote to ask Eckener if she could come on the maiden flight, he regretfully told her that it was impossible. "Perhaps one day I can fly the new Zeppelin with the press on board," he wrote, "and then I'll look forward to having you with me once again." But it was not to be.

On September 14, 1938, Dr. Eckener christened the new ship *Graf Zeppelin II* and commanded it on its maiden flight from Friedrichshafen. Altogether the new *Graf* made a total of thirty flights, most of them "circus flights" over German cities, none with fare-paying passengers on board. The ship was commanded at first by von Schiller, later by Sammt, now recovered from his burns. Once again zeppelin fever overwhelmed the German people. Wherever it went brass bands played and adoring crowds came out to wave and cheer.

Then, confirming Harold Ickes's fears, the *Graf Zeppelin II* was taken over by the signals department of the Luftwaffe and sent on nine electronic spying missions along the British coastline and the Czech frontier, usually under the command of Sammt. On September 22, 1938, barely a week before Czechoslovakia was forced to cede to Hitler's territorial claims, the ship under Eckener's command carried out a spying mission along the Czech border—the last flight Eckener was ever to undertake—and the one he was loath to admit. On July 12 through 14, 1939, the *Graf II* made another spy flight of just under forty-five hours along the east coast of England in an attempt to determine the frequencies of the British radar defense network. On August 2 through 4, only weeks before the outbreak of World War II, it made a similar flight, getting as far north as Scotland before Royal Air Force Spitfires intercepted it and turned it away. The *Graf Zeppelin II* failed to discover anything of value concerning Britain's radar defenses. Had it succeeded, the outcome of the Battle of Britain, and therefore of the whole war, might have been different.

At the outbreak of the war, the new *Graf II* was taken out of service and laid up in a hangar in Frankfurt. In the spring of 1940, on the orders of Hermann Goering, both the old *Graf Zeppelin* and the *Graf Zeppelin II* were broken up, on the pretext that their aluminum was required for military aircraft manufacture. Shortly afterward the two zeppelin hangars that had housed them were blown up on Goering's orders. It was the end.

By the time of its demise, Dr. Eckener's dream machine, the old and ever popular *Graf Zeppelin*, had made 590 flights, including 144 ocean crossings; flown over a million miles; spent 17,177 hours (the equivalent of two years) in the air; carried 34,000 people, 13,110 of whom were fare-paying passengers, together with a total of 78,661 kilograms of freight. No one had ever been hurt on the dream machine, nor a single letter lost.

As for Eckener, he had stayed with the Zeppelin Company in the hope that he could keep the dream alive and carry on again when peace came. But when it became clear that airship construction had been formally terminated, he broke his ties with the company, handed back the honorary citizenship that Friedrichshafen had bestowed upon him, and turned his back on his zeppelin past. He was not as disappointed at the total extinction of the zeppelin as he might have been. "Often, when people greeted it so enthusiastically when it appeared in the heavens," he wrote years later, "I felt as if they believed they were seeing it as a sign and symbol of lasting peace, or at least as a symbol of the universal dream of lasting peace. Amidst all the regret for the unreasonable demolition, I was not entirely dissatisfied, for Hitler's concepts were in the most fundamental sense irreconcilable."

The *Hindenburg* had been a magnificent but flawed flying machine, a supreme example of one evolutionary branch of aeronautical development. Though it was fire that destroyed the ship, it was the folly of politics and war that destroyed this branch. As Hans Pruss, the last commander of the last passenger zeppelin, was to pronounce before his death in 1960: "It was not the catastrophe of Lakehurst which destroyed the Zeppelin, it was the war."

# Epilogue

In 1997, sixty years after the terrible demise of Hugo Eckener's dream, a NASA hydrogen-fuels expert named Addison Bain reexamined the newsreel footage of the fire that destroyed the *Hindenburg*. Frame by frame, over and over again, he cranked through those terrible black-and-white images: the first terrifying flash on the top keel aft, the blowtorch blast of white fire through the ship's nose, the stern crumpling in a vast inferno on the ground, the lurching figures stumbling out, some on fire, running and falling.

Watching the footage, Bain was puzzled to see the *Hindenburg*'s bow bounce as it hit the ground. "It bounced!" he exclaimed in surprise. "The bow *bounced!*" If it had been a hydrogen fire, the bow couldn't have bounced, because the hydrogen would have burned up and there would have been no lift; the bow would simply have crashed. Bain concluded that it was not the hydrogen that caught fire first, but the ship itself. "We now realise how flammable the Zeppelin was from stem to stern," he reported. "The cloth, dope, pigment, the cells, adhesives, cords, even the Zep silk tapestry, were enough to make a terrific bonfire." Static electricity had ignited the *Hindenburg*'s cotton outer cover, which had been doped with flammable reflective aluminum paint. The aluminum in the paint reacted with the carbon in the fabric, the hydrogen in the gas cells, and the oxygen in the air, producing a chemical composition like rocket fuel and an explosion very like the launch of a present-day space rocket.

Bain contended that the German investigators of the *Hindenburg*'s destruction were aware of this. In the month following the disaster, one of them wrote in a report that was suppressed for political and insurance reasons, "The actual cause of the fire was the extreme easy inflammability of the covering material brought about by discharges of an electrostatic nature."

Though there are experts who disagree with Bain's interpretation, it seems that Hugo Eckener's dream machine might have been a flying bomb all along. Whatever the cause, even if the *Hindenburg* had never caught fire, the story of the great airships would soon have come to an end. The world was now at war—a war that would be fought in the air by Spitfires and Messerschmitts, Flying Fortresses and flying bombs. In such a war there was no room for the slow-flying, low-flying, gas-filled zeppelins.

Though the Zeppelin Company no longer made airships, it stayed in business during the war, turning its hand to assembling the long-range V-2 rocket missiles that were aimed at Britain in the later stages of the conflict. When this became known to Allied intelligence, British and American bombers flattened the Zeppelin works at Friedrichshafen—and, en passant, most of the town, including the home of Hugo Eckener and his wife, who spent the remainder of the war with their daughter Lotte in Konstanz.

Eckener was not the only old zeppelin hand to survive the war. Former Commanders Pruss, von Schiller, and Sammt also came through safely, as did Eckener's son, Knut, and a number of crew members, including Chief Steward Heinrich Kubis, engine mechanic Eugen Bentele, and others. Notable zeppelin passengers like Commander (now Rear Admiral) Charles Rosendahl, Arthur Koestler, Bill Leeds, Japanese Commander (now Admiral) Fujiyoshi, and Lady Grace Hay-Drummond-Hay also survived into the peace, though in Lady Hay's case not for long. She was in the Philippines when the islands fell to the Japanese early in 1942 and endured the rest of the war in a civilian prison camp, dying in New York not long after her release from a heart attack brought on by extreme exhaustion.

For Dr. Eckener the story was not quite over. Even after the war, the best part of a decade after the last flight of the last zeppelin, the U.S. Navy was still committed to furthering the development of rigid airships for both military and commercial purposes and was therefore deeply interested in learning the fate of the Zeppelin Company, its airships, personnel, and former chief, Dr. Eckener, who was then seventy-seven years of age. In the summer of 1946 a U.S. Naval Reserve lieutenant named J. Gordon Vaeth was sent to Konstanz, in the French zone of occupied Germany, with the mission of locating Eckener. Years later he would recall:

> As I walked along the shore of picturesque Lake Constance I found myself wondering what kind of reception I could expect. I was about to meet a man whose home, personal possessions and lifework had been destroyed, largely by my own countrymen. "Will he be bitter?" I asked myself. "Will he even see me?"
>
> I found the house largely through the help of a passer-by who told me, "It is always an honour and a pleasure to do something for Dr. Eckener!" It was a substantial yet modest house. I went up the front walk and rang the bell. Someone came to the door. I was admitted and ushered into the living room, where a heavily built man rose to greet me.
>
> "Dr. Eckener?" I said.
>
> I really didn't have to ask. I had studied his pictures and would have known that massive and furrowed face, that goatee, and those intelligent eyes anywhere. But he looked thinner and more tired than in his photographs. The war years had obviously taken their toll.

They sat down. Eckener's powerful, dynamic profile, silhouetted against the window, made Vaeth think of the determination and strength of character for which he was so well known. A magnificent oil painting hung on the wall, showing Eckener as captain of the *Graf*

*Zeppelin.* First Lieutenant Vaeth had something to give Eckener: a rectangular box wrapped in stiff brown paper. "I had been carrying it ever since leaving the States," he recalled. "It had caught the eye of every customs officer I had met in England, France, Switzerland and Germany. It was a box of the finest Havana cigars, a gift from his friend Rosendahl. The old gentleman beamed and his eyes sparkled as he lit his first cigar in many months."

"Lieutenant," he remarked, "I didn't know who it would be, but I was sure that sometime someone in the U.S. Navy would get in touch with me again."

There was a lot for Vaeth to find out. Since 1939 next to no information had come out of Germany about Dr. Eckener and the Zeppelin enterprise. Then they turned to the future. Vaeth recalled: "He talked of starting again, of building new airships, and of reweaving a web of commercial Zeppelin passenger and cargo routes. I wondered, as I left him that afternoon, whether he could in fact begin once more. Certainly not in Germany. But how about America? Could the Zeppelin be reborn there?"

On April 30, 1947, at the instigation of his old colleagues Paul Litchfield and Karl Arnstein, chairman and vice-president of the Goodyear Aircraft Corporation in Akron, Ohio, Hugo Eckener once again found himself on the way to America, this time on board a C-54 airplane of the U.S. Army's Transport Command out of Frankfurt, the *Hindenburg*'s old base. For seven months the old man remained in the States as a special consultant to Goodyear Aircraft, helping to prepare proposals and plans for the first postwar airship of the zeppelin type. The new ship was to be a huge affair, 950 feet in length, 10 million cubic feet in capacity, with a seven-thousand-mile range and a top speed of ninety miles per hour. Two hundred fifty-two passengers could be carried in the ship in Pullman-type accommodation, or a little less than half that number in deluxe staterooms. Alternatively, the ship could be used as a flying hospital, carrying up to 248 casualties, or as an aerial freighter, carrying 180,000 pounds of cargo.

"But the idea had no takers," Vaeth wrote. "American businessmen, and the government as well, considered the airplane had progressed too rapidly and too far for the dirigible to catch up. The commercial dirigible had lost its commercial appeal."

Eckener returned to Friedrichshafen, where, in a villa by the shore of Lake Constance on a street that bore his name, he settled down to write his memoirs (published in Germany in 1949 and in Britain in 1958) and live out his life in busy retirement. He maintained an active correspondence with his many friends throughout the world, taking a keen interest in international politics, disarmament, and in particular the unification of divided postwar Germany. In his favorite haunt, a small pavilion near the shore, the old man would sit by the hour, puffing on a cigar and looking out over the lake. Nighttime passers-by knew when he was there by the red glow as he sat smoking, thinking and reminiscing. In one of his last letters, he wrote of his greatest unfulfilled ambition, to increase world cooperation and make for better international trade and understanding by the use of the zeppelin airship. On August 14, 1954, four days after his eighty-sixth birthday, the "Magellan of the Air" died quietly at home from a heart ailment.

The end of the great rigids was not the end of airships altogether. A number of U.S. Navy blimp (nonrigid) squadrons were formed when America entered the Second World War, and they saw service as convoy escorts and submarine scouts in the Pacific, Atlantic, Caribbean, and Mediterranean. Some flew all the way across the Atlantic, the first blimps ever to do so. Altogether they escorted eighty-nine thousand merchant ships through coastal waters, and not a ship was lost to enemy action while they were in attendance.

In 1956 U.S. Navy airships became part of the early-warning radar network of the North American Air Defense System. They were much bigger than the wartime blimps and repeatedly broke air endurance records. In 1957 the ZPG-2 airship *Snowbird* flew across the Atlantic to Portugal, then down the west coast of Africa and back across the Atlantic to Florida nonstop, a distance of 8,261 nautical miles: eleven days, fourteen minutes, and eighteen seconds spent entirely in the air. In 1958 another ZPG-2 flew nine thousand miles to deliver supplies to a scientific expedition deep in the Canadian Arctic, and in the same year the biggest blimp ever built, the 403-foot-long, 1.5-million-cubic-foot-capacity ZPG-3W, bigger even than the earliest zeppelins, made its maiden flight. But improved early-warning radar stations began to replace the navy airships. One by one they were decommissioned, and in 1964 the last airship group of the U.S. Navy was disbanded.

Today Goodyear and other organizations continue to operate a number of blimps around the world for a variety of purposes, from goodwill flights and aerial advertising to scientific surveys, television sports photography, and traffic and police observation. They are handy, safe, and fun and can be used in ways that planes and helicopters cannot.

In the early years of the twentieth century, it had seemed that powered flight would develop along two different but parallel lines: on the one hand, the heavier-than-air plane, on the other, the lighter-than-air airship. In those days there was room for both. If in the end the big rigid appeared to fail, it was not because there was something fundamentally wrong with the concept: buoyant flight is the application of a physical principle, and physical principles do not become obsolete. It failed for a variety of reasons that are now avoidable: inadequate information about the weather, unevolved technology, pilot error due to insufficient experience, the use of flammable hydrogen gas.

Technology has taken huge strides since then. From a technical point of view alone, there is nothing to stop anyone from building a big, strong, safe, efficient rigid airship. The real problem is economic. Can a big rigid pay its way? It is unlikely that rigids will ever be major passenger carriers—they would be no cheaper than a jumbo jet, and five times slower. But as long-distance cargo carriers, especially of bulky, prefabricated loads, they would seem to have very good prospects. How else could you deliver, say, a bridge, or a boiler, or an oil derrick, or a generator, straight from a factory to a work site thousands of miles away, nonstop, in the shortest possible time? Planes and helicopters couldn't do it, because the bigger you build them, the heavier they become and the less load they can carry. The opposite is true of airships. The bigger they are, the more efficient they become.

Airships have other advantages. They don't pollute the atmosphere as much as do airplanes. They are not such a noise nuisance. They use only a fraction of the fuel of a plane, because they don't need power to keep themselves up. They are less liable to have midair collisions. They are not bound to crash if an engine fails, but can hold off, stop in midair, or fly backward out of danger. And when the day comes that there is no more petrol left in the world, they can go nuclear and keep flying.

Since the end of the Second World War, there have been several projects to reintroduce the rigid airship for one purpose or another. Following the immediate postwar Goodyear project involving Dr. Eckener, for example, a design study was made in America for a nuclear-powered ship of 12.5 million cubic feet that could carry five hundred people and circle the Earth repeatedly without refueling; Russia talked of three-hundred-mile-per-hour rigids that could help develop natural resources in the wilds of Siberia; Germany contemplated a revival of the zeppelin passenger service to America; and Shell Petroleum planned to develop a colossal rigid, eighteen hundred feet long and 100 million cubic feet in capacity, to airlift natural gas from the Sahara. Though small-scale pressure airships continue to fly and carry out a variety of aerial tasks in a number of countries around the world—Germany, Russia, Singapore, the United States, and elsewhere—no rigid or large-scale airship has taken to the air since the era of the great zeppelins. But that situation seems about to change.

At the old *Graf Zeppelin* base at Friedrichshafen these days the Zeppelin Company is flying a new, 246-foot semirigid airship with a one-ton payload called the NT (New Technology), which is designed for air tourism. At the old R-101 airship base at Cardington a British company called Advanced Technologies Group is developing a revolutionary twin-hulled airship in the shape of a giant aerofoil called the SkyCat (short for Sky Catamaran) designed for long-distance air freighting (perhaps with military potential), and is also building a six-hundred-foot, vertically launched, unmanned space airship called StratSat that can operate as a satellite transmitter at a fraction of the cost of the conventional kind.

Meanwhile, at a former Soviet military airfield near the town of Briesen-Brand, south of Berlin, a phoenix is rising out of the ashes of the old zeppelins of an era gone by—a new state-of-the-art, high-tech "super-zeppelin" called *CargoLifter,* due to enter operational service in the relatively near future.

A colossal semirigid, sixteen feet longer than the *Hindenburg* but with nearly three times the volume of lifting gas (helium), *CargoLifter* will be the largest airship (or aircraft of any kind) ever built. Using the old and tested principles of yesteryear, the new airship has the advantage of the latest materials and technologies. But it is not so much the technology that is revolutionary as the purpose to which it will be put.

For *CargoLifter* is in effect a flying crane that can transport oversize, unwieldy, or heavy cargoes in one piece, up to 150 feet in length and 160 tons in weight, over distances as far as sixty-two hundred miles without landing, independent of existing transport infrastructures and overflying all obstructions en route. In this way, fully assembled loads heavier than anything that can be transported by air at present (heavy machinery and plant components, for example, or two whole battle tanks and a field gun) can be air freighted from factory to site intercontinentally—Chicago to Patagonia, say, or Essen factory to Yangtse dam—in a fraction of the time and complexity of current methods, with major savings in time and cost.

In ten years it is reckoned that both long-haul and short-haul transportation of heavy, oversize freight will be inconceivable without *CargoLifter*, and that there will be a worldwide demand for about two hundred airships with *CargoLifter*'s capacity. Though critics have raised doubts about the project's viability, claiming the new airship is still subject to the same inherent handling problems in the air and on the ground as the giant airships of the past, *CargoLifter* looks to be unstoppable, and the maiden flight approaches apace.

Already the central production hangar—the largest self-supporting hall in the world—has been completed, and a scaled-down experimental version of the airship is already in service for pilot training and flight and load tests. The company that is building *CargoLifter* is now one of the top one hundred quoted companies on the German stock exchange and is already moving into America, where refueling stations are being built coast to coast and a site for a second *CargoLifter* manufacturing facility has been found in New Bern, North Carolina. In Germany production of the first *CargoLifter* prototype is due in the autumn of 2001 and industrial series production will start in 2004.

The magic of bouyant flight, the dream of worldwide airship travel, remains as irresistible and irrepressible as ever. In retrospect, it is possible that as a concept Doctor Eckener's Dream Machine was ahead of its time, rather than behind—it was the backup technology then available that was unable to match up to the vision. Now it seems likely that Hugo Eckener's faith in his ill-fated Dream Machine may be vindicated, and that great airships may perhaps once again take to the skies to thrill and amaze all below—reliable, safe, and filling a market niche no other transport mode can match.

# Bibliography

*World Flight: August–September 1929 (Chapters 1 and 5)*

Baker, Russell. "The Chief: The Life of William Randolph Hearst." In *New York Review* (August 10, 2000).

Colsman, Alfred. *Luftschiff Voraus!* Stuttgart and Berlin, 1933.

Dresden Cigarette Co. "Welt-Fahrt 1929." *Zeppelin-Weltfahrten.* 1932–34. Vol. 1, Dresden, 1934.

Eckener, Hugo. *Instructions for Piloting Rigid Airships.* Friedrichshafen, 1919.

Eckener, Hugo. "The First Airship Flight Round the World." *National Geographic* (June 1930).

Eckener, Hugo. *Im Luftschiff Zeppelin über Länder und Meere.* Flensburg, Germany, 1949 (English ed: *My Zeppelins.* London, 1958).

Eckener, Hugo. "Die Weltfahrt des Graf Zeppelins." In Rolf Italiaander, *Hugo Eckener: Die Weltschau eines Luftschiffers.* Husum, Germany, 1980.

Geisenheyner, Max. "Auf Weltfahrt mit Graf Zeppelin." Gütersloh, Germany, c. 1941.

———. *Mit Graf Zeppelin um die Welt: Ein Bildbuch.* Frankfurt, 1929.

———. *E. A. Lehmann: Zeppelin-Kapitän.* Frankfurt, 1937.

Gerville-Réache, Léo. *Autour du monde en Zeppelin.* Paris, 1929.

Hay-Drummond-Hay, Lady Grace, Karl von Wiegand, and Sir Hubert Wilkins. News dispatches on the World Flight to the Hearst Press, *Chicago Herald-Examiner* and *New York American*, 1929.

Italiaander, Rolf, *Ein Deutscher namens Eckener.* Konstanz, Germany, 1981.

———. *Hugo Eckener: Die Weltschau eines Luftschiffers.* Husum, Germany, 1980.

———. *Hugo Eckener: Ein Moderner Columbus.* Konstanz, Germany, 1979.

Langsdorf, Werner von. *LZ-127 Graf Zeppelin: Das Luftschiff des Deutschen Volkes.* Frankfurt-am-Main, 1928.

Lehmann, Ernst A. *Auf Luftpatrouille und Weltfahrt.* Leipzig, 1938. (English ed.: *Zeppelin.* London, 1938.

———. "Wie steuert man ein Luftschiff um die Welt?" In *Zeppelin fährt um die Welt* Berlin, 1929.

———, and H. Mingos. *The Zeppelins.* London, 1927.

Lüdecke, Meta. *Der Welt- und Siegesflug LZ-127.* Berlin, 1929.

Luschnath, H. *Zeppelin-Weltfahrten: Vom ersten Luftschiff 1899 bis zu den Fahrten des LZ-127 Graf Zeppelin 1932.* 2 vols. Dresden, 1933.

Megías, Dr. Jerónimo. *La Primera Vuelta al Mundo en el Graf Zeppelin, 15 Agosto–4 Septiembre 1929.* Madrid, 1929.

Nielsen, Thor. *The Zeppelin Story: The Life of Hugo Eckener.* London, 1955.

Rackwitz, Erich. *Reisen und Abenteuer im Zeppelin (Nach Erlebnisse und Erinnerungen des Dr. Eckener).* Neuenhagen, Germany, 1960.

Rosendahl, Charles E. *Up Ship!* New York, 1931.

Sammt, Albert. *Mein Leben für den Zeppelin (mit einem Beitrag von Ernst Breuning, bearbeitet und ergänst von Wolfgang von Zeppelin und Peter Kleinheins).* Wahlwies, Germany, 1980.

Schiller, Hans von, *Kapitän Hans von Schillers Zeppelinbuch.* Leipzig, 1938.

———. *Zeppelin: Aufbruch ins 20 Jahrhundert.* Bonn, 1988.

———. *Zeppelin: Wegbereiter des Weltluftverkehrs.* Bad Gödesberg, Germany, 1967.

———, and Joachim Breithaupt. "Die Weltfahrt des Graf Zeppelins." In *30 Jahre Zeppelin Luftschiffahrt.* Eilenburg, Germany, 1930.

Seilkopf, Heinrich. *Eindrücke und Meteorologische Erfahrungen auf der Weltfahrt des Luftschiffs* Graf Zeppelin. Germany, 1930.

———. "Zeppelin-Weltfahrt und Wetterdienst." In *Zeppelinfährt um die Welt.* Berlin, 1929.

Tittel, Lutz. *Zeppelin Sammlung Heinz Urban.* Friedrichshafen, Germany, 1986.

*21 Tage um die Welt: Bildbericht vom Zeppelinflug um die Erde.* Berlin, 1929.

Vaeth, Gordon. *Graf Zeppelin.* New York, 1958.

*Zeppelin, marsch!* Berlin, 1936.

*Zeppelinfahrt um die Welt: Das Gedenkbuch der Woche.* Berlin, 1929.

"The Zeppelin's Triumph." *The Times* (August 30, 1929).

### *Origins, Pre–World War I (Chapter 2)*

Baum, Edgar. *Der "närrische" Graf: Streifzug durch ein Heldenleben.* Berlin, c. 1938.

Belafi, Michael. *Graf Ferdinand von Zeppelin.* Leipzig, 1987.

Biedenknapp, Georg. *Graf Zeppelin.* Braunschweig, Germany, c. 1910.

DELAG. "Passenger Trips by Zeppelin Airships." Brochure, Germany, 1911.

Eckener, Hugo. *Graf Zeppelin: Sein Leben.* Stuttgart, 1938; Essen, 1996. (English ed., *Count Zeppelin: The Man and his Work.* London, 1938.)

Goldsmith, Margaret. *Zeppelin: A Biography.* New York, 1931.

Hacker, Wolfgang. *Die erste Zeppelinabwurfpost.* Leipzig, 1961.

Hamburg-America Line. "Passagier Fahrten mit Zeppelin." Brochure, Hamburg, 1914.

Hesse, Hermann. *Spazierfahrt in der Luft.* Germany, 1911.

Hörnes, Hermann. *Lenkbare Ballons.* Leipzig, 1902.

Hoogh, Peter. *Zeppelin und die Eroberung des Luftmeeres.* Leipzig, 1909.

Jane, Henry T. *Jane's All the World's Airships 1909.* London, 1909.

Knäusel, Hans G. *LZ-1: Der erste Zeppelin: Geschichter einer Idee 1874–1908.* Bonn, 1985.

———. *LZ-1: Eine Dokumentation.* Friedrichshafen, Germany, 1975.

Linke, Franz. *Die Luftschiffahrt von Montgolfier bis Graf Zeppelin.* Berlin, c. 1909.

Meyer, Henry Cord. *Count Zeppelin: A Psychological Portrait.* (Auckland, New Zealand, 1998.

Saager, Adolf. *Zeppelin: Der Mensch, der Kämpfer, der Sieger.* Stuttgart, 1915.

Scherl, August. "Zeppelin." *Die Woche* (Berlin, c. 1908).

Tittel, Lutz. *Die Fahrten des LZ-4 1908.* Friedrichshafen, Germany, 1983.

Vömel, A. *Graf Ferdinand von Zeppelin: Ein Mann der Tat.* Konstanz, Germany, 1908.

Zeppelin, Graf Ferdinand von. *Erfahrungen beim Bau von Luftschiffen.* Berlin, 1908.

*Zeppelin: 15. Sonderheft der "Woche."* Berlin, 1908.


## *World War I (Chapter 3)*

Anon. *"Z-181": Im Zeppelin gegen Bukarest.* Berlin, 1916.

———. *Zeppeline gegen England.* Berlin, 1916.

Beith, Margaret. *The Story of the WWI Raid on Eldon, April 1916.* Chester, England, 1999.

Brown, John W. *Zeppelins over Streatham.* London, 1996.

Buttlar Brandenfels, Freiherr Treusch von. *Zeppeline gegen England.* Leipzig, 1931 (English ed.: *Zeppelins over England.* London, 1932).

Carstens, Heinz. *Schiffe am Himmel.* Bremerhaven, Germany, 1989.

Charlton, L. E. O. *War over England.* London, 1936.

Cross, Wilbur. *Zeppelins of World War I.* London, 1991.

Dieckerhoff, Otto. *Deutsche Luftschiffe 1914–18.* Walluf, Germany, 1973.

Falcke, C. von. *Gasluftfahrzeuge und Kriegsverwendung.* Stuttgart, n.d.

Goebel, J., and Walter Förster. *Afrika zu unsern Fuessen.* Berlin/Leipzig, 1925.

———. *40,000 km Zeppelin Kriegsfahrten.* Leipzig, 1933.

Goote, Thor. *Peter Strasser der F.d.L.* Frankfurt, 1938.

Hacker, Georg. *Die Männer von Manzell: Ersten Zeppelinkapitäns.* Frankfurt, 1936.

Hearne, R. P. *Zeppelins and Super-Zeppelins.* London, 1916.

Holmes, Lieutenant Gerard. *Christmas 1914.* Privately printed.

Klein, Pitt. *Achtung! Bomben Fallen!* Leipzig, 1934.

Marben, Rolf. *Zeppelin Adventures.* London, 1931.

Meighörner-Schardt, Wolfgang. *Wegbereiter des Weltluftverkehrs wider Willen.* Friedrichshafen, Germany, 1992.

Mielke, Otto. *Verwegener Flug nach Afrika.* Munich, 1968.

Mieth, Otto. "Shot Down by the British: A Zeppelin Officer's Story." *Living Age* (April 1926).

Monson, E. C. P. *Air Raid Damage on London.* London, 1923.

Morison, Frank. *War on Great Cities.* London, c. 1920.

Morris, Captain Joseph. *The German Air Raids on Britain 1914–18.* London, 1969.

Mühler, Alfred. "Mit LZ-37 aus 2,000 m. Brennend Abgestürzt." *Kyffhäuser* (May 8, 1938).

Poolman, Kenneth. *Zeppelins over England.* London, 1960.

*Punch,* articles on the Zeppelin war, 1915–18.

Rawlinson, A. *The Defence of London 1915–18.* London, 1923.

Rimell, Raymond L. *The Airship VC.* Bourne End, England, 1989.

———. *Zeppelin: The Battle for Air Supremacy in World War One.* London, 1984.

Robinson, Douglas H. *The Zeppelin in Combat.* London, 1962; 2d ed. 1971.

Schmalenbach, Paul. *Die Deutschen Marine-Luftschiffe.* Herford, Germany, 1977.

Smith, Peter J. C. *Zeppelins over Lancashire.* Manchester, 1991.

Wright, C. E. *The Fate of the Zeppelin L-32.* Billericay, England, 1977.

Wyatt, R. J. *The Zeppelin Raids over Norfolk 1915.* Norwich, England, 1990.

## *Run-Up to the* Graf *(Chapter 4)*

*Flight* magazine (November 22, 1923).

Heinen, Anton. *Die Fahrt des Luftschiffes Bodensee nach Stockholm.* Germany, 1919.

Kleinheins, Peter. *LZ-120 Bodensee u. LZ-121 Nordstern.* Friedrichshafen, Germany, 1991.

Mielke, Otto. *Ein Leben für die Luftschiffahrt: Luftschiff ZR-3/"Los Angeles."* Munich, 1957.

Pochhammer, Bruno. *ZR-III: Das Deutsch-Amerikanische Verkehrluftschiff.* Freiburg, 1924.

Scott, Major George H. Confidential letter to Dr. Hugo Eckener on the problem of insuring airships. H.M. Airship Station, Pulham, England, May 3, 1923.

Wittemann, A. *Die Amerikafahrt des ZR-III.* Wiesbaden, Germany, 1928.

## *Pre–World Flight (Chapter 4)*

### FIRST ATLANTIC PASSENGER FLIGHT: OCTOBER 1928

Brockdorff, R. von. *LZ-127, Graf Zeppelin.* Munich, 1927.

Dettman, Ludwig. *Mit dem Zeppelin nach Amerika, 1929: Des Wunder von Himmel und Ozean.* Berlin, 1930.

Dresden Cigarette Co. "Amerika-Fahrt 1928." *Zeppelin-Weltfahrten.* 1932–34. Vol. 1. Dresden, 1934.

Dürr, W. E. "Das neue Luftschiff *Graf Zeppelin.*" In *Schiffbau und Schiffahrt.* Heft 19 (1928).

Eckener, Hugo. *Die Amerikafahrt des "Graf Zeppelin."* Berlin, 1928.

Grzesinski, Albert. *Im Zeppelin nach Amerika: Notizen aus dem Tagebuch des Preussisch Ministers des Innern.* Berlin, 1928.

Hay-Drummond-Hay, Lady Grace. Letters to her mother. Typescript, October–November 1928.

Kleffel, Walther, and Wilhelm Schulze. *Die Zeppelin-fahrt im Luftschiff nach Amerika und zurück.* Berlin, 1928.

Rosendahl, Charles E. *Up Ship!* New York, 1931.

Scherz, Walter. "Das Luftschiff Graf Zeppelin." In *Illustrierten Flug-Woche.* Berlin, 1928.

von Wiegand, Karl, and Lady Grace Hay-Drummond-Hay. *The Story of a Great Adventure: The First Trans-Oceanic Voyage on a Commercial Air-Liner.* New York, 1928–29.

### EASTERN MEDITERRANEAN: MARCH 1929

Blau, Fred F., and Cyril Deighton. *Die Orientfahrt des LZ-127* Graf Zeppelin. Lorch, Germany, 1991.

Dresden Cigarette Co. "Orient-Fahrt 1929." *Zeppelin-Weltfahrten.* 1932–34. Vol. 2. Dresden, 1934.

Leder, Dieter. "Von ungünstigen Winden verhindert, Ägypten zu uberfliegen: einer Aerophilatelische Studie über die Orientfahrt des LZ-127 Graf Zeppelin." Ms. made public for the first time.

**WESTERN MEDITERRANEAN: APRIL 1929**

Dresden Cigarette Co. "Spanien-Fahrt 1929." *Zeppelin-Weltfahrten.* 1932–34. Vol. 1. Dresden, 1934.

**SECOND ATLANTIC FLIGHT: MAY 1929**

Nicholson, Frank Ernest. "When the Graf Broke Down." *Collier's National Weekly* (March 8, 1930).

**SWITZERLAND: JULY 1929**

Schiller, Hans von. *Im Zeppelin über der Schweiz (55 Bilder von Ernst E. Haberkorn, eingeleitet von Hans von Schiller).* Zurich, 1930.

———. "Schweizfahrt Graf Zeppelin." *Veedol Kurier* 36 (1929).

*Post–World Flights*

**SWITZERLAND: SEPTEMBER 1929**

Conrad, Ludwig. "Herbst-Fahrt." *Zepp durch die Schweiz* (September 27, 1929).

Dresden Cigarette Co. "Schweiz-Fahrten." *Zeppelin-Weltfahrten.* 1932–34. Vol. 2. Dresden, 1934.

**HOLLAND/BALKANS/SPAIN:**
**OCTOBER 12–13/OCTOBER 15–17/OCTOBER 23–24, 1929.**

Dresden Cigarette Co. "Holland-Fahrt/Balkan-Fahrt." *Zeppelin-Weltfahrten.* 1932–34. Vol. 2. Dresden, 1934.

Duggan, John. Graf Zeppelin *to the Balkans.* Ickenham, England, 2000.

**ENGLAND: 1928–32**

Dresden Cigarette Co. "England-Fahrten." *Zeppelin-Weltfahrten.* 1932–34. Vol. 1. Dresden, 1934.

Duggan, John. Graf Zeppelin *Flights to England.* Ickenham, England, 1998.

**TRIANGULAR FLIGHT TO AMERICA: MAY–JUNE 1930**

Breithaupt, Joachim. *Das ist Luftschiffhart: Die grosse Dreiecksfahrt des Luftschiffs* Graf Zeppelin. Berlin, 1930.

———. "Die Südamerikafahrt des *Graf Zeppelin* unter ihre voraussichtlichen Aus-wirkungen." In *Das Luftschiff.* 1930.

———. *Mit* Graf Zeppelin *nach Süd- und Nord-Amerika: Reiseeindrucke und Fahrt-erlebnisse.* Lahr/Baden, Germany, 1930.

Dresden Cigarette Co. "Süd-Amerika-Fahrt." *Zeppelin-Weltfahrten.* 1932–34. Vol. 1. Dresden, 1934.

Zwicky, J. F. *Mit* Graf Zeppelin *nach Marokko-Brasilien-Newyork-Spanien-Norwegen und Island.* Chur/St. Moritz, 1930.

**NORWAY AND ICELAND: JULY 1930**

Dresden Cigarette Co. "Nordland-Fahrten 1930." Dresden, 1930.

Hürlimann, Martin. "Zwischen Bodensee und Spitzbergen." *Atlantis* Magazine (1930).

Zwicky, J. F. *Mit* Graf Zeppelin *nach Marokko-Brasilien-Newyork-Spanien-Norwegen und Island.* Chur/St. Moritz, 1930.

**MOSCOW: SEPTEMBER 1930**
Dresden Cigarette Co. "Moskau-Fahrt 1930." *Zeppelin-Weltfahrten*. 1932–34. Vol. 1. Dresden, 1934.

**GERMANY AND AUSTRIA: 1929–31**
Dresden Cigarette Co. "Österreich-Fahrten 1929/31." *Zeppelin-Weltfahrten*. 1932–34. Vol. 2. Dresden, 1934.

**EGYPT: APRIL 1931**
Blau, Fred, and Cyril Deighton. *Die Ägyptenfahrt des LZ-127* Graf Zeppelin. Lorch, Germany, 1991.
Bruer, Carl. *Mit dem Luftschiff* Graf Zeppelin *nach Kairo vom 9 bis 13 April 1931*. Goslar, Germany, 1931.
Dresden Cigarette Co. "Ägypten-Fahrt 1931." *Zeppelin-Weltfahrten*. 1932–34. Vol. 1. Dresden, 1934.

**ICELAND: JULY 1931**
Bruer, Carl. *Mit dem Luftschiff* Graf Zeppelin *nach Island vom 30 Juni bis 3 Juli 1931*. Goslar, Germany, 1931.

**ARCTIC: JULY 1931**
Dresden Cigarette Co. "Arktis-Fahrt 1931." *Zeppelin-Weltfahrten*. 1932–34. Vol. 2. Dresden, 1934.
Koestler, Arthur. *Arrow in the Blue*. London, 1953.
———. *Von Weissen Nächten und Roten Tagen*. Kharkov, Ukraine, 1933.
Kohl-Larsen, Dr. Ludwig. *Die Arktisfahrt des* Graf Zeppelin. Berlin, 1931.

**MEMMINGEN: OCTOBER 1931**
Lapatki, Roland. *Vom Schwabenmeer zur Theaterstadt im Luftschiff*. Memmingen, Germany, 1982.

*Technical and Operational (Chapter 4)*

Eckener, Hugo. *Instructions for Piloting Rigid Airships*. Friedrichshafen, Germany, 1919.
U.S. Navy. "Rigid Airship Manual 1927." Washington, D. C., 1928.

*First Scheduled Transatlantic Service: 1931–1937 (Chapter 6)*

Bruer, Carl. *Mit dem Luftschiff* Graf Zeppelin *nach Pernambuco vom 17 bis 28 Oktober 1931*. Goslar, Germany, 1931.
Dresden Cigarette Co. "Südamerika-Fahrten 1931/32." *Zeppelin-Weltfahrten*. 1932–34. Vol. 2. Dresden, 1934.
Dresden Cigarette Co. "Deutschland-Fahrt am 1 Mai 1933"; "Rom-Fahrt am 30 Mai 1933." *Zeppelin-Weltfahrten*. 1932–34. Vol. 2. Dresden, 1934.
Duggan, John, and James W. Graue. *Commercial Zeppelin Flights to South America*. Valleyford, Washington, 1995.
Hamburg-America Line. "Sailings and Fares: Zeppelin South America Service 1935." Brochure. Hamburg, 1935.
Jacob, Heinrich Eduard. *Mit dem Zeppelin nach Pernambuco: Poetische Luftbilder einer ungewönlichen Reise*. Berlin, 1992.
Kohl, Hermann. "Mit dem Zeppelin nach Südamerika." In *Hillgers Deutsche Jugendbucherei*. Germany, 1934.

Lambrecht, Wolfgang. "Transoceanic Dirigible Service," *American Traveller's Gazette* (1933).

Mayer, Josef. *Mit dem Zepp in neun Tagen nach Südamerika und zurück 5 bis 13 April 1932.* Stuttgart/Ravensburg, 1932.

Sonntag, Albert. *Mit* Graf Zeppelin *und Kondor-Flugzeugen Europa-Brasilien.* Bonn, 1932.

### *The* Hindenburg *(Chapter 7)*

Ahner, Hans. *Die Zeppelin Katastrophe.* Berlin, 1985.

Brandt, Rolf. *Mit Luftschiff* Hindenburg *über den Atlantik.* Berlin, 1936–37.

Bruer, Carl. *Erste Fahrt des Luftschiffe* Hindenburg *nach Nordamerika 6–14 May 1936.* Goslar, Germany, 1936.

Danner, James F. *They Flew on the* Hindenburg. New York, 1978.

Hoehling, A. A. *Who Destroyed the* Hindenburg? New York, 1962.

*Die Katastrophe von Lakehurst.* Report of the German Investigation.

Knäusel, Hans G. *Sackgasse am Himmel: Anmerkungen zur Luftschiffahrt damals und heute.* Bonn, 1988.

Knight, R. W. *The* Hindenburg *Accident.* Report No. 11, Washington, D.C., August 1938.

Langsdorf, W. von. *LZ-129* Hindenburg. Frankfurt, 1936.

Medem, W. G. *Cabin Boy Werner Franz of the* Hindenburg. Berlin, 1937.

Mooney, Michael M. *The* Hindenburg. London, 1972.

Robinson, Douglas H. *LZ-129* Hindenburg. Dallas, 1964.

Sinz, Herbert. *Die Letzte Fahrt der* Hindenburg. Freiburg, 1985.

Stein, R. Conrad. *The* Hindenburg *Disaster.* Chicago, 1993.

Tanaka, Shelley. *Die Katastrophe der* Hindenburg. Nuremberg/New York, 1993/94.

Tittel, Lutz. *LZ-129* Hindenburg *1936–37.* Friedrichshafen, Germany, 1987.

*Zum Gedenken an LZ* Hindenburg. Friedrichshafen, Germany, 1937.

### *Recent Explanation of* Hindenburg *Disaster (Epilogue)*

Matthews, Robert. "Paint Now Blamed for *Hindenburg* Disaster." *Sunday Telegraph* (June 27, 1999).

Peake, Norman. *What Happened to the* Hindenburg? Television program *Buoyant Flight,* Lighter-than-Air-Society, Akron, Ohio (April 30, 2000).

Treuren, Richard G. Van. "Odorless, Colorless, Blameless." *Air & Space,* Smithsonian Institution (April–May 1997).

———, and Addison Bain. "The *Hindenburg* Fire at Sixty: Part One, Flammable Containers of Hydrogen." *Buoyant Flight,* Lighter-than-Air-Society, Akron, Ohio (March–April 1997); Part Two (July–August 1997).

### *Post–World War II (Epilogue)*

Ambers, Henry J. *The Dirigible and the Future.* New York, 1970.

Harris, Martin J. *The Use of Weather Satellite Pictures in Airship Operations Worldwide.* Oxford, England, 2000.

Kirschner, Edwin J. *The Zeppelin in the Atomic Age.* Urbana, Ill., 1974.

Knäusel, Hans G. *Sackgasse am Himmel: Anmerkungen zur Luftschiffahrt damals und heute.* Bonn, 1988.

Litchfield, Paul, and Hugh Allen. *Why? Why Has America No Rigid Airships?* Akron, Ohio, 1945; 2d ed. 1976.

Rosendahl, Charles E. *What About the Airship? The Challenge to the United States.* New York, 1938.


## CargoLifter (Epilogue)

CargoLifter GmbH. *Geschäftsbericht 1998/99.* Berlin.

CargoLifter GmbH. *Lifter News.* Brand, Germany, September 1999.

CargoLifter GmbH. *The Power of Zero Gravity.* Brand, Germany, 2000.

Hall, Allan. "Lesson One, Check Your Air Brakes," *Evening Standard* (October 17, 2000).

Hooper, John. "Giant Airship is no Flight of Fancy," *Guardian* (February 3, 2001).

Major, Tony. "Flotation Marks Revival of an Old Mode of Transport," *Financial Times* (May 30, 2000).

Paterson, Tony. "German Airship Plan Backed by EU Flies Into Trouble," *Sunday Telegraph* (January 21, 2001).

Steere, Mike. "The Baron's Big Balloon," *Wired* (August 2000).


## General Histories

Allen, Hugh. *The Story of the Airship.* Akron, Ohio, 1931.

Anon. *Der neue Zeppelin und das Schicksal der Anderen: LZ-1–LZ-129.* Stuttgart, 1936.

Archbold, Rick. Hindenburg: *Reliving the Era of the Great Airships.* New York, 1995.

Aust, Siegfried, and Stefan Lemke. *Abenteur Zeppelin.* Ravensburg, Germany, 1988.

Baden-Württemberg Zeitschrift (Sonderausgaben). *150 Jahre Ferdinand Graf von Zeppelin.* Baden-Württemberg, 1988.

Botting, Douglas. *The Giant Airships.* Alexandria, Va., 1980.

———. *Shadow in the Clouds.* BBC-TV, 1966.

———. Personal correspondence with Squadron Leader Ralph Booth (Commander of British rigid R-100), General Umberto Nobile (Commander of North Pole airship *Italia*), Captain Hans von Schiller (Commander of the *Graf Zeppelin*), Oberleutnant zur See Werner Vermehren (Commander of L-65 and last-ever combat mission by Zeppelin), Dr. Douglas Robinson (U.S. Zeppelin historian).

Brooks, Peter W. *Historic Airships.* London, 1973.

———. *Zeppelin: Rigid Airships 1893–1940.* London, 1992.

Clausberg, Karl. *Zeppelin: Die Geschichte eines unwarscheinlichen Erfolges.* Augsburg, Germany, 1990.

Collier, Basil. *The Airship.* London, 1974.

Dick, Harold G., and Douglas H. Robinson. *The Golden Age of the Great Passenger Airships,* Graf Zeppelin *and* Hindenburg. London, 1987.

"Dirigibles." In *The Guinness Book of Firsts.* London.

Dolfus, Charles. *Les Ballons.* Paris, 1960.

Dresden Cigarette Co. *Zeppelin-Weltfahrten.* 2 vols. Dresden, 1934.

Engberding, Dietrich. *Luftschiff und Luftschiffahrt in Vergangenheit, Gegenwart und Zukunft.* Berlin, 1928.

Grieder, Karl. *Zeppeline: Giganten der Lüfte.* Zurich, 1971.

Griehl, Manfred, and Joachim Dressel. *Zeppelin: The German Airship Glory*. London, 1990.

Hansen, Hans Jürgen. *Blick aus dem Zeppelin 1929–33*. Hamburg, 1974.

Hartcup, Guy. *The Achievement of the Airship*. Newton Abbot, 1974.

Hedin, Robert. *The Zeppelin Reader*. Iowa City, 1999.

Heiss, F. *Das Zeppelin Buch*. Berlin, 1936.

Horton, Edward. *The Age of the Airship*. London, 1973.

Jackson, Robert. *Airships*. London, 1971.

Kleinheins, P. *Die Grosse Zeppeline*. Düsseldorf, 1985.

Knäusel, Hans G. *Zeppelin and the USA: An Important Episode in German-American Relations*. Friedrichshafen, Germany, 1981.

Langsdorf, Werner von. *LZ-127 Graf Zeppelin: Das Luftschiff des Deutschen Volkes*. Frankfurt-am-Main, 1928.

Litchfield, Paul, and Hugh Allen. *Why? Why Has America No Rigid Airships?* Akron, Ohio, 1945; 2d ed. 1976.

Louis, Richard. *30 Jahre Zeppelin Luftschiffahrt*. Eilenburg, Germany, c. 1931.

Meighörner, Wolfgang. *Giganten der Lüfte: Geschichte und Technik der Zeppeline in ausgwählten Berichten und zahlreichen Fotos*. Erlangen, Germany, 1996.

Meyer, Henry Cord. *Airshipmen, Businessmen and Politics 1890–1940*. Washington, D.C., and London, 1991.

Meyer, Peter. *Das Grosseluftschiffbuch*. Mönchengladbach, Germany, 1976.

Mowforth, E. *The Airship: A Technical History*. London, 1973.

Nitske, W. Robert. *The Zeppelin Story*. South Brunswick, N.J., 1977.

Pudor, Dr. Heinrich von. "Der Zeppelin von 1900 bis 1935," *Der Deutsche Techniker* 15 (1935).

Robinson, Douglas. *The Zeppelin in Combat*. London, 1962; 2d ed. 1971.

———. *Giants in the Sky*. Henley-on-Thames, England, 1973.

Sinclair, J. A. *Airships in Peace and War*. London, 1934.

Spanner, E. F. *About Airships*. London, 1929.

———. *Gentlemen Prefer Aeroplanes*. London, 1928.

———. *This Airship Business*. London, 1927.

———. *The Tragedy of R-101*. 2 vols. London, 1931.

Sprigg, Christopher. *The Airship: Its Design, History, Operation and Future*. London, c. 1931.

Stelling, A. von. *12,000 Kilometer im* Parseval. Berlin, 1911.

Straub, Heinz. *Fliegen mit Feuer und Gas*. Stuttgart, 1984.

Toland, John. *The Great Dirigibles*. New York, 1957 (2d ed. 1972).

Topping, Dale. *When Giants Roamed the Sky: Karl Arnstein and the Rise of Airships from Zeppelin to Goodyear*. Edited by Eric Brothers. Akron, Ohio, 2001.

Ullstein Verlag. *Zeppelin Marsch!* Berlin, 1936.

Vaeth, Gordon. Graf Zeppelin: *The Adventures of an Aerial Globetrotter*. New York, 1958.

Ventry, Lord, and Eugene M. Kolenski. *Airship Development: Jane's Pocket Book*. London, 1976.

Waibel, Barbara, and Renate Kissel. *Zu Gast im Zeppelin: Reisen und Speisen im Luftschiff* Graf Zeppelin. Friedrichshafen/Weingarten, Germany, 1998.

*Zeppelin: Ein bedeutendes Kapitel aus der Geschichte der Luftfahrt*. Friedrichshafen, Germany, 1983.

*Zirkel, Zangen and Cellon—Arbeit am Luftschiff*. Friedrichshafen, Germany, 1999.

### Eye-Witness Accounts by Zeppelin Crew Members and Others

Bentele, Eugen. *Meine Fahrten 1931–38: Ein Zeppelin-Machinist erzählt.* Friedrichs-hafen, Germany, 1991.

Colsman, Alfred. *Luftschiff Voraus!* Stuttgart and Berlin, 1933.

Eckener, Hugo. *Im Luftschiff Zeppelin über Länder und Meere.* Flensburg, Germany, 1949 (English ed.; *My Zeppelins.* London, 1958).

Geisenheyner, Max. *E. A. Lehmann: Zeppelin-Kapitän.* Frankfurt, 1937.

Italiaander, Rolf. *Ein Deutscher namens Eckener.* Konstanz, Germany, 1981.

———. *Hugo Eckener: Ein Moderner Columbus.* Konstanz, Germany, 1979.

———. *Der Weltschau eines Luftschiffers.* Husum, Germany, 1980.

Lehmann, Ernst A. *Auf Luftpatrouille und Weltfahrt.* Leipzig, 1938 (English ed.; *Zeppelin.* London, 1938).

———, and H. Mingos. *The Zeppelins.* London, 1927.

Nielsen, Thor. *The Zeppelin Story: The Life of Hugo Eckener.* London, 1955.

Rackwitz, Erich. *Reisen und Abenteuer im Zeppelin (Nach Erlebsnisse und Erin-nerungen des Dr. Eckener).* Neuenhagen, Germany, 1960.

Sammt, Albert. *Mein Leben für den Zeppelin (mit einem Beitrag von Ernst Breuning, bearbeitet und ergänst von Wolfgang von Zeppelin und Peter Kleinheins).* Wahlwies, Germany, 1980.

Schiller, Hans von. *Kapitän Hans von Schillers Zeppelinbuch.* Leipzig, 1938.

———. *Zeppelin: Aufbruch ins 20 Jahrhundert.* Bonn, 1988.

———. *Zeppelin: Wegbereiter des Weltluftverkehrs.* Bad Gödesberg, Germany, 1967.


### Aviation

Allen, Oliver E. *The Airline Builders.* (Alexandria, Va., 1981.

Gibbs-Smith, Charles. *Aviation: An Historical Survey.* London, 1970.

Jackson, Donald Dale. *Flying the Mail.* Alexandria, Va., 1982.

Macmillan, Norman. *The Air Traveller's Guide to Europe.* London, 1929 and 1930.

Taylor, John W. R., and Kenneth Munson. *History of Aviation.* London, 1978.

# Acknowledgments

In writing this book I have been particularly grateful to Anthony
Smith, Chairman of the Airship Heritage Trust and President of
the British Balloon and Airship Club, for his invaluable information and feedback at all stages; David Kirch, for the loan of crucially valuable research material from his major airship collection in
Jersey, Channel Islands; Giles Camplin of CargoLifter, Germany, for
help regarding the *CargoLifter* project and the acquisition of rare
German-language research material; Barbara Waibel, for her help in
locating many of the photos in the Zeppelin Archives at Friedrichshafen; Daniel Lehmann of Hilterfingen, Switzerland; Michael Cuddy
and John Blake for their help in acquiring valuable specialist texts; and
Dr. Patrick Carter, Emeritus Fellow of Downing College, Cambridge,
for his judicious assessment of the text during the preparation of this
book. I am also most grateful to Richard Johnson and Robert Lacey,
my editors at HarperCollins in London; Melanie Haselden, picture
editor at HarperCollins; and Elizabeth Stein, my editor at Henry Holt
and Company in New York; for their highly professional input in
preparing this book for publication; and to Andrew Hewson, Elizabeth Fairbairn, and Stuart Krichevsky, my literary agents in London

and New York, for their valuable support and encouragement from start to finish.

My thanks are due to the Hearst Press, USA, for permission to quote from the exclusive World Flight reports of Hearst special correspondents Lady Hay-Drummond-Hay, Karl von Wiegand, and Sir Hubert Wilkins, along with staff reporters on the ground, in the *Chicago Herald-Examiner* between 15 August and 4 September 1929; to Penguin Putnam, New York, for permission to quote from *My Zeppelins* by Dr. Hugo Eckener (Putnam, London, 1958); and to the PFD Agency, London, on behalf of the Estate of Arthur Koestler, for permission to reprint from *Arrow in the Blue* by Arthur Koestler (London, 1953).

# Index

# About the Author

Douglas Botting is a writer, journalist, and biographer whose interests include travel, exploration, wild places, and conservation matters. His previous works include *Gerald Durrell: The Authorized Biography* and *The Saga of Ring of Bright Water: The Enigma of Gavin Maxwell.* He took part in the first balloon flight across East Africa and has flown in Goodyear airships over England. He lives near London.